Series in
Legal Information and
Communication Technologies

Volume 8

Volume Editors' Biographies

Daniele Bourcier, doctorate in Public Law, is director of research at the Centre National de la Recherche Scientifique, CERSA, Paris. She is associated professor at the University of Paris 1 in eGovernment. Scientific lead of CC France, she works on Commons Governance and Regulation. She wrote 16 books (collective or not) and many papers in the field of IT, Cognition and Law. She is an appointed member of the Comite d'Éthique des Sciences (CNRS).

Pompeu Casanovas, director of the UAB Institute of Law and Technology (http://idt.uab.cat) and professor of Philosophy of Law at the Universitat Autònoma de Barcelona. He has an extended PI experience in several international and national research projects on legal ontologies, sociolegal studies, and the Semantic Web. He is the author of many books and scientific papers. He is general editor of *La Razón Aurea* (Ed. Comares, Granada), *IDT Series* (Ed. Huygens, Barcelona) and, with Giovanni Sartor, of *Law, Governance and Technology* (Springer, Berlin, Heidelberg), and EPAP Series in *Legal Information and Communication Technologies* (Florence).

Melanie Dulong de Rosnay is a researcher in law and information science. She is the publications manager of Communia, the European network on the digital public domain coordinated by Politecnico di Torino. Member of the Creative Commons Netherlands team at the Institute for Information Law of the University of Amsterdam in 2009-2010, she was a fellow at the Berkman Center for Internet & Society at Harvard Law School and at Science Commons in 2007-2008. She co-founded Creative Commons France at CERSA of University Paris 2 in 2003.

Catharina Maracke is a German qualified lawyer and Associate Professor at the Graduate School for Media and Governance, Shonan Fujisawa Campus, Keio University. She graduated from the University of Kiel and the Hamburg Court of Appeal, Germany, with the first and second state examination. While studying she obtained a scholarship from the Max-Planck-Institute for Foreign and International Patent, Copyright and Competition Law in Munich to write her PhD thesis on the History of the German Copyright Act of 1965. As international Director at Creative Commons she has overseen the international licensing projects for more than 3 years.

INTELLIGENT MULTIMEDIA

Managing Creative Works
in a Digital World

Edited by

Danièle Bourcier, Pompeu Casanovas,
Mélanie Dulong de Rosnay, Catharina Maracke

EUROPEAN PRESS ACADEMIC PUBLISHING

ISBN 978-88-8398-063-3
Copyright © 2010 by European Press Academic Publishing
Florence, Italy
www.e-p-a-p.com
www.europeanpress.eu
Printed in Italy

Contents

SECTION II
MULTIMEDIA AND LAW: MANAGING DIGITAL CONTENTS

Foreword: Intelligent Multimedia

This volume stems from the encounter between two communities: Creative Commons (CC) and Artificial Intelligence and Law, especially those people devoted to the development of Multimedia Technology. The Institute of Law and Technology (IDT-Universitat Autònoma de Barcelona) and the CC French chapter (CERSA-Université de Paris 2), together with leads from other CC jurisdictions, are united in one common effort to discuss CC values, technology and innovative solutions.

We think that authors contributing to this volume share the following trends:

1. *Commons-oriented management*: Humans are able to organize collective action on a much larger scale than predicted by theories of individualistic rationality. Intelligent multimedia means that collaborative work on access and reuse is more efficient for building a common good of digital texts and images.

2. *Open Access*: Technologies develop and promote interoperability standards when building ontologies, interfaces, documents, platforms, and in the reuse of software and tools to facilitate the efficient dissemination of content. The Open Access Initiative (Declaration of Budapest, 2001) has its roots in the open access and institutional repository movements. Universal access to information and knowledge is a key principle in UNESCO's overall mandate to promote the free flow of information and thus to place information and knowledge through multimedia platforms at the doorsteps of communities.

3. *Free Culture and public data*: This movement states that all citizens are free to participate in the transmission and evolution of knowledge and culture, without setting artificial boundaries on who can participate or how to. The Free Culture movement seeks to develop knowledge, creativity and participation by promoting principles such as public domain, communication and free expression or citizens' civil liberties, and offer technological means to practice and develop their liberties.

4. *A common interest in multimedia creation, imaging and management*: Accessibility means flexibility and the possibility of an easier and more effective readability and use of the shared content. As emphasized by the African, Asian and Latin-American experiences, people seek for a faster and cheaper communication to organize their lives and their social bonds. This is coming to be essential either in hard or safer environments. The Social Web is becoming the Web of (linked) Data. Multimedia and Mobile technologies are the next step for such a programme.

8

Moreover, this book is the follow-up of a first work edited in 2004 by two of the editors when the Creative Commons France licenses were launched in Paris[1]. Since then, the Creative Commons International Project expanded its main research subject matters. Communities of academics, lawyers, economists, sociologists or commoners are going along with Semantic Web developers to design new intelligent tools, to analyze experiences coming from the Social Web, and to work out better regulations and governance. The European Thematic Network on the digital public domain Communia (2007-2010) is on the track. It is our contention that the CC initiative will participate increasingly into world commons movements, at large.

However, we know that the values promoted by the commons cannot be absolute. We do not think they can be imposed or even enforced through a positivistic conception of the law. We are convinced that we all live in a mixed, hybrid, global, complex culture. As shown by the experience of the Free Access to Law movement, the creation of a public space to create and share knowledge and innovative works is not necessarily incompatible with the implementation of rights in a global market. This is the real issue for the next decade. Dialogue among all stakeholders — authors, users, service providers, companies, institutions and states — is essential to preserve and develop creativity. Our volume is conceived to foster this kind of dialogue as well.

Last but not least, we would like to thank Emma Teodoro, Núria Galera, Sílvia Gabarró, Olga Baranowska, Paula Ruiz-Alfaro, and Meritxell Fernández-Barrera, as well as Jane Park and Michelle Thorne, for their invaluable help. Without them, the work of editing would have been much more difficult. Projects TSI-020501-2008, CSO-2008-05536-SOCI, TSI-020110-2009-374, SGR-CIRIT, made possible the final edition of this volume.

May 2010

Danièle Bourcier
Pompeu Casanovas
Melanie Dulong de Rosnay
Catharina Maracke

---

[1] D. Bourcier & M. Dulong de Rosnay (eds), *International Commons at the digital age. La création en partage*, Romillat, Paris, 2004.

Introduction: Creative Commons, Intelligent Multimedia, and Web 3.0

Danièle Bourcier[*], Pompeu Casanovas[°], Melanie Dulong de Rosnay[+], Catharina Maracke[#]

[*] *CERSA-CNRS, Paris (France)*
[°] *UAB Institute of Law and Technology, Barcelona (Spain)*
[+] *Politecnico di Torino (Italy)*
[#] *Graduate School of Media and Governance, Shonan Fujisawa Campus, Keio University (Japan)*

1. An apple and the idea of an apple

Perhaps one of the funniest criticisms on the idea of intellectual property comes from Laurence Sterne. It is the well-known paragraph of *Tristram Shandy* (1759-1767) in which the writer makes the analogy between the property of an apple and the intellectual property of a belief, opinion or discourse.

[...] that the sweat of a man's brows, and the exudations of a man's brains, are as much a man's own property as the breaches upon his backside; —which said exudations, &c., being dropped upon the said apple by the labour of finding it, and picking it up, and being moreover indissolubly wasted, and as indissolubly annexed, by the picker up, to the thing picked up, carried home, roasted, peeled, eaten, digested, and so on, —'tis evident that the gatherer of the apple, in so doing, has mixed up something which was his own with the apple which was not his own; by which means he has acquired a property; —or, in other words, the apple is John's apple.

With the same stroke, Sterne goes on to say that everything which is intellectually produced by John is John's exclusive property: his opinions, beliefs, ideas and all the products of his mind.

By the same learned chain of reasoning, my father stood up for all his opinions: he had spared no pains in picking them up, and the more they lay out of the common way the better still was his title.—No mortal claimed them; they had cost him, moreover, as much labour in cooking and digesting as in the case above; so that they might well and truly be said to be of his own goods and chattels. Accordingly, he held fast by 'em, both by teeth and claws — would fly to whatever he could lay his hands on, —and, in a word, would entrench and fortify them round with as many circumvallations and breast-works as my uncle Toby would a citadel.

The isolated legally citadel-mind idea, that Sterne was nicely and elegantly ridiculing, has attracted all kind of criticisms in the last two centuries. But only with the coming of the Internet, and the real possibility to expand and freely share almost universally the products of the mind, the discussion on the nature and boundaries of intellectual property has reached its peak. The story has been most told, and it has reached even Wikipedia, but we will reproduce it here because it constitutes a new starting point for the defense of public domain.[1]

There are three main milestones for this discussion, all rooted in the US: the *Digital Millenium Copyright Act* (DMCA) in 1998, the *Sonny Bono Copyright Term Extension Act* (CTEA) of the same year (that extended the US copyright protection up to ninety-five years), and the Supreme Court ruling *Eldred vs. Ashcroft 537 U.S.* of January 15th 2003 (which backed the extension of the protection against the complaint presented by the Internet publisher Eric Eldred).[2] The law was both *prospective* and *retroactive*: for works published before January 1st 1978 the term was extended to 95 years; for works authored by individuals after January 1st, the term was extended to equal the life of the author plus 70 years. It was quite clear to everybody that behind the case, argued by Lawrence Lessig for the plaintiff against Solicitor General Theodore Olson, there were the private interests of the broadcasting and movies industry. The Supreme Court final ruling prevented a number of works — Mickey Mouse among them— from entering the public domain.

From 1998 to 2004, this legal turmoil originated the reaction of the US legal scholars and an explosion of papers and books on intellectual property rights. Some lawyers, especially the minority that have been paying special attention to the development of the Internet and the Web, displayed a lot of energy to defend the free generation, use, reuse and circulation of ideas and works through the Web.[3] In 2001, Lawrence Lessig, Hal Abelson, Eric Eldred and a few others came up with the idea of *Creative Commons* (CC). In 2004, James Boyle made the announcement of his Manifesto following up "the Second Enclosure Movement". Boyle's position was quite reasonable, claiming that WIPO — The World Intellectual Property Organization— could take into account the function to balance legitimate private and public interests[4]:

---

[1] See http://en.wikipedia.org/wiki/Eldred_v._Ashcroft

[2] CTEA extended existing copyright terms by an additional 20 years from the terms set by the Copyright Act of 1976. The Supreme Court, leaded by Justice Ginsburg, ruled that as long as the limit is not forever, any limit set by Congress can be deemed constitutional. Justices Breyer and Stevens, dissented. See http://www.copyright.gov/docs/eldrdedo.pdf

[3] To quote just a few: Benkler (2000), Litman (2001), Vaydhyatan (2001), Biegel (2002), Boyle (2003).

[4] In fact, he anticipated what it is known as the Geneva Declaration, available at: http://www.cptech.org/ip/wipo/genevadeclaration.html

The ideas proposed here are not radical. If anything they have a conservative strand - a return to the rational roots of intellectual property rather than an embrace of its recent excesses. Patents, for example, have a restricted term and were always intended to work to fuel the public domain. Copyrights were intended to last only for a limited time, to regulate texts, not criminalize technologies, to facilitate rather than to restrict access. Even the *droits d'auteur* tradition was built around the assumption that there were social and temporal limitations on the author's claims; natural right did not mean absolute right. Neither Macaulay and Jefferson, nor Le Chapelier and Rousseau would recognize their ideas in the edifice we have erected today. In the name of authorial and inventive genius, we are creating a bureaucratic system that only a tax-collector or a monopolist could love. But genius is actually less likely to flower in this world, with its regulations, its pervasive surveillance, its privatized public domain and its taxes on knowledge. Even if the system worked exactly as specified, it could not solve some of the most important human problems we face, and it would likely hamper our most important communications technology. And now we foist that system on the world, declaring that anyone who does not have exactly the same legal monopolies as we do is distorting trade. True, WIPO's power to undo these trends is limited at the moment. Trade negotiations have become the preferred arena for expanding rights still further. But if these trends are to be reversed there will need to be an international, informed, democratic debate about the trajectory we are on. WIPO's role in that debate is a central one. It should embrace that role, rather than seeking to jump onto the bandwagon of ever-expanding rights.

The balance Boyle was calling for is far from easy, because — as Sterne reminded in *Tristram Shandy* — after picking up an apple in the state of nature, the natural tendency of the picker is biting it. Ten years ago, a Federal Trade Commission (FTC) survey showed that more than 97% of the existing websites collected personal information from the consumers; 88% informed the users about it; but only 20% followed the FTC policies of transparent information (Steinke, 2002). After all, through the Internet, you can grasp not only the apple but, for the first time, the idea of an apple (as it appears in multiple representations in texts, images and movies).

There is a tension among practices and routines companies follow under economic pressure within the web markets, legal national frameworks, and protocols and principles issued from the Internet technical rulers (such as WIPO, ICANN and W3C).

2. The Creative Commons project: legal and technical aspects of multimedia

The development of affordable and user-friendly computer technology coupled with technical and economic advances in multimedia technology have enabled the large scale transformation of users from a passive role of cultural consumers to an active role of cultural creators. The notion of

"Intelligent multimedia" - which is also the title of this book - summarizes this social and technical transformation.

Since the technical barriers to create and disseminate copyrightable works were lowered, the path towards large scale cultural creation and edition was opened. The results of this change are visible in all types of works from text to images, from audio to video and all the multimedia combinations in between. Today, copyright law itself has to be changed due to the paradox Lawrence Lessig pointed out in the Foreword of our previous book on international questions raised by Creative Commons[5]: "First, copyright is essential to the dignity and often the incentives of creative authors. Second, the existing system of copyright is insanely complex and often harmful to the interest of creators". Creative Commons was developed as a method for overcoming this final barrier.

In the meanwhile, the cyberspace had also evolved: an initial freedom and opportunity was being given up. Cyberspace looks more and more like real space — regulated, concentrated, controlled. An *ecology of innovation* made changes to the architecture considered as a commons, which has built the greatest revolution in creativity we have seen. The Net was open source, the Net has to stay open: a common resource that produces a common good.

In December 2002, Creative Commons launched a set of copyright licenses that would enable people to mark the freedoms associated with their work and build a commons of culture and science which would be free to remix and share. Soon after the launch, Creative Commons initiated a project that would enable lawyers in countries outside the United States to 'port' CC licenses to their own national jurisdiction. According to Creative Commons founder Lawrence Lessig, the license porting project was key to the CC strategy. Most of the chapters on Creative Commons presented in this book are the results of reflections led by these CC leads in their country.

How is the Creative Commons web-based platform organized? Creative Commons, a not-for-profit organization, promotes the creative re-use of intellectual and artistic works. Through its free copyright licenses, Creative Commons offers authors the choice of a flexible range of protections and freedoms that build upon the "all rights reserved" concept of traditional copyright to enable a *voluntary* "some rights reserved" approach. Eight years after the launch of Creative Commons, which has revolutionized the modalities of sharing the creation on the Internet, this collective book on intelligent multimedia, edited by three members of the international CC network as editors, gathers the experiences of CC project leads on various topics: Legal Matters and national rights, Governance and common

---

[5] Lessig, L. (2004) *Foreword*, in Bourcier, D. and Dulong de Rosnay, M. (Eds), "International Commons at the digital age. La création en partage", Romillat, Paris.

property on the Internet, Open Access policies, New models of the Free Culture and Open Education.

What will Creative Commons be in 30 years? These essays reveal new collective practices and controversial issues in the field of copyright and open licensing. They also make an important contribution to contemporary debates on Open Access movement and Internet communities. In view of current debates and experiments in social theory and legal governance, we may rephrase this theoretical question underlying the project: is Creative Commons an answer to the conflict between modernity and post-modernity, positivism and empiricism, or a step to experiencing democracy?

2.1. THE LICENCING OF GOVERNMENT AND EDUCATIONAL MATERIAL

The question of reusing publicly funded material has become a critical issue: works, data, databases produced by governments, local authorities and public bodies are crucial for creative, educational and scientific purposes. Reuse by the public, the industry and scientists or by other governments is demanded. The management of these inaccessible materials has become one of the most significant issues for government in the knowledge age.

Technological developments have changed the way digital content is devised, stored, delivered, preserved, accessed and used, and together with business models for transacting digital content, they raise policy challenges to governments. With the advent of the internet-induced sharing opportunity, educational, business and even governmental actors started to open up a little by offering free access to information and collaborating in open content projects. In an evaluation of the Directive 96/9/EC on the legal protection of databases[6] in Europe, data.gov projects such as data.gov.uk (to be compared with data.gov US website) appear to have been rather slowly implemented due to some other legal barriers: "There has been a considerable growth in *database* production in the US, whereas, in the EU, the introduction of "sui generis" protection appears to have had the opposite effect."

In Australia, as explained by the overview of recent Australian developments, **Neale Hooper, Anne Fitzgerald, Brian Fitzgerald and Tim Beale** explained how the use of Creative Commons licensing enables

---

[6] First evaluation of Directive 96/9/EC on the legal protection of databases, December 12 2005.
http://ec.europa.eu/internal_market/copyright/docs/databases/evaluation_report_en.pdf

Open Access to Public Sector Information and publicly funded research results.

The concrete ways to use these licenses in a given legal system in Europe are interesting to quote. **Juan Carlos De Martin**, lead of CC Italy and coordinator of Communia, the European Thematic Network on the digital public domain, and **Andrea Glorioso** explore the SeLiLi project developed by the Piedmont region (Italy). This region has teamed with the Politecnico of Torino to create SeLiLi – Servizio Licenze Libere (Free Licenses Service), a project based in Torino and aimed at providing individuals and small businesses with information and, when necessary, consulting services on the licenses. This chapter describes the main characteristics of SeLiLi and summarizes the results of its first year of activities.

A new initiative has sprung on the path created by the Open Access (OA) movement: Open Education (OE). In order to achieve this goal, several international institutions, such as UNESCO and OECD, have published reports, surveys and documents to help educational institutions in this endeavor. This global initiative needs a legal framework; as a result, efforts thus far have usually resorted to Open Licensing (OL), especially Creative Commons licensing. In fact, as a response to this new movement, Creative Commons launched a new program, *ccLearn*[7], which recognizes open licensing's impact on education and directly supports the idea of open educational resources (OER). **Carolina Botero and Ignasi Labastida** analyze the current situation focusing on two local situations, the Colombian and the Catalan experiences with open educational projects at higher education level.

2.2. INTRICATION BETWEEN LEGAL, INSTITUTIONAL AND TECHNICAL CONSTRAINTS

The relationship between law and multimedia technology in the realm of copyright is strongly intertwined. **Melanie Dulong de Rosnay**, lead of CC France discusses what additional legal regulation may be required to allow full accessibility, which includes not only a legal authorization to perform certain rights, but also the technical possibility to effectively access and reuse material. She examines what technical infrastructure may better support the enforceability of CC licensing terms, namely a framework automating certain actions and pedagogy tools.

Collecting societies were solutions to the cultural and industrial revolutions of the past, the online licensing initiatives seem to provide

---

[7] http://learn.creativecommons.org

answers to the digital world. **Herkko Hietanen** of CC Finland describes the functions and the scope of collective licensing and examines the overlap among the individual, collective and the CC public licensing procedures. Can such institutions coexist? How? By using CC licenses, the rights owner reserves rights to collect royalties from the uses that are not covered by the license. However, in some jurisdictions, some rights cannot be waived and are mandatory managed by collecting societies. The question of rights owner's autonomy has to be examined beyond a paternalistic approach of copyright. Should the authors be allowed to manage their rights, even if it could lead to unknown or negative consequences?

Global interest in the CC licenses prompted a discussion about the need for national versions of the CC licenses. Creative Commons international is working with CC jurisdiction teams to port the core Creative Commons licenses to different copyright legislations around the world. The porting process includes both linguistically translating the licenses and legally adapting the licenses to a particular law to make them comprehensible and legally enforceable in the local jurisdiction. **Catharina Maracke**, a former director of Creative Commons international, presents an overview of her experience in this international porting process and its legal and promotional aspects.

2.3. THE FUTURE OF DIGITAL COMMONS

With the emergence of digital technology and the Internet, in many places and regions of developing countries (especially in the "peripheries"), technology arrived earlier than the idea of intellectual property. **Ronaldo Lemos**, project lead for Creative Commons in Brazil, and chair of iCommons describes the idea of *legal commons* in contrast with the idea of *social commons*. While the idea of *legal commons* can be understood as the voluntary use of licenses such as Creative Commons in order to create a "commons", the idea of *social commons* is related to the tensions between legality and illegality in developing countries. These tensions appear prominently in the so-called global "peripheries", and often make the legal structure of intellectual property irrelevant, unfamiliar, or unenforceable for various reasons. The Creative Commons project was launched without thinking especially about governance.

Several years after, the question of governance as a logic of collective action rises. Creative Commons provides creators and licensors with a simple way to express which freedoms they want their creative work to carry. The notion of *commons patrimony* will be proposed to analyze if Digital Common Goods do not ask for a new type of governance: what we call a *patrimonial governance*. The various concepts of property, commons and patrimony will be first revisited to understand the fundamentals of the CC project. **Danièle Bourcier**, lead of CC France, analyzes the various aspects of governance experienced through the CC Community and compares with some research on patrimonial goods.

Is a Tech Commons possible? **John H. Weitzmann**, lead of CC Germany, wonders if a commons of technological register rights content would be suitable for Open Innovation. According to the view presented here, a possible Tech Commons License should be accompanied by a registering support system and an incentive system that preserves at least some market effects.

Commons Based Peer Production (CBPP) represents a variety of distributed non–hierarchical and non–market–based forms of production. **Prodromos Tsiavos and Edgar Whitley**, London School of Economics and Political Science, explore the degree to which the widest adopted form of Open Content licensing, the CC licences, are produced. The analysis shows that as a regulation building project the CC case involves the production of both meaning and actual regulatory instruments.

3. Multimedia, Web 2.0 and Web 3.0

We live in a world in which economics, politics, and law have been definitively pervaded by technology. The WWW has changed as well in the last years. In the market, people are acting more as *prosumers* than as consumers. In the Internet, the web has turned into the *Social Web* (Web 2.0). Flickr, Wikipedia, Facebook, YouTube... are now familiar, and millions of interacting people add content and value into them. On the other way round, social reality is changing through and by means of changes produced in the Web. Semantic content, the creation of meaning through the possibilities and use of the new web languages enacts new patterns of social behavior as well.

The challenge is the connection and organization of this content, which is now disseminated all along the web, to facilitate its sharing and reuse. Therefore, the next step is the so-called Web 3.0 or Web of Data, and the construction of Semantic Web Services (SWS) which may operate through different kind of interfaces and easy accesses based on platforms or mobile technologies. Images, movies, films... constitute perhaps the most difficult part of the content to be properly indexed, classified and organized. For instance, multimedia ontologies have faced during the past decade what is known as "the semantic gap", the difficult enduring problem to automate the representation of content through images alone (and not only trough the apposite linguistic tags).

Quite understandably, so far, Web 3.0 and SWS are more an aspiration than a reality. But it is not wishful thinking; it is just the next step to be reached. The second part of the volume points to the description of innovative tools applying semantics to structuring and indexing multimedia data, or presenting some projects in this direction. This leads to the intertwining algorithmic, ontologic and Natural Language Processing (NLP) methodologies to produce hybrid approaches to the problem of acquiring, representing, inferring and retrieving multimedia knowledge.

As the reader will quickly notice, hybrid methodologies also match with a hybrid kind of regulation which does not consist only in legal norms, but in rules, principles, contexts, behavioural patterns and self-regulated institutional and professional systems. Soft law, technical protocols, governance and relational justice are being developed at the same time, and sometimes in the same places where legislation, administrative rules and court rulings try to reordering the moves of broadcast companies and internet servers.

Victoria Camps, Joan Barata, Emma Teodoro, Núria Galera and Pompeu Casanovas, who have been working together within the Project of the Code of Best Practices of the CPAC (Col.legi Professional de l'Audiovisual de Catalunya), reflect on this kind of self-regulated field through their experience as co-regulators. As they show, this field is particularly segmented, crossed by opposite interests and different professional profiles, and organized according the leverage of the agents acting in the field (from huge broadcast companies to individual script writers). Moreover, in the Spanish case, there is a powerful company manager acting as a prosecutor of the violations of property rights.

Those are the real settings, turmoil and present legal fights. From this point of view, social participation, downloads, and especially content sharing and new forms of computer grid coordination, represent a problem to be tackled in the Courtrooms. However, as **Nardine Osman, Carles Sierra, Jordi Sabater-Mir, Joseph R. Wakeling, Judith Simon, Gloria Origgi, Roberto Casati** are able to explain, even in the scientific field, people communicate faster and safer through blogs, wikis and other publishing tools allowing modifications and enrichments of the author's original content. They call them liquid publications.

On the other side of freedom in the Web are privacy and digital rights management. Privacy Enhancement Technologies (PETs), ambience intelligence, and ubiquitous computing, have to be balanced with CC and open source works. This is a particularly apt field to represent rights in combination with a conceptual framework allowing both data protection and open management. **Antoni Roig** reflects on privacy-preserving digital rights management in social networks applications. **Víctor Rodríguez Doncel, Jaime Delgado, Roberto García and Rosa Gil** show how ontology construction may participate in the governance and control of copyright, using NLP techniques. Copyright and copyleft may be combined at different ontology linguistic levels to be enacted in contracts or management of rights. **Jaime Delgado and Víctor Rodríguez Doncel** work out a legal ontology for creative works. Digital licenses for end users beyond the Rights Expressions Langage standard (REL) are modeled into an ontology focusing on the property value chain (Media Property Rights Ontology). In this sense, language engineering may become social engineering as well. To us, what it matters is showing the possibilities of linguistic ontological governance when applied to digital rights.

Finally, the volume ends up with two concrete applications. **Elena Sánchez-Nielsen and Francisco Chávez-Gutiérrez** introduce a tool to personalize the retrieval of Parliamentary Proceedings (including the regular videotaping of the sessions. **Pompeu Casanovas, Marta Poblet, José Manuel López-Cobo, Alvaro Cabrerizo and Juan Antonio Prieto** present Ontomedia, an example of a Semantic Web Service to provide annotated content and tools both to users and to professional mediators.

Within the same project, **Ciro Gracia, Xavier Binefa, Emma Teodoro, Núria Galera, and Jorge González-Conejero** face two different techniques to annotate multimedia content coming from courts and mediated interactions. The first one is diarization, the mathematical segmentation of the audio linked to the images of court procedures. The second one is semantic annotation, using light MPEG ontologies to annotate the content of legal videotapes. Both techniques are applied to the result of an empirical knowledge acquisition process. Moreover, **Ciro Gracia and Xavier Binefa** present the interesting subject of the extraction and representation of emotions in multimedia interchanges.

All technical contributions of the SW in the Web of Data can and should be coupled with CC ideas and developments. This turns into social advance towards a more habitable world.

Acknowledgements

This volume and its Introduction has been developed within the framework of these different projects: TSI-020501-2008, CSO-2008-05536-SOCI, TSI-020110-2009-374, SGR-CIRIT.

References

Benkler, Y. (2000) *From Consummers to Users: Shifting the Deeper Structures of Regulation*, Federal Communications Law Journal, Vol. 52, pp. 561.

Biegel, S. (2002) *Beyond Our Control? Confronting the Limits of Our Legal System in the Age of Cyberspace*, The MIT Press, Cambridge Mass.

Bourcier, D. and Dulong de Rosnay, M. (Eds) (2004), *International Commons at the digital age. La création en partage*, Romillat, Paris.

Boyle, J. (2003) *The Second Enclosure Movement and the Construction of the Public Domain*, Law & Contemporary Problems, Vol. 66, pp. 33-74.

Boyle, J. (2004) *A Manifesto on WIPO and the Future of Intellectual Property*, Duke Law & Technology Review, num. 0009, 9/8/2004. Available at: http://www.law.duke.edu/journals/dltr/articles/2004dltr0009.html   (accessed 6/3/2010).

Casanovas, P. (2004) *Derecho, Internet y Web Semántica*, Derecho a la intimidad y nuevas tecnologías. Cuadernos de Derecho Judicial IX, pp. 13-44.

Casanovas, P. (2009) *The Future of Law: Relational Law and Next Generation of Web Services*, Meritxell Fernández Barrera, Primavera de Filippi, Norberto Nuno, Andrade, Mario Viola de Azevedo Cunha, Giovanni Sartor, Pompeu Casanovas (Eds.) "The Future of Law and Technology: Looking into the Future. Selected Essays, European Press Academic Publishing, Legal Information and Communication Technologies Series, vol. 7, Florence, 2009, pp. 137-156.

Casanovas, P. and Poblet, M. (2008) *Justice via the Internet: Hopes and Challenges of Law and the Semantic Web*, G. Peruginelli, M. Ragona (Eds.), "Law via the Internet. Free Access, Quality of Information, Effectiveness of Rights", European Press Academic Publishing, Florence, pp. 347-359.

Claffy, K.C. (2008) *Ten Things Lawyers should Know about the Internet*, 2008, http://www.caida.org/publications/papers/2008/lawyers_top_ten/   (accessed 7/03/2010).

Kenneally E. and Claffy, K. (2009) An Internet Data Sharing Framework For Balancing Privacy and Utility, in "Engaging Data: First International Forum on the Application and Management of Personal Electronic Information" Oct. 2009, MIT (accessed 7/03/2010).

Hetcher, S. (2008a) *User-generated Content And the Future of Copyright: Part One — Investiture of Ownership*, Vanderbilt Journal of Entertainment & Technology Law, Vol. 10, pp. 863-892.

Hetcher, S. (2008b) *User-generated Content And the Future of Copyright: Part Two — Agreements Between Users and Mega-Sites* Santa Clara Computer and High Technology Law Journal, Vol. 24, Issue 4, pp. 829-867.

Hunter, D. (1999) *Cyberspace as Place and the Tragedy of the Digital Anticommons*, California Law Review, Vol. 91, pp. 439-519.

Lessig, L. (2004) *Foreword*, in Bourcier, D. and Dulong de Rosnay, M. (Eds), "International Commons at the digital age. La création en partage", Romillat, Paris.

Lessig, L. (2001) *The Future of Ideas. The Fate of the Commons in a Connected World*, Vintage Books, New York.

Litman, J. (2001) *Digital Copyright*, Prometeus Books, Amherst, New York.

Steinke, G. (2002) "Data Privacy approaches from US and EU perspectives", Telematics and Informatics, n. 19, pp. 193-200.

Sterne, L. (1847) *The Works of Laurence Sterne, containing the Life and Opinions of Tristram Shandy, gentleman*. Vol. 1. London, John James Chidley.

Steinke, G. (2002) *Data Privacy approaches from US and EU perspectives*, Telematics and Informatics, n. 19, pp. 193-200.

Vaidhyathan, S. (2001) *Copyrights and Copywrongs. The Rise of Intellectual Property and How It Threatens Creativity*, New York University Press.

Wagner, R. P. (2003) *Information Wants to Be Free: Intellectual Property and the Mythlogies of Control*, Columbia Law Review, Vol. 103, pp. 995-1034.

SECTION I

Creative Commons and Digital Rights: a New Kind of Governance

Digital Commons Works: Thinking Governance

Danièle Bourcier
CERSA – Université de Paris 2

Abstract. The Creative Commons (CC) Project was launched with no particular thinking on governance. Its primary aim was simply to share a common resource with common digital management. Several years on, the question of governance, as a logic of collective action, is arising. Between legicentrism and over-privatization, can both CC governance and governance by CC be seen as an alternative solution for managing future projects on common property *in common*?
Creative Commons oversees a system of common rights that provide creators and licensors with a simple method of indicating what freedoms they would like to pertain to their creative work. The notion of *commons patrimony* will be proposed in order to analyze whether Digital Commons necessitates a new type of governance: what we could call "patrimonial governance". The varying concepts of property, commons and patrimony will first be reviewed to give an insight into the fundamentals of the CC project. I will then analyze the various aspects of governance experienced through the CC Community and compare these with research on patrimonial goods.

Keywords: Governance of Digital Commons, Creative Commons, Public Domain, Patrimonalization, Global Commons.

1. Introduction

How should common goods on the borderline between commercial and non-commercial be managed? This has been the subject of recent works on cultural, genetic and environmental goods (Barrère, Barthélémy, 2005). Other studies explore the relationship between commons, community and property.[1] Even before the current increase in digital commons, the subject of this article, E. Ostrom (1990) drew attention to the importance of governing commons. The first body of work sought ways of managing a common resource, but did not directly address digital commons. However, these commons are specifically non-excludable and non-rival; this alters the relationship between commoners and common goods.

Creative Commons is a project that enables the sharing of digital cultural goods through a range of licenses that can be applied to a work, according to the terms desired. It is based on copyright, but with a new rationale of patrimony. That potential for conceptual innovation has let to

---

[1]   "Community and Property", Special Issue, *Theoretical Inquiries in Law,* vol. 10, N. 1, January 2009, The Berkeley Electronic Press http://www.bepress.com

the success of this "singular legal object",[2] but has, however, also attracted criticism. In essence, this initiative is at the center of new tension between the logics of economics (commercial/non-commercial) and the law (exclusive ownership or shared use). How can we analyze these new institutional formats whose equivalents are seen in other contexts, and which require us to review certain legal concepts?

At this juncture, our focus is on questions of property, common goods, patrimony and governance.

We will firstly explain the difficulty of defining the goods and contracts concerned, then we will turn to *patrimony* with a view to renewing our approach to this notion. In point of fact, considering only the property regime (purely questions of property) means that some analyses have little relevance to the topic in hand. The question of patrimony goes beyond a simple distinction between public and private goods, for to administer is first to ensure management, that is, the best management possible in response to specific objectives. In other words, the notions of community and patrimony determine new choices of governance. This chapter looks at these choices.

When the market and the state were considered to have different roles, a balance could be found between individual and general interest. However, since the demarcations between market and state intervention are now becoming less clear, as in cases where the state distorts competition and innovation by strengthening regulation in favor of the market, new types of governance - Lehavi (2009) distinguishes between intentional, planned or spontaneous governance - are appearing. These are put into place to manage new types of goods. In the USA and Europe, the most recent legislation related to intellectual property led directly to the founding of Creative Commons (CC).

Following a description of some concepts used in Creative Commons we will postulate that the concept of patrimony takes on the role of *driver*: it is responsible for the selection and institution of works that carry the identity of their holder and also the global identity. It imposes a type of governance that will be called patrimonial governance. Will this notion of patrimonial goods enable an understanding of some features of the CC project?

2. Property Rights and Governance

Goods relevant to CC are immaterial and/or digital goods,[3] and may be private or "public". However, this category of "public goods" is difficult to

---

[2]   P.Y. Thoumsin, *Creative Commons Le meilleur des deux mondes?* http://creativecommons.org/licences/by-nc-nd/2.0/be

[3]   The CC licences can be also used for material goods (books for example).

clarify. For economists, a public good is characterized by non-rivalry and non-excludability. Water, for instance, is not a public good since appropriation of this resource may give rise to rivalry. In this, we see the first signs of possible confusion between economic and legal vocabulary: as far as lawyers are concerned, public informational goods are those subsidized by public funding, intended to be accessible to the public, while the law deals with private goods under the concepts of property and private heritage. The question of governance arises when the goods are in a gray area between private property and public service.

2.1. RECONSIDERING TRADITIONAL NOTIONS

In the case of copyright, some aspects of ownership have been extended to include intellectual property. Creative Commons and Science Commons have reintroduced the concept of commons. We will now return to these fundamental concepts to give a clearer appreciation of their development.

2.1.1. *Property Rights*

Ownership was defined in the Civil Code at the beginning of the nineteenth century, on the basis of the Roman law de Justinien (*plena in re potestas*): [4]

> Civil Code Art. 544
>
> Ownership is the right to enjoy and dispose of things in the most absolute manner, provided they are not used in a way prohibited by statutes or regulations.

Some characteristics of property such as *exclusivity* are increasingly put into question. From a political standpoint, Angell (2009)[5] stated that property may be considered not as "something owned" but as a government-sanctioned monopoly right which is legally enforced by courts.

However, over the last two centuries, this exclusivity has become limited, particularly where land property and areas covered by the rise in urban planning are concerned. There is now a distortion between fact and law and a growing number consider that a new definition would be desirable. It has been said that this change was the revenge of Greece on Rome, of Philosophy on Law. The Roman concept that justified ownership in relation to its source (family, dowry, inheritance) has been overtaken by a teleological concept that justifies ownership through its aim, its service, and its function. The first draft of the French Constitution in 1946 was thus

---

[4]   *Institutes* 2,4,4.

[5]   Ian Angell, "All (Intellectual) Property is Theft?" Presentation, Fifth Communia Workshop, Accessing, Using, Reusing Public Sector Content and Data, 26-27 March 2009, London School of Economics, Proceedings.

written: *"Ownership cannot be exercised unless it is of social utility"*.

Some lawyers have attempted to bring together notions of general interest and public domain, with a view to changing the current position. The use of a plot of land is forbidden if this is contrary to the designation of the land. Ownership will be removed if the use goes against collective interest.

The term "property" has been used in the field of intellectual property. Property is more than a metaphor: for Elkin-Koren (2006), "It constitutes an effective legal mechanism that allows exclusion". In this legal field, in fact, the changes have been the exact opposite: this right is used increasingly "in the most absolute manner". The CC project was one of the responses to this "insanely complex system" of copyright (Lessig, 2004).

2.1.2. *Common Goods*

Common goods are goods that have owners: thus they may not be appropriated by third parties, whereas *res nullius* (goods that belongs to no-one, such as wild game) and *res derelictae* (abandoned goods or waste) have no specific ownership. Common Goods are resources that are not divided into individual portions of property but rather are jointly held so that anyone may use them without special permission: for example, public streets, parks, waterways, and works in the public domain. According to the Oxford English Dictionary *"A commons is a legal regime in which multiple owners are each endowed with the privilege to use equally a resource, and no one has the right to exclude another"*. This means that no-one needs permission for access or use. Some rules may define particular rights *a priori*. No-one is owner because no exclusive right can determine if a resource can be let to the other.

A common is not only defined by its nature (water, beaches, or the theory of relativity) but also by its function in the community (Lessig, 2001). A policy choice decides on the organization. For Lessig, several factors may justify the creation of common goods. Firstly, common goods imply certain values that would vanish if these goods were privatized. Secondly, some resources may be more *efficiently* used if they are held in common. Nuances have now been introduced into this notion.

When commons are referred to, there may be some confusion between the notions of a community of rights and common management.

For example, management of a common good may be undertaken as a result of a decision taken between a group of commoners and the owner. However, this management may also be handed over to a public person. In 1792 during the French revolution, the laws stated that every Municipality was the owner of several types of goods: commons goods ("bare and indeterminate land") in the stricter sense, and productive goods.

A common land (a common) can be a piece of land owned by one person but over which other people may exercise certain rights: this is considered a semicommons, which would in reality come under CC (Loren, 2007). Older texts use the word "common" to denote any such right but modern usage refers to particular rights of common and reserves the word "common" for the land over which the rights are exercised. By extension, the term "commons" has come to be applied to any resource to which a community has rights or access.

In reality, common land does not mean there is no owner. Rather, it signifies only that people other than the owner have rights: these are known as commoners. The owner may retain certain rights and any common rights abandoned by the commoners. The commoner may be interested in particular plots of land, but most of the time the rights of common are unconnected with ownership or tenure of land: these rights include pasture, *piscary*, *turbary*, *mast* and *pannage*, and *estovers* (small trees and fallen branches).

The term "commons" denotes a resource over which a group has access and rights of use, under certain conditions. This is used even more widely than the term "public domain." The first aspect is the *size* of the group that has *access* rights. Some would say it is a commons only if the whole community has access. The second aspect represents the extent of the restrictions on *use*. A commons may be restrictive. For example, some open source software gives the user the freedom to modify the software on condition that their own contributions will also be freely open to others. There is some discussion on what exactly should be considered as commons: all agree on water, but not on education, health, or the environment (Kiss,1989). The issue of software, genes, and seeds are points of contention between those who wish these to be commons and others who want to extend patents. Developed societies tend to have a preference for private property over public interest. For John Sulston, Nobel Prize Winner for Medicine, the human genome was sequenced as an open project; consequently this type of collaboration and increase in knowledge is inalienably a common patrimony of humanity. The Global Earth Observing System of Systems (GEOSS) is a major international initiative which proposes that "all shared data, metadata and products will be made available with minimum time delay and at a minimum cost" to develop "coordinated, comprehensive and sustained earth observations and information".[6] Wikimedia Commons is free, unlike image and media banks that come under GNU licensing, where it is possible to use and modify the information. This lack of agreement on the size of the commons and the rights of use requires the involvement of the notions of public interest

---

[6]   P. Uhlir, Global Change in Environmental Data Sharing: Implementation of the GEOSS Data Sharing Principles, *Communia Workshop Proceedings*, Torino, July 2009.

patrimony and human patrimony. This hypothesis will be explored in Section Three.

2.1.3. *Public Domain or Commons?*

The term "public domain" is ambiguous since it may be related to Public Law[7] and copyright. In copyright, the public domain is not a commons: it is a *status* into which works whose use is no longer compulsorily subject to permission are put. These are public or private goods that are not open to private appropriation. By its very nature, some "public" content is part of the public domain (the unedited versions of Official Journals). Private works may also "fall" into the public domain after the rights expire, or in exceptions to copyright (quotation), or be put there voluntarily by the author.[8]

For US copyright law, those who do not wish to have a legal monopoly can omit the usual phrase on copyright for their work: it would then pass into the public domain.[9] The default position would become freedom and the dead weight would disappear. Also, given the changing role of knowledge in society, the Australian government is redefining the concept more broadly to mean *open knowledge*: information that may be readily accessed, redistributed, and reused. According to J. Boyle (2008) "W*e have to invent the public domain before we can save It*". CC0, the final licensing option in CC, is a way of putting goods into the public domain by waiving all copyrights and related contiguous rights such as moral rights (to some extent waivable), and database rights that protect the extraction, dissemination and reuse of data. In the same way, Science Commons launched the Protocol for Implementing Open Access Data, a method for ensuring that scientific databases may legally be integrated into each another. The protocol is built on the public domain status for data in many countries and provides legal certainty for data deposit and data reuse.

2.2. GOVERNANCE OF CULTURAL GOODS

The "Governance of Goods" describes the types of management that regulate use of these goods. The management rules may be established by law, and complemented by individual contract for copyright, or in a form developed by the rights holders where common goods are concerned.

---

[7]   There is a theory of public domain in public law that concurs with management of goods of a special nature, known as public domain or national domain by a public body. The goods must be assigned to public use.

[8]   This status has been the subject of numerous discussions in the CC Community: the European Communia project is based on this theme: www.communia-project.eu

[9]   With a period of time during which the author could claim copyright retrospectively if the phrase were omitted by accident.

Composite positions may be defined as a result of public policy or democratic principles (open access, for example) related to patrimony or the public domain.

The conditions for production of and the needs of the public with regard to informational or cultural goods have radically changed, to such an extent that property rights and particularly copyright, and also the size of the commons along with public domain status have had to adapt to a movement towards *copyleft*. These changes have been necessary firstly because production of these goods, whether public or private, is increasingly the result of collective effort, and a new culture of collaborative work has emerged. This culture is linked to the new technological possibilities offered by Web 2.0, with its orientation toward user interactions via participatory portals. Users are active players and, consequently, authors. They feed content into databases, websites, blogs and wikis. Secondly, cultural goods are now more likely to be produced and disseminated by public bodies. Lastly, there is a public desire to use digital works for themselves, in order to modify and diversify the usages although digitalization of some holdings appears to have changed the conditions for access.[10] In this context, the mode of governance becomes capital, as suggested by Garrett Hardin (1968) in the (ideological) fable relating the Tragedy of the Commons: a community of sheep farmers who share a commons of pastureland may choose a dangerous type of management that leads to overexploitation of the resource and environmental deterioration. Garrett concludes that in order to overcome this paradox of the commons it will be necessary to reinstate appropriation by the state, or, even better, by the private sector, in the same way that in 1960 Ronald Coase advocated privatizing the environment so that it could be managed more effectively. Some believe that certain mechanisms restricting access to resources managed by the state must be extended. In fact, this is now the case for databases, as will be seen later. Nevertheless, there are other solutions. The two aspects of common property and free access must not be confused.

Private knowledge is governed by intellectual property law, with the complex restrictions of exclusivity denounced by believers in the opposite tragedy, anticommons. Public knowledge may be the result of a public service mission or material produced by public servants. Some public knowledge may be ordered by copyright law (abstracts of judicial cases) or in the "public domain" (Official Journals). The status of public knowledge is varied, as demonstrated under "legal information" in public sites

---

[10]   An investigation into public library websites in France showed that one third of the sites carry NO legal indications and that a large number of indications were biased or totally illegal.
http://www.slideshare.net/calimaq/bibliothques-numriques-et-mentions-lgales-un-aperu-des-pratiques-en-france

constructed for museums and libraries. Public bodies often produce works and manage them as enclosures: these are made available to closed groups of users. For several years now these goods have become more accessible because of the Internet. However, opening public informational goods remains subject to exceptions. In addition, under European law, databases benefit from protection *sui generis* that prevents direct access to the content. Legal databases are an example of the tensions currently allied to the functions of information in a democratic society funded through circulation of content.[11] In the sphere of politics and public policy, environmentalism presents a *remarkable diversity of organizational forms and missions.* We are at the beginnings of the replication of that *institutional diversity in the world of intangible property.*

3. Managing Digital Commons: The Creative Commons Project

Intellectual property rights are based on the regime of exclusive property and limited access to the resource, whether the property be *individual, collective* or *common.* Creative Commons has changed the given by immediately questioning how to best manage rights holders' freedoms in a digital commons, and how these management "rules" could be part of a minimal agreement between authors and the public.

In the Tragedy of the Commons, the commoners were invited into the area but no-one had defined the limits of the resource. For Garrett Hardin, only the right of the state (which regulates individual property and internalizes management on the part of each owner) is effective because common goods will inevitably be subject to anarchy of use until the moment they disappear. Two institutional modes of managing these knowledge pools have therefore been detailed: the market and the state. In the Internet world, the question has shifted from exclusion to access. Many resources now have different modes of access. The fact that digital goods are not rivalrous broadens the variety of agreements and types of cooperation, even though the cooperation is weak. These commons, considered by economists to be positive externalities, are facilitated by *social media* and Web 2.0 applications.

---

[11]   For instance: The State of California publishes its laws on the Internet. Its copyright claims mean that people have to pay to download or print state laws and regulations. A user decided to digitally scan the 33,000 pages and put them online for free on the website The State claimed that this user needed its permission to put state laws online. This user wanted to provide open access to common public resources. If documents are in standardized formats companies can improve services (annotation of codes, wikis). The point is that government information is monopolized by the State and above all by exclusive vendors. This content is therefore not a commons. Lessig (2001) responds: "The essence in other words is that no one exercises the core of a property right with respect to these resources – the exclusive right to choose whether the resource is made available to others".

Mediated communities are asking the State to develop all possible means to enable better circulation of information, for example to develop high speed broadband against outside company monopolies and to ensure arbitrage between differing collective preoccupations. However these communities believe there is another tragedy, that of *private goods*: *enclosure* models are closed in the short term. Although neither altruistic nor completely individualistic, communities of creators, such as Creative Commons, share a common vision and aim for equality of rights to the resource, with no limits to access, when the licensor waives his conditional rights.

3.1. THE OBJECTIVES OF CREATIVE COMMONS

The aims of CC are thus to facilitate simple, legal sharing and reuse of creative, educational, and scientific content. To this end, it provides free legal and technical tools in order to: *"promote collaboration between content creators and users around the globe. Creative Commons supports a world in which people actively engage in — and don't just passively consume — cultural, educational, and scientific material around them and build a pool of creative, educational, and scientific content that can be freely and legally accessed, used, and remixed".*[12]

CC falls into the category of open information models. Any use that is not to the detriment of the common may be made. However not all the conditions are totally to the advantage of a community: non share-alike, non-derivative, non-commercial (Eechoud, Wal, 2008).

The notion of *anticommons* characterizes a resource that is not used for maximum benefit. Whereas a common good is a good that all can draw on, an anticommon is subject to vetoes on its use. The Nobel Prize winning economist J. Buchanan has shown that as too many people have the right of veto over patents, the resource has become underused. Thus private property rights combined with rights pertaining to databases result in some resources lying dormant. It is therefore necessary for the right attached to a good or a work to be returned to its original source. The costs for use are too high. This exploitative monopoly has become a hindrance to the free circulation of information, works, and services.

3.2. COMMON GOODS IN CREATIVE COMMONS

James Boyle's book puts forward the view that we are in the middle of a second enclosure movement. Things that were formerly considered to be

---

[12]   http://creativecommons.org/

common property, or "uncommodifiable," or completely outside the market, are now being covered by new, or newly extended, property rights.

Take the human genome, for example: supporters of enclosure have argued that the state was right to step in and extend the reach of property rights. However, opponents of enclosure have claimed that the human genome belongs to all, that it is literally the common heritage of humankind, and that it should not and perhaps in some sense cannot be owned. Here it is impossible to exclude economic factors from legal values. The point of property is that it may be destroyed, and also confiscated. When scientific progress is concerned, this method of managing the resource may be particularly unfavorable to the common good of health.[13] We have noted that "A common is a piece of land owned by one person but over which other people can exercise certain rights". A work created by the mind, like a piece of land, has an owner (the author) but other persons may also exercise some rights.

Moreover as the term "commons" has come to be applied to any resource to which a community has rights or access, it is agreed that all in the CC and more can access the piece of common. What exactly is *shared* in the CC project? At first sight it may be said that this is all works in the virtual pool. However, my hypothesis is that the Commons shared in CC is not simply limited to *private ordering* but that it applies to all the facilities and services put in common in this project.

3.2.1. *The Size of the Commons*
The knowledge pool is made up of all works that authors have placed under CC license. These multimedia works (books, reports, articles, images, photographs, music, films etc.) are produced by independent authors or producers; however, they may also be produced by public bodies. It must be borne in mind that all the works in question must be protected by copyright because the author chooses the type of license.

The commons includes rights over these productions because they are copyrighted, unless they are CC0 licensed or fall into the public domain.[14] What is put in common is open, free access to works: a non-exclusive general authorization to produce, distribute and communicate the work to the public, at no charge. This applies also to collective works and P2P networks. Other optional conditions apply to certain rights that the creator has relinquished: the possibility of altering the work, of using it

---

[13]   Health is considered to be part of common goods or global public goods by the United Nations Development Program (in English) (UNDP).

[14]   CC0 is similar to the current allocation to the public domain; but in the case of CC0 the rights waiver will also have more force because there is a platform for reputable systems to develop the copyright status of content on the basis of who has done the certifying.

commercially or non-commercially, and of circulating it under the same conditions.

A movement towards a community-oriented philosophy that views exclusion from content as undesirable has now been set in motion. Licensed content is accessible via search engines such as Yahoo and Google, and is thus completely open. The number of works online has now reached around 200 million, but as there is no central count of works, authors or users the number of commoners is unknown.

The larger the body of work online the greater will be the choice and the use of the commons. Bell & Parchomovsky (2009) explain this choice in terms of cost: *"The CC movement was born out of a sense that in the information age the cost of excluding others from most informational works is too high"*. This means that the free commons (where there is no question of entry or exclusion) diminish "costs of transaction and governance", and are thus particularly efficient. There is therefore no need to register in order to use the services of the commons: there are no controls and no sanctions regarding the use to which they are put.

3.2.2. *Digital License Platform*
CC offers open, free access to the platform providing the licenses.[15] A license is a contractual document that specifies what can and cannot be done with a work. It grants permission, and states restrictions: access, reuse and redistribution, with few or no restrictions. It is possible for example to print, to share, to publish, to make alterations and additions to it, to incorporate it in another piece of writing, and to use it as the basis for a work in another medium.

Six options, combinations the different criteria, are available to authors. Once the author has chosen the license for a particular work, the platform produces three personalized documents: one in html format, one that is simplified, and, thirdly, a legal document. Currently there are more than fifty-two sets of national licenses that have ported the generic license in national legal systems.

3.2.3. *The Creative Commons Tag*
Creative Commons is more than simply a resource or a service: it is also an identity. CC upholds a certain number of objectives and values. Some conditions are optional (individual values) while others are common (collective values). Authors who deposit their work in CC commit to making it available at a minimal level of access, at the least.

The Australian Culer report contains a strong recommendation endorsing the use of CC licenses for public information. CC licenses can

---

[15]   Under French jurisdiction: www.fr.creativecommons.org

become the means for implementing Open Access policies. In particular, these increase the delivery of government services on line. This approach fosters participatory democracy with a two-way commitment between the state and the citizen.

3.3. THE GOVERNANCE OF CREATIVE COMMONS

An understanding of the way in which the Commons are governed is necessary. However, the choice of management method is not linked solely the concept of the "cost of governance". Overall governance of the project is under neither the control of the authors who provide their works *a priori* nor of those who will use them.

The resource management system has not eliminated authors' rights and none can currently predict whether it will move towards more, or less, open access. Demsetz' hypothetical model that postulates the development of a rights regime moving from Commons to exclusive rights is no more provable than the opposing model, wherein there is an ineluctable movement towards open access.

The CC empirical governance model has not been aimed at *good governance* or optimal management of the resource (by giving more rights to commoners or initiating more organized governance); but it has been led by the increase in goods, the development of collaborative work, and freedom of choice between those who wish to relinquish their rights and others who want to manage their patrimony. When this is compared to the *Open Source Movement,* there access is open in the same way as for CC, but the license is a mechanism that manages the future of the resource: use and adaptation are reserved to those who accept the terms of the Open Source License. In CC, externalization costs have been borne by CC but authors continue to manage their own goods individually, with no collective commitment to the future. In the following part, we describe the current method adopted to manage CC globally.

3.3.1. *The Collaborative Mode of Developing the Licenses*
As the rules on Intellectual Property Rights come under national jurisdictions, - in spite of the existence of international law - an international organization has been set up to adapt CC licenses to every legal system. Creative Commons International was established to develop and coordinate worldwide national chapters. Questions common to several chapters may sometimes be discussed (moral rights). Vertical relationships are associated to questions that for the most part relate to legal and technical expertise. The different steps in the porting show some tension in the efforts to keep close to the (US) originals, in order to maintain the

greatest degree of similarity possible between the licenses. This expertise belongs to the Commons.

3.3.2. *Management by National Chapters*

The national Project Lead team is a volunteer. This would constitute an expert in copyright law, often a law professor, a junior researcher or an artist generally associated with the institutions or a law practice. In most cases, university law faculties have volunteered.

Governance is based on subsidiarity, and coordination.

These relationships are coordinated by a CC International (Berlin) authority, separate from headquarters (San Francisco). The chapters have tried to form regional groupings: these attempts have led to several initiatives in the Asia Pacific region and in Europe. The 2009 CC Asia Pacific Regional Conference, recognizing its "cultural and language diversity" proposed to adopt an action strategy in an Action Plan Statement. Their aim is to play a proactive role in expanding and building the CC Communities in Asia and the Pacific areas with the objective of administering a Common web portal to establish a "regional identity".

Discussions regarding the region of Europe are now in progress. These are expected to lead to similar regional organization. However, for the moment no decision has been made on the creation of these regional levels positioned between the national and global bodies.

3.3.3. *No Central Committee and No Centralized Governance of Owners*

To Richard Epstein an experiment such as open source (close to the CC project) must inevitably end in failure because it cannot scale up to meet its own success. Then Epstein asks for a "central committee" from which insiders will be unable to cash out – a mixture of communist and capitalist metaphors. "*All governance systems - including democracies and corporate boards - have problems. But so far as we can tell, those who are influential in the free software and open source governance communities feel that they are doing very well indeed.*"

In the 1980s and 1990s a large body of literature taught us that property-like governance mechanisms could and often do emerge in the absence of formal property rights. Robert Ellickson and Elinor Ostrom described governance regimes to allocate resources and coordinate activities when property rights were nonexistent or ineffective. In this process, order, allocation, and coordination were not always synonymous with formal property rights. For CC, formal rights are managed by the legal systems and the licenses are self-managed. In the same vein, some interesting real-world situations – where in effect public resources emerge against a backdrop of private entitlements – have been described. "The upshot is the same: private re-engineering of the entitlement structure, in the interest of people getting things done" (Merges, 2004).

3.3.4. *The Relationship between Commoners*

CC commoners, whether authors or users, have a variety of relationships, as already described in the sociology of social networks. In effect a social network is shown as a chart of relationships and interactions between individuals, and may be based on geography, work organization, or simply on informal connections (Barnes, 1972). With CC, the network does not exist prior to its creation. The very fact that the commons pool is not centralized (through a database) and that there is no relationship between authors and users – or a system of representation – makes it a network of informal relationships where the network is mainly used to create a global identity or to determine the "social capital" of individual participants.

In reality the project is based on the digital universe wherein the idea of territory is relatively weak. The system does exist at territorial level but only in relation to the transposition into a particular legal system. The organization of production and circulation is reduced to a minimum due to the externality of the platform and the transparence of procedures and documents. The social spread of informal relationships is described *a posteriori*. However the Legal Leads community has created a Thematic Network on the Public Domain at European regional level in response to a European invitation to tender (COMMUNIA).[16]

3.4. GOVERNANCE, THE LAW AND REGULATION IN CC

The terms "Governance" and "Regulation" are often used together and sometimes interchangeably. However, there is a clear distinction: regulation pertains to the development of new forms of interaction between law and society, while governance aims to find new equilibriums between law and society (Bourcier, 2002) where a parallel form of State regulation is sought. We will argue that the CC project relates in part to both approaches. What is Creative Commons vis-à-vis the State? Is it self-governance? What is the underlying institutional question? For the majority of the problems relevant to Commons, the issues are typically of governance and institution.

First, Creative Commons is a complementary form of State regulation. However, public interest is replaced by the "civil society of Internet users" at the core of the freedom related to creation. This might be considered a new method of coordination between agents. Agents are iCommoners as well as users. This method of governance is a manner of responding to the

---

[16]   www.communia-project.eu

creator's offer and the needs of new creators and users.

Second, CC licenses constitute a learning process enabled by the exchange of works, information, and experiences. CC creates a new form of social governance by means of "soft self-regulation" providing a dynamic that is worth looking at from both a national and international point of view. This approach can be seen as a reaction to legal complexity. However, the CC instruments also define a new equilibrium between law (statute) and contract. The CC contract is proposed under conditions chosen by the contracting parties.

Here, the issue at stake is to find a balance between freedom and rules. Authors must be paid but at the same time they cannot have complete control over their works: in legal parlance, the rules are more those of liability than of property. In fact all the questions concern rivalry or non-rivalry; and in a world of non-rivalry and innovation, it is necessary to allow for openness, but also to make rules for the common pool. Common practice may be more effective than the State or the market. Management of property rights in a customary system or a social network is able to self-organize (Rose, 1986).

Finally the CC approach introduces a new logic moving from "management by regulation" to "management by coordination". It represents an incremental approach where breakthroughs are measured in real practice more than through normative texts (Bourcier, 2007).

In this context, large-scale centralized coordination is impossible: the process of creation must be modular, with units of differing sizes and complexities, each requiring slightly differing expertise, all of which can be added together to make a complete whole. However, the total enterprise will be much, much, greater than the sum of its parts. Governance processes may be assembled through local systems in a global network, by people with widely varying motivations and skills.

4. Patrimonial Governance for Digital Goods: Reinventing the Notion

The CC project has thus created a common resource that can be shared, and to which all have access. In addition, CC has allowed those who wish to share, following certain conditions, to choose and to circulate their options; CC has also created open collaborative works in progress, an open collaborative Commons that will become a future Commons. Membership is not necessary, but there is a kind of moral "contract" based on an economy of exchange, of give and take. A CC community is developing in every country and participating in the dissemination of the project. The Commons is not one of ownership, but it creates a pool that may be accessed. The Commons draws up the conditions for use. As a result, these Commons, far from falling into decline, are likely to increase their spread.

The question I will ask in this final section on CC is whether a new form of institution is coming into being, one with a will for preservation and a potential to create new goods that have the express characteristic of being accessible. The traditional notion of patrimony is becoming multidimensional. Successively, patrimony has been familial, genetic, cultural, national, in land now close to World Heritage status, and in Humanity. We will explore whether it is possible to go beyond the simple notion of common property, and to extend the concept to common heritage. Cultural heritage is not limited to the material, such as monuments and objects preserved over time: the notion also encompasses living expressions and traditions that countless groups and communities worldwide have inherited from their ancestors and now transmit to their descendants, in most cases orally. In the field of Creative Commons, there are also many works, especially of music, that we cannot protect other than by making them live.

4.1. THE NOTION OF PATRIMONY

The notion of patrimony is evolving from the strict civilist notion (patrimonial rights) to that of Human rights: *"Patrimony is the set of goods of a person, considered as forming an universality of rights"*.[17] CC requires attributes from each of these concepts of patrimony.

For positivist lawyers, patrimony is an individualistic notion and can refer only to monetary values. Where copyright is concerned, patrimonial rights differ from moral rights. Patrimonial rights give the author "the possibility of living off his work". They confer the exclusive right to authorize third parties to use his creations, through agreement on transfers or licenses with these third parties. Here, the notion of exclusivity proper to the notion of property reappears. The author decides on the conditions for use and may instigate proceedings against imitation in the case of any non-authorized exploitation of his work. This concept could explain the origin of copyright laws. Moral rights, without monetary value, are outside of the concept of patrimoniality.

The notion of patrimony is currently changing dramatically (World Common Heritage) due to conflicts in patrimonial management. Formerly, patrimony was defined by its source and origin more than by its future, affectation, and use. However, the notion has evolved: it is now not enough to preserve heritage, it is necessary to exploit it, to display it in cultural inventories. The notion of common heritage may be a pathway between private and public heritage. Given the origin of the private conception of patrimony, public bodies are not comfortable with the notion of public

---

[17]   Cf. a traditional book in French doctrine: Aubry & Rau, *Droit civil français*, t. IX, 6th Ed.

patrimony. This notion of patrimony could re-qualify a resource. It allows for re-appropriating some goods and some rights. Indeed, patrimony is also the expression of the capacity for use (Declaration of Human Rights 1789, Art. 1). It is inherent in personality. To be entitled to a patrimony means to hold a power to be included in a circulation of goods and to be registered in a relationship of exchange. For Ollagnon, patrimonialization is a way of constituting a community between participants – not to solve conflict or earn money but to affirm identity. Patrimonialization can become an *operational* tool, with the aim of administering/governing (economic value) or managing (patrimonial value). Patrimony can be seen as an alternative to property rights: it is a way of finding other institutional solutions. In the long term, patrimonialization can take on a social identity.

4.2. THE OBJECTIVES AND VALUES OF CC AS PATRIMONY

CC responds to the main points we have described above.

Micoud[18] demonstrates that the role of patrimonalization (in environment) was firstly to conserve and to protect. Now the issue of governance is a major consideration where resources are concerned: "Patrimoniality is a way of building a community". The use of this notion can prevent exclusive appropriation, particularly in the case of scarce resources such as fish.

In the digital world, reuse is at the heart of common interest. The main advantage is to be able to access, sort, and consult intermediate pools. However, reuse is a new type of production. In fact, the issue is also not to create a new work for an individual but to build collaborative space. The new paradigm is to bridge the gap between production and creation. The term "patrimonial economy more than commercial or patrimonial capitalism is debated".

Governance of this patrimony has led to the development of new property rights: the right to access, the right to regulate, the right to dispose, the right to be transparent (right to expression, and related preferences).[19] The right to property becomes more varied. This is based on an implicit patrimonial convention whose principal aims are laid out below.

---

[18]   Patrimony in Environmental field has been broadly analyzed in : A. Micoud, "Redire ce qui nous relie?", C. Barrière, D. Barthelemy, M. Nieddu, F.D. Vivien (eds), *Réinventer le patrimoine, De la culture à l'économie, une nouvelle pensée du patrimoine ?* Paris, L'Harmattan, p. 81 and ff.

[19]   Recommendation at the National Meeting of Internet Players, Autrans, France, January 2009 (300 participants): For free access to public data: to change the legislation and practice in favour of access and reuse in order to develop a knowledge-based society – to indicate the conditions for use clearly in all public data financed by public budgets; these rights could be guaranteed by licences such as CC and Art Libre.

4.2.1. *To Create a Safe Global Commons*

The project was not set up to help individuals and to assemble an aggregation of individual works. On the contrary, it was created to share something different, something new. It was more than simply a series of isolated actions. The ensuing result was the creation of a global "commons" of material that was open to all, provided the terms of the licenses were adhered to. Any contract must be in accordance with the rules selected by individuals, and must conform.

This patrimony is based not only on access to a work for private use but also on co-production. In this context CC is similar in some ways to the world of Free Software: it has followed on from the opportunity offered by file sharing applications. In fact, all the bywords used in free software development have their counterparts in the theory of democracy and open society. With open source the production process was transparent, and the result of that process was a "product" which out-competed other products in the marketplace. In his noteworthy book on "distributed creativity" and the sharing economy, Yochai Benkler (2006) sets the idea of "peer production" alongside other mechanisms for market and political governance and puts forward powerful normative arguments regarding that future. Eric Von Hippel (2005) shows that innovation happens in more places than we have traditionally imagined, particularly in end-user communities. This reinforces the theme that "peer production" and "distributed creativity" is not something new, merely something that is given considerably more salience and reach by the Web. In addition, Jonathan Zittrain (2008) argues that "the main force of Creative Commons as a movement has not been in the Courts but in cultural mindshare".

Other examples of commons-based, non-proprietary production exist all around us. The present teaches us about the potential of a new "hybrid economy" (Lessig), one where commercial entities leverage value from sharing economies. That future will thus benefit both commerce and community.

4.2.2. *To Preserve All Cultural Patrimony Through Open Acess*

Offering open access to a complete knowledge pool, or placing it under CC license, may prevent "pirating" of works in the public domain for which individuals with few scruples request patents or copyright at the time of their digitalization. In India, this was the case for traditional yoga postures found in ancient texts. The Indian government has begun scanning the documents in order to store and preserve them in an encyclopedia, The *First traditional knowledge digital library*, which will be open to free access.[20] A second example concerns digital archives that disappear because they have been purchased.

Even the term "reuse" may be subject to different conditions, depending on individual, commercial or non-profit reuse. Where private authors are concerned, solely the author should be able to decide what is authorized. However, reuse also enables the content to be extended, so that works which are Creative Commons (Wikipedia, for example) become new universal pools that are added to voluntarily by users. Thus, Global Commons, part of the United States Library of Congress, and therefore repository of a body of work produced through public funding, is constituted of a group of individuals and institutions who wish to make their "treasures" available to the widest possible public. Similarly, Flickr contains photographs from all over the world and users are invited to expand on descriptions by adding tags. We are now in a period where services are exchanged and information is extended, where facts produced by a private author or by an authority can coexist in the same common work...

In this way we now see the question of licenses in a different light: they are not limited to accessibility, but now also concern making material available, reusing it, adding to it and even patrimonial preservation of digital content within the public domain. Producers of content are not determined by the public or private nature of works. Creators now have tools they can trust that, while respecting ownership of their rights, offer a public the potential of using and reusing their content *a priori* and without *intermediary*.

4.3. COLLECTIVE PATRIMONY: FUNDAMENTAL RIGHTS AND PUBLIC DEBATE

The justification for property rights to be included in patrimonial governance may also be supported by the change from a system where rights are reserved in the name of ownership of goods towards a system where these goods are preserved "in the name of a common patrimony and of universal access to knowledge and culture" (Bourcier, Dulong de Rosnay, 2004). For V. Hugo, the work as thought belongs to humankind.[21] Moreover, public space and public debate need to be developed, as

---

[20]   Where asanas are concerned, the UK daily www.telegraph.co.uk recently reported that there have been more than 130 yoga-related patents, 150 copyrights and 2,300 trademarks in the United States alone. And in the USA alone, the yoga business brings in $5.7 billion a year, according to Yoga Journal, including money spent on yoga classes and products. http://www.communia-project.eu/node/217 (July 10 2009).

[21]   V. Hugo, Discours d'ouverture du congres littéraire international de 1878, available on http://www.freecape.eu.org/biblio/article.php3?id article =93

promoted by Habermas. Overpropriatarization and the enclosure of works could put an end to the circulation of ideas (Dussolier, 2005).

4.3.1. *The Relationship between Commons and Publicly-funded Goods*

Exclusive rights, the prerogative of private property, have also invaded the non-commercial public sector, that pertaining to the general interest and public service.

In fact, there are different approaches: one based on the notion of public service or general interest that dominates management of the state public domain, and one based on ownership of public assets. Thus the copyright of public persons has continually been reaffirmed by the French Council of State.[22] These two approaches are conflictual which would show that over-patrimonialization has penetrated all sectors of society. In France in fact a study[23] has been set up to attempt to understand why informational goods subsidized by public persons are not explicitly open to access. States' lack of capacity to deal with environmental issues has now led lawyers to develop the concept of the "common heritage of mankind". The traditional status of *res communis* as applied to certain resources is not suitable (free access and free exploitation). However, the central question remains how can "mankind" manage this heritage? The Rio Convention on Biological Diversity (1992) omitted this concept, but recognized the creation of new copyrights that assist indigenous local communities. The subjective individualistic nature of patrimony is a significant impediment to the conceptualization of a new framework for cultural patrimony. The right recognized as pertaining to a community is not an individual right but an agreement for the exercise of a specific activity, legally attributed to the holder of the right: it is no longer a property right. In private law patrimony and property are closely bound. All goods in the patrimony are submitted to property rights. On the other hand Creative Commons creates a new link between individual works, commons deposits and collective governance. We are now in a culture of availability rather than authorization and a *"mutual sharing of knowledge as the collective property of mankind"*.[24]

4.3.2. *Reinventing Heritage*

The categories of public, community and private must thus be examined and brought to the fore through the notion of patrimony. The traditional approach to good property governance was through familiar institutions:

---

[22]   Public data can thus be "Works of the Mind" which do not belong to the civil servant authors, but to the public person itself: CE, Ass. 10 juillet 1996, Sté Direct Mail Production, AJDA, 20 février 1997, p. 189, Note H. Maisl.

[23]   http://www.bicoop.net/index.php/BICOOP,_des_Biens_public_biens_communs

[24]   R Stallman, The Copyleft and its Context, *Proceedings of the Copyright. Copywrong*, Nantes, 2003, ed. MemO, 2003.

the government, the market, communal management, or through property rights. Some recommend that the state control the majority of natural resources in order to prevent their destruction; others advocate that privatizing these resources will resolve the problem. Nevertheless these solutions are not uniformly successful in enabling individuals to sustain long-term productive use of natural resources. *"Communities of individuals have relied on institutions resembling neither the state nor the market to govern some resource systems with reasonable degrees of success over long period of times"* (Ostrom, 1990). At present we do not have the relevant intellectual tools and models to integrate the governance and management of these issues. The notion of Market and State cannot contribute to this reinvention of models. Many communities (commons), groups, and entities need to be reconstituted around the notion of patrimony and of governing how they coordinate and cohabit. The concept of patrimony shows that in addition to the notion of *general values* there is a way of more effectively managing the resource and conforming to collective interest. We recognize a new trend in public policies: the state is founded on the notion of general interest and social contact. Today, new communities are able to help the State to find a new legitimacy through regulating the way that common goods and public goods can be managed by new players who are not private but patrimonial, particularly where cultural heritage is concerned.[25]

4.3.3. *From the Environment to Cultural Goods*

Over the last forty years, the notion of patrimony, which first appeared in the context of the environment, has been a genuine, new institutional innovation. For economists it seemed a means of escaping market logic, of upsetting market rationality. It became fair to change the terms of the debate: the right of ownership confers the right to use but also the "right to destroy". It is in this area that debate on the environment can add to the general debate. In the digital world, this right to destroy is equivalent to *enclosing* cultural resources. However, the notion of patrimony highlights the necessity of preserving, adding to and transmission. It brings collective management solutions to the fore, since common goods require a communal approach to patrimony (Ollagnon, 1979). Thus in this situation there is collective appropriation with a multitude of rights holders and uses. This is known as "transappropriation" or "transpropriation" (Ost, 1995). In real terms this means that anyone may exercise a right of ownership but that maintaining the good quality of the resource depends on all players and

---

[25]   Public law historians have raised a new topic of discussion: that in Europe the role of Public Administration has been linked to a rationale of management since the beginning of the nineteenth century. "To govern is to apply law to manage *common* interests."

managers involved. A changing perspective of patrimony consists of seeing this common good within a *"system of circulation and exchange not only between successive owners but also between the sphere of being and having"*. Patrimony is something that can be exchanged: it remains synonymous with belonging and continuity, coinciding with different degrees of fluidity and transitivity. However, a management structure (non-private, non-state) must be created above and beyond these rights. Patrimonial mediation falls into this category. It is necessary to first identify then draw up patrimonial objectives. Next management procedures must be set out and conditions for access and control specified. The final stage is ritualization, that is, a phase of public legitimization. The notion of property is reductive: the notion of patrimony opens new perspectives for assigning wealth, and for its visibility and sustainability in the digital world.

5. Conclusions

The CC project oversees a facility for sharing, where works are open to free access because rights holders waive their exclusive rights. This is a *common* facility, but the works concerned are not considered common property: they may be used according to certain conditions. Owners do not waive their rights except in the CC0 license (no rights reserved). Other concepts such as *patrimonialization* must be looked into. However, in a situation where the right of (intellectual) property is still central, what are the fundamentals and identity of this type of patrimony? Certain points must be clarified to enable an understanding of how this form of organizing may establish new balances and renew social effectiveness. Where circulation, sharing and collaborative work in the digital world are concerned, the divisions between private and public goods appear somewhat difficult to operate in reality. Following our account of certain concepts used by Creative Commons, we have demonstrated that the concept of patrimony may be the *driver*, as seen in other domains such as the environment. Within this concept of patrimony works that carry the identity of their holder, a global identity, and above all, public rights, are selected and put in place. This imposes a type of governance known as patrimonial governance of the digital commons, which bases copyright on the freedom to receive and to communicate ideas, that is, on fundamental rights.

References

Barnes, J.A. (1972), *Social Networks*, An Addison-Wesley Module in Anthropology, Module 26, pp. 1-29.

Barrère, C. and Barthélémy, D. (2005), *Réinventer le patrimoine: de la culture à l'économie, une nouvelle pensée du patrimoine?*, Editions L'Harmattan, Paris.

Bell A. and Parchomovsky G. (2009), *The evolution of Private and Open access property*, Theoretical Inquiries in Law, Vol. 10, No. 1, available at: http://www.bepress.com/til/default/vol10/iss1/art4/ (accessed 3 May 2010).

Benkler, Y. (2006), *The Wealth of Networks: How Social Production Transforms Markets and Freedom*, New Haven, Conn. Yale University Press.

Bourcier, D. (2002), *Is Governance a New Form of Regulation? Balancing the Roles of the State and Civil* Society, IWM Working Paper 6/2002, Vienna, pp. 2.

Bourcier, D. and Dulong de Rosnay, M. (2004), *Introduction*, in Bourcier, D. and Dulong de Rosnay, M. (Eds.), "International Commons ou la Création en partage", Paris, Romillat.

Bourcier, D. (2007), *Creative Commons: An Observatory for Governance and Regulation through the Internet*, in Casanovas, P.; Noriega, P.; Bourcier, D.; Galindo, F. (Eds.), "Trends in Legal Knowledge the Semantic Web and the Regulation of Electronic Social Systems", Firenze, EPAP, pp. 41-52.

Boyle, J. (2008), *The Public Domain, Enclosing the Commons of the Mind*, Yale University Press New Haven & London, Preface pp. xvi, available at: http://www.thepublicdomain.org/download (accessed 3 May 2010).

Dussolier, S. (2005), *Droit d'auteur et protection des œuvres dans l'univers numérique*, Bruxelles, Larcier, pp. 231.

van Eechoud M. and van der Wal B. (2008), *Creative Commons Licensing for Public Sector Information Opportunities and Pitfalls*, IVIR, University of Amsterdam, available at: http://www.ivir.nl (version 3.0 Def.Jan 2008), (accessed 3 May 2010).

Elkin-Koren, N. (2005), *What Contracts Can't Do: The Limits of Private Ordering in Facilitating a Creative Commons*, Fordham Law Review, Vol. 74.

Elkin-Koren N. (2006), *Creative Commons: A Skeptical View of a Worthy Pursuit*, in Hugenholtz, P. B. and Guibault L. (Eds.) "The Future of the Public Domain", Kluwer Law International, available at: http://papers.ssrn.com/sol3/papers.cfm?abstract_id=885466 (accessed 5 May 2010).

Hardin, G. (1968), *The Tragedy of the Commons*, Science, Vol. 162, No. 3859, pp. 1243-1248

von Hippel, E. (2005), *Democratizing Innovation*, Cambridge, Mass.: MIT Press.

Kiss A. (1989), *L'écologie et la loi: le statut juridique de l'environnement*, Paris, L'Harmattan.

Lehavi, A (2009), *How Property can Create, Maintain or Destroy Community*, Theoretical Inquiries in Law, Vol. 10, No. 1, The Berkeley Electronic Press, available at: http://www.bepress.com (accessed 5 May 2010).

Lessig, L. (2001), *The Future of Ideas, The Fate of the Commons in a Connected World*, Random House New York, available at: http://www.the-future-of-ideas.com/download/ (accessed 8 May 2010).

Lessig, L. (2004), *Foreword*, in Bourcier, D. and Dulong de Rosnay, M..(Eds.), "International Commons at the Digital Age: La création en partage", Romillat, pp. 7.

Loren, L. (2007), *Building a Reliable Semicommons of Creative Works: Enforcement of Creative Commons Licences and Limited Abandonment of Copyright*, Geo.Mason Law Review. Vol. 14, No. 2, pp. 271.

Merges, R. P. (2004), *A New Dynamism in the Public Domain*, University of Chicago Law Review, Vol. 71 pp. 183-203.

Ollagnon, H. (1979*), Propositions pour une gestion patrimoniale des eaux souterraines : l'expérience de la nappe phréatique d'Alsace*, Bulletin interministériel pour la rationalisation des Choix budgétaires, No. 36, pp. 33.

Ost, F. (1995), *La nature hors la loi*, Paris, La Découverte, p. 323.

Ostrom, E. (1990), *Governing the Commons: The Evolution of Institutions for Collective Action*, Cambridge: Cambridge University Press.

Rose, C. (1986), *The Comedy of the Commons: Custom, Commerce, and Inherently Public Property*, University of Chicago Law Review, Vol. 53, pp. 742.

Zittrain, J. (2008), *The Future of the Internet — And How to Stop It*, New Haven, Yale University Press, pp. 225.

From Free Culture to Open Data: Technical Requirements for Access and Authorship

Melanie Dulong de Rosnay[*]
[*]*Politecnico di Torino*

Abstract. Creative Commons tools makes it easier for users, who are also authors, to share, locate and distribute reusable content, fostering remix and digital creativity, open science and freedom of expression. But reuse could be made even easier by the licensing framework, which does not yet handle the diversity of legal and usage situations pertaining to technical accessibility and reuse modalities of works and data.

This paper will first discuss what additional legal regulation may be required to allow full accessibility, which includes not only a legal authorization to perform certain rights, but also the technical possibility to effectively access and reuse material. Then, based on the example of attribution and authorship requirements for reproduction and performances of works and derivative works, it will be examined what technical infrastructure may better support the enforceability of these licensing terms, namely a framework automating certain actions and pedagogy tools.

From legal accessibility to technical accessibility and technical support of open content licenses, this article illustrates the intricate relationship between law and technology in the realm of copyright and focuses on access and authorship, two fundamental elements of (free) culture and (open) science.

Keywords: Creative Commons licenses, open access, open data, free culture, technical accessibility, attribution, authorship, credit, derivative works.

1. Introduction

Creative Commons (CC) offers a set of copyright licenses for authors who want to grant flexible rights to the public. The licenses are generated though a web interface which delivers a piece of HTML code to the user. The licenses have various formats which are linked to one another. The HTML code describes a license button, which is a logo with an embedded link to the human-readable Commons Deed summarizing the provisions developed in a Legal Code, the actual text of the license. The machine-readable layer of the licenses makes it possible for search engines to locate content marked with CC metadata. All licenses have in common the requirement that the licensee attribute the work and retrain a link to the CC license for any use or redistribution. Various options allow the author to retain or grant commercial rights and the rights to make derivatives. The licenses combine several elements around core clauses expressing the rights granted and restrictions which may apply, as well as general conditions.

In a first part, I will discuss which legal and technical conditions make it possible to reuse works licensed under a CC license and what could be added to make reuse more effective. In a second part, I will explain that reuse requires correct attribution and how this task could be better supported.

2. The conditions of technical accessibility

Open content licenses intend to facilitate sharing and reuse. All CC licenses authorize the public to reproduce and publicly perform their work, including in a collection (a selection or an arrangement of several unmodified works, such as an encyclopedia or an anthology). The rights granted "may be exercised in all media and formats (and) include the right to make such modifications as are technically necessary to exercise the rights in other media and formats"[1].

Some CC licenses allow adaptations, which "means a work based upon the Work, or upon the Work and other pre-existing works, such as a translation, adaptation, derivative work, arrangement of music or other alterations of a literary or artistic work, or phonogram or performance and includes cinematographic adaptations or any other form in which the Work may be recast, transformed, or adapted including in any form recognizably derived from the original", including the synchronization of music on moving images.

Therefore, it is expected that the original work can technically be modified, not only to make adaptations, but also (and anyway in all the licenses) to transfer it to other medias or formats, or to reformat it to include it in a broader collection. This permission requires delivery in a format that effectively enables reuse. After defining the notion of open access and proposing to include technical accessibility, the concept will be applied to scientific publications, scientific databases and cultural works.

---

[1] All definitions and excerpts of the CC licenses come from the legal code of the version 3.0 of the licenses, for instance http://creativecommons.org/licenses/by/3.0/ for the CC Attribution license.

2.1. DEFINING OPEN ACCESS

Culture and science are being built incrementally. Artists take inspiration by others' works, and scholars also reuse previous articles and data. All aim to broadly disseminate new culture and the knowledge they create into society. The Free Culture movement "promotes the freedom to distribute and modify creative works using the Internet as well as other media"[2]. "A free culture is one where all members are free to participate in its transmission and evolution, without artificial limits on who can participate or in what way."[3] The Open Access (OA) movement seeks to take advantage of the opportunities offered by digital publishing and distributing to share scientific results more quickly. Both movements aim to facilitate education, culture and access to knowledge, and CC licenses are one of the tools towards these objectives. What steps can further free culture, open education, open science and scholarship? Should licenses simply ensure access without a fee while granting some legal rights, or should the licenses do more to improve that access, such as including technical capabilities for finding, extracting, modifying, editing, remixing, annotating, compiling and otherwise tweaking the content in order to make better use of it? In order to define OA, this subsection draws examples from the situation of OA in respect to scientific publications, which has a longer history than Open Science or Open Data and Free Culture, which will be discussed in the next subsections.

Based on the Budapest Open Access Initiative definition for Open Access, "free availability (...) without financial, legal, or technical barriers"[4], three categories are fundamental for OA material. They constitute a typology to define the different forms of OA: **economic OA**, **legal OA** and **technical OA**[5]. Usually, the emphasis is put only on the two first categories and I propose to give a specific attention to the technical barriers to OA which are often hidden or neglected.

2.1.1. *Economic OA*

Research available only for a fee cannot be read by researchers from financially disadvantaged institutions and countries where libraries cannot

---

[2] http://en.wikipedia.org/wiki/Free_culture_movement

[3] http://freeculture.org/

[4] http://www.sorors.org/openaccess/read.shtml

[5] The three following subsections defining legal, economic and technical open access come from Mélanie Dulong de Rosnay (2008), « Opening Access in a Networked Science », in *Publius Project, Essays and conversations about constitutional moments on the Net collected by the Berkman Center*, June 2008. http://publius.cc/2008/06/13/melanie-dulong-de-rosnay-opening-access-in-a-networked-science/

afford the subscription to a particular journal or online database. The public also will likely not afford these articles either. Economic OA grants basic access rights by making articles and data available for private reading.

Economic barriers to access can be waived though different options. Publishers can issue OA journals that do not charge their readers and they can develop alternative publication models: this is the golden road to OA. Authors can also self-archive their articles in pre-print or post-print versions in an institutional repository. Many non-OA journals allow authors to do so, and this is Green OA. Several policies are available for those authors who want to but can not. Authors may add a contractual opt-out clause[6] to their publishing agreement to retain some of their rights. Finally, universities and research funders may mandate the archiving of articles in OA repositories.

2.1.2. *Legal OA*

Legal OA is an additional condition that allows redistribution, and it goes beyond the removal of financial barriers to accessing and reading. Removing permission barriers grants the public rights to use material beyond simple access. Like economic OA, legal OA, or "Permission-barrier-free" scholarship relies on contractual agreements. Authors must indicate that they are publishing their output without legal restrictions. Otherwise, third parties will not be aware that they may have additional permissions beyond the right of reading. Without an explicit declaration that additional rights are granted to the public, the right to copy, distribute and make derivatives may be impeded by transaction costs associated with permission requests. Libraries, professors, and other curators and aggregators may wonder if they can reproduce, translate, and redistribute material on websites or in course packs without an expensive rights clearance process. Adding a clear license to a journal, repository, or conference website will allow creative and confident usages. The Creative Commons Attribution license[7] complies with the Budapest Open Access Initiative definition and makes legal OA a reality. However, other Creative Commons licensing options that reserve commercial rights and derivative rights do not comply with this definition and can not lead to legal OA. In these instances for example, one may redistribute legal OA articles only for non-commercial purposes, or one may not translate them or distribute derivative works without additional authorization.

2.1.3. *Technical OA*

Just as in the case of price and rights clearance, technology can create barriers to access, redistribution and reuse of articles and data. But

---

[6] For instance http://scholars.sciencecommons.org/
[7] http://creativecommons.org/licenses/by/3.0/

technical choices can also help remove barriers. Technical OA should ensure that materials can be actually and effectively reused, mined, processed, aggregated, integrated, and searched by both humans and machines. Technical barriers can include the following: protection measures that prevent copying, compulsory registration before download, design features that add hidden costs to search and processing, complexity of all sorts prior to full accessibility of the content in a data format allowing any sort of processing. For example, it can be more or less easy to interact with a document because of the publication format. HTML pages are more convenient to browse a large amount of articles compared to PDF files which require download. HTML and wiki allow comments and editing; two-column articles are difficult to read quickly on most screens but are the norm for scientific articles. Poor indexing or lack of metadata also prevent some modes of use.

The opening of this triple architecture of market, law and technology allows broader and better access. More and more journals and book editors are becoming aware of OA's social benefit and potential impact on innovation and aim to share their results. If they wish to do so, they should make sure that not only economic and legal, but also technical restrictions have been effectively removed, so that researchers and the public can not only access, but also redistribute and reuse materials in any way, including ways that initial creators had not considered.

2.2. ACCESSIBILITY FOR SCIENTIFIC DATABASES

Removing technical restrictions to full OA has a different meaning for scientific publications than for scientific data, and data curators may wonder what accessibility or open formats mean for scientific databases.

Contractual requirements such as Creative Commons Attribution policy[8] and the complexity of these requirements[9] constitute a legal barrier to

---

[8] Science Commons suggests to distribute data under simple and understandable terms as close as possible to the public domain, free of copyright, contractual, database and other controls. Nguyen Thinh, « Freedom to Research: Keeping Scientific Data Open, Accessible, and Interoperable », Science Commons Reading Room. http://sciencecommons.org/wp-content/uploads/freedom-to-research.pdf

[9] Legal simplicity and predictability can be achieved by waiving copyright and other contractual restrictions, allowing data integrators to reuse, modify and redistribute large datasets, towards the freedom to integrate according to Wilbanks John, "Public domain, copyright licenses and the freedom to integrate science", *Journal of Science Communication*, volume 07, issue 02, June 2008.

downstream reuse of data. But legal accessibility is not the only hurdle to data integration. Technical accessibility as defined above should be ensured in order to allow scientists to download data easily and use them in any way, including ways that the initial creators, curators and contributors had not considered.

The objective of the research[10] presented hereafter has been to assess the accessibility of databases by analyzing their access interfaces and their reuse policies. Databases' openness will be measured by analyzing a set of technical access interfaces and legal terms of use. A taxonomy of technical and legal restrictions applicable to databases in life science will be presented and used to assess a sample of databases. Based on these criteria, I propose a set of questions for database curators to assess their own data's technical and legal openness. It intends to help to define what can be changed or specified in open content licenses to better support full accessibility in the context of databases of scientific data.

2.2.1. *The design of a taxonomy*

This research started with analyzing the terms of use for databases from the Molecular Biology Database hosted by the Nucleic Acids Research Journal (extend link to whole name), and assessing them regarding open access criteria as described in the Science Commons Open Data Protocol[11]. A sample of policies has been retrieved and analyzed. The next step identified barriers to open access and reuse of data based on these database policies and built a taxonomy of restrictions. These restrictions can be of legal or contractual nature, but they can also be technical, e.g. the impossibility of downloading the whole database if its results can be accessed only through a field-based search. A systematic analysis of more database policies hosted by the Life Science Resource Name (LSRN) Schema registry allowed us to confirm this taxonomy and to refine it by adding other terms.

---

[10] This section reuses substantial parts of a paper the author wrote with Shirley Fung entitled « Legal and Technical Accessibility for Life Science Databases », Proceedings of the Second Communia Conference: Global Science & Economics of Knowledge-Sharing Institutions, Torino (Italy), 28-29-30/06/2009 available at: http://www.communia-project.eu/node/333 which was itself developing a preprint (Mélanie Dulong de Rosnay, "Check Your Data Freedom: Defining a Taxonomy for Access and Reuse of Life Science Data", *Nature Precedings*, July 2008) the author wrote as the output of a fellowship at Science Commons on a research project developed under the auspices of the Science Commons Data project and building upon the Science Commons Open Access Data Protocol proposing requirements for interoperability of scientific data available at: http://sciencecommons.org/projects/publishing/open-access-data-protocol/
[11] http://sciencecommons.org/projects/publishing/open-access-data-protocol/

Technical and legal accessibility conditions as well as restriction values will be defined. The purpose of identifying controls and restrictions applicable to databases is twofold. First, it will enable the understanding of the terms of use and other requirements governing the access to molecular biology databases especially identifying the control that prevents the free sharing of data. Second, these restrictions will be clustered into classes, making it possible to systematize the analysis of databases and to easily identify the data that can be reused by the scientific community.

Two types of control can be exercised on databases: technical restrictions embedded in the design of the database, and legal restrictions expressed in the terms of use.

Technical restrictions affect databases that cannot be searched or processed in any possible way. Technical openness is ensured by the possibility of downloading the whole dataset and reusing and integrating data, in the same way the Science Commons Neurocommons project provides a data mining platform allowing machine-readable representation and interpretation of data, or that Basic Local Alignment Search Tool (BLAST) finds similarities between sequences. Semantic web processing applied to scientific data should improve the way science is performed and allow network effects by connecting knowledge from various datasets. Databases that require registration before access, or offer only a batch processing or a query-based mechanism to retrieve data after a specific search, do not comply with the technical requirements necessary to make data open.

Terms of use, licenses and access policies are legal texts describing authorized and unauthorized usages. The legal rules are expressed by the entity distributing a product such as software or scientific data. The infringement of these self-declared rights can lead to lawsuits. Terms of use can be difficult to understand, even for lawyers, while scientists need to know quickly whether they can use a dataset.

Therefore, a set of questions has been designed to understand whether databases are, in fact, fully accessible and whether the data can be reused, redistributed and integrated.

Technical accessibility

Downloadability
Is there a link to download the whole database?
YES or NO
If YES, include the URL

Batch
Is it possible to access the data through a batch feature?
YES or NO

Query
Is it possible to access the data through a query-based system?
YES or NO

Registration
Finally, is registration compulsory before downloading or accessing data in the ways described above?
YES or NO

Legal accessibility

Terms of use
Does the database have a policy?
YES or NO
If YES, include the URL and assess whether the policy authorize reuse, redistribution, integration

Are there any restrictions on the right to reformatting and redistributing?
If NO
If YES, which restrictions?

Fields to describe restrictions are
Attribution Contractual Requirements
Non-Derivative Use
Non-Commercial Use
Share Alike
Others (to be described).

Figure 1. Set of questions to process databases

The questions in Figure 1 allow the processing of databases. A subsequent database has been developed with information describing databases technical and legal accessibility.

Five answers can be provided to these questions and together constitute a taxonomy to assess technical and legal openness, as presented in Figure 2 below.

1. DOWNLOADABILITY
The website provides a file transfer protocol or a link to download the whole dataset without registration.
The ability to download the whole dataset without registration constitutes the double requirement to be considered as technically accessible.

2. TECHNICAL RESTRICTION: the database can be accessed only through registration, batch or query-based system.
Technical accessibility is not achieved.

3. PUBLIC DOMAIN POLICY: the website provides simple and clear terms of use informing users that the data are in the public domain.
Data are thus free to integrate. Legal accessibility is achieved.

4. NO POLICY: the website does not provide terms of use.
Legal accessibility is not achieved.

5. LEGAL RESTRICTIONS: the terms of use impose contractual restrictions, such as heavy contractual requirements for attribution, limitation to non-commercial usages, prohibition to modify data, or other constraints on their redistribution or modification.
Legal accessibility is not achieved. The data are not free to integrate.

Figure 2. Databases qualification

2.2.2. *Databases analysis according to the taxonomy*

Samples of the Nucleic Acids Research (NAR) Molecular Biology Database Collection MBDC[12] and Life Science Resource Name (LSRN)[13] Schemas databases have been analyzed to define the taxonomy. Then one third of the LSRN databases (60 databases) have been systematically analyzed. A subsequent database[14] has been created, gathering for each of these databases:

- The name and URL of the database,
- URL of the download page and URL of the terms of use,
- Extracts of the terms of use for further review and comments,
- Values for technical accessibility and legal accessibility features as described in Figure 1.

Technical openness

Four values have been identified to assess technical accessibility: Downloadability, Batch features, Query-based system and Registration.

---

[12] http://nar.oxfordjournals.org/cgi/content/full/gkm1037/DC1/1

[13] http://lsrn.org/lsrn/registry.html

[14] A user interface has been built by Shirley Fung using PHP and MySQL to host the dataset assessing databases technical and legal accessibility. It is available at http://labs.creativecommons.org/demos/mbdb/

The only combination qualifying the database as technically open is the ability to download without registration. Indeed, registration before access and the possibility to perform only batch or query-based searches prevents automated data mining. However, it can be useful to have access to several systems to retrieve and analyze data. Therefore, the database indicates whether it is possible to retrieve data also through batch and query in addition to download.

Another technical restriction that has not been analyzed is the presence of standardized annotations or comments allowing users to understand data collected by others. This feature has been disregarded because of a lack of expertise to assess the relevance and quality of annotation for external reuse.

Legal openness

Values that have been used to define legal accessibility are the following: **Policy Available, Public Domain Policy, Attribution Contractual Requirements, Non-Derivative Use, Non-Commercial Use, Share Alike** and **Other (to be described)**.

In order to be open, a database must have a policy, and this policy must not impose any restriction to the redistribution and the modification of data. The absence of any terms of use or policy on the database website could imply to some people that, in the absence of any expressed restrictions, data are free. But rights unknown to the user might be applicable by default. Indeed, the Science Commons Protocol states that "any implementation MUST affirmatively declare that contractual constraints do not apply to the database." Policies should be clear and have only one possible legal interpretation. The absence of a clear and understandable policy is equivalent to the absence of a policy because it leads to legal uncertainty.

Legal restrictions to redistribute and modify of data can be diverse. Four values have been identified, corresponding to Creative Commons licenses options: Attribution Contractual Requirements, Non-Derivative Use, Non-Commercial Use, Share Alike. However, the definition for these legal restrictions in the context of this research is broader than the Creative Commons definitions.

The Attribution requirement may constitute a restriction on the reuse of data. Instead of strong contractually binding requirements on how data should be attributed, a request of acknowledgment according to scientific norms should be sufficient. According to the Protocol, "any implementation SHOULD define a non-legally binding set of citation norms in clear, lay-readable language". Furthermore, "community standards for sharing publication-related data and materials should flow from the general principle that the publication of scientific information is intended to move science forward. An author's obligation is not only to release data and materials to enable others to verify or replicate published findings (as journals already implicitly or explicitly require) but also to provide them in a form on which other scientists can build with further research."[15]

The Non-Commercial and Non-Derivative requirements prevent many types of data use. They are defined as restrictions based on the commercial nature of the user or of the usage, and as restrictions on the distribution of modified versions of the database.

The Share Alike requirement is present in the original taxonomy. This option requests modifications to be offered under the same open terms and should encompass all copyleft policies. No policy in the analyzed sample contains this requirement.

Other possible restrictions may affect terms of use. For instance, an embargo on publishing before the data producer, the existence of patents and the absence of warranties against third-party rights are legal restrictions which have not been taken into account in this first analysis.

In many cases, the database is offered with no restrictions in place by the database curator, but nevertheless without warranties on the legal status of the data submitted by contributors. Data may contain elements protected by copyright or any applicable right. The database curator did not clear the rights, or did not request from the contributors a rights waiver or no rights assertion before data upload, or does not want to be held liable in case the previously described processes would present a failure. This warranties disclaimer can be seen as a hurdle to the usage of these data. Both uncertainty for the end-user and absence of responsibility for the curator might be avoided by offering contributors a seamlessly integrated data sharing agreement prior to submission. Although this procedure might disincentive some contributors, the burden of checking the legal status of data and avoiding possible claims by third parties should not rely on the data user, forcing her to hire a lawyer. Besides, these disclaimers do not identify which data are free and which parts of the database might be copyrighted or covered by other rights.

2.2.3. Results

Databases which can be considered legally and technically open, and compliant with the Science Commons Open Data Protocol, are those that are downloadable without prior registration and under a simple policy close

---

[15] Board on Life Sciences (BLS), Sharing Publication-Related Data and Materials: Responsibilities of Authorship in the Life Sciences (2003).
http://books.nap.edu/books/0309088593/html/R1.html

to the public domain. The impossibility or the difficulty of downloading and reformatting the dataset does not fulfill technical accessibility requirements. Databases available only through batch or query interfaces are not considered technically open, but those offering these features in addition to downloadability will be compliant.

Besides databases created by the National Center for Biotechnology Information (NCBI) and the European Bioinformatics Institute (EBI), only a couple of databases among the 60 first schemas of the LCRN registry analyzed sample can be considered as both technically and legally open, without restrictions.

2.2.4. *Checklist to assess databases openness*

The following checklist may assist data curators in opening their data, and to make sure that the database's design and terms of use will allow others to access, reuse and build upon their data. All answers should be positive.

A. Check your database technical accessibility

A.1. Do you provide a link to download the whole database?
A.2. Is the dataset available in at least one standard format?
A.3. Do you provide comments and annotations fields allowing users to understand the data?

B. Check your database legal accessibility

B.1. Do you provide a policy expressing terms of use of your database?
B.2. Is the policy clearly indicated on your website?
B.3. Are the terms short and easy to understand by non-lawyers?
B.4. Does the policy authorize redistribution, reuse and modification without restrictions or contractual requirements on the user or the usage?
B.5. Is the attribution requirement at most as strong as the acknowledgment norms of your scientific community?

Figure 3. Database openness checklist

2.3. TECHNICAL ACCESSIBILITY FOR LITERARY AND ARTISTIC WORKS

The absence of economic and legal restrictions expressed in clear and simple terms of use is not enough to ensure full accessibility to scientific articles or data. Distribution should ensure that materials can be effectively reused and processed by humans and machines. Several features typical of a bad design should be avoided in order to facilitate data mining and further aggregation and integration in collections and derivative works:

registration, abuse of PDF or format which is cumbersome to process and edit, difficulty in downloading an entire set or the content of a website within a few clicks.

Can these requirements be useful beyond science? Are these remarks applicable to literary and artistic works? Could the CC licenses encourage technical accessibility? After having defined what is technical accessibility for science, I will try to define how the technical barriers and requirements above can be transposed to other works.

Technical accessibility and the ability to manipulate software are conditioned by the release of the source code in an open format and OA to the relevant documentation. The GNU Free Documentation License[16] is the standard license for software documentation. It contains in its first clause a definition of open format crafted for textual software documentation:

> A "Transparent" copy of the Document means a machine-readable copy, represented in a format whose specification is available to the general public, that is suitable for revising the document straightforwardly with generic text editors or (for images composed of pixels) generic paint programs or (for drawings) some widely available drawing editor, and that is suitable for input to text formatters or for automatic translation to a variety of formats suitable for input to text formatters. A copy made in an otherwise Transparent file format whose markup, or absence of markup, has been arranged to thwart or discourage subsequent modification by readers is not Transparent. An image format is not Transparent if used for any substantial amount of text. A copy that is not "Transparent" is called "Opaque".
>
> Examples of suitable formats for Transparent copies include plain ASCII without markup, Texinfo input format, LaTeX input format, SGML or XML using a publicly available DTD, and standard-conforming simple HTML, PostScript or PDF designed for human modification. Examples of transparent image formats include PNG, XCF and JPG. Opaque formats include proprietary formats that can be read and edited only by proprietary word processors, SGML or XML for which the DTD and/or processing tools are not generally available, and the machine-generated HTML, PostScript or PDF produced by some word processors for output purposes only.

This definition allowing human editing and machine processing applies to textual media in the current state-of-the-art text editors and technical standards. OGG is the free and open format for audio while MP3 is a de facto distribution standard. Music players and editors necessary to reproduce, perform and adapt MP3 files may require the payment of a fee at some stage, which may conflict with economic OA at some point.

But the situation is more complicated for media types other than text. Again taking the example of music, having an audio file in a free and open

---

[16] http://www.gnu.org/copyleft/fdl.html

format may not be sufficient to remix it. Instructions such as information enclosed in a MIDI file and other data such as music notation or explanation for performers could, when they exist, also be released. Some of these issues can be solved through project-oriented online communities which would encourage or require uploading complete project-files in addition to the media.[17]

Open media means more than distributing a file in non-proprietary format under an open content license. CC licenses, as we will see in the coming section, contain very detailed requirements on the way to attribute authors. They could also contain requirements to facilitate technical accessibility and allow a true remix culture. Guidelines for each community or media type could be developed and, without being as specific as the GFDL clause, a provision could request the licensor to release the work in a format suitable for manipulation and with the information necessary for its manipulation in a reasonable manner appropriate to the media. This implies a different perspective than the current CC approach which places restrictions on the licensee rather than on the licensor.

3. Technical contributions to authorship

Now that I defined what technical accessibility could mean for free culture and open media to ensure full access and facilitate reuse beyond a CC license grant, I propose to accompany open content licensing with a technical framework facilitating authorship and attribution. The concept of attribution is central to copyright from a civil law country perspective with strong moral rights, but not exclusively. Citing the author is a social norm beyond legal and contractual obligations. The Attribution element is standard in all the CC licenses; they all require the original author to be credited for her work when copying, performing or remixing it.

3.1 THE CC ATTRIBUTION CLAUSE

The Creative Commons Attribution provision addresses not only the name of the author, but also the name of one or several individuals or entities who can be not only authors or performers but also licensors, rightholders, publishers, sponsors, etc. as well as the URI associated to the work. The attribution provision is expressed in the CC Commons Deed, the human-readable summary, as follows:

---

[17] Cheliotis Giorgos, "From open source to open content: Organization, licensing and decision processes in open cultural production", *Decision Support Systems*, Volume 47, Issue 3, June 2009, p. 229-244.

"Attribution — You must attribute the work in the manner specified by the author or licensor (but not in any way that suggests that they endorse you or your use of the work)."

Besides, all the licenses require the user to also include the license when they reuse the work:

"Notice — For any reuse or distribution, you must make clear to others the license terms of this work. The best way to do this is with a link to this web page."

The right to make derivatives granted in some of the licenses is stated as:

"to Remix — to adapt the work"

The attribution provision has a long definition with specific requirements located in three subclauses:

1. In the license grant clause for the licenses authorizing adaptations to condition the exercise of this right to the identification of the changes made to the original work[18],
2. In the second subclause of the restrictions clause as a positive obligation of the licensee to attribute the author or licensor as she requests, including the attribution of adaptations if they are authorized, and the way to exercise this obligation,
3. And at the end of the first subclause of the restrictions (4.a.) as a negative obligation to remove upon request of the licensor such attribution from collections and adaptations to the extend they are authorized.

The text, which varies among licenses authorizing adaptations and licenses that do not, reads as follows, with provisions related to derivatives in italic and a modified layout and order of the excerpts to present them in the order they are to be exercised, starting with requested attribution, including for adaptations, followed by non endorsement and unwanted attribution requirements:

"If You Distribute, or Publicly Perform the Work or any Adaptations or Collections, You must, unless a request has been made pursuant to Section 4(a), keep intact all copyright notices for the Work and provide, reasonable to the medium or means You are utilizing:
(i) the name of the Original Author (or pseudonym, if applicable) if supplied,

---

[18] This provision "The original work was translated from English to Spanish" could be clustered with the next one "French translation of the Work by Original Author": even if the first is addressing the original work and the second the author of the original work.

and/or if the Original Author and/or Licensor designate another party or parties (e.g., a sponsor institute, publishing entity, journal) for attribution ("Attribution Parties") in Licensor's copyright notice, terms of service or by other reasonable means, the name of such party or parties;
(ii) the title of the Work if supplied;
(iii) to the extent reasonably practicable, the URI, if any, that Licensor specifies to be associated with the Work, unless such URI does not refer to the copyright notice or licensing information for the Work; and
(iv) consistent with Section 3(b), in the case of an Adaptation, a credit identifying the use of the Work in the Adaptation (e.g., "French translation of the Work by Original Author," or "Screenplay based on original Work by Original Author").

(in clause 3 License grant)
to create and Reproduce Adaptations provided that any such Adaptation, including any translation in any medium, takes reasonable steps to clearly label, demarcate or otherwise identify that changes were made to the original Work. For example, a translation could be marked "The original work was translated from English to Spanish," or a modification could indicate "The original work has been modified.";

The credit required by this Section 4(c) *or 4(d)* may be implemented in any reasonable manner; provided, however, that in the case of a *Adaptation or* Collection, at a minimum such credit will appear, if a credit for all contributing authors of the *Adaptation or* Collection appears, then as part of these credits and in a manner at least as prominent as the credits for the other contributing authors.

For the avoidance of doubt, You may only use the credit required by this Section for the purpose of attribution in the manner set out above and, by exercising Your rights under this License, You may not implicitly or explicitly assert or imply any connection with, sponsorship or endorsement by the Original Author, Licensor and/or Attribution Parties, as appropriate, of You or Your use of the Work, without the separate, express prior written permission of the Original Author, Licensor and/or Attribution Parties.

If You create a Collection, upon notice from any Licensor You must, to the extent practicable, remove from the Collection any credit as required by Section 4(b), as requested.
If You create an Adaptation, upon notice from any Licensor You must, to the extent practicable, remove from the Adaptation any credit as required by Section 4(b), as requested."

Figure 6. CC licenses Attribution provisions

To summarize, the license allows the licensor to require from the licensee a particular way to attribute the work by citing:

- The name of the author, licensor or any party,
- The title of the work,

- The source URL (not URI?) of the work,[19]
- For derivatives, a credit identifying the original author, the use of the original work and changes which have been made.

3.2 FACILITATING ATTRIBUTION AND AUTHORSHIP

The Attribution requirements are difficult to fulfill. An initial solution could be to simplify the wording of the Attribution clause in the CC licenses. Meanwhile, this final section describes difficulties raised by the high standard of attribution in the CC licenses and proposes possible solutions for better compliance.

The licensor may require that these elements be cited to the extent she supplies them (except for the last one requiring to identify changes made to the original work in a derivative because it is not possible). It is not clear how the licensee should fulfill this obligation in case no or insufficient information has been provided by the licensor who may not have the skills or the energy necessary to express this information. Sometimes the original licensor did not correctly, fully or entirely express attribution of the original work in the first place.

Some websites provide useful guidelines[20]. The standard of attribution is "a reasonable manner" except for adaptations and collections, where it should follow as a minimum the attribution standard of the other components.

---

[19] But not the source URL of the original work for derivatives, which could be useful, as allowed by the fields on the license chooser interface: http://creativecommons.org/choose/

[20] See for example the attribution policies or guidelines published by Global Voices hosting articles authored by bloggers and translated by others, providing a recommended model to attribute as well as expressing the wish to have the logo of the institution included in additional to the name of the author and the hosting website, corresponding to the "publishing entity" as defined by the CC license attribution clause: "Please note: in the case of images and multimedia we have sourced from others you need permission to republish from the creators, as they may have different copyright terms from Global Voices. Please include a link to the original article. An example:

This article by Jane Doe was originally published by Global Voices Online, a website that translates and reports on blogs from around the world.

If you want to make us extra happy, please include our logo in the attribution. To make it easier, you can copy and paste the code below to make the image appear in your blog or website."

http://globalvoicesonline.org/about/global-voices-attribution-policy/

In the case of complex mash-ups of artistic and literary works, it is sometimes difficult to know whether a final collage will be considered as a collective work. This qualification matters because the CC licenses attribution provision stipulates that "in the case of an Adaptation, a credit identifying the use of the Work in the Adaptation (e.g., "French translation of the Work by Original Author," or "Screenplay based on original Work by Original Author"" is needed. Attribution must be expressed in a specific way and conform to the format, medium or means employed to convey the work. Finally, the copyright notice must solely express attribution: no connection, sponsorship or endorsement by the original author may be asserted by the licensee reusing the work. The licensee should not use the credit to imply the author, licensor or party is endorsing the licensee or her use of the work. The licensee must be ready to remove the credit from adaptations and collections upon request from the licensor. This requirement raises practical questions. The licensor may never notice the work, or notice it late and make it impossible for the licensee to remove credits on works which have already been circulated, shared and reused.

Attribution requirements are not only considerable for complex works reusing numerous prior contributions or collections and successive adaptations which might be difficult to trace. Attribution is often not fulfilled by licensees because they do not know how to proceed. They may provide the name of the author, but not the link to his webpage nor to the CC license, or mention that the work is under a CC license and link to its source without crediting the author. A common example where attribution is badly handled is found in newspapers reusing Flickr photos without proper credit, possibly creating a copyright infringement, a violation of the license (and thus the termination of the grant), and the impossibility of subsequent users properly attributing the work if they wish to reuse it or incorporate it in their own work.

An initial technical solution could be to better assist the licensor and the licensee with filling in adequate fields with appropriate information. This task can be facilitated by applications that would automate the process for both 1) licensors, who when selecting a license to apply to their file[21], should enter correct and complete data in the license chooser interface which already contains fields for optional additional information, and 2) licensees when editing and redistributing a modified work. It is already possible for the licensor to indicate the following in the CC metadata: 1) the format and the title of the work, 2) the name users of the work should give attribution to, 3) the URL users of the work should link to, the source work URL and 4) an URL for additional permission. If this option was

---

[21] http://creativecommons.org/choose/

more widely used and further developed, licensees would receive proper information in the work's metadata, and further applications or editors plugins could help provide correct attribution when they redistribute the work or reuse it otherwise. A simple specification of attribution elements[22], would help authors and licensors to be attributed the way they are entitled to request, and to help licensees to respect these requirements. Then, attribution elements would follow the work along its life-cycle.

The burden of legalese requirements should be kept minimal in order to not deter creativity and discourage innovation: the goal of open content licenses is to make circulation, use and reuse easier, not to add complexity for licensors to indicate how they want to be attributed and for licensees to respect these contractual expectations.

A second solution also involving the support by technology is the development of more tutorials, comics or games describing the role of authors and reusers and conveying authorship ideas which are behind the attribution clause. Explaining how to attribute a work can also be seen as the first step to teach how to create, use and reuse creative works, and give a sense of what constitute an act of authorship when one creates or modifies someone else's work. Beyond sophisticated legal clauses and technical applications to convey attribution elements, users may lack necessary media literacy and copyright law skills to understand what is authorship and what constitutes an adaptation. The New Media Literacy team[23] developed an attribution module within an online learning environment the Learning Library[24]. Challenges, or sequences of a game to teach media literacy and participation, involve activities around copyright, fair use and the CC licenses.

With the NML team, solving the difficulties of understanding authorship and reuse were identified as prerequisite to using a CC license. To indicate proper attribution for both potential licensors and licensees, I suggested this simple three-step pattern of reuse:

1. An author creates a work.
2. Someone else modifies this original work.
3. The result constitutes a new work.

---

[22] Which can take the format of trackbacks and of RDF tags supported by the CC Rights Expression Language (ccREL) described at
http://wiki.creativecommons.org/CcREL
[23] http://newmedialiteracies.org/
[24] http://newmedialiteracies.org/library/

Understanding authorship should help to express attribution as follows: "This is a work by [name of the author of the adaptation] that is [modification action] from [title and link to original work], by [name of the original author]."

Conclusion

Works and data made available under a CC license may require more freedoms than the licenses offer to maximize possibilities of reuse and remix. They should be made available in ways and formats that technically enable modifications, editing and processing and the licenses could also foresee to waive technical restrictions. Technology can also help ensure attribution accompanyies media files. Pedagogy is also necessary for both licensors and licensees to understand authorship and build a free culture.

Acknowledgements

The author is grateful to Shirley Fung for her work on the databases user interface, to Shunling Chen, Erin Reilly, Anna van Someren, Victoria Stodden, John Wilbanks and Carolina Rossini for many valuable discussions, and to Michelle Thorne for her useful comments.

References

Cheliotis G. (2009), *From open source to open content: Organization, licensing and decision processes in open cultural production*, Decision Support Systems, Volume 47, Issue 3, June, pp. 229-244.

Dulong de Rosnay, M. (2008a), *Opening Access in a Networked Science*, in Publius Project, Essays and conversations about constitutional moments on the Net collected by the Berkman Center, June.

Dulong de Rosnay, M. (2008b), *Check Your Data Freedom: Defining a Taxonomy for Access and Reuse of Life Science Data*, Nature Precedings, July.

Dulong de Rosnay M., Fung S. (2009), *Legal and Technical Accessibility for Life Science Databases*, Proceedings of the Second Communia Conference: Global Science & Economics of Knowledge-Sharing Institutions, Torino (Italy), June, 28th-30th.

Nguyen, T. (2008), *Freedom to Research: Keeping Scientific Data Open, Accessible, and Interoperable*, Science Commons Reading Room. http://sciencecommons.org/wp-content/uploads/freedom-to-research.pdf

Wilbanks J. (2008), Public domain, copyright licenses and the freedom to integrate science, Journal of Science Communication, Vol. 07, Issue 02, June 2008.

URLs were last accessed by 26 November 2009.

Creative Commons International
The International License Porting Project — Origins, Experiences, and Challenges

Catharina Maracke[*]
[*]Dr. iur., Associate Professor, Graduate School of Media and Governance,
Shonan Fujisawa Campus, Keio University

Abstract. When Creative Commons was founded in 2001, the core Creative Commons licenses were drafted according to United States Copyright Law. Since their first introduction in December 2002, Creative Commons licenses have been enthusiastically adopted by many creators, authors, and other content producers – not only in the United States, but in many other jurisdictions as well. Global interest in the CC licenses prompted a discussion about the need for national versions of the CC licenses. To best address this need, the international license porting project ("Creative Commons International" – formerly known as "International Commons")[1] was launched in 2003. Creative Commons International works to port the core Creative Commons licenses to different copyright legislations around the world. The porting process includes both linguistically translating the licenses and legally adapting the licenses to a particular jurisdiction such that they are comprehensible in the local jurisdiction and legally enforceable but concurrently retain the same key elements.
Since its inception, Creative Commons International has found many supporters all over the world. With Finland, Brazil, and Japan as the first completed jurisdiction projects, experts around the globe have followed their lead and joined the international collaboration with Creative Commons to adapt the licenses to their local copyright. This article aims to present an overview of the international porting process, explain and clarify the international license architecture, its legal and promotional aspects, as well as its most recent challenges.

Keywords: Creative Commons, Creative Commons licenses, Creative Commons International, Moral Rights, Private International Law, Case Studies, Interoperability

1. Introduction: Creative Commons – a global project to foster culture and innovation

Over the past decade, we have seen an enormous change in the way we disseminate and exchange information. The advent of widespread adoption

---

[1] http://creativecommons.org/international/ The author was the former Director, Creative Commons International (2006 to 2009). This paper is also available at http://www.jipitec.eu/issues/jipitec-1-1-2010/2417/dippadm1268743811.97.pdf

of digital technologies has enabled a new generation of content creation and exchange. Technical advances have made it possible to distribute works in a variety of formats and of a high, often professional quality. It has become much easier and cheaper to work collaboratively across contexts and different media and to create new, derivative or collective works on a global level.

The downside of these new technical developments is that they can more easily facilitate a contradiction of law. Most of the digital content being accessed through the Internet is subject to copyright and owned by a particular person or company. But because of how digital technologies function, most of these uses necessarily make a "copy"[2] of the original work and/or require distribution, which can cause friction under the default terms of copyright: By enabling temporary and permanent copies, copyright's right is exercised and, from these copies, interpretive reuse is possible, which in turn implicates another copyright rule, the derivative works right.[3]

Current copyright regulation maintains the absurdity that while on the one hand, digital technology can provide a much bigger scope of access and distribution, such access will be unlawful unless either the law allows that specific access, or the respective copyright owner gives permission.[4] However, it is unquestioned that the flow and exchange of information is key for a well functioning society, be it on a cultural or economic level. This dilemma has prompted a discussion about making the law more suitable for the digital age in many different national jurisdictions around the world. Since debating and reforming law naturally takes time, many users realized that a much more valuable and immediate solution would be to work with new types of voluntary mechanisms that would operate within the currently existing copyright framework. Creative Commons aims to provide such voluntary mechanisms by offering creators and licensors a simple way to say what freedoms they want their creative content to carry. Through its free copyright licenses[5], Creative Commons offers creators and

---

[2] The World Intellectual Property Organization has described the Internet as the world's biggest copying machine. For details, see World Intellectual Property Organization, Intellectual Property on the Internet: A survey of issues (2002), available at:
http://www.wipo.int/export/sites/www/copyright/en/ecommerce/pdf/survey.pdf
[3] See also Garlick, Creative Commons Licensing – Another Option to enable online
Business Models, available at http://webarchive.nationalarchives.gov.uk/+/http://www.hm-treasury.gov.uk/d/creative_commons_418_p2_218kb.pdfls
[4]   In short, every information flow in the digital environment has the potential for copyright infringement – a reproduction or a communication to the public (see the general overview Fitzgerald/Olwan, 2009). For a detailed analysis about the balancing of interest in the European context, see Peukert (2004), page 11-46 (25 et seq.).
[5] Creative Commons has made available free legal and technical tools to enable authors and other creators to publish their content more easily, to have their creative works found by others more rapidly, and most important to have their creative works used on more flexible

other authors a legal way to structure their rights. Content and information
can be set free for certain uses, consistent with the author's specific intent,
opening the stage for a more flexible flow of content and information.[6]

While the origins of Creative Commons, including the project's
founder, lie in the United States,[7] many people around the world have
entered the discussion and joined the initiative to make Creative Commons
a truly global project, one that builds a distributed, international
information "commons" by encouraging copyright owners to make their
material available through open content licensing protocols and thereby
promote better identification, negotiation, and reutilization of content for
the purposes of creativity and innovation.

2. Creative Commons Licensing Infrastructure

The Creative Commons licensing suite consists of public standardized
licenses, which allow authors to decide whether others may make
commercial use of their work, whether to make derivative works, and if
derivative works are allowed whether those derivative works must be made
available under the same licensing terms.[8] All licenses require attribution.[9]
Attribution is a key element - not only regarding some of the legal
questions, but also in terms of cultural norms and acceptance.[10]

---

terms than the traditional „all rights reserved" approach of default copyright protection (for
a general overview see Garlick (2005)).

[6] For details about Creative Commons' mission see http://creativecommons.org/about/what-
is-cc as well as Garlick (2009).

[7]   Creative Commons was founded in 2001 by Stanford Law Professor Lawrence
Lessig and other Cyberlaw and Intellectual Property experts. For details, see
http://creativecommons.org/about/history/

[8]   This way, the licenses are designed to provide creators with the ability to clearly
signal their approval of certain uses of their work whilst reserving some rights – in other
words „some rights reserved" as opposed to the default „all rights reserved" level of
copyright protection. For further reading, see http://creativecommons.org/about/what-is-cc

[9]   The "Attribution" element can then be mixed and matched with the other terms
of the core Creative Commons licensing suite into the following 6 licenses: Attribution
(BY), Attribution ShareAlike (BY-SA), Attribution NonCommercial (BY-NC), Attribution
NoDerivatives (BY-ND), Attribution NonCommercial ShareAlike (BY-NC-SA), Attribution
NonCommercial   NoDerivatives   (BY-NC-ND).   For   details   see
http://creativecommons.org/about/licenses/

[10]   The first version of the original Creative Commons licenses allowed for a license
without the attribution element (for details see the original legal code of the CC SA license
version 1.0, available at http://creativecommons.org/licenses/sa/1.0/legalcode). However,
most of the users opted for a license requiring attribution, which resulted in a new version of
the Creative Commons licensing suite. Since then, Attribution became standard and the
number of licenses was reduced from eleven possible to six making the license selection
user interface much simpler. For details see http://creativecommons.org/weblog/entry/4216

A license, once selected, is expressed in three different ways: 1) the "human readable" format (Deed), 2) the lawyer readable format (Legal Code), and 3) the machine readable format (Resource Description Format, metadata). The latter enables online content and information, licensed under a Creative Commons license, to be searched for and identified based on the work's licensing terms.[11] The "Deed" is drafted to be understood by anyone without any legal background, and the "Legal Code" is the actual "license", a legal document drafted to be read by lawyers, courts, and those with a particular interest or involvement in the legal details. These three different layers of the Creative Commons licenses are often described as one distinction between Creative Commons licenses and other Open Content licenses such as the GNU Free Documentation License[12] or the Free Art License[13]. Another important distinguishing feature of Creative Commons licenses is its internationalization.

3. Creative Commons International – the global porting project

Global interest in Creative Commons soared as did license usage worldwide. Because of this and – most importantly – because of the international structure of the Internet per se, it became clear that Creative Commons could not stay as an US project only. Building on the work initiated in the United States, Creative Commons International was founded to coordinate and support the growth of an international network responsible for porting the original US licenses and other tools to local jurisdictions. The goal of this international porting project is to create a multilingual model of the licensing suite that is legally enforceable in jurisdictions around the world.

To achieve this aim, Creative Commons International works with local experts in the intellectual property and technology fields to evaluate national copyright legislations and how these national legislations would potentially interact with Creative Commons licenses. This evaluation is a prerequisite to producing high quality localized versions of the Creative Commons licenses. To guarantee such high quality, Creative Commons International has developed a set of guidelines for the porting process, a detailed ten-step program through which each participating jurisdiction project works firstly to indentify local Project Leads and Affiliate

---

[11]   See advanced search options at Google, Yahoo, etc. (e.g. http://www.google.com/advanced_search?hl=en)
[12]   http://www.gnu.org/copyleft/fdl.html
(http://en.wikipedia.org/wiki/GNU_Free_Documentation_License)
[13]   http://artlibre.org/licence/lal/en/ (http://en.wikipedia.org/wiki/Free_Art_license)

Institution, followed by the license drafting, public discussion, license revision, technical arrangements and translation, and launch event.[14] Once a local host institution and a national legal expert are identified and appointed to act as "Project Lead" for the respective national CC project, the actual works begins with a first draft of a localized Creative Commons license, literally translated into the national language and legally adapted to the national copyright law. An English retranslation and a detailed explanation of all substantial legal changes describe what revisions have been made to fit the Creative Commons licenses into the local legislation and allow for a fruitful and efficient discussion with the Creative Commons International team.[15] After that, a public discussion of the national license draft is called, in which the license draft and supporting documents are used to gather input from potential local stakeholders and user groups. After careful review and approval by the Creative Commons International team, the Creative Commons *jurisdiction licenses* are officially made available and can be accessed through the Creative Commons license chooser.[16]

To date, 52 different national Creative Commons projects have successfully launched national versions of the original Creative Commons licenses.[17] With Thailand and the Czech Republic being the most recent to join the global project and with Armenia, Azerbaijan, Georgia, Russia as well as Indonesia, Vietnam, and several other countries in progress, Creative Commons International has been able to expand its projects beyond the better known traditional copyright jurisdictions and into Asia Pacific, Eastern Europe, and the Post Soviet States. Whereas the legal framework forms an important component of the international porting project, there have also been significant educational and promotional efforts undertaken as part of the internationalization strategy. To begin with, some of the legal aspects will be highlighted, followed by a short outline of the project's "promotional" efforts.

3.1. LEGAL ASPECTS

The most important reason for developing an international licensing model is to address the differences and particularities in understanding "copyright" according to national legislations around the globe. Differences in the legislation and licensing practices among jurisdictions reveal several

---

[14]   http://wiki.creativecommons.org/International_Overview
[15]   See archives for each national Creative Commons project, available at http://creativecommons.org/international, e.g. details for the Serbian project at http://creativecommons.org/international/rs/
[16]   http://creativecommons.org/license/
[17]   http://creativecommons.org/international/

legal issues that do not appear in the US context and vice versa. Some problems arising under local law, e.g. German law can only be addressed by a German version of the core Creative Commons licenses, namely a version which is translated into German language and adopted to German law. Only such a localized version of the CC licenses will assure enforceability in local courts.[18]

Moral Rights: One of the most significant legal issues addressed in porting the Creative Commons licenses is moral rights. Moral rights, to describe them briefly, are distinct from any economic rights tied to copyright. Even if an author has assigned his or her rights to a third party, he still maintains the moral rights to his work. Moral rights recognize an author's personal attachment to their work and seek to protect that connection. The concept of the author's moral rights goes back to the early days of copyright in the Continental European regimes.[19] The theory behind moral rights according to European Continental law is that authors of copyrightable works have inalienable rights[20] in their works that protect their moral or personal interest and that complement the author's economic rights. In this way, the moral rights serve to protect the inherent link between the author and his intellectual and mental creative work.[21] While there can be many different moral rights depending on the jurisdiction, all member states of the Berne Convention[22] are required to provide legal protection for at least two specific moral rights, which subsequently are the main rights currently present in most countries around the globe: the moral right of *attribution* and the moral right of *integrity*. As stated in Art. 6bis of the Berne Convention, these two moral rights give the author of a copyright-protected work the right to claim authorship of the work and to object to any distortion, mutilation or other modification of, or other derogatory action in relation to, the said work, which would be prejudicial to his honor or reputation.[23]

---

[18] For details especially regarding the German Creative Commons licenses see Metzger (2004).

[19] For details regarding theory and history of the *droit d'auteur* approach and Copyright in Continental European *droit d'auteur* jurisdictions, see Wandtke/Bullinger (2008), Einleitung/Introduction marginal number 25, as well as Pessach (2003), page 250-270 (255).

[20] In most European jurisdictions, this is often referred to as „unbreakable bound" between author and work.

[21] See Pessach (2003), page 250-270 (255).

[22] Berne Convention for the Protection of Literary and Artistic Works, as amended on September 28, 1979: http://www.wipo.int/treaties/en/ip/berne/trtdocs_wo001.html

[23] Article 6bis of the Berne Convention: "Independently of the author's economic rights, and even after the transfer of the said rights, the author shall have the right to claim authorship of the work and to object to any distortion, mutilation or other modification of, or other derogatory action in relation to, the said work, which would be prejudicial to his honor or reputation."

Since all Creative Commons licenses require attribution,[24] there is less of an issue regarding the author's moral right of attribution. However, the author's right to object to any derogatory treatment of his work has the potential to impact the freedom to modify the work and exercise the right to make derivatives. A derivative work will likely always qualify as an alteration of the original work, and there may be some instances where it is arguable that it is prejudicial to the original author's reputation or honor.[25] While this hasn't been much of a problem in the US and when drafting the US Creative Commons licenses, the freedom to modify the work has provoked many legal issues in traditional "droit d'auteur" jurisdictions like France and Germany.

It might sound contradictory that the freedom to modify the work poses legal problems in European jurisdictions like Germany or France but not in the US even though all three of those jurisdictions are signatories of the Berne Convention. There is, however, a feasible explanation. The Berne Convention only assures that moral rights exist, but it does not address the question of a potential waiver of moral rights. Each individual member state has to determine in its own legislation to which extent – if any – an author is able to waive such rights.[26]

The possibility of waiving moral rights, plus its legal effectiveness and the potential scope of a waiver, is one of the most pressing questions for Creative Commons licenses. This is especially true with regard to the Continental European copyright regimes, such as France, which is considered to be the birthplace of the moral rights doctrine.[27] Traditionally, France and other "droit d'auteur" jurisdictions have provided a much stronger and broader protection of moral rights than most of the copyright regimes based on common law. The French legislation currently states that moral rights are "inalienable", and although upon the author's death they may be transmitted to his or her legal successors, they may not be otherwise transferred or assigned. Consequently, French courts have determined that "1) authors cannot legally relinquish or abandon the rights of attribution or integrity altogether, 2) advance blanket waivers are unenforceable, and 3) narrowly tailored waivers that involve reasonably

---

[24] See footnote 11: Attribution became standard in version 2.0 of the Creative Commons licenses (http://creativecommons.org/weblog/entry/4216)
[25] See Garlick, Creative Commons Version 3.0 licenses – A brief explanation, available at http://wiki.creativecommons.org/Version_3
[26] For further reading about how a potential waiver has been handled in different jurisdictions, see the detailed report *Moral Rights in Puerto Rico and the Creative Commons 3.0 licenses* –available at http://mirrors.creativecommons.org/international/pr/moral-rights.pdf
[27] For details regarding theory and origin of moral rights in France see Schmidt-Szalewski (1992), page 187-194 (187 et seq.) as well as Pessach (2003), page 250-270 (250 et seq.).

foreseeable encroachments on the author's moral rights are generally valid."[28]

Most other Continental European copyright jurisdictions follow the French tradition in their own regulation of moral rights. Despite the current debate in Germany about whether it might be possible to partially waive copyright including moral rights[29], there has not yet been room for any different understanding of moral rights. German courts and most scholars still accept assignments only under the condition that the changes are specified, meaning that the author must have a realistic chance to foresee any changes that will be made.[30] This option is rather unlikely, if not impossible, within the context of standardized open content licenses such as the Creative Commons licenses.[31] France and Germany being only two examples of how moral rights are conceived as "inalienable" and thereby proscribing any assignment or waiver of such rights, many other jurisdictions can be found to follow the French approach.[32]

On the other hand, most common law countries have traditionally favored the protection of economic rights within the copyright regimes, although moral rights have found their way into the copyright laws by other means.[33] In the past decades countries like the United Kingdom and Australia have developed a moral rights concept in their national legislation but simultaneously allowed a waiver of such rights.[34] Between these two different approaches to moral rights, there are some jurisdictions such as the Netherlands, which traditionally follow the Continental European "droit d'auteur approach" but allow a partial waiver under certain circumstances.[35] Under Canadian copyright law, which is heavily

---

[28]   See Rigamonti (2006).

[29]   For further reading about the discussion in Germany and France, see Metzger (2003), page 9-23 (9 et seq.).

[30]   Ibid.

[31]   Ibid.

[32]   See the detailed examination about the situation in Spain, Mexico, and other jurisdictions in the report *Moral Rights in Puerto Rico and the Creative Commons 3.0 licenses* available at http://mirrors.creativecommons.org/international/pr/moral-rights.pdf

[33]   Dietz/Schricker, Urheberrecht, Vor §§ 12 ff. Marginal number 21. See also report *Moral Rights in Puerto Rico and the Creative Commons 3.0 licenses* –available at http://mirrors.creativecommons.org/international/pr/moral-rights.pdf

[34]   The possibility of a waiver has led some scholars to question the level of compliance to their international obligations – for details, see Dworkin (1995).

[35]   "Section 25(3) of the Dutch Copyright Act allows authors to waive some of their moral rights (the right to attribution and to oppose slight changes made to the work). However, the moral right Section 25(1) under d. to oppose 'any distortion, mutilation or other impairment of the work that could be prejudicial to the name or reputation of the author or to his/her dignity as such' cannot be waived." For details, see Hendriks, Developing CC Licenses for Dutch Creatives, available at http://fr.creativecommons.org/articles/netherlands.htm as well as the detailed report "Moral

influenced by the civil law tradition of Quebec, moral rights may not be
assigned but may be waived in whole or in part.[36] However, the act of
assigning a copyright in Canada does not in itself constitute a waiver of any
moral rights. Therefore, any act or omission contrary to one of the author's
moral rights is, without the author's consent, an infringement of his or her
moral rights.[37]

Finally Japan deserves a separate analysis. Under Japanese law, any
modification "against the author's will" could be a violation of the moral
right of integrity.[38] If the modification is made in a way "where it is
possible to directly perceive the essential characteristics of the original
work" such a modification can be a violation of the moral right of integrity
if the author's consent is missing.[39] Even though it can be argued that by
allowing derivative works through a Creative Commons license implies
that the author gave his consent and that at least part of the moral right of
integrity is "licensed", there remains a risk of violating the moral right of
integrity if the resulting derivative work is outside the scope of what the
author thought he was licensing.[40]

Different regulations and interpretations of moral rights make their
adaptation in various jurisdictions one of the most important legal issues
when working with Creative Commons licenses. One approach could be to
not mention moral rights in Creative Commons licenses at all.[41] Not
addressing moral rights in the legal code could be argued as leaving the
legal code open for interpretation by the respective court in the case of an
infringement. But what would be the consequence if Creative Commons
licenses did not provide for any regulation regarding moral rights? Would
the court simply recognize moral rights as they are implemented and
executed in the respective national law? And what impact could this have
for the existence of the license, especially for the section allowing
derivative works?

Rights in Puerto Rico and the Creative Commons 3.0 licenses" –available at
http://mirrors.creativecommons.org/international/pr/moral-rights.pdf

[36] http://creativecommons.ca/index.php?p=moralrights and
http://mirrors.creativecommons.org/international/ca/english-changes.pdf

[37] See the report "Moral Rights in Puerto Rico and the Creative Commons 3.0
licenses" –available at http://mirrors.creativecommons.org/international/pr/moral-rights.pdf

[38] Article 20 Japanese Copyright Act available at
http://www.cric.or.jp/cric_e/clj/clj.html

[39] Supreme Court of Japan:
http://www.courts.go.jp/english/judgments/text/1980.03.28-1976.-O-.No.923.html

[40] Tokyo High Court, dated 1999.9.21. (Heisei 11 (ne) 1154)

[41] Creative Commons licenses version 1.0 did not address moral rights at all. For
details see the overview of different license versions available at
http://wiki.creativecommons.org/License_versions

Taking again the German situation as an illustrative example, the whole section of the Creative Commons license that allows for derivative works would most likely be considered invalid under the German law of standard terms.[42] Creating and distributing derivative works would be impossible. To avoid such a risk of invalidity, moral rights have to be dealt with in Creative Commons licenses if these licenses are to be used whenever German law is applicable. Similarly, most other Continental European jurisdictions licenses have to deal with the specific and mostly very restrictive moral rights regulation in their respective national legislation.

Because of this uncertainty and especially because of the fact that interpretation by local courts cannot be clearly foreseen, it was discussed and decided amongst the global Creative Commons International Network to address moral rights in the Creative Commons licenses. Instead of not mentioning moral rights at all, with the hope that local courts would implement it adequately, moral rights are now dealt with in the Creative Commons licenses. To provide clarity regarding the treatment of moral rights, it was agreed to explicitly retain the moral right of integrity in those jurisdiction licenses that have to deal with a strong level of protection for the moral right of integrity, as evidenced by the risk that local courts would take a dim view of a license which does not expressly include moral rights.[43]

Consequently, the next question when evaluating the Creative Commons licenses in terms of moral rights is whether those rights should be waived or not. Since most jurisdictions throughout the world grant moral rights to authors, but only some of them allow for a waiver, the issue of a potential waiver presents a challenge for Creative Commons licenses. Many users within the community are in favor of a license that permits creators to "completely" waive moral rights, because only such a license would ensure that the freedom to create derivatives and build upon other's works can be exercised to the fullest extent possible. On the other hand, it has again been argued that the Creative Commons licenses would face the risk of being vulnerable to judicial validity in the case that the respective national copyright legislation conceives moral rights as "inalienable" and therefore proscribes any assignment or waiver of such rights. Thus, the policy question to be evaluated is which uncertainty is more tolerable: the one brought by the possibility of claims against (downstream) users for

---

[42]   See Article 306 of the German Civil Code which states that "To the extent that the terms have not become part of the contract or are ineffective, the contents of the contract are determined by the statutory provisions (Verbot der geltungserhaltenden Reduktion)" available at http://www.gesetze-im-internet.de/englisch_bgb/englisch_bgb.html

[43]   See Garlick, Creative Commons Version 3.0 licenses – A brief explanation, available at http://wiki.creativecommons.org/Version_3#Further_Internationalization

integrity rights violation or the uncertainty brought by having the licenses per se vulnerable to attack for providing moral rights waiver.[44]

To make it even more complicated, not only does this question have to be discussed on a national level for each respective jurisdiction license, but it also has an impact on an international level, since all Creative Commons licenses have to work globally as well. When drafting the moral rights wording for a national version of the Creative Commons licenses while at the same time looking at the different regulations for moral rights in different jurisdictions, the question of applicable law becomes relevant. Will the respective national copyright legislation necessarily always provide the basis for discussions and interpretation of the moral rights section of that particular associated Creative Commons license? Hence, the issue about moral rights proves perfectly how almost every legal question regarding Creative Commons licenses coincides with rules of Private International Law. In the case of moral rights, and after careful consideration and consultation with the international legal network, it was agreed that most jurisdictions should implement a simple wording stating that moral rights remain untouched by the respective Creative Commons license, so as to ensure validity of the license but allows for the exercise of the rights provided by the license to the fullest extent permitted by applicable law in order to respect the freedom to modify the work as broadly as possible. For most of the national jurisdiction licenses, the following simple wording served as a basis for discussion during the porting process: "Moral Rights remain unaffected to the extent they are recognized and not waivable by applicable law."

This approach[45] allows the user to exercise the rights under the license to the fullest extent possible, while also protecting the license from any challenge and potential risk of invalidity based on an improper or void waiver. It also leaves enough room for interpretation at the respective national level and at the same time fits perfectly into the overall international harmonization efforts of the global porting project.

---

[44]   This question had to be evaluated and answered for many different jurisdiction licenses. As an example, please see the detailed report for the porting process in Puerto Rico *Moral Rights in Puerto Rico and the Creative Commons 3.0 licenses* –available at http://mirrors.creativecommons.org/international/pr/moral-rights.pdf

[45]   It has to be emphasized that this approach is only used as a starting point for discussion for each national CC project. Based on this approach, a specific wording for the respective national jurisdiction license needs to be elaborated and implemented to best match the situation given by the national legislation which can end up to be the same wording or end up in something more specific, such as the Dutch solution available at http://mirrors.creativecommons.org/international/nl/english-retranslation.pdf, or the wording in the CC licenses for New Zealand, available at http://creativecommons.org/licenses/by/3.0/nz/legalcode

Neighboring Rights and especially the European Database Directive: In addition to the traditional protection of "copyrightable works", most European copyright systems[46] also provide protection for "related rights" ("neighboring rights") and through the European Database Directive[47] for databases ("sui generis database protection").[48] Similar to the argumentation for the protection of neighboring rights, the Database Directive allows for the special protection of a database "which shows that there has been qualitatively and/or quantitatively a substantial *investment* in either obtaining, verification or presentation of the contents to prevent extraction and/or reutilization of the whole or of a substantial part, evaluated qualitatively and/or quantitatively, of the contents of that database"[49]. Obviously, the rationale behind protection is not the personal intellectual creation, as it is the prerequisite for copyright protection in most European jurisdictions[50], but rather the *investment* shown by the maker of a database.[51]

In the past, some of the European localized and translated versions of Creative Commons licenses (see Belgium, France, Germany and Netherlands) contained a reference to the respective national legislation passed pursuant to the Database Directive by defining a "work" to include databases protected by these laws.[52] However, most other European

---

[46]   See Directive 2006/115/EC of the European Parliament and of the Council of 12 December 2006 on rental right and lending right and on certain rights related to copyright in the field of intellectual property, which harmonizes the situation regarding rental right, lending right and certain related rights as to provide a greater level of protection for literary and artistic property in Europe. Similarly to the European situation, most Latin American jurisdictions recognize "neighboring rights" or "related rights" as well. As an example, see the situation in Guatemala explained in the summary of substantial legal changes for the Guatemalan Creative Commons licenses available at http://mirrors.creativecommons.org/international/gt/english-changes.pdf

[47]   Directive 96/9/EC of the European Parliament and of the Council of 11 March 1996 on the legal protection of databases.

[48]   Whereas the US concept of Copyright may protect all creative expressions, including the performing rights, such rights are separately qualified as "related rights" in EU jurisdictions. For Details see Hendriks, Developing CC licenses for Dutch Creatives, available at http://fr.creativecommons.org/articles/netherlands.htm

[49]   Directive 96/9/EC of the European Parliament and of the Council of 11 March 1996 on the legal protection of databases. For details about the database right, see also http://en.wikipedia.org/wiki/Database_right

[50]   See definition of "copyrightable work" in Section 2 of the German Copyright Act available at   http://www.iuscomp.org/gla/statutes/UrhG.htm#2

[51]   For details regarding the US and Dutch use of the term "copyright" and the addition of related rights see Hendriks, Developing CC Licenses for Dutch Creatives, available at http://fr.creativecommons.org/articles/netherlands.htm

[52]   See the Dutch Creative Commons licenses version 1.0 and the explanation of the substantial   legal   changes   available   at http://mirrors.creativecommons.org/international/nl/english-changes.pdf   as well as the

licenses did not mention the database rights at all, even if the Database Directive had already been implemented in their national legislation. Neighboring rights and in particular the database right turned out to be one of the most controversial and the most inconsistently treated aspects in the European licenses.

The main argument for addressing these rights in the European licenses is that these rights are defined so broadly that, without addressing them, the national versions of the Creative Commons licenses are not complete, nor exercisable in practical applications, particularly in Internet collections. The main argument follows that without the neighboring rights and database right included, the Licensor would still hold some exclusive rights in the work, which were intended to be licensed. To resolve this problem, it was suggested to explicitly incorporate the neighboring rights as well as the database right in the license text by extending the definition of "work" so that neighboring rights are listed concurrently with the definition of work, namely as being the "copyrightable work of authorship".

On the other hand, there have been significant concerns regarding the inclusion of database rights in the Creative Commons licenses. It was argued that Creative Commons licenses, when including the sui generis database right via the definition of "work", can become especially problematic as they pose the danger that, through the use of a Creative Commons license, protection of the sui generis database right can be "imported" to a jurisdiction without any sui generis database right protection. In other words, by using a national version of the Creative Commons licenses for a jurisdiction which both a) has implemented the European Database Directive and b) where the national Creative Commons licenses reflect the legislation through an amendment of the definition of work and an inclusion of the database right as an exclusive right, the use of such a license could actually lead to the assumption and confusion that these rights are intended to be respected even if they are not protected by national law.

As a result of the debate between the advantages and disadvantages of implementing neighboring rights and the very specific problem of the European database rights, it was agreed to include these rights in the Creative Commons licenses where they are recognized by the national legislation. But at the same time, a "geographic boundary" assures that those Creative Commons licenses that define the term "work" to include neighboring rights as well as databases protected by the national implementation of the Database Directive, should have territorial limitations regarding these rights by stating that these are only included in

---

German Creative Commons licenses version 2.0
(http://creativecommons.org/licenses/by/2.0/de/legalcode)

the definition of work "to the extent they are recognized and protected by applicable law".[53] Additionally, for the database right, an unconditional waiver will ensure that these rights are disqualified in the scientific context. Concretely, this means that those national Creative Commons jurisdiction licenses which have included the database protected by the national implementation of the European Database Directive as a consequence of following a harmonized treatment of neighboring rights must waive these specific database rights obtained under the sui generis right. A simple sentence in the end of the license grant ensures the resolution for European licenses:

> "Where the Licensor is the owner of the sui generis database rights under the national law implementing the European Database Directive, the Licensor will waive this right."

3.2. LANGUAGE: SPREADING THE WORD AND PROMOTIONAL ASPECTS

As indicated above, license internationalization also has tremendous impact on the worldwide usage of Creative Commons licenses and by extension, on the growth of the global "commons" as a pool of pre-cleared content that can be mixed and shared in an international dimension. Linguistically translating the licenses into a jurisdiction's national language encourages license acceptance and usage beyond the English-speaking world. In addition, officially recognized license translations lead to increased global adoption by institutions and public organizations, including governments.[54] Not only can we find an enormous number of Creative Commons licensed content via popular search engines such as Google, Yahoo or others[55], some concrete examples[56] of Creative Commons license usage qualitatively demonstrates the global impact of Creative Commons over the past years. These examples provide evidence of how Creative Commons licensed content fits into other projects and helps build a system of networked informational exchange in the Internet.

In December 2008 the German Federal Archives[57] donated a significant amount of historical German images to the Wikimedia Commons project.[58]

---

[53] See e.g. the solution in the Dutch Creative Commons licenses version 3.0: http://mirrors.creativecommons.org/international/nl/english-retranslation.pdf

[54] http://wiki.creativecommons.org/Government_use_of_CC_licenses

[55] http://search.yahoo.com/web/advanced?ei=UTF-8&fr=yfp-t-501 and http://www.google.com/advanced_search?hl=en&output=unclesam&restrict=unclesam

[56] For a detailed report about how Creative Commons licenses have been used by creators and institutions along with an explanation of their motivations please see "Building and Australasian Commons" available at http://creativecommons.org.au/materials/Building_an_Australasian_Commons_book.pdf

[57] http://www.bundesarchiv.de/

These images are now licensed under the German Creative Commons Attribution Share Alike 3.0 license. Their availability to the public through the Wikimedia Commons is part of a cooperation between Wikimedia Germany and the Federal Archives, whose collaboration also developed a tool to link the images to their respective German Wikipedia article and file in the German National Library. Another significant boost for Creative Commons emphasizes that Creative Commons licenses are not only important to private users and amateurs. Shortly after the news from Germany, the Australian (Queensland) government launched a new website for their Government Information Licensing Framework project (GILF) under the Australian Creative Commons Attribution 2.5 license.[59] Through this website, the GILF project is working to further promote the benefits of using and re-using of Public Sector Information. These benefits can be measured for the Australian community in terms of innovation, creativity, and economic growth: *"The GILF makes it easy for people who use public sector information to understand the rights of use associated with PSI material. GILF comprises a simple open content licensing framework, designed to assist in the management of government intellectual property, and encourage the use of public sector information through increased availability and accessibility..."*[60] Encouraged by the preceding national debate arguing that *"owing to Creative Commons' status as an international movement, and its recognition as a standard for flexible copyright licensing, the government can gain significant leverage from adopting Creative Commons. No point in needlessly re-inventing the wheel..."*[61] the Australian GILF can be seen as one of the most innovative governmental projects in the world.

The list of case studies can be extended and seen as the best proof that developing the international porting project and working with local Project Leads and Affiliate Institutions in different jurisdictions on national versions of the core CC licenses becomes, automatically, the best promotional tool for Creative Commons. It remains the key factor for the international adoption of Creative Commons licenses.

When porting the licenses to different national jurisdictions around the world, Creative Commons International has simultaneously established an international network of IP and IT experts. With the patronage and enormous support of this network, the idea of Creative Commons as a new type of voluntary mechanism for legal questions within the digital age has entered the local debate about copyright law on a national legislative level.

---

58   http://commons.wikimedia.org/wiki/Commons:Bundesarchiv
59   http://www.creativecommons.org.au/node/229 and http://www.gilf.gov.au/
60   For details, please http://www.gilf.gov.au/
61   http://wiki.creativecommons.org/Government_Information_Licensing_Framework
and http://www.creativecommons.org.au/node/229

The greatest success of Creative Commons is its unshakable presence in the discussion of a pragmatic legal system that deals with questions arising with the advent of the Internet.

4. Challenges for Creative Commons and its international licensing model

Private International Law: The previous examples as well as the legal evaluation of only two potential issues for Creative Commons licenses demonstrates that there is a need for the international porting project and that the licenses have to be adapted in many different ways to prevent misunderstandings and invalidity. We cannot ignore the fact that some provisions of a US license would be invalid insofar as European law is applicable. However, at the same time, this perception opens the discussion about the applicable law and a potential choice of law clause in the Creative Commons licenses. In other words, a "multi–jurisdictional" approach raises an array of private international law issues. The key question to be investigated arises when Licensor A, a resident of Germany, is licensing his picture on his German website under the German Creative Commons licenses Attribution (BY) and Licensee B, a resident of New Zealand is using the picture on his New Zealand website without giving attribution at all. In the case that Licensor A wants to sue Licensee B alleging that B's activities infringe the terms of the German Creative Commons license, which court would be competent to hear the claim and – more importantly – which law would be applicable? And finally how can the ruling be enforced elsewhere?

Not all of these questions can be covered in this article, whose purpose is to raise the issues rather than solve them. In terms of the applicable law, and according to the rules of private international law, two different issues have to be considered. The first one is how to deal with questions regarding copyright, the second relates to other parts of the law, such as contract law.

For all questions regarding copyright, such as questions about the existence, duration of copyright, moral rights or even questions regarding fair dealing or limitations and exceptions of the exclusive copyright, the rule of territoriality will have to be applied. According to Art. 8 of the recently adopted Rome II regulation, at least for the European Union, it is stated that *"The law applicable to a non-contractual obligation arising from an infringement of an intellectual property right shall be the law of the country for which protection is claimed."*[62] On an international scale, many scholars consider Art. 5 II of the Berne Convention as also mirroring

---

[62]   http://eur-
lex.europa.eu/LexUriServ/LexUriServ.do?uri=OJ:L:2007:199:0040:0049:EN:PDF.

this approach.[63] However, especially for copyright issues, the rule of
territoriality is still controversial.[64]

Irrespective of how to interpret the wording of the Berne Convention,
and without a detailed analysis of all arguments, the current tendency is to
stick with the rule of territoriality to questions of copyright, especially
regarding the existence, duration of copyright and neighboring rights,
moral rights or even questions about fair dealing or limitations and
exceptions of the exclusive copyright.[65] Consequently, all these copyright
questions are governed by the respective national legal order. Instead of
"*one global* copyright", the copyright holder has a "bundle of different
national copyrights", which can be seen as some kind of "mosaic-like"
approach.[66]

For contractual issues, the answer is even more complicated. According
to Article 4 of the Rome I Convention of 2008 on the law applicable to
contractual obligations[67], the applicable law is considered to be the national
law of the jurisdiction "where the party required to effect the characteristic
performance of the contract has his habitual residence" – unless the parties
have agreed on a different choice of law in the contract. To the extent
Creative Commons licenses are deemed to be a contract, a choice of law
clause could be helpful to complete the picture of a nationally adapted
license. By making sure that the German version of the Creative Commons
licenses will be governed by German law, some level of legal certainty can
be reached. However, as mentioned above, the potential choice of law
clause can only help for contractual issues of the Creative Commons
licenses and only if the Creative Commons licenses themselves are
considered to be a contract. For questions regarding copyright, the rule of

---

[63]   Art. 5 II of the Berne Convention: *"The enjoyment and the exercise of these rights
shall not be subject to any formality; such enjoyment and such exercise shall be independent
of the existence of protection in the country of origin of the work. Consequently, apart from
the provisions of this Convention, the extent of protection, as well as the means of redress
afforded to the author to protect his rights, shall be governed exclusively by the laws of the
country   where   protection   is   claimed."*   available   at
http://www.wipo.int/treaties/en/ip/berne/trtdocs_wo001.html#P109_16834.   For   an
interpretation as conflicts rule see Goldstein (2001), pp. 103-104; Katzenberger in Schricker,
Urheberrecht, Vor §§ 120ff, marginal number 120; Ulmer (1975), marginal number 1, 16.

[64]   See, e.g., Schack (2007), page 458 et seq.; Boschiero (2007), *pp.* 87, 94 et seq.

[65]   See § 301 of American Law Institute, *Intellectual Property: Principles Governing
Jurisdiction, Choice of Law, and Judgments in Transnational Disputes*, 2007 and Articles
3:102, 3:201, 3:301, 3:601 of European Max Planck Group on Conflict of Laws in
Intellectual Property (CLIP), Principles for Conflict of Laws in Intellectual Property, Second
Preliminary Draft (6 June 2009), available at www.cl-ip.eu .

[66]   Jaeger/Metzer, Open Source Software, 2nd edition, marginal number 356.

[67]   http://eur-
lex.europa.eu/LexUriServ/LexUriServ.do?uri=OJ:L:2008:177:0006:0016:EN:PDF

territoriality is internationally mandatory and cannot be eluded by any additional choice of law clause in the license.[68]

To summarize, these questions regarding private international law are probably the most crucial and most difficult to be investigated when working with Creative Commons licenses in the digital age, since any use on the Internet tends to cross borders. One potential starting point for further research and discussion could be the relationship between different national versions of the Creative Commons licenses. Because of how Creative Commons licenses are functioning and especially because they are *non-exclusive*, the Licensor is free to choose more than one license and also combine different license versions, which can be used on parallel. Once different licenses are used in parallel, the only missing point will be a mechanism to ensure that each license is used in the correct and adequate context, e.g., the German license should be binding if German law is applicable. For contractual issues, this result can be reached by implementing a choice of law clause (see above), and for copyright issues this can be assured by adding some kind of restriction to the respective jurisdiction.[69] Whether and how the same effect can be reached or at least be supported by technical advancement needs to be investigated and further discussed.

Interoperability: The idea of open content licenses is not new, and Creative Commons did not invent the first free public licenses for digital content. Following the Free Software Foundation's initiative to build a public license for software, there were many others to follow and to release free licenses designed for creative content instead of software. The aforementioned Art Libre License[70] and the Free Software Foundation's GNU Free Documentation License (GNU FDL)[71] are probably the most famous, but others can be found for different types of works and content. [72]

All these open content licenses share a common goal, which is to give authors, creators, and other rights holders the ability to offer important freedoms and share with others. However, there remains an issue when remixing content that has been licensed under different open content licenses.[73] Generally speaking, the copyleft or ShareAlike element of any

---

[68]   Jaeger/Metzer, Open Source Software, 2nd edition, marginal number 356.

[69]   One possible wording for such a clause could be: "This license shall apply only if German copyright law is applicable. German copyright law is to be applied if you copy or distribute the work or make it available on German territory. In this case, the license shall also be governed by German law". For details see Metzer (2004).

[70]   http://artlibre.org/licence/lal/en/

[71]   For details please see http://www.fsf.org/licensing/licenses/fdl.html

[72]   See   Liang,   Guide   to   Open   Content   Licenses   –   available   at http://www.pzwart.wdka.hro.nl/mdr/research/lliang/open_content_guide

[73]   For details, see Lessig, CC in Review: Lawrence Lessig on Compatibility, available at http://creativecommons.org/weblog/entry/5709

open content license requires derivatives to be licensed under the same license only. Consequently, content available under an open content license that includes a ShareAlike element cannot be used together and remixed with content that has been licensed under another open content license, even if this license also includes a ShareAlike or copyleft element.

In the past, this was a major issue for the Wikipedia project. Before the most recent change in license adoption for Wikipedia articles[74], if someone wanted to put together a movie based on a Wikipedia entry, supplemented with images licensed under a Creative Commons license on Flickr, this was not legally permitted even if it was technically possible.[75] The same was true for pictures, music or other content licensed under Creative Commons license BY-SA. If licensed under CC BY-SA, these materials could not legally be remixed with other creative content that was licensed under another open content license, even another copyleft license.[76] Obviously, the idea of building a common pool of easily accessible and pre-cleared, freely available content would fail if this problem were not addressed in the near future. One of the most important features of the digital technologies, the possibility to take images, music and other content, remix it, and produce something new at relatively low costs yet often of high quality, would be diminished if the content were restricted to the respective license terms. Instead, without interoperability, many different but not overlapping pools of creative content would be established.

In terms of the Wikipedia project, this issue has just recently been addressed by a new version of the CC BY-SA as well as a new version of the GNU FDL. Creative Commons licenses at version 3.0 allow for a new Share Alike structure in their CC BY-SA, which enables Creative Commons to certify particular licenses as being compatible with the CC BY-SA.[77] Once certified as being compatible, licensees of both the CC BY-SA version 3.0 and the certified "CC compatible license" will be able to relicense derivatives under either license.[78] Similarly, the Free Software

---

[74]　　　Just recently, the Wikipedia community and the Wikimedia Foundation board approved the adoption of the Creative Commons Attribution ShareAlike license as the main content license for Wikipedia and other Wikimedia sites. For details and background see http://creativecommons.org/weblog/entry/15411

[75]　　　See Lessig's example at http://creativecommons.org/weblog/entry/5709

[76]　　　The old version 2.5 of the CC BY-SA similarly required derivatives to be licensed under *"the terms of this license, a later version of this license with the same license elements as this license, or a Creative Commons jurisdiction license that contains the same elements as this license."*

[77]　　　Garlick, Creative Commons Version 3.0 licenses – A brief explanation, available at http://wiki.creativecommons.org/Version_3

[78]　　　E.g., under either the CC BY-SA license or the certified CC compatible license. See Garlick, Creative Commons Version 3.0 licenses – A brief explanation, available at http://wiki.creativecommons.org/Version_3

Foundation released an update of the GNU FDL.[79] This new version was drafted specifically to allow Wikipedia and other projects in a similar position to make licensing changes.[80] Interoperability between GNU FDL and CC BY-SA, and especially the move from GNU FDL to the CC BY-SA as the primary content license for all Wikimedia Foundation's projects, will foster a broader usage of Wikimedia project content including Wikipedia articles as they will be more interoperable with existing CC BY-SA content and easier to re-use.[81] Assuring this interoperability certainly means *"a critical step towards making this freedom work"*, as Lessig commented on the announcement of the licensing decision.[82] There is no doubt of the significance and meaningfulness of this huge step within the free culture movement, which will hopefully serve as a template for others. But the general dilemma remains: Copyleft licenses automatically restrict the respective content. This sounds particularly absurd since the motivation behind copyleft licenses is to keep the content "open" and within the pool of freely licensed material, while at the same time these licenses restrict the ability to reuse and remix.

6. Conclusion and perspectives

Creative Commons' licenses and other tools provide an additional option for copyright creators and right holders to structure their rights in a more flexible way. This way, the "best-of both-worlds" is offered: a way to protect their creative works while encouraging certain uses of them, tailored to each creators individual preference. Creative Commons' global porting project ensures that this new way of balancing copyright can be exercised on an international level and at the same time helps to increase the global commons of easily accessible content. Concurrently, a network of international legal and technical experts has been built to collaborate on the internationalization of the core Creative Commons licensing suite, license maintenance and legal commentary on new license versions.

Although, with the support of the international network, the Creative Commons licensing suite has been successfully ported to more than 50 jurisdictions, there are still some interesting legal questions to be discussed and researched. In particular, questions of Private International Law and

---

[79]   http://creativecommons.org/weblog/entry/10443   -   details   available   at
http://www.gnu.org/licenses/fdl-1.3.html
http://meta.wikimedia.org/wiki/Licensing_update/Questions_and_Answers
[80]   http://arstechnica.com/open-source/news/2009/04/wikipedians-to-vote-on-
creative-commons-license-adoption.ars
[81]   See Press release on dual licensing (May 21, 2009) available at
http://wikimediafoundation.org/wiki/Press_releases/Dual_license_vote_May_2009
[82]   http://wikimediafoundation.org/wiki/Press_releases/Dual_license_vote_May_2009

how the Creative Commons licensing can best interact with and become
compatible with other open content licensing models are two topics that
need to be addressed in order to complete the international project and
achieve an internationally functioning structure. There is no doubt that
there are still many problems to be solved, but there is also no doubt that
many of these issues can be resolved by the international network and the
global Creative Commons community itself. The latest news regarding the
voting for Wikipedia contributors to use the Creative Commons BY-SA
license is the best example to show that community members have to push
for their needs and use their influence to refine and adjust the tools so that
they serve their purpose.

Similarly, some of the legal questions have already been on the agenda
of Creative Commons' global conferences. With the first initial meeting in
Harvard in 2005, followed by other regional and global conferences[83],
including last year's Creative Commons' Legal Day in Sapporo, Creative
Commons project leads and team members from many different
jurisdictions came together to discuss legal aspects like moral rights and
other specific questions regarding Creative Commons licenses such as
licensing of derivatives works and statistics on the global growth of
Creative Commons licensed content.[84]

It is hoped that the series of global meetings will persevere and that the
international network can build upon the initiative that began in Rio de
Janeiro in 2006 and continued in Dubrovnik in 2007 and Sapporo in 2008.
Only a sustained discussion on an international level will help to clarify and
solve the open questions. National and regional debates can help but would
not replace a truly international approach, since the diversity of copyright
regimes around the globe needs to be discussed. Many scholars have
already provided input and joined the dialogue.[85] The issues presented
above may be a starting point for further research and discussion, and it
hopefully invites others to take part. But most importantly, this article gives
an insight in some essentials of the internationalization process, and in this
manner can also be seen as an acknowledgement to the global network.

To conclude, the users themselves, be it the international Creative
Commons network or other associations, communities, and contributors are
in the best position to shape the advantages of the digital age to best fit
their needs.

---

[83]   See   http://creativecommons.org/weblog/entry/10399,
http://creativecommons.org/weblog/entry/11099,
http://creativecommons.org/weblog/entry/9686,
http://creativecommons.org/weblog/entry/9249
http://creativecommons.org/weblog/entry/11162
[84]   http://wiki.creativecommons.org/CCi_Legal_Day_2008
[85]   http://www.icommons.org/articles/the-cci-legal-day-in-dubrovnik-highlights

References

Boschiero (2007), *Infringement of Intellectual Property Rights, A Commentary on Article 8 of the Rome II Regulation,* IX Yearbook of Private International Law 87, 94 et seq.

Dietz/Schricker (2006), *Urheberrecht,* 3rd edition, Vor §§ 12 et seq.

Dworkin, R. (1995), *The Moral Right of the Author: Moral Rights and the Commons Law Countries,* 19 Columbia VLA J.L. & Arts 229.

Fitzgerald/Olwan (2009), *Copyright and Innovation in the Digital Age: The United Arab Emirates* (UAE) available at http://slconf.uaeu.ac.ae/papers/PDF%201%20English/e9.pdf

Garlick, *Creative Commons Version 3.0 licenses – A brief explanation,* available at http://wiki.creativecommons.org/Version_3#Further_Internationalization

Garlick (2005), *A Review of Creative Commons and Science Commons,* Educause Review, Vol. 40, No.5 , September/October 2005 available at http://www.educause.edu/EDUCAUSE+Review/EDUCAUSEReviewMagazine Volume40/AReviewofCreativeCommonsandSci/158002

Garlick (2009), *Creative Commons Licensing – Another Option to enable online Business Models,* available at http://www.hm-treasury.gov.uk/d/creative_commons_418_p2_218kb.pdf

Goldstein (2001), *International Copyright: Principles, Law and Practice,* page 103-104.

Hendriks, *Developing CC Licenses fur Dutch Creatives,* available at http://fr.creativecommons.org/articles/netherlands.htm

Jaeger/Metzger (2006), *Open Source Software,* 2nd edition.

Katzenberger/Schricker (2006), Urhebberrecht, 3rd edition, Vor §§ 120 et seq.

Lessig, CC in *Review: Lawrence Lessig on Compatibility,* available at: http://creativecommons.org/weblog/entry/5709

Liang (2004), *Guide to Open Content Licenses* - available at http://pzwart.wdka.hro.nl/mdr/pubsfolder/opencontent/

Metzger (2004), *Free Content licenses under German Law.* Talk at the Wissenschaftskolleg, Berlin, June 17, available at http://lists.ibiblio.org/pipermail/cc-de/2004-July/000015.html

Pessach (2003), *The Author's Moral Right of Integrity in Cyberspace – A Preliminary Normative Framework,* IIC, pp. 250 – 270.

Peukert, *Der Schutzbereich des Urheberrechts und das Werk als öffentliches Gut - Insbesondere: Die urheberrechtliche Relevanz des privaten Werkgenusses,* in Reto M. Hilty, Alexander Peukert (Hrsg.) "Interessenausgleich im Urheberrecht", 1st edition 2004, page 11 – 46.

Rigamonti (2006), *Deconstructing Moral Rights,* 47 Harv. Int'l L. J. 353.

Schack (2007), *Urheber- und Urhebervertragsrecht,* 4th edition.

Schmidt-Szalewski (1992), *Die theoretischen Grundlagen des französischen Urheberrecht im 19. und 20. Jahrhundert,* GRUR Int. 1992, page 187-194.

Ulmer (1975), *Die Immaterialgüterrechte* im IPR, marginal number 1, 16.

Wandtke/Bullinger (2008), *Urheberrecht,* 3rd edition.

Open Sourcing Regulation: The Development of the Creative Commons Licences as a Form of Commons Based Peer Production

Prodomos Tsiavos[*], Edgar A. Whitley[°]
[*]London School of Economics and Political Science and University of Oslo
[°]Information Systems and Innovation Group, Department of Management, London School of Economics and Political Science

Abstract. Commons Based Peer Production (CBPP) as an abstraction of a variety of distributed, non–hierarchical and non–market–based forms of production may be seen to apply in a variety of production phenomena from Free / Libre Open Source Software to Free Open Content, Open Hardware and Social Networks. While much of the existing literature on the implications of CBPP has confined itself to tracing its potential implications in relation to Copyright law, this study explores its implications on the form and process of copyright–related regulation. More specifically, it explores the degree to which the widest adopted form of Open Content licensing, the Creative Commons (CC) licences, are produced in a way that resembles the CBPP model. Through a qualitative analysis of the production of the basic CC licences this paper argues that CC follows a form of CBPP. The analysis shows that as a regulation building project the CC case involves the production of both meaning and actual regulatory instruments. In this case, pure CBPP can only be achieved by increasing the levels of skills of the participants to enable the requisite excess capacity required for CBPP. In the absence of this capacity, CBPP models may tend to return to more traditional hierarchies and controlled network structures. It is unclear, however, whether such a move is a temporary stage in the regulatory development process or something more permanent.

Keywords: Creative Commons, Commons Based Peer Production, Free Libre Open Source Software

1. Introduction

The profile of Free / Libre Open Source Software (FLOSS) in recent years has highlighted what some describe as a new mode of production that applies both to software and other forms of technology such as Personal fabrication / Open Hardware (Seaman, 2002) or content, for example, Wikipedia and other cultural goods (Tapscott & Williams, 2008). In an attempt to generalise this new mode of production, Benkler describes it as a Commons Based Peer Production (CBPP) model. He has identified a number of constituent elements of any CBPP project (Benkler, 1998; Benkler, 2002; Benkler, 2006), which we present in section two.

Benkler presents CBPP as a model that is both very likely to emerge as a result of the existence of certain technological conditions and as a desirable model to be achieved when it does not "naturally" emerge. Cases such as Linux are examples of the former scenario. The careful organization of production in a mode that tries to resemble CBPP in the case of corporations such as Nokia or IBM is closer to the latter scenario.

The proliferation of cases where some form of CBPP is applied supports Benkler's argument regarding the potential prevalence of CBPP as a dominant production model for a ubiquitously networked environment. At the same time, as Benkler frequently notes, CBPP calls for a serious reconsideration of the regulatory environment supporting innovation and creativity. In a world where the problem to be addressed is not just one of incentives but also involves the abolition of frictions, the legal or regulatory system should aim to reflect these organizational realities. Benkler, following a stream of earlier theorists such as Moglen (1997) and Boyle (1997) argues that the current intellectual property rights system for regulating innovation and creativity falls short in terms of supporting CBPP forms of production (Benkler, 2006).

Benkler focuses his critique on the *content* of the current regulatory regime arguing that it is one that is seeking to provide incentives, rather than one aiming at reducing frictions. Regulation is also affected by *form*. Regulation is increasingly effected by a mixture of technological standards, applications and End User Licence Agreements (EULAs) (see, for example, Elkin-Koren, 1998; Littman, 1997). Behaviour on a platform like Facebook is limited both by the applications that govern end user behaviour and the EULA that defines the permissible uses of content on such a service (Lessig, 1996b; Lessig, 1998). The issue of the regulatory impact that CBPP has on the way we produce and experience regulation is of great importance as it sets the background against which most of human activity in technology intensive environments takes place (Mlcakova & Whitley, 2004).

This change of form has raised substantial questions regarding the extent to which these new forms of regulatory intervention reflect the same values and adhere to the same standards of participation, accountability and transparency that traditional legislation is supposed to follow. This problem of "substitution" of one type of regulatory form for another leads to questions of *process*: what is the process of development of these new regulatory forms that should be followed in order to achieve a result that most closely resembles the democratic standards seen in the more traditional forms of regulation (Lessig, 1998; Lessig, 1999a; Lessig, 1999b; Brownsword, 2005; Brownsword, 2006; Black, 2000; Black, 2001). Thus, we reach the key questions that this paper seeks to address: can we apply the organising principles of CBPP to the production of a legal instrument, such as a EULA? And what are the implications of such an attempt?

The application of CBPP as a model for the production of a standardized licence itself supporting CBPP seems to be desirable both for reasons of efficiency (lower production costs) and relevance (closer reflection of the needs of the users of the licence).   However, the feasibility of such an endeavour needs to be tested by an actual case.

The case examined in this paper is that of the Creative Commons suite of six licences.   Understanding the development of these licences offers an illuminating case as it constitutes both an extreme case for testing the boundaries of the CBPP model (being a non–functional object with strong regulatory properties) and a good illustration of why and how CBPP may be applied in a regulatory instrument alternative to the mainstream legislative instruments.

2. Commons based peer production

The model of Commons Based Peer Production was initially proposed by Benkler (2002) to provide an abstraction of the organizational structures underlying the production of FLOSS (Benkler, 2006). He highlights the role of the incentives necessary for creative production (Moglen, 1999), their changing nature as a result of the advent of the internet and the management of complexity that may arise (Raymond, 2001).   CBPP can therefore be seen as ensuing from the existence of excess capacity as a result of a great number of potential contributors and the natural tendency of this capacity to be transformed into something creative provided the right organisational structures are in place.   Thus, Benkler's work is particularly significant as it helps identify the conditions under which CBPP is likely to be preferred over a hierarchy or market.

The CBPP model has three basic constituent parts, relating to three aspects of the production: (a) the kind of artefact that is to be produced by the project and particularly its granularity; (b) the decentralized, non–hierarchical and self–selected mode of peer production based on excess capacity; and (c) the organisational integration of these contributions in some form of Commons.

These three aspects are presented in Table 1 and are illustrated with examples from FLOSS.

CBPP aspect		Aspect as found in FLOSS
Project features	Open ended	Ongoing software development
	Modular	Individual modules / interfaces
	Fine granularity	Subroutines for very specific purposes

	Heterogeneous granularity	e.g. User interface modules, real-time processing modules, security and encryption modules
Form of excess capacity		Programmers interested in contributing to FLOSS project, Users willing to report bugs
Integration		General Public License (GPL), Concurrent Version System (CVS)

Table 1 Aspects of CBPP as found in FLOSS

2.1. PROJECT FEATURES

Benkler refers to features of a peer production project rather than simply an artefact or product. This allows CBPP to apply in the provision of services (e.g. ratings of products or sellers on auction sites) or concentration capacity (e.g. processing cycles) and not just the development of products (such as software or texts). Projects have to be "modular" and the resulting granularity allows many contributors to operate in a more decentralized fashion. The modularity and granularity also determine the level of effort required for a minimal contribution. The lower this barrier, the more likely that individuals will join the project. A distinct set of diverse modules opens up the possibility of contributions from individuals with varying backgrounds and skills. Finally, the project should be open–ended or potentially always unfinished: this provides space for continuous development and operates as an attractor for contributors. For example, in a web browser such as Firefox or an encyclopaedia like Wikipedia there is always scope for improvement.

2.2. FORMS OF EXCESS CAPACITY

In order to succeed, CBPP requires 'excess capacity' in the community of potential contributors and whilst the modular structure of a project can facilitate this, structure alone is not a sufficient condition. Benkler identifies two conditions where this excess capacity can arise. The first is when there is unused capacity in terms of physical goods (e.g. car seats for car sharing, or processor cycles for computer processing). The second arises when the object of production is information and hence is non–rivalrous (e.g. software or content). Given the importance of excess capacity, it is necessary to have in place mechanisms that ensure such excess capacity is available both legally and technically. This is one of the reasons why Commons or Commons Based Property regimes, such as the ones sustained by copyleft licences, are so important in the case of information goods: they ensure that access to common resources remains a legal possibility.

2.2. INTEGRATION

The final feature of Benkler's model is concerned with organization and integration. This refers to the process of gathering the contributions and positioning them in a coherent whole. Ideally such integration should be low cost and unobtrusive. Mechanisms for integration may include co–ordination, channelling, filtering and error correction of individual contributions. Forms of integration include formal legal rules (e.g. GPL), social norms (e.g. netiquette), technical systems (e.g. CVS) or hierarchy (e.g. the editorial board of a scientific journal). An example of a centralized integration model is the peer review process for a scientific journal. FLOSS projects typically have more decentralized integration models.

CBPP appears to be a better production system than markets or hierarchies in cases where self–identification of the relevant talent is crucial for the achievement of particular goals (Benkler, 2002). The benefits of CBPP are enhanced by effective error–correction mechanisms. The power of CBPP as an organizational model is its capacity to aggregate dispersed contributions by peers that have excess capacity but are unable to produce any value on an individual basis.

3. How to include citations

The literature regarding regulatory conditions of CBPP in the legislative level has mainly focused on the way in which Copyright exceptions (or Fair Use / Fair Dealing) need to be expanded and harmonized internationally to deal with the intricacies of a digitally networked environment (e.g. Boyle, 1997; Boyle, 2006; Samuelson, 2001; Samuelson, 2003; Hugenholtz, 2000a; Hugenholtz, 2006; Litman, 2004; Vaidhyanathan, 2001). Though not necessarily explicitly related to CBPP this relevant literature has argued for a regulatory system which supports the conditions for CBPP, namely the minimization of legal friction in collaborative production and the establishment of a healthy public domain. The literature on FLOSS has also been focused on the degree to which FLOSS licences are compatible with the existing copyright, commercial and contract laws (e.g. Katz, 2006; Hunt, 2004-2005; Elkin-Koren, 1997; Elkin-Koren, 1998).

Authors like Elkin–Koren (2005; 2006) and Dusollier (2006) have questioned both the validity of such contracts and the ability to produce the desired effects, i.e. the removal of legal obstacles for a CBPP–like production mode. This literature presents two basic arguments: First, critical legal theorists agree that licensing seems the preferable means of regulating legal relations on the internet because of its proximity in form to the features of the technological environment which they seek to regulate. Licences are flexible, have a mass application and are micro enforced. In addition they are complemented by technological measures that make their enforcement even more immediate than what their naked legal form would allow. However, such theorists are also critical of the ways in which the internet is regulated by such "private instruments" as they raise issues of transparency, accountability and participation in the formation of such instruments. Individuals do not have access to the formation of such private instruments and their effectiveness makes such lack of access even more risky for the way in which society is regulated.

A similar concern is expressed by two other groups of theorists. One is that of the critical international copyright theorists and the second that of critical regulation theorists.

The former, (e.g. Drahos & Braithwaite, 2004), question the ways in which international IPR instruments are produced. The decisions are made at the international level with little or no real input from the average – especially not professional– content creator. They are then diffused to regional or national legislative instruments whose ability to make substantial changes to their regulatory content decreases just at the time when the level of participation, transparency and accountability increases (cf Hosein, 2004). The outcome is similar to the concerns raised above: alienation of the content of regulatory instruments from the subjects of regulatory force.

The second category critically examines the way in which technology regulates human behaviour. Theorists have raised the issue of the implications of technology when operating as a regulatory form. In the context of U.S. constitutionalism, Lessig has posed the question of how we should increase participation, transparency and accountability when regulation is produced (Lessig, 1996a). Brownsword has identified the process of technology–as–regulation–building as the key moment when such questions should be asked and answered (Brownsword, 2005; Brownsword, 2006). Finally, Black has extensively worked on the issues of the *proceduralization* of regulation, i.e. the investigation of the conditions of participation in the production of regulatory instruments so that they most acutely reflect the needs of the social context which they set to regulate (Black, 2000; Black, 2001).

Lessig has suggested the FLOSS model of production of technology as the closest to the democratic system of producing regulation. Such a claim introduces an interesting and practical suggestion even if the validity of the parallel is open to question.

4. Creative Commons and its licences

The Creative Commons is a project that provides a set of licences that support the share, reuse and remix of digital content primarily in online environments (Creative Commons, 2010b). The Creative Commons project was founded by Lawrence Lessig while he was a professor at Harvard Law School's Berkman Centre for Internet and Society. The core concept of the project was to allow novel forms of creativity, that were taking place on the internet, to be conducted in a legal way. Underlying this was the acknowledgement that they were often based on pre–existing works and that the obtaining of permission from the original rights–holders was becoming increasingly difficult (Creative Commons, 2010b). The idea was to reduce legal frictions to commons–based forms of creativity. Lessig and colleagues initially sought a solution via the U.S. Copyright Office, however when the office suggested that there was no available legal instrument to solve the problem, Lessig proposed introducing a novel regulatory instrument: the Creative Commons licences (Creative Commons, 2006). These would exist in the middle–ground between no–rights–reserved (i.e. public domain) and all–rights–reserved (as used by copyright based industries) licenses.

At a legal level, there are six variations of the licences: a combination of one fixed [Attribution (BY)] and three variable Licence Elements [ShareAlike (SA), NonCommercial (NC), NoDerivative Works (ND)]. The CC licences are thus of a modular nature: they comprise of two parts: First, a basic template, common in all licences allowing free verbatim copying of the content as long there is proper attribution and all copyright notices remain with the work. Second, the three variable Licence Elements (SA, NC and ND) constitute distinct modules of legal functionality that may be freely combined to produce the six CC licence variations. Once licensors decide to distribute a work under a CC licence, they follow a "licence wizard" on the Creative Commons website. This helps them to choose the appropriate combination of elements for their licence and also allows them to tag the work with appropriate meta–data describing the licence chosen. This meta–data allows search engines to locate works with particular licences, e.g. all photographs that can be commercially shared with attribution. Because CC licences are intended to be used by a broad range of individuals, most of whom will not be legal specialists, the licences are expressed in plain language and use simple icons so that they are both easy to use and easy to understand.

4.1. INTELLECTUAL ORIGINS OF THE CREATIVE COMMONS PROJECT

The Creative Commons was founded in late 2001 in an effort to support the public domain. Its forerunners included the Constitutional Commons, Counter Copyrights and Copyright Commons projects (Moody, 2006a; Moody, 2006b; Moody, 2006c). The Open Law project (Open Law, 2003) is another relevant forerunner as this project used a mailing list to produce legal instruments. One of the key original intellectual drivers behind the Creative Commons has been a concern to protect and support the Public Domain as an instrument for further enhancing creativity. Lessig has argued that free access to cultural works is necessary for reasons of free speech and, in the case of Eldred vs Ascroft (Jones, 2004), that the expansion of copyrights runs counter to the U.S. constitutional conceptualization of intellectual property rights and does not contribute to creativity of innovation (Lessig, 2004). In particular, Lessig (2002) and Benkler (2003) have argued that in order to support creativity and innovation it is necessary to reduce all forms of friction on the creative process, where legal friction in the form of traditional copyrights are probably most significant.

A particular problem that Lessig and others have noted is that whilst on the one hand, there are increasingly inexpensive technologies that allow greater and more active participation by individuals in the creative process, on the other hand there is also increasingly restrictive legislation that seeks to constrain such activities both normatively and technologically (e.g. the Digital Millennium Copyright Act (Samuelson, 2003) or the EU Copyright Directive (Hugenholtz, 2000b)).

Part of the problem arises that the legal instruments introduced range from high level, international intellectual property rights treaties to low level restrictions such as End User Licence Agreements. The high level instruments introduce a form of regulatory "alienation" in that they are implemented in environments where the average regulated subject does not have access to regulation building and political accountability is limited (Drahos & Braithwaite, 2002; Yu, 2007; Hugenholtz, 2000a) whilst the low level instruments are neither balanced nor subject to any "public interest" test. They are massively applied and micro–enforced, creating what have been described as "private regulatory regimes" (Elkin-Koren, 1998; Hutter, 2006).

As such, Creative Commons licences can be seen as occupying the space between international IPR treaties and individual EULAs allowing the creator to define the property rights about how their creations can be used. They are more fine grained and provide more freedoms for the user of the work than the national level provisions found in Copyright legislation (e.g., Fair Use in the U.S. and the more restrictively defined limitations or exceptions to author's rights in European Copyright systems or Fair Dealing in the UK). However, they are also dependent on the individual creator adopting them, making them expressions of individual autonomy. In that sense, the CC licences are private regulatory instruments that seek to achieve public purpose objectives. The Creative Commons project has a utilitarian rather than purist orientation: it seeks to use the available tools (i.e. licences) to support CBPP rather than opting for legal reform. CC is, hence, in its current form, a rationalization of Copyright excesses rather than a Public Domain project. This approach has often been criticized by more radical proponents of the Commons.

From this perspective, interventions in the level of Copyright licensing seem less costly than alternatives and offer options for speedy and plastic regulatory instruments (Littman, 1997). This kind of understanding is reflected both upon the organizational structure of Creative Commons and the actual implementation of the licence production process. Both are structured in such a way that they manage to address most of the regulatory problems that have given rise to the emergence of the CC project itself. In particular, the organizing of CC and the CC licence production process attempts (a) to reduce the costs of institutional change by choosing an easier to form regulatory instrument (a licence); and (b) to mitigate the "regulatory alienation" phenomenon and thus reduce high enforcement regulatory costs by introducing more participatory structures in the production of the CC licences.

4.2. CC ORGANIZATIONAL STRUCTURE

Structurally, CC consists of: (a) CC headquarters; (b) CC International[1]; and (c) the network of CC national projects run by national CC project leads (Creative Commons, 2010a). It is important to note at this stage that the national CC affiliates, project leads and their respective projects do not have any hierarchical relationship with the CC headquarters. Their relationships are primarily governed by Memoranda of Understanding as well as legal and / or public affiliate agreements (Creative Commons, 2005). A hosting institution is a legal entity existing in the jurisdiction where a new CC licence is to be transferred or "ported". It undertakes to do all the necessary legal work for the licences to be legally applicable in its jurisdiction. The hosting institution is limited in the ways it may use the CC logo and other CC trademarks.

---

[1]   This description reflects the CC organisational structure in late 2008 when this study was conducted. It needs to be stressed out that CC International is part of the CC Headquarters, and not an independent organisation, though it is located in Berlin and not in San Fransisco as CCHQ.

Besides the formal organizational structure of CC, a series of formal and informal, physical and virtual fora have emerged. Here licences and CC policies are discussed and developed. CC initiated fora are the iSummit annual meeting and the various CC related mailing lists.

Various mailing lists have been set up and are used as means of discussion between the members of the wider CC community. The analysis in this paper is based on three lists: (a) the *cc–licenses* mailing list that deals with the development of the CC licences; (b) the *cc–community* mailing list that deals with various issues related to the CC licences but not necessarily their development; and (c) the *cc–i* list that is used by national CC affiliates. The first two lists are public whereas the latter is private with access restricted to CC national affiliates. The *cc–community* list is unmoderated. Moderation was introduced on the *cc–licenses* list in February 2007 in response to concerns about "noise" unrelated to the development of the licences.

As mentioned above, the use of mailing lists for the development of legal instruments was not new for the founders of the CC project. Copyright's Commons, the direct ancestor of Creative Commons, was part of the larger Open Law project hosted at Berkman Centre for the Internet and Society, a project using a FLOSS–like mailing–list based process in order to develop legal instruments (Open Law, 2003).

In addition to the mailing lists, CC headquarters, regional (e.g. Europe and Asia) meetings and global events (the iSummit), complemented by informal conversations amongst participants, all play an important role in the development of the licences.

Overall the CC licences can be seen to be developed in two broadly described modes: one is in the normal course of the life of a licence where different issues related to its implementation and interpretation are discussed; and a second one, is during an expressed period of public or semi–public consultation preceding the introduction of a new licence version (e.g. CC v.3) or new licence (as in the case of CC Zero). The accumulation of comments and potential issues in the former period normally informs the amendment of the licences and leads to a new version or it raises issues that lead to the need for a new licence. Both implicitly and explicitly CC has been against the proliferation of licences (Linksvayer, 2008) and actively tries not to introduce new licences unless there is an absolute need to do so. Such an inescapable need emerges when there are expressed and verified legal and practical problems with existing licences that may be resolved through amendment (need for a new version) or require a totally new legal instrument [withdrawal of licences (e.g. Developing Nations Licence) or new licence (e.g. CC Zero[2])]. The good

---

[2]   CC Zero operates in two levels: in the first level it consitute a declaration of waiving all the economic and moral rights on copyright subject matter. In those jurisdictions

operation of the national versions of CC licences is hence a condition for the smooth operation of the international CC Ecology.

For that reason the collection of input both from jurists from all the CC hosting institutions' jurisdictions and from users of the CC licence is invaluable for CC. At the same time CC has been adamant that the decision making and strategic orientation of the licensing project needs to remain with the headquarters. This dual nature of CC is reflected on the organization of the licence development process.

The decision for the development of a new licence or the initiation of a new revision cycle rests ultimately with the CC headquarters in consultation with the international network, especially for version 2.5 and 3.0. The decision is taken by the CC Board of Directors and then actioned by the CC general legal counsel, who is responsible for the coordination of all the legal work in relation to the discussion of the licences. During the days of the first legal counsel, Glen Otis Brown, and as we see in the first period of the licence development such consultation was pretty loosely defined with only some pointers to be discussed on the cc licenses mailing list, at the time the only list in existence for the cc communications.

5. Viewing CC licences in terms of CBPP

5.1. PROJECT FEATURES

According to Benkler's model of CBPP (Benkler, 2002), the produced artefact should be: (a) open ended; (b) modular; (c) of fine granularity; and (d) of heterogeneous granularity. In many ways, the CC licenses satisfy these requirements.

The CC licences constitute *open ended texts*. They are potentially always open to amendment and improvement because of their dynamic and normative nature. Indeed, the decision to go down the licence route was in part driven by a need to offer low–cost, plastic regulatory instruments. There have already been four versions of the CC licences (1.0, 2.0, 2.5 and 3.0) and another one (3.01) is currently under discussion.

The open–ended nature of the licenses is also punctuated by the need to port the various licences to different jurisdictions and so, in a manner similar to stable and unstable FLOSS releases, there is a period of dissemination for every version of the licence. The development of the licences therefore moves in cycles: after the unported version of the licence has been upgraded to a new version, its development is halted until a substantial number of national jurisdictions move to the new version. This

---

, where such statement has no effect, these provisions are to be interpreted as a licences having a similar effect.

is the stage where the CC licence development project is right now following the release of version 3.0 of the licences in February 2007. Each new version of the licence constitutes the expressed point of compromise between the various stakeholders in the international community.

The openness of the licences is further enhanced by the continuous discussion of the implementation of the CC licences on the various mailing lists, which occurs often in parallel with the discussion on the amendment of the licences or the introduction of new ones. Such discussions not only pose questions regarding the operation of the licences but are the source of most of the suggestions for amendments that will then be addressed during the revision process.

The licences are also, to some extent, *modular* texts, as they consist of a basic template and Licence Elements but also because of their architecture consisting of a combination of one and three elements (the BY element remains stable whereas the NC, ND, and SA elements may be combined to produce the six variations of the licences). A second layer of modularity emerges from the discussions on the mailing lists, where a variety of questions are *de facto* clustered around the structure of the licence. Such clustering is evident by the recurrence of discussions around the same issues following the Licence Elements or the structure of the licence. For instance, Attribution has been part of the cluster of emails about "moral rights" but has also generated a series of other email smaller clusters on the question of "non–endorsement", the removal of attribution and "integrity right" issues. In terms of the Non–Commercial Licence Element, similar clusters can be found in the link between "collecting societies" and Creative Commons and the ShareAlike element has generated email clusters about, for example, compatibility with other Open Content licences and in particular compatibility with the Free Documentation Licenses, the General Public Licences and other specific FLOSS licences. Some of these clusters have also led to the creation of *ad hoc* working groups such as the "CC and Collecting Societies" or "CC and governance" groups that have organised relevant face–to–face meetings.

There is some *granularity* in the licence modules, though it is debatable how fine such granularity really is. For example, the granularity of the Licence Elements and the basic template is not very fine. This is one area where CC licence development diverts from the CBPP ideal. Each of the issues that such items raise requires considerable expertise to be tackled. Moreover, finer granularity of these modules, for example, the further breaking down of the SA topic into issues of GPL compatibility, is typically created informally by the community in the course of the discussions over the mailing lists. As a result the cost of contributing is markedly higher than in mainstream CBPP projects. For example, the modular structure of most FLOSS projects means that key user interface or language porting elements are easily identified and separated out.

The CC case also illustrates the interlinking between heterogeneity and modularity: the lack of clear definition of the modules and the limited range of the clearly defined ones limits their *heterogeneity*. It also indicates the different ways in which modularity and granularity are managed in different facets of the project: whereas modularity and granularity is actively sought where there is the objective of specifically building a licence or upgrading to a newer version, there is no similar effort for the everyday discussions regarding the application of the CC licences.

5.2. FORMS OF EXCESS CAPACITY

The lack of excess capacity in the level of the peers has led to the gradual withdrawal of legal project leads from public mailing lists. CC national affiliates are able to provide comments or answers on the mailing lists but they rarely do. There are a number of reasons why this may happen including: (a) lack of time and incentives to make such time available for the production of the CC licences without direct recognition; (b) increased "noise" on the list—a direct result of non–expert participation; (c) lack of understanding of how the list works or what the current theme in the discussion on the list is; and (d) fears of their opinion affecting their professional career (e.g. having clients that may object the CC project). As a result, much of the final filtering and editing of the licences is done internally in the way a classic legal team would have worked.

It is important to note that while the CC leads are reluctant to participate to the public mailing lists, they are more likely to contribute to the cc–i list where they feel that their comments will not be accessible by the general public. It seems, hence, that while the participation in the production of shared meaning is dominated by non–legal experts, the production of legal documents remains a task for the experts. Even in that case, the role of the network of affiliates remains reactive rather than proactive as they primarily use the cc–i list to respond to comments raised by the CC Headquarters. The introduction of web–questionnaires for the discussion of the CC–Zero licence has further moved the whole development process toward the model of public consultation rather than discussion in the sense that the comments are not publicly discussed before all are collected. This model seems to address the problem of noise but to bring the whole production process further away from a CBPP–like model.

5.3. INTEGRATION MECHANISMS

Managing and integrating the Commons is a key aspect of any CBPP process. In the case of the CC project the collection of contributions occurs at three levels. The mailing lists are used in order to collect contributions from a general public (*cc–licenses* and *cc–community*) or the network of affiliates (*cc–i*). These include comments on specific issues related to the operation of the licences, suggested changes in the text of the licences or responses to specific questions a consultation may have raised. The active moderation of the *cc–licenses* list by Mike Linksvayer has allowed a channelling of some of these messages in two types of mailing lists: a high–volume generic mailing list (*cc–community*) and a low–volume specialized private mailing list (*cc–i*). However, in practice, this has had little effect on the overall volume of comments as many of participants have simply migrated from the *cc–licenses* list to the *cc–community* list directly. In addition, the legal experts on the *cc–licenses* have moved off the list, preferring to use traditional means of communication (e.g. phone, direct emailing or physical meetings) or the private *cc–i* list.

A second level of collecting contributions appears in the formal and informal communication between national CC project leads and CC International at the iSummit and regional meetings. These contributions are particularly important for the implementation of the licences in national jurisdictions although they also give rise to comments or concerns in relation to the unported licences. There is no set procedure for how these comments are passed on to the licence developers, although they do generally feed into that process.

In the third level contributions for the development of the licences takes place within the organizational structure of the CC project itself. The legal counsel and the CC international director, together with the board of directors, decide which changes are to be incorporated in the text of the licences or which direction the licences are to follow. In making their decisions they increasingly take into consideration the national project leads whilst limiting consideration of the discussions on the mailing lists.

The storing of the contributions happens in a rather centralized fashion. All formal documentation, existing approved versions of the national and unported CC licences, draft national CC licences, CC policies and CC wikis are stored on the CC central servers. However, most national projects also have their own websites where they store information and news in local languages. There is no standard for the kind of data stored in different countries, though there is a standard layout for the sites to facilitate easy browsing. The discussions over the mailing lists are archived with access linked to contribution rights but there is no classification or other structuring of the content.

Finally, the CC headquarters with the assistance of the CC International operate as the final judge in the porting process. The international license porting project is managed by the Creative Commons International judgement and needs to be approved by the CCi director. Various comments are incorporated in the text of the licences after they have been received through (a) the general audience through the mailing lists; (b) the national CC legal project leads through private channels of communication or the CC legal days; and (c) the members of the CC board, the legal counsel and the CC International director.

CBPP aspect		Aspects as found in CC licences
Project features	Open ended	New versions of licenses in development
	Modular	Licence Elements
	Fine granularity	Further breaking down of Licence Elements by the discussants on the mailing lists
	Heterogeneous granularity	Variety of types of modules (e.g. ND vs. SA)
Form of excess capacity		Free access to the licence code (artefact capacity) Domain and legal knowledge (peer capacity)
Integration		Mailing lists / Legal Counsel / CC – International coordination

Table 2 Aspects of CBPP as found in the CC licence development process

6. Analysis: Open Sourcing Regulation?

While the licences are modular, their designed modularity does not appear fine enough to immediately satisfy Benkler's conditions for CBPP, see Table 2. Moreover, there does not appear to be enough obvious heterogeneity to attract sufficient contributions from a general audience. Interestingly, the study of the mailing lists reveals that once the licences are discussed finer modularization emerges as a result of a self–selection process by the involved peers. For example, within the first 1½ years of the CC project 23 categories of discussion topics can be identified from the cc–licenses mailing list.

However, the finer granularity that is produced is limited by the (current) lack of mechanisms for structured storing and integrating the comments of peers from the mailing list. Hence, the benefits from the peer–produced fine granularity are lost in the absence of their crystallization as categories to further work on. This is an obvious area where software CBPP has a distinct advantage, for example, with the use of version control systems and documentation tools.

The problem of explicitly created and maintained finer modules is a very practical one. It reflects upon the costs of repeatedly having to deal with the same issues over the mailing lists and severely hinders the creation of a Commons at the level of the licences: as time passes only the consistent users of the mailing lists are able to follow the discussion on the licences or are fully aware of the range of applications of the CC licences. Such a situation can lead (a) to a fragmentation of the common regulatory space that the CC licences seek to produce; (b) to the *de facto* establishment of at least two classes of users (power and peripheral users); (c) to the under–utilization of the regulatory commons; and (d) consequently to the reduction of the benefits that a CBPP model for the production of licences could provide.

6.1. REGULATORY COMMONS AND SOCIAL MEANING

While the expressed objective of the CC project as an effort to produce instruments contributing to the rationalization of the Copyright system is materialized in the development of the licences, a closer look into the types of peers producing and commons produced during this process reveals that two different kinds of commons are developed.

We have seen that a major part of the development of the licences is implemented in a layered fashion where the general audience is free to express questions or make suggestions about the future of the licence but is unable to have any direct effect on the text of the licences. This raises the question of the nature of the general audience's contribution.

The fact that the CC mailing lists are primarily an instrument for the creation of regulatory meaning and only indirectly an instrument for the production of the licences does not diminish their importance. On the contrary, it makes us sensitive to the importance of the production of a more subtle and often more effective and pervasive regulatory instrument, that of social norms. The production of social meaning can be seen as one of the key objectives of the CC machinery and is ubiquitous in all aspects of the organization: the logos used, the public events that operate as rituals, the videos on the website and the great emphasis in the adherence to trademark policies through the MOUs are all expressive of CC's effort to control the production of copyright related social meaning.

It thus makes sense to talk of two analytically distinct types of commons produced by CC. First, the production of social meaning that is primarily effected through a mildly controlled CBPP system based on the CC mailing lists; and second, the production of the CC licences that is primarily produced by hierarchical organization that is also open to inputs integrated through a basic CBPP system (the cc mailing lists).

6.2. SOCIAL MEANING AND REGULATION PRODUCTION

At this point it is important to return to the original intellectual foundations and objectives of the CC project in order to appreciate the way in which CBPP might be seen in this context. CC is founded on the assumption that the current Copyright system is inconsistent with the dominant creative practices on the internet that require reuse of the existing material at minimum cost. In addition, the production of legislative instruments does not involve all classes of creators but only a small subset of them. The CC founders, Lawrence Lessig and James Boyle, have conceptualized the problems with the existing Copyright regime as ones of fundamentally institutional nature: the change of existing institutions regulating creativity is extremely costly to be effected in one step and at the legislative level. The CC project is thus poised to provide the platform for such a change by attempting to bring the regulatory instruments closer to creative practices and the creators closer to the regulatory instruments.

This double move results in the hybrid CBPP – hierarchy model we experience in the CC case. It is reflected on the use of a CBPP–like model for the production of regulatory meaning and the use of a hierarchy–like model for the production of the legal instruments, i.e. the CC licences.

The core concept of any CBPP model is the existence of excess capacity not merely in the form of the produced artefact, whether we refer to physical or information goods (what we have called artefact excess capacity), but also in the form of excess creative capacity or time that an individual contributor possesses (what we have called peer excess capacity). In an ideal CBPP scenario in the same way that the outcome of one contributor instantly becomes the raw material for another in the form of some commons–based regime, the roles of contributor and user should coincide in the same person. Whereas, the former condition has been explicitly expressed in the CBPP and FLOSS literature, the latter has attracted less attention or been conceptualized as a motivation / organizational problem. What the CC case illustrates is that both are types of excess capacity and contribute to the sustainability of the CBPP structure. If the contributor is not a user of the produced artefact, then she is not able to maximize the benefits from the participation to the CBPP process and sometimes lacks significant understanding of the way in which the artefact operates feeding thus back negatively to the production process.

In other words, the more distant the contributor is from the use of the artefact the less is her excess capacity. Accordingly, if the user of the artefact cannot be a producer as well, then she does not make any real use of the facility of being able to influence the production of the common resource and thus extract value from its customization to her needs.

6.3. EXCESS CAPACITY AND HYBRID CBPP-HIERARCHY STRUCTURE IN THE CC PROJECT

The ideal CBPP model assumes that the roles of user and developer coincide and thus excess artefact and peer capacity as well as maximum utilization of the commons are possible. The FLOSS literature and the CC case indicate that such an ideal scenario rarely occurs in practice. In this paper we argue that CC is seen as attempting to reduce the under–utilization of the commons and its dual hierarchy– CBPP organizational structure is the result of such an effort.

The CC case demonstrates that even from the population of active participants (i.e. participants that have made at least a single posting on the CC mailing lists) only a fragment is responsible for the majority of the comments. From this minority only a segment is able to substantially influence the process of licence development either by setting the agenda or by attracting multiple comments. However, even this segment of the participants on the list rarely contributes directly to the formation of the licences. It is more likely that these participants elucidate and form the meaning of the licences and thus only indirectly influence the wording of the licence. As we have seen above the formation of the licences occurs mainly in other non–CBPP for a, such as physical meetings, the closed cc–i mailing list, consultation documents or the CC HQ legal department.

The reasons behind this two tier structure are to be found in the skill–set that the peers have. The skill–set is what defines the area in which they are most susceptible in developing excess capacity. Lay users who do not hold any formal legal training are unlikely to resolve specific technical problems of licence drafting. On the contrary, they are domain experts and they have knowledge of the application of the CC licences or the problems they pose that are beyond the knowledge horizon of the legal experts. In addition they have an incentive for correctly appreciating the regulatory meaning of the licences or participating in their formation. In that sense, they have an excess capacity in the production of its meaning. They express such capacity by raising questions about the operation of the licences or answering questions that relate to the technicalities of their domain. Thus, the artefact that is produced as a result of their engagement in a CBPP–like production is directly linked to the domain of their excess capacity, which in the CC case is that of regulatory meaning. It is not a coincidence that a significant percentage of the discourses developed on the mailing lists relate to the operation not merely of the CC licences but also of Copyright law itself. When the "creative commoners", as the cc mailing list participants are often referred to by CC, reach a stage of understanding of the Copyright system and the operation of the CC licences that is more technical, then they are able to move to the second type of artefact development, that is the development of the licences themselves.

At the same time, the legal teams producing the licences in the national level and comprising of prominent jurists in the respective jurisdictions are often less than adept to appreciate the ways in which the licences may be practically applicable. Being practitioners with a clientele who are unlikely to have used or being interested in the near future in open content licences, they may only contribute to the drafting of the licences. Their contribution is in a sense symmetrical to that of non–qualified, non–experienced users: they cannot actively participate in the formation of the licences or actively direct its future development; instead, they are confined in the technical task of "porting" the licences to the local legal system. In a way similar to the case of non–legal cc mailing list participants, there are legal experts that have a good understanding of the domain and are able to contribute to the construction of meaning over the mailing lists as much as being involved in the technical task of licence drafting. These legal experts together with the power users are the ones who are most likely to drive the innovation process of CC licence development. In fact, some of these experts also participate in the cc mailing lists (public or private) and have an impact in the way the discussions flow. However, their contribution to the development of the licences or CC as an organization is more likely to be effected in off–line or private on–line discussions with the CC headquarters.

6.4. WAYS TO SOLVE THE PROBLEMS OF UNDER-UTILIZATION OF THE COMMONS

What the trajectory of the CC licences in their five years of existence has proven is that there are some *de facto* ways in which any CBPP system self–corrects this under–utilization of the commons. The one relates to the users and the other to the object produced and the way integration organically happens. The major obstacle for a better participation to both layers of the commons (meaning and licences) is the lack of peer excess capacity, either of the legal system or the problem domain.

In that sense, it is necessary to increase the skills of the peers or decrease the knowledge requirements for participating to the production process. The former happens through participation on the list and the use of the licences. Comments by more experienced members or CC staff allow the consistent participants to increase their technical skills. The latter happens through the process of de facto granularization of the thematic areas. As the discussion evolves, thematic areas are identified and are pursued further operating at the same instance as integration and filtering mechanisms.

However, as already indicated, such an organic or non–interventionist approach is very likely to stratify participation and after an initial stage where a growing number of participants on the lists or off–line discussions improve their skills, we reach a plateau: as time passes skills improve but the number of expert users grows very slowly. Accordingly, the off–line discussions exhibit a similar pattern, where the most informed and knowledgeable participants clustered and new-comers face the challenge of having to go through a learning curve in order to be able to meaningfully participate in the discussions. The cc–i mailing list which sits somewhere in between the public mailing lists and the private physical meetings illustrates a more evenly distributed pattern of participation than the public mailing lists, but is still dominated by national affiliates with greater experience or better funded projects. The more experienced affiliates have greater peer excess capacity because of their accumulated knowledge, whereas participants to more well funded projects have the ability to increase their knowledge as they are funded to research CC related issues. These are differentiated from national affiliates with no funding or that have more recently joined the project and which do not have much excess peer capacity to offer.

The CC case illustrates some potential ways in which such education of the participants could take place. This is essentially done by enhancing the trends already present in the CC project, i.e. *education of the peers* and *reduction of the skill threshold*. It seems thus that in order to qualitatively improve the contributions of the participants it is necessary to put in place a series of mechanisms that aim at increasing the excess capacity of the contributors. These mechanisms follow a lifting–lowering model: They may be in the form of educational programs (focus on increasing the knowledge of the individual – lifting of expertise level) or in the form of training material (focus on the finer granularization and modularization of the primary material that is to be used by the individual – lowering of the knowledge threshold). Mailing lists primarily aim at producing collective meaning and, in that respect do not require much additional mechanisms. Even in the case where mailing lists operate in their simplest form the collective meaning production function is adequately served. However, when we are to move either toward a cumulative meaning production direction or to produce more technical products, such as the CC licences, training and granularization is necessary in order to produce the required excess capacity that could support a CBPP model.

Such functions –at least in the early stages of the project– require organizational forms that are closer to the hierarchical or small network model than CBPP. Education or training is achieved primarily through physical meetings such as CC seminars or attaching CC projects to formal university level courses; the granularization of the material is made –if at all– by the CC staff or national CC project leads; exchange of experiences and expertise happens in the regional (e.g. CC Europe and CC Asia Working Groups) and international (iSummit) meetings. The elements of the CC project that do not follow a CBPP but rather a hierarchical model are thus the ones that serve such functions. However, in the course of time, the effort seems to be to moving more and more modules of the project to the CBPP mode of production primarily through increasing the number of legal experts and introducing hybrid virtual – physical communities. This is seen in the examples of the CC Europe mailing list and physical meeting and the combined operation of the cc–i mailing list and iSummit Legal Day events.

7. Conclusions

As the CBPP production model matures in time we experience two parallel phenomena: first, the "low hanging fruits" in terms of issues to be easily identified and tackled are gradually exhausted; and second, as a result of this exhaustion, either there will be repetition of the same discussions on the list or there will be an increasing need for more sophisticated dialogue between the members of the relevant community. Returning to our original point regarding the life–cycle of a CBPP project, such a project needs to continuously evolve; else it will collapse and die.

The emergence of CBPP models is a direct result of excess capacity both in the level of technology (artefact excess capacity) and human skills (peer excess capacity). Social meaning seems to be the artefact that humans are quick to produce and inherently have an excess capacity for. This is particularly true in relation to the application or implementation of the CC licences in specific domains. In that sense the CBPP model is almost immediately used for the production of collective meaning on the use of the licences or the broader issues of Copyright law. On the contrary, more technical applications require a more structured approach and a training cycle that is achieved either through formal education (e.g. legal training, CC national project leads legal days, specialized mailing lists) or through a lengthy process of interaction which requires consistency and persistence (e.g. active participation on the mailing lists for long periods of time).

Precisely because CBPP is a goal rather than a given, it seems that in its initial stages we will have a form of separation between those participating in the production of meaning and those participating in the production of the actual technical artefacts. In order to bring these two groups together organizations like CC put mechanisms in place that lead to the establishment of hybrid hierarchy–CBPP structures. Such hybrid structures aim at increasing excess capacity both in the level of meaning and technical production. In order to increase the technical understanding of the project and to allow its progress, the CC should try to establish mechanisms that will either increase technical skills or lower the knowledge thresholds for participating in this process. We have seen that raw mailing lists do not really support such strategies. Wikis are also not really used by the relevant communities unless there are individuals who are entrusted with the task of updating them. This has been partially done by the CC headquarters and the CC Europe working group. In addition the existence of a variety of documents or reports encapsulating the current status of the discussions and the knowledge related to the CC licences discussions could also contribute to such a direction. Finally the Regional (CC Europe and Asia) meetings and the annual iSummit events as well as the linking of CC national projects with educational institutions or courses could also facilitate the creation of highly motivated and domain savvy CC experts.

While most of the existing literature has emphasized the importance of CBPP as a means for learning and education, what we have argued in this paper is that learning and education is also a condition for the setting up of any CBPP model. If there is not enough knowledge the excess capacity in the level of the individual is missing and hence the CBPP model cannot emerge or sustain itself. Once a CBPP organizational model is in place learning may also be facilitated and a virtuous learning cycle is initiated. Our analysis has also indicated that even in closed CBPP models as the one seen in the cc–i mailing list, the participants who are most likely to contribute actively are the ones that have somehow managed to pass a certain knowledge threshold and are able to sustain their knowledge capacity through time. This realization necessarily brings forward the issue of cost of this knowledge capacity building. The better funded CC projects are the ones that are most likely to have the peer excess capacity to participate. There seems thus to be an important capacity cost in any CBPP model that needs to be further explored.

Finally, the nature of the artefact produced plays a great role in deciding whether or not and how to adopt a CBPP model. The CC project is devoted in the production of regulatory artefacts, i.e. the CC licences. As we have seen in the theory section of this paper regulation operates through the application of meaning or association constructions. The same is true for most of technology–as–regulation artefacts. By allowing participation in the level of meaning construction any CBPP project essentially reverses most of the assumptions of existing technology or regulatory artefacts: instead of seeking to impose a certain normative program, CBPP structures seek to absorb the practices of the human being and the technological environment that surrounds it. If CC is to resolve any of the problems raised by the regulatory alienation that Copyright legislation suffers from, it needs to move closer to a CBPP model for licences–as–regulation production. We urgently need to think of ways to devise regulatory models that do not only reflect CBPP in terms of content, such as public domain friendly regulation, but also reflect CBPP in form and process, such as the open sourcing of licence production. By allowing a collective construction of meaning and providing the tools for the construction of the technological associations as well, CBPP projects constitute the primary means for participation in a society where the construction–cultivation of technology coincides with the construction–cultivation of regulation. This is CBPP's primary contribution and ultimate challenge.

References

Benkler Y (1998) Communications, Infrastructure Regulation and the Distribution of Control over Content. *Telecommunications Policy* Vol. 22 No. 3, pp. 183-196.

Benkler Y (2002) Coase's Penguin,or Linux and the Nature of the Firm. *Yale Law Journal* Vol. 112 No., pp. 369.

Benkler Y (2003) Freedom in the Commons: Toward a Political Economy of Information. *Duke Law Journal* Vol. 52 No. April, pp. 1245-1276.

Benkler Y (2006) *The Wealth of Networks: How Social Production Transforms Markets and Freedom.* Yale University Press, New Haven and London.

Black J (2000) Proceduralising Regulation: Part I. *Oxford Journal of Legal Studies* Vol. 20 No. 4, pp. 597-614.

Black J (2001) Proceduralising Regulation: Part II. *Oxford Journal of Legal Studies* Vol. 21 No. 1, pp. 33-58.

Boyle J (1997) A Politics of Intellectual Property: Environmentalism for the Net. *Duke Law Journal* Vol. 47 No., pp. 87.

Boyle J (2006) Cultural Environmentalism? *Financial Times* (20 February) Archived at http://www.ft.com/cms/s/2/cc8e24ce-a242-11da-9096-0000779e2340.html

Brownsword R (2005) Code, control, and choice: why East is East and West is West. *Legal Studies* Vol. 25 No., pp. 1-21.

Brownsword R (2006) Neither East Nor West, Is Mid-West Best? *Script-ed* Vol. 3 No. 1, pp. 15-33.

Creative Commons (2005) Amended Memorandum of Association of Creative Commons International Limited. Company Limited by Guarantee

Creative Commons (2006) Who started Creative Commons Retrieved from http://creativecommons.org/faq#About_Creative_Commons

Creative Commons (2010a) About Retrieved from http://creativecommons.org/about/

Creative Commons (2010b) Creative Commons Home Page Retrieved from http://creativecommons.org/

Drahos P and Braithwaite J (2002) *Information feudalism : who owns the knowledge economy?* Earthscan, London.

Drahos P and Braithwaite J (2004) *Who owns the knowledge economy? : political organising behind TRIPS.* Corner House, Sturminster Newton.

Dusollier S (2006) The Master's Tools v. the Master's House: Creative Commons v. Copyright. *Columbia Journal of Law & the Arts* Vol. 29 No. Spring, pp. 271-293.

Elkin-Koren N (1997) Copyright Policy and the Limits of Freedom of Contract. *Berkeley Technology Law Journal* Vol. 12 No. 1, pp. 93.

Elkin-Koren N (1998) Copyrights in Cyberspace -- Rights Without Laws? *Chicago Law Review* Vol. 73 No., pp. 1115.

Elkin-Koren N (2005) What Contracts Cannot Do: The Limits of Private Ordering In Facilitating a Creative Commons. *Fordham Law Review* Vol. 74 No. November, pp. 375-422.

Elkin-Koren N (2006) *Exploring Creative Commons: A Skeptical View of a Worthy Pursuit.* In "The Future of the Public Domain" (Hugenholtz B and Guibault L, Eds), Kluwer Law International.

Hosein IR (2004) The Sources of Laws: Policy Dynamics in a Digital and Terrorized World. *The information society* Vol. 20 No. 3, pp. 187-199.

Hugenholtz B (2000a) The Great Copyright Robbery. Rights allocation in a digital environment. In *A Free Information Ecology in a Digital Environment Conference*, New York University School of Law.

Hugenholtz B (2000b) Why the Copyright Directive is Unimportant, and Possiby Invalid. *European Intellectual Property Review* Vol. 22 No. 11, pp. 499-505.

Hugenholtz B (2006) *The Future of the Public Domain: An Introduction.* In "The Future of the Public Domain" (Guibault L and Hugenholtz B, Eds), Kluwer Law International, Amsterdam. pp 1-6

Hunt WS (2004-2005) The Supreme Court's Mixed Messages on the Public Domain: Cases Interpreting Section 43 of the Lanham Act. *Kentucky Law Journal* Vol. 93 No., pp. 787-811.

Hutter BM (2006) The Role of Non-State Actors in Regulation. *The Centre for Analysis of Risk and Regulation*, The London School of Economics, London, pp 1-24.

Jones M (2004) Eldred v. Ashcroft: The Constitutionality of the Copyright Term Extension Act. *Berkeley Technology Law Journal* Vol. 19 No., pp. 85-106.

Katz Z (2006) Pitfalls of Open Licensing: an Analysis of Creative Commons Licensing. *IDEA: The Intellectual Property Law Review* Vol. 46 No., pp. 391-413.

Lessig L (1996a) Post Constitutionalism. *Michigan Law Review* Vol. 94 No. May, pp. 1422-1470.

Lessig L (1996b) The Zones of Cyberspace. *Stanford Law Review* Vol. 48 No. May, pp. 1403.

Lessig L (1998) The New Chicago School. *Journal of Legal Studies* Vol. 27 No. June, pp. 661-691.

Lessig L (1999a) *Code and Other Laws of Cyberspace.* Basic Books, New York.

Lessig L (1999b) The Law Of The Horse: What Cyberlaw Might Teach. *Harvard Law Review* Vol. 113 No. December, pp. 501.

Lessig L (2002) The Architecture Of Innovation. *Duke Law Journal* Vol. 51 No. April, pp. 1783-1801.

Lessig L (2004) How I Lost The Big One. *APR Legal Affairs* Vol.   No. March/April, pp. 57-63.

Linksvayer M (2008) Interview with Mike Linksvayer in Sapporo, Japan. Sapporo, Japan.

Litman J (2004) Sharing and Stealing. *Hastings Communications and Enterprise Law Journal* Vol. 27 No., pp. 1.

Littman J (1997) Copyright NonCompliance (or Why We Can't "Just Say Yes" to Licensing). *New York University Journal of International Law and Policy* Vol. 29 No. Fall-Winter, pp.

Mlcakova A and Whitley EA (2004) Configuring peer–to–peer software: An empirical study of how users react to the regulatory features of software. *European Journal of Information Systems* Vol. 13 No. 2, pp. 95-102.

Moglen E (1997) The Invisible Barbecue. *Columbia Law Review* Vol. 97 No., pp. 945.

Moglen E (1999) Anarchism Triumphant: Free Software and the Death of Copyright   4(8)   Archived   at http://firstmonday.org/htbin/cgiwrap/bin/ojs/index.php/fm/article/viewArticle/6 84/594

Moody G (2006a) Gutenberg 2.0: the birth of open content Retrieved from http://lwn.net/Articles/177602/

Moody G (2006b) Learning the lesson: open content licensing Retrieved from http://lwn.net/Articles/181374/

Moody G (2006c) Open Content III: the code Retrieved from http://lwn.net/Articles/183907/

Open Law (2003) OpenLaw Home Retrieved from http://cyber.law.harvard.edu/openlaw/

Raymond ES (2001) *The cathedral and the bazaar : musings on linux and open source by an accidental revolutionary.* O'Reilly, Cambridge, Mass.

Samuelson P (2001) Toward a New Politics of Intellectual Property. *Communications of the ACM* Vol. 44 No. 3, pp. 98-99.

Samuelson P (2003) Digital Rights Management {and, or, vs.} the Law. *Communications of the ACM* Vol. 46 No. 4, pp. 41-45.

Seaman G (2002) The Two Economies Or: Why the washing machine question is the wrong question. *Second OEKNUX Conference*, Technische Universitaet Berlin, Technische Universitaet Berlin.

Tapscott D and Williams AD (2008) *Wikinomics : how mass collaboration changes everything.* Atlantic, London.

Vaidhyanathan S (2001) *Copyrights and copywrongs : the rise of intellectual property and how it threatens creativity.* New York University Press, New York.

Yu PK (2007) *Intellectual property and information wealth : issues and practices in the digital age.* Praeger, Westport, Co.

Is a Tech Commons possible? Enabling a Commons of Technological Register Rights Content Suitable for Open Innovation

*John H. Weitzmann
Saarland University

Abstract. In the past two decades several well-founded and influential legal tools have been developed to correct detrimental monopolization and perceived over-protection of copyrightable material. For immaterial objects outside the scope of copyright, nothing even remotely close has been devised yet. This paper tries to look into some of the reasons for this imbalance. Accordingly, the central subject matter of this article is access to immaterial goods – not necessarily present in digital form – which aren't subject to instant protection through copyright regimes, but rather protectable through institutionalized registering and/or patent systems only. The term design is used here in the sense of a "model for technological action", a technological construction or solution,[1] in order to discuss the special properties of this kind of content and whether a pool of easily accessible and re-usable material could be set up without legislative action, i. e. through a model along the lines of private order. Most technological designs are protectable only if – and as long as – they are new in a factual or a certain formal way, compared to the state of the art in the relevant technological field. Thus, the most obvious idea to ensure unlimited access to those designs would be to generate sufficient publicity. That could destroy the novelty status of otherwise protectable solutions and make them state of the art, which would in effect prevent monopolization. In some contexts a single proven public display of a new invention can render its design common expert knowledge.[2] If such an attempt goes well, it enables the design information to enter the public sphere; although, certain issues would persist, one of which is proof of the publicity status. That is why it is argued here that private order models can offer benefits in regards to keeping technological designs accessible. But the article tries to argue that it probably takes more than just a licensing model to get a real tech commons off the ground. In a way, the result would equal a system that produces the disclosure effect of patents without granting a protection period, and would instead combine the disclosure process with a standard licensing and remuneration scheme. According to the view presented here, a possible Tech Commons License should thus be accompanied by a registering support system and an incentives system that preserves at least some rewarding mechanisms and market effects.

Keywords: Tech Commons, immaterial goods, patents,

---

1 Regarding patent law in Germany, see Kraßner (2009). These are patents and utility models only. The term is not menat to include other non-technological register content, like trademarks, aesthetical models and appearances referred to as "industrial design".
2 Kraßer (§ 16 A IV S. 272).

1. Introduction

This article wants to explore some key aspects of whether and how a standard legal tool could be devised to reach out beyond the copyright / database protection world into the area of register rights in technological design (including but not limited to hardware design). The rationale of this would be to build a kind of voluntary commons there, too, comparable to the commons developing through the application of free licensing to copyrighted content. A key benefit of such an approach could be to provide a way to sustain what is sometimes referred to as "collective invention" (Meyer, 2003) or "open innovation", beyond the point where it disappears again through re-appropriation, unclear protection status or for other reasons.[3] There are obviously fundamental differences in both the matter that such a new tool would need to deal with and the way it would need to work, compared to what is already achieved through free licensing of creative works. Several concepts of copyright law are not entirely counterparted in register rights in general and in patent systems in particular. At the same time the ways to achieve protection are also different compared to what copyright law offers, as is the effect of the protection. All these aspects would need to be a taken into account when drafting a kind of Tech Commons License (a TCL, to stay in the common tradition of abbreviations). Not all of them can be covered in this article, which is rather meant to be thought provoking and tries to highlight as many aspects as possible. Many points made will need further investigation in order to lead to a viable concept of a tech commons.

It needs to be stressed here that the term "design" in this article is meant to describe the way something is constructed technologically, a specific technological solution, where the solution itself can be an object of protection independent from the medium or work describing it. Design in this sense is about technological solutions for problems to the extent that they are not to be regarded as creative work but rather as discoveries, as results of logical reasoning, engineering, research or serendipity and are protectable – at least in principle – through documents describing them.

The kind of content covered by this meaning is technological inventions and utility models only. Other content that might be described using the term design is non-technical in nature and consists of shapes, colors, logos, trademarks and other modes of appearance of objects or companies. Although this non-technical, aesthetic content might also be protectable through registration, it has a different purpose than functional technology. It is used to make products and services unique and distinguishable from

---

3   A community of steam engineers, sharing their knowledge and innovative ideas, disappeared in the 19th century due to patent law becoming more influential, see Rishab Ghosh, FN 14.

the competition. As such, this aesthetic industrial content is in its nature much closer to copyrightable content, and sharing and re-use of such identification markers has little benefit, if any. The boundary between technological design and aesthetical design is not always clear. Both can be present within the same object, and they often are, especially in the subject matter of industrial design. Sometimes the aesthetics of an object amount to being a work in the eyes of copyright law, sometimes they do not but are legally protected on a somewhat lower level. All this is not the topic of this article. This article is about functionally technical design as in "*defective by design*".[4]

2. Creative content licensing models when applied to design

In a growing number of cases, copyright licenses are applied to specific technological designs. Yet, although they do have some effects there too, they don't work very well for this kind of content. The Creative Commons Public Licenses (CCPL), for example, are not targeting non-creative, objectively devisable discoveries, which becomes apparent in the licenses' wording and the way they work legally.[5] This is not to say that they are very far away from being suitable, and they are actually used in an increasing number of cases in contexts where (according to the point made here) a legal tool or set of tools tailored to the idiosyncrasies of tech content would be desirable.

One prominent example for this was OpenMoko,[6] the mobile phone platform based on free software and open hardware concepts. In addition to the mobile phone software being "free as in free speech", the CAD files for the hardware were been put on the internet under a CC license. The problem here is, that while it is perfectly valid to license pictures under CC, even if they are mainly technological descriptions, these graphics are just that: Descriptions of technological concepts, not the concepts themselves. Just because a technological concept needs at least one conclusive description to successfully be identified, communicated and transferred, that does not mean that any such description and the copyright protection it might carry do the trick for protecting the technological concept described. And if there's no protection present, no protection regime can be instituted

---

4 The name of a campaign against DRM systems, brought forward in 2006 mainly by the Free Software Foundation.
5 To name just a few points here: Copyright licenses assume that protection exists from and through creation itself, without the need for registration; they grant rights to reproduce the works themselves, not the production of things described in the works; they deal with moral rights and fair use principles, which do not in the same way apply in patent law.
6 See http://www.openmoko.com/ , now with a different business model than initially.

to generate permanent accessibility in the way private ordering does through copyleft licensing.

A similar example is the VIA OpenBook design. Some of the CAD files necessary for developing additional parts for the mini-note concept have been released under the CC-BY-SA license.[7] This licensing behaviour is not without effect: If VIA Technologies Inc. would now sue a re-user claiming infringement of any patents they might have in the designs (with the descriptions previously released under CCPL), the case could probably be struck out on the grounds of misrepresentation or implied terms.[8] It would with little doubt amount to contradictory behavior to first give open access to CAD files on the internet under a license contract allowing reproduction of the construction plans themselves, and later sue someone for damages because he makes use of them to build physical objects.[9] Still, it's not at all definite that things would go this way. There are usually problems of establishing proof of facts regarding the exact wording of websites at some given point in time. Secondly, CC licenses expressly give no warranty of any kind that the rights licensed are actually in the hands of the licensor. This gets aggravated if the files are accessible not only from the site they were first published on. Thirdly, some design features might not follow directly from the CAD illustrations, but rather from certain things left out in them. Therefore, it becomes apparent that there are questions here that CC licenses are not able and are not meant to answer; for example, are designs that are not directly shown in the CAD files, but can be concluded from them indirectly, also covered by the license?

Furthermore, copyright protection aims at an object fundamentally different from the one that technological protection aims at. The low level, "automatic" protection of creative content is usually justified through the dichotomy of concept vs. instantiation. Because theoretically there are infinite different ways to instantiate the same concept, each instance is very closely related to the originator's personality.[10] At the same time, to protect one of those instances is – in view of all the other possible ones – not as detrimental to the public interest as to outweigh the individual interest. In technology on the other hand, things look quite different, because technological effects are only possible within the scope of the laws of physics. If the options are significantly more limited, as they are with technological solutions, each solution inevitably carries comparatively less

---

7 The files cover the external panels of the mini-note reference design, see http://www.viaopenbook.com/index.php?option=com_content&task=view&id=5&Itemid=1 0

8 For the UK see for example *Misrepresentation Act* 1967, sections 1 b) and 2.

9 In some jurisdictions, e. g. Germany, the scope of copyright to a technical plan also reaches out to physical executions of the plan, by covering „the essence" contained in the work.

10 See for the situation in Germany Tetzner (1983).

personality than a creative work usually does, and its monopolization through protection is (at least potentially) much more prohibitive and therefore more detrimental to society as a whole. Another aspect lies in the way objects of copyright and patent-like register rights are used. While copyrighted works are protected as ends in themselves, as pieces of literature to enjoy for example, the author cannot prohibit the further use of ideas and facts contained in his or her text – as long as the work itself is not reproduced or a derivative made. Contrary to that, patented solutions are just means to do other things, to solve technological problems, to produce goods and the like.[11] They are therefore much closer to the commercial realm and must be fit for detailed proof and testing, must be available to trade and transfer as commercial assets. These differences are, at large, what speaks in favor of the automatic long-term protection of creative works, and in favor of demanding additional steps to be taken to gain protection for inventions. The latter represent concepts, not instantiations of concepts.[12]

Notwithstanding these differences, there is also a certain internal contradiction present when trying to apply one of the CCPL to technological designs: CC licenses expressly state that nothing in them "... *is intended to reduce, limit, or restrict any uses free from copyright or rights arising from limitations or exceptions that are provided for in connection with the copyright protection under copyright law or other applicable laws.*" (Section 2 in all CC licenses under the heading "*Fair Dealing Rights*"). Apart from the fact that protection through patents is in a legal sense different from copyright protection, and that Fair Dealing is hard to argue in patent contexts, it becomes clear from the wording of the CCPL that these licenses are meant to repair something that has (at least in the view of many) gone wrong because of the automatic protection of content under copyright law. It is this automatism that does not exist in the field of technological design in the first place. For technological designs, the simplest available status resembling open access would be one where the technological solution in question is known publicly, and is nonetheless not registered. The technological design is then part of "the state of the art" and can no longer be monopolized by an individual or company. Thus, the right decision from the CCPL stance would be not to register such a piece of content in the first place. Of course, if registration has already happened, the situation is somewhat similar to the copyright situation, because then

---

11 Troller A., in the journal *Computer und Recht*, 1987, 213, 217.

12 It would be against the rationale of copyright law, if one could get any kind of protection for the concept of the story of, say, a pirate fighting a number of supernatural beings in a tropical setting of the 18th century, but of course it is perfectly reasonable to offer copyright protection to Disney's "Pirates of the Caribbean", for that is just an instantiation of the aforementioned concept.

there is a strict protection that – in order to reach the status of open access – needs to be removed to some extent. But to use the CCPL in such a context where the protection first has to be initiated in order to later remove it again to free the content , is quite remote from the original CCPL idea.

3. The tea pot example

One very strange idea to try to make CC licenses work as design protection (in this case covering both meanings of the term, i. e. functional design and aesthetical design) highlights how the idea behind the CCPL can be misunderstood. This was actually suggested at a discussion around the launch of the CCPL version 3.0: 1. Use an animation program to render a 3-D morphing sequence between two extreme shapes of a chosen object, lets say a non-dripping tea pot with a remarkable look. In this make sure the sequence goes through any perceivable alteration that could reasonably be made to the appearance while preserving the non-dripping feature; 2. Attach a CC Attribution Share-Alike license, and 3. Claim that anyone producing a tea pot resembling one of the frames of the animation a) cannot appropriate the design of that one single shape because as part of the animation it is covered by copyright, b) needs to attribute you and c) is obliged to keep sharing when producing corresponding tea pots.

Is that an easy way to free multiple designs at once? It is not, of course, although you can give legal freedoms to the animation itself this way. But you don't have stronger rights than anyone else in any of the specific non-dripping tea pot designs morphed through in the sequence, because there might not even be one specific tea pot design present here, in the legal sense. But even if there were, the non-dripping clue is outside the scope of copyright law, thus neither gets automatically protected nor subsequently freed by the copyleft CC license.

The tea pot example also stands when using the GPL, even though that license does deal with basically technological issues, just like the ones a Tech Commons License would aim for. After all, the GPL is a tool to keep technological solutions reached through software available for everyone. But this works for software only, because software – unlike other technological design types – belongs to the realm of automatic protection. Copyright law is behind this curiosity that ultimately enables the GPL to work at all, for there is usually no registration needed for written code according to national and/or TRIPS rules. So, even though formal software patents exist in some regions, they are no prerequisite for building up the protection regime that the GPL (and the CCPL) rely on because protection is granted even without registration, just like in creative works.

This, however, is not the case in the context of inventions or technological solutions that someone found rather than created or coded. They belong to an *a priori* different kind of content. A license system is able to bring copyleft to this kind of non-code technological content doesn't exist yet. It would need to actually deal with the question of registration and require any licensor – in the sense of a strict condition – that a registration has already taken place before any licensing statement is made. Otherwise, this Tech Commons License could be too easily used in a misleading manner, to arrogate protected rights where actually there are none. But there is no such strict condition in either the GPL or the related GFDL, neither would it make sense there after all, because code is automatically protected. In addition to that, these two licenses are also not quite suitable for patentable content other than software, because they explicitly relate to copyrighted or copyrightable works only. The GFDL could in fact be used to set (and keep) the describing documents of technological solutions free, but in relation to the invention, the design as such, it is not the GFDL that destroys a solution's patentability but rather the publicity alone.

4. Publicity as a means to ensure freedom of design

The assessment of the commonly-used licenses above almost inevitably leads to another idea: Why not focus simply on publicity and use that as a very simple tool to keep technological designs free for everyone? After all, publicity is a core principle of patent law and the most important result of registering something with the patent authorities[13] (without any doubt it can be more detrimental to society to have businesses refrain from patenting and still use the solutions they found while hiding them in the closet). So, it would indeed be very neat if there were an effective way of reaching enough publicity so as to solve the problem discussed here. A known technological solution is usually not eligible for patent protection anymore, because it has already been released into common knowledge. But the world is not that simple. Firstly, publicity is not worth much without sufficient proof, and the best way to gain this proof might be through simply making use of the services already established by public institutions offering this function, i.e. registering with patent authorities. Secondly, there is a very fundamental principle of territoriality of register protection, and it is thus rather expensive to reach worldwide publicity by private means alone. This fact gives abusers the opportunity to outpace the

---

13 This becomes apparent from the word "patent" itself, which is derived from latin "patens", meaning "open" or "openly visible"; only what has been properly disclosed can be defined and assessed by the authorities and become part of the patent protection.

publicity and register the particular design in places where it was not yet heard of. Again, the international regime already in place can be used to help out. International treaties like TRIPS, as controversial as they may be, provide the means to get legally enhanced publicity, because – depending on the process – one registration will have an instant legal effect in many areas around the globe. Also, only these international regimes can bridge many gaps between national jurisdictions and provide for viable arbitration procedures.

Also, a license added to existing protection regimes does prove preferable over mere publicity especially because publicity alone does not in itself carry any clear intentions of the person publishing the content. Businesses wanting to make use of published designs would probably not be willing to take the risk of using a specific invention where the intention of a potential rights holder is unknown to them. And last but not least, a license based on formal registration also opens a door to open up designs already long registered. The latter could, however, quite as well be achieved through the cancellation of registrations, but apart from potentially producing additional costs, this option often means an end to the attribution that is so very important to many inventors.

5. Administrative costs and lack of incentives

The largest practical obstacles in establishing a tech commons system as described here would be the cost of utilizing the international registering infrastructures and the potential economic loss of the individual licensor compared to the regular situation, i. e. compared to exploiting monopolies coming from patents until their term ends. This is somewhat different from the well-known incentives arguments in the copyright context, where easier access often raises the revenues coming from sales rather than diminishing them. In addition to that, when looking at creative works, there is a hard-to-quantify but surely large amount of content that was and is created for radically different reasons than personal gain. There is a lot of material created by lay persons parallel to a strong commercial sector. This content is created for the pure fun of creating something or because of emotional involvement or numerous other reasons. The personal cost of adding new creative content has dropped dramatically since the technologies needed for creation and distribution have gone digital. Under these circumstances it is arguably not too hard to establish a sort of self sufficient pool of truly free content, and Creative Commons as a licensing model has helped this process significantly. Also, if there is one not freely licensed piece of content suitable for a certain purpose, there probably are other pieces online that can be used instead. That is what makes it a valid claim to say "*there is no point today in clinging to monopolizing copyright constructs; we could and should find new business models for being professionally creative."*

When it comes to technological solutions, however, the costs of reaching the solutions have hardly dropped at all compared to the early days of invention. Of course there were some geniuses out there that tinkered around on their own, producing cutting edge technology much like artistic minds do when producing new art on their PC at home. But as technology progresses, the space for new inventions made in the garage by the talented hobbyist shrinks more and more. Many sectors of technology have reached a state of development where improvements increasingly come out of highly effective research labs or well-endowed universities. So, while the potential cost of failing and the idea of remuneration through monopolies has lost much of its importance in the copyright world, it remains strong for technological problem solving (although that in turn doesn't necessarily mean that monopolies in this context actually support progress[14]). Furthermore, logic has it that there is always a lesser number of alternative solutions for a given technological problem than there are ways to express a given topic artistically (see above). This is not to say that art has less value than technological design, but the value of art has much looser ties to the regulatory model of commerce – fortunately. That's why the tech design field can't avoid getting attributed with economic questions, chances and constraints. One might regret that, but the world will probably not change too quickly in this respect. So, for building a tech commons the principles of the market will have to be considered.

6. Market mechanisms put to work

The simplest and most free-as-in-free-speech approach would mainly resemble the liberation mechanisms that copyleft uses for copyright protected content. It must depend on reciprocal altruism to be widespread and strong enough to get people to contribute designs to the tech commons. As with free software, copyleft has basically been used to re-initiate an environment that had once developed by itself, i. e. the freely sharing community of coders of the 1960s and 70s who together pushed a new technology forward. Such communities have existed via less virtual technologies as well, but they have subsequently vanished at some point (McHugh, 1980). And although the success of free software suggests that copyleft could have an equally beneficial resurrecting effect in fields other than software, it might fail as a concept for a tech commons simply for psychological reasons. (The community of cooperating steam engineers f.

---

14 Shown for example by Rishab Ghosh in the steam engine example, see http://communia-project.eu/communiafiles/COMMUNIA-ghosh.pdf

e. has been gone for so long that hardly anyone could imagine that such a community could re-emerge or function in the first place).

And it may in many cases simply take too much infrastructure to enter the game of technological design just like Open Source entered the world of software. One needs a lot more resources to develop machines, in comparison to just the laptop and internet connection needed by a Debian developer to improve the code of a software module. Considering this, it might be accurate to state that copyleft came just in time to re-animate the dying sharing traditions in software programming, and that comparable traditions are gone too long in other industries to take the same approach that Stallman and others took with GNU. So, for several reasons, the inventor or the discovering body might, in addition to renouncing legal monopolies, not want to or not be able to pay for such an act of release. In this case, someone else would have to bear the overall costs to make a design enter the tech commons. What could be done to overcome this?

At least three possible approaches to monetary issues come to mind. A foundation could be formed to collect funds for freeing designs and distribute them, based on democratic decision processes. Or there could possibly be something like a patronage set up for designs on a per case basis. But these approaches would need to achieve a certain scale to have even the slightest chance of being effective. If none of them would prove feasible, however, or raise sufficient funds or support, a more market-minded approach could be taken. This approach would quite clearly depart in many respects from the principles that Creative Commons and free software are based on.

Possibly, things unthinkable for open access in copyright would need to be thought of for open access in tech design. This fourth option could, for example, consist of developing a system of standard royalties. The use of a TCL-licensed solution would then lead to the obligation to pay royalties in a percentage relation to the profit made directly from that solution (only in case that there actually are profits, the licensor himself being excluded from this obligation of course). The money could either exclusively go into financing the freedom of new designs or, to push the idea to a maximum market view, could partly go to the licensor. A system like this would help leave intact key steering mechanisms of the business world, but would also carry the big disadvantage of establishing a considerable amount of bureaucracy. This approach would, there is no doubt here, be located far away from "free", both as in free speech and as in free beer. On the other hand, it would be quite close to what is factually already at hand through the combination of CC non-commercial licensing with the now-established CC+ features. Only it would be a little more honest. It's obvious that the popularity of the Creative Commons NC license type is based on the attitude "*I set this content free in a way, but nobody shall get rich with it or if someone does, I want my share"*. A standard royalties model would basically say the same, but would do so openly. At the same time, through linking royalties to the amount of profits actually made, this approach would let such persons or entities make use of designs without limitations that a) work as not-for-profits, b) just fail to make any profits or c) act privately as hobbyists.

7. What would the key features of a TCL need to be?

To get back to the legal basis for all this, the question is what should and should not be included in a Tech Commons License in order for it to make practical sense. As noted above, the license model would need to make previous registration a *conditio sine qua non*. Otherwise it could - intentionally or by accident - be used to arrogate rights and obligations where there actually are no grounds for them, or be used to cause confusion about designs that have a status subject to a dispute. In addition to this, easy ways (APIs, standards, ...) to verify the actual registration status of content would not only be much easier to push than they are in the copyright world, but would also be nothing short of crucial to make things work smoothly for small companies and private users.[15]

While strictly making previous registration a condition, the license should not less strictly require this registration to be limited to the minimum registration period. This requirement could be secured through an unconditional waiver of any right to extend the period or, respectively, an assertion not to exercise the right. This is important for several reasons. After something has been registered under patent law, it cannot be protected again once the period ran out.[16] So, after the minimum period of registration is over, the main goal of setting the design free is reached, and any extension can only make things worse. Given the scenario of competent patent authorities, no expired patent can be re-appropriated, and thus the need for a supporting tool like a TCL disappears. For similar reasons, Share-Alike mechanisms in copyright context turn detrimental as soon as the work enters the Public Domain, because they effectively add restrictions by misleadingly alleging obligations that have no grounds anymore.

---

15 It is noteworthy here that Creative Commons began exploring into registry building in Spring of 2008, which might provide further insight also for the tech commons idea.

16 Through the disclosure following registration it has entered public knowledge as part of the "state of the art" or "prior art" and is granted a limited time of protection. After that protection runs out, there is an absolute obstacle to re-registration as there is an official publication with the same content, see for example § 3 (1) of the German Patent Code.

Secondly, the licensee of a TCL must be put in the position to assess the period of time that any terms and conditions will be binding. For copyright content, this is usually done on the basis of very few easily accessible facts. Even though in some cases the term calculation might be rather tricky, the copyright term itself is at no discretion of the copyright holder. To the contrary, in most jurisdictions the registration of patents and other register rights can be extended up to a certain maximum by paying additional fees and/or other administrative action.[17] It would cause uncertainty and the need for additional communication between licensor and licensee if the licensor could at his discretion decide whether to extend registration or not (although many licensors would possibly refrain from it because of additional costs). To immediately limit registration to the minimum period would be the most straightforward way around this. A third reason for limitation would be the fact that in case certain clauses of the license grant are successfully challenged in court, the damage done by a residual registration would be minimized.[18]

A license for creating a pool of tech commons material would of course need to be irrevocable regarding its liberation part, at least. If legally possible, the license should be drafted to also effectively limit the licensor's ability to delete the registration, and it should provide ways to deal with the situation of a registration deleted due to external reasons. There should be clauses in the license that regulate the ways of arbitration proceedings, because conflicts about the exact nature of a certain design allegedly protected by a patent, or about the validity of competing patents, would not be a long time coming. A strict non-commercial option on the other hand would make much less sense for a Tech Commons License than it possibly does for example in the CCPL context. CC licenses are to a good extent used by lay persons or semi-professionals and mostly affect content that has at least some potential for home use. Quite on the contrary, a possible TCL would largely have very different groups of licensors and licensees compared to the CCPL (less different to that of the GPL, though). Most technological solutions stem from a context where only few tools are at hand for private users that would allow them to make use of those solutions. For example, while today almost everyone has access to software tools enabling sophisticated creative work in digital media, the machines to produce mobile phone parts following the OpenMoko designs are rarely at hand for home use. So, at the moment there is no real point in limiting the freedom of a certain design to the world of non-commercial activities. In private home use, that would simply be pointless.

---

17 See for example § 16a of the German Patent Code.
18 Although patent protection is very similar around the world, there would be a problem with minimum protection periods differing between jurisdictions, as the Paris Convention leaves that point largely to the members own discretion.

Derivatives are another concept from the realm of creative work not quite fitting into the context of designs protected under (and possibly set free through) a TCL. Whenever a dispute arises about a specific design violating a certain patent, an assessment needs to be made whether a violation actually occurred. The way to proceed is quite different from what happens when courts have to decide whether something is derived from or only inspired by a copyright protected pre-existing work. Where we in fact have a continuum in the creative context – something most judges would of course deny – there is more of a black-white situation when assessing technological designs (or rather, that would be the case if patents authorities would guard and defend the principle of unambiguous description as a prerequisite for patent protection the way they should). Either the design in question contains solutions directly resembling what is in the patent, and then it's a violation, or otherwise there is at least some relevant physical difference identifiable in the function of it, then there's no violation. The actual distance between two different technological solutions is much less relevant as long as they are significantly different at all. If one would try to introduce the notion of derivatives here, the attempt would be rather futile, for a patent is meant to protect one precise design only, not an area of related solutions.

At the core of the license there would need to be the grant of a non-exclusive right to use the respective design to solve any kind of problem, not limited to the working(s) described in the patent letter. Even though restrictions like "you are entitled to use this design for the purposes X, Y and Z only" or "... for non-military purposes only", or similar restrictions are thinkable, they would produce massive interpretation problems and most probably ruin the central liberating character of such a license altogether. A possible and not very onerous restriction could be a clause along the lines of an attribution requirement, because, while personality rights as such do not have much relevance in the commercially biased context of tech design, the attribution for a very useful invention is still an important factor.

8. Attempts already made

Is the point made in this article such a new idea after all? No, there are several approaches that have been offered elsewhere, also headed for a similar goal as the tech commons. While making no claim to be complete in this listing, I'll try to comment on some of them. There are well known pledges and promises by corporations, to start with, like Microsoft's "Open Specification Promise"[19] for example. Such promises are a step in the right

---

19 See http://www.microsoft.com/interop/osp/default.mspx

direction, and it would be a rather simple task to draft something similar for other technological solutions than software. However, apart from being non-standard and thus making it a necessary to re-evaluate the often far reaching conditions for every conceivable type of promise, these statements do not really grant any rights, but simply represent an assertion not to sue if certain rights are violated in a specific way. And the validity of such promises has not yet been clearly established for many jurisdictions.

Another approach is known as the "Eco-Patent Commons"[20] of the World Business Council for Sustainable Development. This is somewhat close to what a TCL could look and work like, although it is not based on a standard license used as a tool for private order, but on a mutual agreement between members, combined with a public pledge. And there are structural downsides, too, the most prominent ones being the required membership in a consortium and the way this approach strongly relies on a "responsible green image" effect as a motivation for the members to contribute. There is no mechanism present to give support to smaller companies who want to participate, which limits the group of potential members to larger corporations for whom registering their solutions is standard procedure. The scope here is strictly limited to "green patents", which is quite obviously reflected by the rather symbolic nature of the whole model.

Back in the world of software, but aiming at register rights in the form of a single specific patent (U.S. Patent No. 5,995,745), there is the Open RTLinux Patent License[21], which allows for royalty-free use of processes resulting in Linux becoming a real-time operating system. Besides the fact that it is debatable whether the basic principles of the RTLinux patent should be protectable in the first place, this license has a very limited scope both in its object and the rights granted. Licensee's software must either run within a RTLinux system or be a GPL licensed piece of software. To the contrary, the patents forming a true tech commons will most probably need to be combinable with non-free designs – as long as they are in effect distinguishable from the non-free parts. If TCL designs would only be combinable with other TCL designs, as in the RTLinux example, that could give non-TCL designs a prohibitive power if there is no completely free alternative set of solutions at hand.

A very recent example of outreach into the realm of patents and corporate research is "GreenXchange",[22] an initiative of Science Commons and two large corporations. It is a project that aims to build patent pools and foster a culture of open innovation. It could, once up and running, be

---

20 See
http://www.wbcsd.org/templates/TemplateWBCSD5/layout.asp?type=p&MenuId=MTU1O
Q&doOpen=1&ClickMenu=LeftMenu
21 See http://www.rtlinuxfree.com/openpatentlicense.html
22 See http://sciencecommons.org/projects/greenxchange/

the closest to a real tech commons yet, but there are two limitations built into this approach that might make it fall short of becoming that far-reaching. Firstly, it is limited from the start to deal only with certain outcomes of corporate research, the ones that usually don't make it into actual products. These results and designs often vanish within the corporations without reaching the public through publications or patents and are lost for anyone outside. GreenXchange wants to counter this effect. While this is surely a good cause, the corresponding limitation is a very extensive one. It is obviously incurred to make it easier for corporations to subscribe to the initiative, because they do not have to depart from the primary principles of asset management they are used to. But it is deemed to exclude some of the most valuable and important innovations from the "innovation ecology" that is to be created. Secondly, here also is a strong focus on "green patents", meaning solutions that support sustainability and a sparing use of resources in general. While this again might make the initiative more attractive for (especially larger) corporations, because it fits well into any kind of green image campaign, both limitations are neither essential nor beneficial for a tech commons in the true sense of the meaning. Free software would without any doubt not be as successful a concept had it been confined to those kinds of coding results that are commercially irrelevant. And hardly any product can be built relying on green patents alone. The latter does act as a hard limit on any patent pool and probably renders the whole approach useless in many ways.

9. Conclusion

When evaluating the different types of content that constitute intellectual property, it becomes apparent that standard ways of making this content available to everyone through easy-to-use legal tools only exist for some of those types of content. They do exist for content protected by non-register rights, i. e. for creative works receiving instant protection through copyright or related rights, for facts receiving sui generis protection through being collected in databases and for software. Register rights, like patents for technological solutions and utility models, are neither directly covered nor coverable by any of the major free licensing models, yet they form an important part of the IP world. To enable the development of a commons of register rights content, certain idiosyncratic features of this content type have to be dealt with. The most prominent one is the registration process itself and its central role in constituting protection. Some concepts important for the copyright world bear little relevance for technological solutions, and vice versa. Especially the notions of derivative works and personality rights are of little use in technology contexts. And the very close ties between patents and commerce might make it necessary to establish standard royalty mechanisms, in order to enable a tech commons to function and grow. These mechanisms would at the same time stand well outside the prevalent concept of freedom now established in copyright contexts. While some attempts are already underway to make and keep certain technological designs available for everyone, all of them are limited in scope and/or to specific applications of design. Thus, it would be worth trying to devise a viable standard system applicable to any kind of registrable technical design, using a Tech Commons License and a supportive infrastructure built around this license.

References

Kraßner, R. (2009), *Patentrecht*, 6th Edition, Munich.

McHugh, J. (1980), *Alexander Holley and the Makers of Steel,* Johns Hopkins University Press.

Meyer, P. B. (2003), *Episodes of Collective Invention*, U.S. Bureau of Labor Statistics, Working Paper 368.

Tetzner V. (1983), *Leitfaden des Patent-, Gebrauchsmuster- und Arbeitnehmererfindungsrechts der Bundesrepublik Deutschland,* 3rd edition 1983, § 1 comment 1, 7.

Open Licensing's Impact on Higher Education Resources Colombian and Catalan Approaches

Carolina Botero [*], Ignasi Labastida [o]

[*] *Grupo Derecho, Internet y Sociedad - Fundación Karisma, Colombia*

[o] *Office for Knowledge Dissemination, CRAI, Universitat de Barcelona*

This text reflects the situation at beginning of 2008

Abstract. A new initiative has sprung on the path created by the Open Access (OA) movement: Open Education (OE). The initiative's aim is to open up all educational resources at all learning levels. In order to achieve this goal, several international institutions, like UNESCO and the OECD, have published reports, surveys and documents to help educational institutions in this endeavor. This global initiative needs a legal framework; as a result, efforts thus far have usually resorted to Open Licensing (OL), especially Creative Commons (CC) licensing. In fact, as a response to this new movement, Creative Commons launched a new program, *ccLearn*1, which recognizes open licensing's impact on education and directly supports the idea of open educational resources (OER). However, there still remain a good amount of open questions: What is happening locally with OL in higher education? How are educational institutions receiving the initiative? How is it that the OL initiative relates to educational resources? Are there local examples of open educational resources (OER)? How do these local instances incorporate CC into their educational frameworks?
To this effect, this analysis aims to focus on the legal approach and specifically on the way the educational sector is using open licenses outside the English speaking world. It will do so by looking at the current situation in two specific scenarios, the Colombian and the Catalan experiences with open educational projects at the higher education level.

Keywords: Open Education, Open Licences, Creative Commons, ccLearn, Educational Resources, Colombia, Catalonia

1. Open Education (OE) now

"Open" (as opposed to "closed") refers to the idea of allowing anyone (open) uses over intellectual productions that are, according to copyright law, the author's privilege to control (to close). The idea of "open" stems from (or is strong tied to) the idea that sharing and spreading knowledge for society, of which there are several related initiatives in different areas, though the free/libre open source software (FLOSS) initiative during the

---

[1] http://learn.creativecommons.org

90's is worthy of note. FLOSS advocates not only shared the idea of openness, but found a juridical solution to fit it within the copyright frame: software licenses to allow everyone to use, copy, share and modify software under the "copyleft" condition. Since then, the use of licenses has become a common tool to modify the scope of the law.

The idea of "open" has also reached the educational sector as a consequence of a remarkable development: the movement for an OA to knowledge in the Sciences and Humanities. Scholars first reacted to this structured alternative to academic publications and are now following the path started by the OA movement in order to develop this new initiative, Open Education (OE), to support joint efforts and standards on the learning process. The OE initiative's aim is to open up all educational resources at all learning levels. Growing interest around this idea in recent years has been focused on the Open Educational Resources (OER) concept. OER is a concept that has evolved since its inception in 1994 when Wayne Hodgins coined the term "learning object", popularizing the idea that digital educational materials could be reused in different situations. Four years later, David Wiley proposed the application of the FLOSS principles to content, introducing the term "open content". In 2001, when MIT announced OpenCourseWare and CC released its first set of licenses, ideas for technological and juridical strategies towards openness were assembled and many could start to use them in practice.

Though the term "OER" was first used at UNESCO's 2002 Forum on the Impact of Open Courseware for Higher Education in Developing Countries[2], there is no agreement on a single definition. UNESCO used the term to refer to "the open provision of educational resources, enabled by information and communication technologies, for consultation, use and adaptation by a community of users for non-commercial purposes". This restriction to non-commercial purposes is contested by some authors like David Wiley, who proposed his own open educational license[3] advocating for a close dedication to public domain to allow any modification without any restrictions. Thus, we may define OER as any educational material or resource that is free (of charge) to be used, modified and combined without any restrictions. Among OER, we may include output from the creation of FLOSS and development tools, the creation and provision of open course content, and the development of standards and licensing tools.

The OE initiative has an important support base. Several institutions, like UNESCO or OECD[4], have joined in the effort and are contributing to

---

[2]   http://unesdoc.unesco.org/images/0012/001285/128515e.pdf
[3]   Wiley, David (2007) Open Education License Draft, Iterating Towards Openness, 8th August 2007, http://opencontent.org/blog/archives/355
[4]   http://www.oecd.org/edu/oer

building standard frameworks for community development, financing publications, reports, surveys and documents to help educational institutions analyze and adopt OER. As with the OA movement, OER adoption needs to address strategies that guarantee "openness", and these strategies should not only address technological concerns but also legal barriers. The fact that ideas like sharing and spreading (both basic to the "open" concept) need a legal framework that works with copyright restrictions is usually resolved by open content licensing, primarily through CC licensing (Fitzgerald, 2007). Surveys show that CC licensing is the preferred legal tool to reinforce "open" strategy (OECD, 2007). As a result, the CC community has shown special support for this educational approach. As an organization, CC started an education program, ccLearn, which recognizes the impact of open licensing on educational resources and explicitly addresses the important issues surrounding OER.

On the other hand, there have always been voices asking for a specific educational license. Inside CC the discussion about the necessity of such a license has surfaced and vanished periodically. The above mentioned proposal from David Wiley to use an open educational license different from the current licenses is the last proposal on this matter. Wiley suggests that any of the existing licenses do not match the needs of OE: reuse, rework, remix and redistribution. His license is almost a dedication to the public domain, something that might be difficult to extend to many jurisdictions.

The international movement to promote and develop open resources for education is strengthened by its growing number of users (Carson, 2006 or OECD, 2007). Regarding users, there is little surprise in finding that surveys on OER projects showed not only an incredible growth rate, but also that the majority of them and their products are located in English-speaking countries in the developed World (OECD, 2007). These numbers bring to the fore a new set of questions regarding OER projects in non-English speaking communities, where data and surveys on usage and impact are scarce.

It is necessary to look at alternative usage scenarios and users. In doing so, we are likely to find not only important initiatives that translate successful projects from the English speaking developed world into other language communities and developing countries (like the Universia-MIT project amply mentioned in the international bibliography), but also local production. This paper aims to discuss alternative local experiences that are outside the current international surveys, and to compare international findings regarding these issues to the specific experiences of Colombia and Catalonia. While doing so, we seek to open new study topics and introduce other considerations into the study field.

This analysis will focus on the legal approach and specifically on the way the educational sector is using the licenses. The adoption of a juridical strategy has been crucial to the design of open standards from its inception, since defining a legal framework becomes necessary to match the institution's philosophy with the "open" idea. Devoid of a legal strategy, the exclusive legal copyright privileges of the rights holder will be a barrier to the desired openness. Therefore, raising the users' and producers' level of awareness of the legal effects of their philosophy is recognized as one of the challenges of the movement. In a global world, this lack of awareness should also be mentioned as one of the causes of the minor impact of OE projects outside the stronger influence area (English speaking developed countries).

Until recently, many of the practices of the educational sector regarding the use of copyright protected material fell outside the scope of copyright law because of its limits (mainly fair use) and the fact that they happen outside of the commercial world. However, technology arrives before legal boundaries and here,here; it swept external legal concerns to the new educational sphere.

The open movement can be seen as a way to explore means to legally and formally keep educational practices in the new technologies environment in spite of legal and technical boundaries arriving with them. The open movement in education appeared and evolved in developed countries where the need to adjust the philosophy to formal technical and legal standards was at stake, with the aim to make it evident to many others. However, the way these concerns are being addressed outside the English-speaking developed world highlights different issues.

The article begins with the Colombian case where, as in many other developing countries, it was only recently that copyright in the educational sector became an issue. In countries like Colombia legal boundaries of copyright are meaningless because in daily practice sharing and spreading knowledge is norm and thus taken for granted[5]. Teachers seem to rely on the "academic" status of educational resources to reuse third party content, without considering that one of the differences between copyright and author's rights system is precisely the scope of the system´s limits. In this later system, academic or educational uses are called limits or exceptions and they have a very narrow legal interpretation scheme. Exceptions grant permission to reuse works for academic purposes but rely on very specific case descriptions. Therefore those exceptions have a very narrow scope, hardly available for the digital world and far from the existing fair use doctrine in copyright systems spread in the web.

---

[5]   This is the case of social commons ideas as described by Ronaldo Lemos for the cultural industry in Brazil (Lemos, 2007).

2. Open licensing in the repositories of the Colombian universities

Colombians (teachers and students) are using Information and Communication Technologies (ICT) to teach and learn as they have always done: without a concrete concern for the legal framework but with the idea of sharing as a social practice. However, the trend to address legal concerns has reached the Colombian educational sector; alternative licenses (like CC) are being used and a call to share and spread is in the discourse, but in the practice, people are addressing recently discovered legal concerns mainly against social practices.

Colombia is a developing country in South America with Spanish as the official language. According to official information in 2007[6] there were 279 higher education institutions (including technical institutions) with 77 universities and 101 university institutions among them. Public institutions' share in this universe was nearly 30%. There were more than one 1.300.000 students (more than a half in public institutions) and more than 80.000 faculty.

Today Colombia is experiencing a breaking point in which awareness of legal barriers and juridical alternatives are at the core of the national discussion and analysis regarding the Educational Resources legal frame. This process has brought forth the more traditional copyright and legal concerns than the possibilities of a legal framework as a tool for sharing. Thus the aim of this part of the document is to show how OL (mainly CC licenses) have been adopted in Colombia through a process motivated by the Repository supported by the Ministry of Education in Colombia where sharing is the central idea. In spite of this, the outcome is public (free access), not open access (free access and reuse) (Maccallum 2007). In this process the copyright issue was addressed as a tool to to face legal concerns, without considering it as a way to share educational practices openly. These shifted the choice from sharing and social practices to economic control and legal models. This can be seen through a discussion of the decision-making process regarding copyright in the Ministry's repository initiative and in the National University.

The first initiative through which the Ministry of Education promoted the use of New Technologies to build and use educational resources was a public competition (2005) to design Learning Objects[7] for a repository. Among the requirements of the contest it was established that participants (universities and their academic staff) would transfer the economic rights[8]

---

[6]   http://snies.mineducacion.gov.co/men/

[7]   http://www.colombiaaprende.edu.co/html/directivos/1598/article-99368.html

[8]   Since in the *Derecho de Autor* regime moral rights are personal rights not transferable and perpetual, they remain with the original individual author Only economic rights are transferable

to the Ministry. As a result of this contest, after all the paperwork (to clean and transfer copyrights) and formal procedures, one-hundred and ninety-nine Virtual Learning Objects (as they where called at the time) were transferred to the Ministry.

The competition's copyright terms entailed several difficulties; on the one hand, the actual transfer of copyright from the author to the Ministry was complicated and costly, both in time and money. There was hardly any awareness among the community on how to "validly" use copyright materials for this type of content while the idea that everything on the Internet is "reusable" prevailed. The feeling amongst the Ministry's staff was that once transferred, there was no incentive for authors to keep working and maintain the Educational Resource, especially to update information and resources. The Ministry confirmed that in Colombia, little attention was being paid to the legal frame that determines the author/rightholder status on Educational Resources projects. Regarding the latter, even if the law provides certain rules to deal with work for hiring contracts, public servant works, rights holder transfer proceedings etc., there are hardly any institutional regulations at the universities to deal with the righholder's status. When they exist, normally no practical measures are taken to actually implement them (considering the formalities imposed by the law). Moreover, the design of Educational Resources projects tend to start in the universities without a previous discussion regarding the legal possibilities when dealing with protected material-

The project inaugurated a second phase in 2006, in which its legal approach changed completely. In 2006 the initiative of the Ministry was to encourage universities to share educational content through institutional repositories of learning objects (Leal, 2007). The content was to be made available for Internet users through the metadata in the National Repository of Educational Resources (*Banco Nacional de Objetos de Aprendizaje*[9]) and the actual content would be placed in the institutional repository at each university.

The Ministry provided a small funding incentive for nine Colombian universities' projects that were to select, catalog and tag the content they already had. The Ministry required that contents should be accessed via Internet without establishing any specific condition on the way they should be accessible avoiding any interference with academic autonomy. However, because a central concern was to promote "valid sharing" in higher education institutions as well as to sustain the repository's content, copyright issues were at stake. The decision this time was that no transfer of copyrights was needed, but that instead each and every university should clearly state the legal conditions under which the content were to be made available to the public at the repository.

---

[9]   http://64.76.190.172/drupalM/

In June 2007 the National Repository of Educational Resources was launched and the content of the nine universities plus the Ministry's content (from the contest) was announced as being, *"open access and downloadable according to the user license defined by each university"*. The preceding quote shows a philosophical intention but does not actually describe the result. Through the project, each university was forced to define the legal grounds in which their content would be made available, and to consider if any special copyright license was going to tag it[10] but OA policy was not requested.

Thus, through this initiative, the participants faced their legal concerns and fears about copyright restrictions and possibilities in different ways. Educational institutions focused their analysis with the fear of loosing control over the content when using a legal tool out of the traditional copyright framework instead of focusing on a new way to confront social educational practices with the legal boundaries. The decision was not a result of the confrontation of the social practices with the legal frame, nor a result of OA initiatives or standards. Regardless, the result was that the nine universities and the Ministry defined the legal approach of the repositories content and in doing so defined their approach towards the repository users. These approaches are presented in Table 1.

Table 1. Legal strategies chosen by participants in the National Repository of Educational Resources.

Universities	Legal Option	Details	Institution Type
EAFIT	Copyright	With some authorizations	Private
Javeriana University (Cali)			Private
National University (Bogota)			Public
Andes University (Bogota)	CC Licenses	by-nc-nd	Private
		by-nc-nd	Public

---

[10]   It is important to note that none of the nine universities nor the Ministry had defined really a legal frame for their educational content before this project required it.

		by-nc-nd	
		by-nc-nd	Private
		by-nc-sa	Private
		By-nc-nd	Private
Pontificia Bolivariana University (Medellín)			
Sabana University			
Minuto de Dios University (Bogota)	Their own license	Not available	Private

The majority of the participants (six) chose a CC license but, as Table 1 shows, all of them chose the non-commercial (NC) condition, and only one of the six institutions allowed modification of content. This university, the Pontificia Bolivariana, would be the only one matching an open standard; the other four and the Ministry itself used the most restrictive CC license (by-nc-nd) and therefore achieved public, not open, standards. The remaining three universities chose to stick to the "all rights reserved" option while the last one, Minuto de Dios, designed its own license that is not available online.

Although the Ministry's intention was a broad approach that sought to favor "open standards", it is evident from Table 1 that it actually only reached "public policies": the material that is placed in the universities' repositories is publicly available, but cannot (as a whole) be copied, redistributed nor modified or reused, unless express authorization is requested, as should be if OA standards were met. As happens in the OA publications, confusion among *open* and *public* is evident. From the OA movement the confusion that this kind of legal statement shows involved mainly the users (Mac Callum, 2007), whereas in the decision making process that we are analyzing, the "confusion" might arise in the beginning by the educational institution itself. Because this decision is made without the open frame, only under copyright concerns, the result can be the opposite of what was originally sought: Projects that are "open" to social educational practices end up being "closed" because of the legal framework chosen.

In the National Repository of Educational Resources experience, the institutions' adoption of CC licenses was a legal strategy to publicly advertise the way the content should be dealt with online, but it was not a means of thinking about open standards since these were neither requested of participants, nor reached.

To understand the scope of their decision it is worthwhile to analyze more in depth the Ministry's and the National University's decisions in particular. They demonstrate how the process in 2006 resulted in more of a legal strategy to face juridical concerns and fears, and not necessarily as a tool to encourage the actual philosophical educational approach of each participant.

Clearly the Ministry's goal was to foster a community of sharing and a wide scope of diffusion as was specifically mentioned. But when the Ministry made the decision as a copyright holder, its choice was to adopt the most restrictive CC license preventing modifications, which are central for openness in this sector.

According to the functionaries in charge, the main reason to adopt this license was the fear that even if a rights holder authorized modifications, it could interfere with the moral right to integrity that would remain with the original author. They feared that this situation might eventually affect the Ministry and hold it liable (due to risk of litigation). This fear was reinforced by the office in charge of copyright policies in Colombia (*Dirección Nacional de Derechos de Autor*), which suggested that the possibility of legal remedies regarding moral rights is still to be measured because of the scarce rate of litigation on copyright issues in Colombia. Furthermore, this office comments on their belief that if this trend changed, new tensions in the current copyright discussions would surface, because litigation by original authors on moral rights grounds would increase.

The moral rights issue has been dealt with extensively in the international community[11] and still no final word exists. Dealing with moral rights in unpredictable environments certainly implies risks and the Ministry is not willing to face them, despite the fact that the actual "social practices" are a legal risk on their own and, despite the importance of localization and sharing that the pedagogical practice claims. The fear of litigation seems to prevail when the institution has to declare the policy, while it is ignored when it exists as a social practice.

---

[11]   In the porting of the CC licenses
http://64.233.179.104/translate_c?hl=es&sl=en&u=http://wiki.creativecommons.org/Version
_3&prev=/search%3Fq%3Dopen%2Bcontent%2Blicenses%2Bmoral%2Bright%26hl%3De
s%26client%3Dfirefox-a%26rls%3Dorg.mozilla:es-AR:official%26hs%3Dcu7_, in the community discussion lists arises from time to time http://lists.ibiblio.org/pipermail/cc-licenses/ , and in papers that approach the issue: Fitzgerald, 2007 or McCraken, 2006.

The other interesting decision-making process is the case of the open courseware project at the National University in Colombia "UNvirtual" that is developed by the *Dirección Nacional de Servicios Académicos Virtuales* (DNSAV). DNSAV has developed a philosophically open project, but when asked to choose the legal strategy to be part of the Ministry's repository, surprisingly, they chose "all rights reserved". UNvirtual is a courseware project that offers e-learning material to support the regular educational activities of the University. UNvirtual's server logs (downloads and visits) show that since its launch, very soon after, the project was recognized in the Latin American internet sphere and its content was being used by users throughout the continent.

The scope of the project was very broad and close to "open" policies, comparable in time and range, but not in its environment or funding, with MIT OpenCourseWare. It was born in 1998, and was designed to provide wide access to the courses it harbored, under the idea that anyone might use them, even allowing download and modification[12]. They expected attribution, but never addressed a specific juridical policy different from "all rights reserved"; actually they were very reliant on social practices, leaving open the possibility of reuse. Technically, they allowed and encouraged open possibilities for free spreading and sharing of the material; furthermore, they felt flattered if it was reused so long as the source was recognized, although some cases of plagiarism have been detected and are viewed as highly problematic. Because of the orientation of their previous efforts, DNSAV's decision confirming the traditional "all rights reserved" approach when joining the National Repository of Educational Resources was totally unexpected.

Why did DNSAV choose "all rights reserved" given their experience and philosophical relation to "openness"? The fact that technology facilitates the "reuse" of content was sensed at the national university as a huge pedagogical possibility and was used to develop a pioneering project like UNvirtual, but, when forced to frame it in a legal context, many concerns and preoccupations arose. The decision was probably influenced by many circumstances: changes in directives, concerns by the public policy copyright office (as mentioned by the Ministry), etc, but it is important to draw attention to the issue of "ownership" linked to the copyright idea.

Being a public university, the law assigns, in many cases, the copyright economic control of the content produced in its context to the state, leaving moral rights to the actual individual authors. As such, public authorities considered that when the university is the rights holder, the content is the state's "property". Therefore, even though the National University would have been glad to agree to an open approach, those responsible were

---

[12]   As they appear drafted in the policies of the institution not yet adopted

concerned in their function as guardians of this "property"[13]. On the other hand, traditionally, the copyright idea related to "ownership" is that by controlling access to the work the rights holder will obtain economic revenue, and will keep an important competition tool especially in areas where resources are scarce. Therefore, functionaries at DNSAV were uncertain regarding the possibilities of losing legal control over the content and then having to face questions on the project's financial sustainability[14] because they were leaving aside an important "competition tool". Here, the paradigm of control as a means to obtain economic resources ("to sell" it, to reinvest in the project) and market competition surfaces clearly and leaves aside social revenue of educational sharing practices.

Today the project is still publicly available through the university's web page and the National Repository of Educational Resources. UNvirtual is still one of the main national online courseware projects with more than 220 courses and more than 26,000 daily visitors from at least 125 different countries[15]. It is still part of the OpenCourseWare project, but with the decision of adding an "all rights reserved" tag to the courses all these steps fall short of open standards. UNvirtual is trying to establish a business strategy for sustainability and trying to define how copyright fits there. Even though UNvirtual switched from a primary OA approach regarding its social practices to a standard "public access" kind of policy, copyright for them is not yet a tool to share, but instead a means to face legal concerns. Therefore the issue is far from settled.

We continue with the Catalan experience where the awareness about copyright is spread but there are a lot of misconceptions. Author's rights are well known but there is a lot of misinformation about exceptions and fair use. There is still a myth about the reuse of any material available on the net: if it is there, it is free to use. However, new projects to disseminate educational resources have transformed the way scholars see those rights when they are applied to them. Although some projects advocate for openness and the use of free licenses, there is an overprotective perspective guiding them to use the most restrictive conditions/licenses.

---

[13]   Joint document for public servants from Dirección Nacional de Derecho de Autor and Procuraduria General de la Nación,
http://derautor.gov.co/htm/legal/directivas_circulares/directivas_circulares.htm

[14]   Not that educational resources projects are good "business" but they believe by loosing copyright control the question will remain open.

[15]   According to the 2005 and 2006 DNSAV annual reports that show that the published courses in the UNVirtual project increased steadily having about 50 courses in 2002, 182 in 2005 and, as the 2006 annual report informs, ended last year with 221.

3. Open licensing in educational projects in Catalan universities

Catalonia is a nation in the kingdom of Spain with an autonomous government that has competences in education, including higher education. The language of the country is Catalan although Spanish is also official. There are twelve universities, eight of them public, with 225,000 students and 16,000 faculties.

In recent years the interest in projects dealing with learning materials is increasing among all the Catalan universities. Following the path started by the MIT, some of them have joined the international OpenCourseWare consortium[16] and others have started their own project to make their educational content available through the net. Although each university is developing its own project, there is also a common effort to build a collaborative educational repository that will harvest content from existing ones and will offer the chance to deposit new content if it is needed. This common repository is still a project but is similar to other consorted repositories developed by CESCA (Supercomputation Center of Catalonia) and coordinated by librarians through the CBUC (Catalan Consortium of University Libraries) as Recercat[17], the Catalan repository for grey literature from research, or TDX[18], the thesis repository. In the first case, Recercat, it hosts collections of preprints, working papers, reports and unpublished documents all under the by-nc-nd license.

In this sense, Catalan universities are imitating their peers around the world, especially the English speaking institutions. Currently the main work in those developing projects is focused on building institutional repositories where any content from academics, including research and learning materials, will be available for all. Nevertheless there is still an unresolved issue: the lack of a general regulation of the intellectual property that arises from those documents.

Almost all the universities have developed a regulation of industrial property including a distribution of benefits from patents and other technological developments. However, no institution has paid much attention to author's rights. Probably the main reason is that the generation of learning materials and its distribution has never been seen by institutions as a possible source of income and therefore, the scholar has never asked for permission to publish educational content anywhere.

The problem arises now when a university wants to establish an open policy concerning the educational resources and it asks itself if an authorization is needed or not. Surprisingly, almost all the projects have begun without a real discussion among the members of the community

---

[16]   http://www.ocwconsortium.org/
[17]   http://www.recercat.net
[18]   http://www.tdx.cbuc.es

about the rights of the content. It seems all the projects are following a trend while some important issues are left aside. The main worries are focused in technology.

The establishment of a repository within an institution could be seen as a good excuse to begin a debate about who holds the rights of a content developed to be used in class. Some universities have regulation on particular cases, but usually there is not a complete regulation about intellectual property. In Spain, the law contemplates the situation of the copyright within a working relation: if the work is created by an author as part of her work, the exploitation rights belong to the employee, though the moral rights will always be held by the author. Normally, this article from the law is not applied in the university in the case of learning materials although sometimes it is used in other cases. This lack of regulation is not an isolated problem in Catalonia; it seems to be a general problem across Europe, with some exceptions.

The exception in Europe can be the United Kingdom where we find clear regulations on copyright though there are different approaches. A report from the Zwolle Group (Friend, 2003) shows three different scenarios: individuals own copyright with a license to the institution, institution own copyrights but the university agrees not to benefit from the individuals' work, or the institution owns intellectual property rights but there are some exceptions[19].

On the other hand, knowledge about intellectual property is very poor among academics. There is awareness about authors rights, but a lot of misunderstandings and disinformation. A scholar can use the fair use doctrine to access any content and reuse it without knowing that the Spanish law has a narrow educational exception not as broad as fair use.

In spite of the lack of an intellectual property regime, the universities have started the projects. From them, we can detect three different groups; the first one includes those institutions restricting access just to members within their own community. In the second group we find those that make their content publicly available, but do not go any further. They are using the well known "all rights reserved" sentence. Finally, we can find a third group that allows a reuse and remixing of their educational resources through the use of the CC licensing model.

Let's talk about this last group. As we have seen, there is not a clear position about the copyright issue and therefore the university allows their teachers to decide which license to use. The first Catalan university using CC licenses was the *Universitat de Barcelona*, its affiliated institution in Spain. Following the MIT model, the university offered its members the possibility of licensing their content under a by-nc-sa license adapted to the

---

[19]   Massive http://cevug.ugr.es/massive/pdf/annex1/Annex_1_IPR.pdf

Spanish intellectual property law and to the university. However, suggested by their own lawyers at the university, it also offered a second choice, their own version of by-nc-nd. Regarding the choices made by scholars so far, one third of the works are published allowing derivative works requiring the ShareAlike condition, and the remaining two thirds are licenses excluding any kind of derivative works. The situation has changed with the new institutional repository and currently the choice is open to any of the six core licenses from CC.

The universities inside the OpenCourseWare consortium are following the MIT model, licensing their materials under a standard CC license. One of the goals of this consortium is making materials available to end users under "open" license terms that allow use, reuse, adaptation, and redistribution. However, it is possible to find materials under the local projects with limited access to members of their own community or materials not allowing derivative works. It is strange that an institution can adopt such a policy not allowing adaptations within a general framework that promote sharing and reuses.

There is also something else to be taken into account when we analyze those open policies: how the universities have reacted to the OA movement. That movement is focused on research, but signing a declaration could imply some kind of openness in an institution. Until now, only four universities have signed the Berlin declarations, beside the former Department of Universities[20] as we can see in Table 2. Only one of the signatories has developed a public repository and its policy is not open at all.

Table 2. Situation of Catalan Universities

University	Berlin	Repository	Educational Resources	Accessibility	Licenses
UAB	no	yes	yes	restricted	No
UB	no	yes	yes	Public to all	Mainly by-nc-nd by-nc-sa
UPC	yes	yes	yes	Public to all – except some materials like the exams	Mainly by-nc-nd
UdG	no	yes	no	---	---
UdL	yes	no	---	---	---
UOC	yes	no	---	---	---
UPF	yes	no	---	---	---
URV	no	no	---	---	---

---

[20]   http://oa.mpg.de/openaccess-berlin/signatories.html

The current situation in Catalonia allows us to say that the universities are following OE projects as a trend or something that has to be done to be socially acceptable, but neglecting a lot of issues that should be taken into account. Some university authorities sign declarations in favor of openness but are not promoting a real debate about this topic within their communities nor establishing any kind of project aimed at opening knowledge.

At this point there are three issues to be discussed: the standard use of the NC clause, the broad use of a Nonderivative requirement in a project aimed to share, and the participation among scholars.

About participation we should say that teaching has never been seen as important as doing research and therefore the reward for innovation or creation of new materials has always been lower than the one obtained for publishing research results. Though tides are changing now, there is still a lack of motivation among scholars to publish their content. Aside from rewards or incentives, scholars are still afraid to share, not only with the public but with colleagues in their departments. In learning materials sometimes the awareness about author's rights is greater than when the same author transfers the copyright to an editor to publish a research paper.

This fear to share is also present when choosing the license. The NonDerivative clause is seen as a way to protect a reputation restricting any adaptation or translation. Maybe this is one of the reasons of the extended use of licenses with that condition, especially among social science scholars. The second requirement, the NC, is a result of the human condition: if someone becomes rich with my work I want my part. The institutions are also imposing this condition in materials that have never been seen as a possible income and if that income arrives no one will be able to distribute it due to the lack of regulation.

Another issue to be taken into account in the case of Catalan universities is the language. Catalan is the usual language used in teaching and therefore is the language used in learning materials. This can be seen as a problem when disseminating educational content because teachers are not motivated enough to spread their knowledge. However the point should not be who will use the materials but we want to share our materials to the world. The world is multicultural and this is a new chance to show it.

To end with the Catalan situation we should mention the adoption of the Bologna process, towards building a common European higher education framework that should be established in 2010. Within this process, some academics have decided to start teaching in English and therefore developing new materials. Those people could see the OE movement as a chance to show the world what they are doing.

4. Some conclusions

Universities have legal concerns regarding their educational resources and their possibilities online. Universities are using these educational resources as pedagogical tools, they are supporting teachers' involvement in similar projects, they are enabling technological support and institutional spaces for these developments and many of them are in practice doing this under open ideas. However, it is only lately that they have started to consider how to deal with the juridical aspects and implications of their decisions. This situation shows two different aspects of pedagogical practices: on the one hand the open practice of using third party materials (believing that internet content is open to public use without copyright restrictions) but deciding to close this possibility when facing their own legal policy towards third party uses. Since universities are looking at the legal framework, not at the context of a philosophical tool for pedagogical and social practices, juridical fears are driving their choices on legal matters. How much of these decisions are influenced by the universities' poor practices regarding the definition of the author/rights holder situation is a question that remains unanswered.

The educational resources projects analyzed show that, as a general trend, people's choice is for restrictive NC licenses. The main preference for the NC clause is that it will restrict the exploitation of materials outside the educational sector, ignoring their different scopes.

Both in the Colombian experience and in the Catalan examples, CC licenses seem to be an interesting and practical way to face the legal copyright framework, but if they are not tied to wider preoccupations, i.e. to match philosophical concerns, as is the case right now, they are not part of open strategies. In the current framework, the fact that the most restrictive CC license is by far the preferred choice should still be seen as a worry for open activists; not only is it discordant with "open" philosophy, it also serves to reinforce the "public"/"open" confusion.

A thorough analysis of the legal standards for open content when applied to the universities' institutional repositories in Colombia and Catalonia shows interest in public access policies. This scenario ratifies the need to raise more awareness on the possibilities and standards of OA (OECD, 2007) because this might be an appropriate moment to find people willing to shift from public to open.

We also point out that this review draws attention to the need to look at social practices, especially since we may have more raw materials for "open practices" in this environment than for legal statements that are part of open standards. Philosophically, the educational sector shares many of the "open" movement claims, but it does not necessarily comply with the formalities that label projects as "open". However, as we have already shown, the risk is that once presented the legal framework, the juridical option will shift the social open practice to a legal public approach or even switch it to a closed option.

Even though in the Colombian case the public initiative, the National Repository of Educational Resources, is certainly the driving force behind the decision making process to address legal frameworks for educational content, it is also important to note that in Catalonia the role of the State should not be downplayed. Public initiatives can push the trend to openness (via public policies) or move the path towards closed (via doctrine), but all those will depend as well on the capacity of the educational sector to demand respect and legal frameworks for their social practices. With different frames, from those of commercial grounds, the educational sector's social practices need to demonstrate how they have also, for decades, searched for balance among users and authors.

We see that without real support from the public sector or private foundations, as in the USA and other English speaking countries, the universities and their staff are left alone with their scarce resources. Moreover, we see how universities have other priorities in addition to difficulties finding sustainability for OE projects' misleading cost and value.. Since successful projects come mainly from the Anglo-American world, that has a very different context from many other worldwide regions, universities outside of this scenario look at them with distrust. We believe that to increase the scope and impact of OE projects, we must build and showcase successful experiences of projects that are built outside of the Anglo-American world and/or that are going in the opposite direction from this current trend, i.e. projects where OE materials are being translated into English.

Consequently, it seems like the actual adoption of OA in certain countries might be reached after legal concerns are cleared; after the decision-making process forces universities to define policies regarding intellectual property. The analysis of the copyright regime vs. the alternatives (especially CC licenses as a possible option) is bringing much needed awareness to universities about the new possibilities and about OA trends that support social practices. It is possible that as a result of such reflections we will find that the number of institutions or academic projects formally adopting open standards will increase, when they realize that legal framework and copyright alternatives can be used as tools for matching existing pedagogical social practices and not only as a means to advertise legal control. This will happen if the institutions start to give value to the projects as part of the institution's needs, as important sources for materials that are otherwise paid for anyway, as important projects that give visibility or status to the institution, as training tools, etc., and not just as a means to obtain economic resources by "selling" them.

Therefore, in the awareness process it could also happen, as in fact it does, that the institutions will define their options with copyright fears and switch to "all rights reserved" (despite the social practices), or authorities in charge of copyright policies will strengthen the fear through concepts that will definitely move all of the sector backwards from the "open" paths. Those responsible will want to define an open practice when the paradigm says that the closed approach is the only path towards economical remuneration for intellectual products.

Finally, by reviewing these experiences, new questions arise. In sharp contrast to what happens in the cultural industry, the educational practices of sharing and spreading intellectual production are at the core of this sector's activity. Therefore, once the legal barriers of the copyright "rule of law" are evident to the people in the sector, will there be a fast and massive decision-making shift in legal strategies? Will many of the institutions and projects formally adhere to open standards? Do we need to measure projects in developing countries including social practices and not only legal statements to really measure OE ideas? Or will the awareness of the legal framework in environments that traditionally are outside the juridical frame have the opposite outcome of making evident to normally open societies the "closed" option? Will this evidence increase the number of institutions adopting "all rights reserved"? How many of them will do so by considering that there is actually some economic revenue by controlling information that they were normally not in the practice of controlling? What will be the role of the state?

References

Carson, S. (2006), *2005, Program Evaluation Findings Report*, MIT OpenCourseWare available at: http://ocw.MIT.edu/ans7870/global/05_Prog_Eval_Report_Final.pdf (accessed 3 May 2010).

Friend, F. J. (2003), *Copyright policies and agreements: implementing the Zwolle Principles*, available at: http://copyright.surf.nl/copyright/files/implem_Zwolle_principles.pdf (accessed 5 May 2010).

Fitzgerald, B. (2007), *Open Content Licensing (OCL) for Open Educational Resources*, CERI - OECD, available at: http://www.oecd.org/dataoecd/33/10/386x45489.pdf (accessed 5 May 2010).

Korn, N. and Oppenheim, C. (2007), *CC licenses in Higher and Further Education: Do We Care?*, Ariadne, Issue 49, available at: http://www.ariadne.ac.uk/issue49/korn-oppenheim/ (accessed 4 May 2010).

Labastida . J. and Iglesias Rebollo, C. (2006*), Guía sobre gestión de derechos de autor y acceso abierto en bibliotecas, servicios de documentación y archivos*, SEDIC Asociación Española de Documentación e Información, available at: http://www.sedic.es/dchos_autor_normaweb.01.07.pdf (accessed 5 May 2010).

Leal, D. (2007), *Iniciativa Colombiana de Objetos de Aprendizaje: situación actual y potencial para el futuro*, Conference presented during the international summit on distance education, University of Guadalajara, Mexico, November.

Lemos, R. (2007), *From legal commons to social commons: Brazil and the cultural industry in the 21st century*, working paper, Centre for Brazilian Studies, University of Oxford.

Maccallum, C.J. (2007), *When is open access not open access?*, Plos Biol 5 (10): e285 doi:10.1371/journal.pbio.0050285.

McCraken, R. (2006), *Cultural responses to open licenses and the accessibility and usability of open educational resources*, Paper for the Expert Meeting on Open Educational Resources, Malmö, Sweden, February, available at: http://www.oecd.org/dataoecd/48/38/36539322.pdf (accessed 8 May 2010).

Wiley, David (2006), *The current state of open educational resources*, "Paper for the Expert Meeting on OER", OECD-CERI, Malmö, Sweden, February, available at: http://www.oecd.org/dataoecd/19/26/36224377.pdf (accessed 8 May 2010).

Special reports on OER

OECD - CERI (2007), *Giving knowledge for free; the emergence of open al resources*, available at: http://www.oecd.org/document/41/0,3343,en_2649_37455_38659497_1_1_1_3 7455,00.html (accessed 8 May 2010).

Olcos Roadmap 2012 (2007), *Open educational practices and resources*, available at: http://www.olcos.org/cms/upload/docs/olcos_roadmap.pdf (accessed 8 May 2010).

The Use of Creative Commons Licensing to Enable Open Access to Public Sector Information and Publicly Funded Research Results: An Overview of Recent Australian Developments

Anne Fitzgerald[*], Neale Hooper[°], Brian Fitzgerald[^]
[*]*Professor of Law Research, QUT Faculty of Law, Brisbane, Australia*
[°]*Legal Project Manager, Government Information Licensing Framework (GILF) Project, Queensland Department of Justice and Attorney General*
[^]*Professor of Intellectual Property and Innovation, QUT Faculty of Law, Brisbane, Australia*

Abstract. This chapter provides an account of the use of Creative Commons (CC) licensing as a legally and operationally effective means by which governments can implement systems to enable open access to and reuse of their public sector information (PSI). It describes the experience of governments in Australia in applying CC licences to PSI in a context where a vast range of material and information produced, collected, commissioned or funded by government is subject to copyright. By applying CC licences, governments can give effect to their open access policies and create a public domain of PSI which is available for reuse by other governmental agencies and the community at large. Although the focus is on Australia, the model described could also be adopted in other jurisdictions which recognise copyright in public sector materials. The application of CC licences to PSI has been supported in several important government reviews and reports, such as the *Venturous Australia* review of the national innovation system in 2008 and the Government 2.0 Taskforce in 2009, and a growing number of government agencies at all levels (local, state and federal) is releasing copyright materials under CC licences.

Keywords: Creative Commons, Copyright, government, public sector information, public domain, Crown, Crown Copyright, Open Access, Copyright licensing

> *Governments are coming to realize that they are one of the primary stewards of intellectual property, and that the wide dissemination of their work - statistics, research, reports, legislation, judicial decisions - can stimulate economic innovation, scientific progress, education, and cultural development.*
> David Bollier, "Viral Spiral: How the Commoners Built a Digital Republic of Their Own", 2008, at p192

1. Introduction

The management of informational works is one of the most significant issues for government in the current era. During the last decade much attention has focused on policies and practices to enable public sector information (PSI)[1] to be more readily accessed and used, as governments have come to appreciate that significant social, cultural and economic benefits stand to be gained from doing so.[2]

This chapter considers how open content licences - specifically, Creative Commons (CC) licences - can be used by governments as a simple and effective mechanism to support the reuse of their copyright-protected PSI, particularly where materials are made available in digital form online or distributed on disk.[3] In Australia, as in other countries worldwide, there is a growing awareness at the governmental level of the advantages of using open content licences when distributing their copyright materials.[4]

In building frameworks to improve the flow of PSI, it is necessary to ensure not only the interoperability of technical systems and document formats but also that legal interests in PSI are understood and effectively managed. The importance of identifying and managing the range of legal interests relevant to PSI, to ensure that they operate to support - not hinder - efforts to improve access and reuse is central to the Organisation for Economic Cooperation and Development (OECD) *Recommendation for Enhanced Access and More Effective Use of Public Sector Information*

---

[1]   The term "public sector information" (PSI) is used here in a broad sense to include information and data produced by the public sector, including materials produced by government employees, materials commissioned by government from non-government parties, materials provided to government by non-government parties pursuant to a legislative obligation and materials that result from publicly-funded cultural, educational and scientific activities. See the European Directive on Access to and Reuse of Public Sector Information, the OECD's *Seoul Declaration on the Future of the Internet Economy* (2008) and the OECD Council's *Recommendation for Enhanced Access and More Effective Use of Public Sector Information* (2008).

[2]   See *Venturous Australia - Building Strength in Innovation*, report on the Review of the National Innovation System, Cutler & Company for the Australian Government Department of Innovation, Industry, Science and Research, 29 August 2008, available at http://www.innovation.gov.au/innovationreview/Pages/home.aspx.

[3]   For a more detailed examination of the issues considered in this chapter, see Anne Fitzgerald, Neale Hooper and Brian Fitzgerald, *Enabling Open Access to Public Sector Information with Creative Commons Licences – The Australian Experience*, in 'Access to Public Sector Information: Law Technology and Policy', Brian Fitzgerald (ed), Sydney University Press, 2010. Full text is available at http://eprints.qut.edu.au/29773/ accessed on 19 May 2010.

[4]   In August 2009, the New Zealand Government released the Draft New Zealand Government Open Access and Licensing Framework (NZGOAL), available at http://www.e.govt.nz/policy/information-data/nzgoalframework.html (accessed 25 January 2010). NZGOAL proposes that government agencies provide open access to copyright works, applying "the most liberal of the New Zealand Creative Commons law licences to those of their copyright works that are appropriate for release," i.e. the CC Attribution (BY) licence.

("the OECD PSI Recommendation").[5] In establishing a primary principle of openness in order to maximise the availability of PSI for use and reuse, the OECD PSI Recommendation requires that any legal grounds that restrict the default presumption of openness should be clearly defined and justified.[6] The OECD PSI Recommendation advocates making PSI available for access and reuse under transparent, broad, non-discriminatory and competitive conditions.[7] Where possible, PSI should be made available online and in electronic form, and unnecessary restrictions on access, use, reuse, combination and sharing should be removed, so that, in principle, all accessible information is open for all to reuse, for any purpose. As most governments worldwide claim copyright in at least some of their PSI (the most notable exception being the United States federal government), in order to give effect to an open access policy, it will be necessary to ensure that the government's copyright is not relied upon to justify (or excuse) restrictions on access, reuse and sharing. While copyright protection does not extend to mere information or facts, many of the informational works created or held by government will fall within the groups of material to which copyright applies (literary, artistic, sound and video recordings) and will be sufficiently original to attract protection. The OECD PSI Recommendation acknowledges that intellectual property rights in PSI should be respected, and recommends that governments exercise their copyright in ways that facilitate reuse, by developing simple mechanisms to encourage wider access and reuse, such as simple and effective automated online licensing systems.[8]

CC licences offer the kind of "simple and effective licensing arrangement" envisaged by the OECD PSI Recommendation, providing non-discriminatory access and conditions of reuse for copyright-protected PSI. This Chapter gives an overview of the key features of the CC licences developed for use in Australia and considers their advantages for governments when distributing their copyright PSI. An account is given of several of the most significant projects in which CC licensing has been applied and the conclusions and recommendations of various government reviews that have considered and supported the use of CC licences on public sector materials.

2. The Complex Flows of Public Sector Information

---

[5]   OECD, *Recommendation of the Council for Enhanced Access and More Effective Use of Public Sector Information*, C(2008)36, OECD, Paris, 2008, available at http://www.oecd.org/dataoecd/0/27/40826024.pdf.
[6]   OECD PSI Recommendation, the "Openness" principle.
[7]   OECD PSI Recommendation, the "Access and transparent conditions for re-use" principle.
[8]   OECD PSI Recommendation, the "Copyright" principle.

Improving the flow of PSI requires a detailed understanding of the kinds of materials produced, how they have been created, and by whom. As these factors all bear upon the existence, ownership and exercise of copyright, they need to be taken into account in any strategy for licensing PSI materials designed to enable PSI to move without impediment among government agencies and between government and the private sector.[9]

Governments at all levels develop, manage and distribute an array of PSI in the form of documents, reports, websites, datasets and databases on CD or DVD and files that can be downloaded from a website. A large amount of PSI material is created within government, through the efforts of government employees and other persons who are not employed by government but produce copyright materials while working as volunteers (e.g. interns, students on work experience placements and members of emergency services teams). However, a significant part of the materials held by government is produced externally, by recipients of government funding (such as research institutes) and parties who are required to provide certain documents and reports to government (e.g. environmental impact assessments and information about water use, greenhouse gas emissions and results of mineral or petroleum exploration activities lodged under statutory or regulatory direction).

Systems to facilitate PSI access and reuse must be designed so that government-produced materials can flow both to other government agencies as well as to non-government users. In addition, government often needs to be able to on-distribute materials generated by a private sector party to others in the private sector. Any model for licensing of copyright PSI materials must be based on an understanding of how PSI is produced and how it flows, both within government and between government and the private sector.

As awareness has grown of the importance of enabling access to PSI, so have the barriers to achieving this objective become more readily apparent. The importance of clear policy frameworks and practices is increasingly well understood. However, as well as developing a policy framework, it is necessary to address the impediments presented by cultural factors and inadequate information management practices. The complexities of PSI creation and use mean that unless the conditions of use are stated in clear and easily understood terms, licensing is likely to prove to be an impediment to information flows.[10] To enable PSI to effectively flow to those who want to use it, the adoption of simple, clear and standardised

---

[9]   See generally, B Atkinson and B Fitzgerald (2008) *Copyright as an Instrument of Information Flow and Dissemination: the case of ICE TV Pty Ltd v Nine Network Australia Pty Ltd.*available at http://eprints.qut.edu.au/15208/ (accessed 29 January 2010).
[10]   See M Heller, *The Gridlock Economy – How Too Much Ownership Wrecks Markets, Stops Innovation and Costs Lives,* Basic Books, New York, 2008.

licences and the transparency of the conditions on which the PSI can be accessed and reused is of crucial importance.[11]

3. Creating a Commons of Public Sector Materials

From a copyright law perspective, the concept of "public domain" traditionally connoted materials that were not subject to copyright protection, whether because copyright had expired or because they did not qualify for copyright in the first place (such as mere facts or information and, in the United States, works produced by the federal government).[12]

During the last decade there has been a rethinking of what the public domain is[13] and how it functions,[14] such that it is now accepted that it has an intrinsic economic and cultural value,[15] and that its openness can be structured and reinforced by law (including copyright and contract).[16] With the changing role of knowledge in society and the economy, the concept of public domain has been recast more broadly to mean "open" knowledge and content – that is, ideas, information and materials that can be accessed, reused and redistributed by participants in an online social community.[17] This public domain – or commons – of openly accessible knowledge and content does not consist only of materials that are not subject to any rights whatsoever but, rather, encompasses materials that are protected by

---

[11]   See KPMG Consulting, *Executive Summary: Geospatial Data Policy Study – Project Report,* 2001, Recommendation 5 at pp 24-25, available at http://www.geoconnections.org/publications/policyDocs/keyDocs/KPMG/KPMG_E.pdf.

[12]   B Fitzgerald, A Fitzgerald et al, *Internet and E-Commerce Law: Technology, Law, and Policy,* Lawbook Co/Thomson, Sydney, 2007 at p 265. See also David Bollier, *Viral Spiral: How the Commoners Built a Digital Republic of Their Own,* The New Press, New York, 2008 at p 42, available at http://www.viralspiral.cc/download-book (accessed 10 December 2009).

[13]   See D Lange, *Recognising the Public Domain* (1981) 44 Law and Contemporary Problems 147.

[14]   See J Litman, *The Public Domain* (1990) 39 Emory L J 965.

[15]   See J Boyle, *The Second Enclosure Movement and the Construction of the Public Domain* (2003) 66 Law and Contemporary Problems 33; B Fitzgerald and I Oi, *Free Culture: Cultivating the Creative Commons* (2004) 9(2) Media and Arts LR 137; L Lessig, *The Future of Ideas: The Fate of the Commons in a Connected World,* Random House, New York, 2001.

[16]   J H Reichman and P F Uhlir, *A Contractually Reconstructed Research Commons for Scientific Data in a Highly Protectionist Intellectual Property Environment,* (2003) 66 Law & Contemporary Problems 315-462; A Fitzgerald and K Pappalardo, *Building the Infrastructure for Data Access and Reuse in Collaborative Research: An Analysis of the Legal Context,* OAK Law Project and Legal Framework for e-Research Project, QUT, Brisbane, July 2007, available online at http://www.oaklaw.qut.edu.au/files/Data_Report_final_web.pdf.

[17]   See Yochai Benkler, *Constitutional Bounds of Database Protection: The Role of Judicial Review in the Creation and Definition of Private Rights in Information,* (2000) 15 Berkley Tech. L J 535.

copyright but are made available for access and reuse under, for example, open source and open content licences.[18]

Based on this broader conceptualisation of public domain, much of the effort directed towards improving access to PSI is not now driven by assumptions that improved access and reuse can only be achieved in situations where copyright does not exist.[19] Although superficially attractive, the deficiencies of a "no copyright" approach towards the structuring of the public domain are now fairly well understood. There is a growing awareness that the key to facilitating access to public sector materials revolves not so much around the issues of subsistence and ownership of copyright, but depends rather on the licensing and pricing arrangements for access to and reuse of the material.[20]

In fact, there are very few jurisdictions worldwide that do not recognise copyright in government-produced materials, the most prominent example being the United States federal government.[21] United States' experience has led to a reappraisal of the appropriateness of the blanket "no copyright" rule, particularly where such works are subsequently included in proprietary products, often without any indication of the source, currency or accuracy of the PSI and absent its accompanying metadata or an explanation of what the material represents.[22] Increasingly, it is apparent that restrictions on access to and reuse of PSI are due less to the subsistence and ownership of copyright in government materials than to the failure to adopt a clear policy position on access and reuse and the lack of established practices (ranging from licensing to use of interoperable file formats)

---

[18]   For a discussion of the concept of "public domain", see R Pollock, *The Value of the Public Domain*, Institute for Public Policy Research, July 2006, available at http://www.ippr.org/publicationsandreports/publication.asp?id=482 (accessed 22 October 2008).

[19]   See Intrallect Ltd (E Barker and C Duncan) and AHRC Research Centre (A Guadamuz, J Hatcher and C Waelde), *The Common Information Environment and Creative Commons, Final Report*, October 2005, Ch 3.6, available at http://www.intrallect.com/index.php/intrallect/knowledge_base/general_articles/creative_co mmons_licensing_solutions_for_the_common_information_environment__1/ (accessed 29 January 2010).

[20]   See the "Copyright" principle, OECD, *Recommendation of the Council for Enhanced Access and More Effective Use of Public Sector Information*, C(2008)36, OECD, Paris, 2008, available at http://www.oecd.org/dataoecd/0/27/40826024.pdf.

[21]   The United States *Copyright Act* 1976, s 105 states: "Copyright protection under this title is not available for any work of the United States Government, but the United States Government is not precluded from receiving and holding copyrights transferred to it by assignment, bequest, or otherwise."

[22]   See Maj. B W Mitchell, *Works of the United States Government: Time to Consider Copyright Protection?*, LLM Thesis, George Washington University School of Law, Washington DC, 2002, available at http://www.stormingmedia.us/81/8166/A816604.html (accessed 10 December 2009).

supporting open access and reuse. As Professor Brian Fitzgerald stated in his submission to the CLRC's Crown Copyright review:

> Ten years ago the question would simply have been whether the Crown should or should not have copyright. Many advocating for no copyright would have been seeking open access to information. However, today we know more about the intricacies of open content licensing. It is arguable that a broader and more robust information commons can be developed by leveraging off copyright rather than merely "giving away" material.[23]

On the specific issue of copyright in judgments, Judge McGill of the District Court of Queensland commented that while abolishing copyright would bring "no obvious practical advantage" (since judgments are already widely disseminated), it could result in unforeseen disadvantages. Copyright ownership of judicial materials was not necessarily "inconsistent with having them readily available, but would be useful in discouraging inappropriate use of them".[24]

Advocates of the abolition of copyright in most or all government materials typically suggest that governments can exercise sufficient control over their PSI by other means, such as imposing contractual obligations on users, technological mechanisms and jurisdiction-specific laws governing the use of official government insignia displayed on government materials. These arguments were considered, but rejected, by the Victorian Parliament's Economic Development and Infrastructure Committee (EDIC) in its *Inquiry into Improving Access to Victorian Public Sector Information and Data*.[25] The Committee concluded that "[a]ccess to and re-use of PSI will be best facilitated by issuing licences in accordance with existing copyright provisions."[26]

---

[23]   Professor Brian Fitzgerald's submission to the Copyright Law Review Committee's review of Crown Copyright (2004) is available at http://www.ag.gov.au/agd/WWW/clrHome.nsf/Page/Present_Inquiries_Crown_copyright_S ubmissions_2004_Sub_No_17_-_Professor_Brian_Fitzgerald. See further B Fitzgerald, *The Australian Creative Commons Project*, (2005) 22(4) Copyright Reporter 138 at p 143.

[24]   Submission 70, p2, referred to in CLRC, *Crown Copyright,* 2005 at p 42, para 4.50.

[25]   Victorian Parliament, Economic Development and Infrastructure Committee, *Inquiry into Improving Access to Victorian Public Sector Information and Data (Final Report)*, June 2009, available at http://www.parliament.vic.gov.au/edic/inquiries/access_to_PSI/final_report.html accessed on 30 June 2009. See para 6.1.2 at p 66 and para 6.1.2.2 at p 67.

[26]   Ibid.

4. Advantages of a Copyright-based Licensing Approach

Adoption of a copyright-based, licensing approach for PSI has some distinct advantages that are not readily achievable otherwise. The most readily identified benefits of this approach are that it enables governments to achieve their open access policy objectives, ensures that information about the provenance of PSI is distributed along with it and avoids government and citizens being locked out (through pricing or technical barriers) from accessing and using materials produced with public funding.

4.1 SUPPORTS GOVERNMENT'S OPEN ACCESS POLICY OBJECTIVES

Where, as in Australia, governments own copyright in a very extensive range of materials, they are in the position of being able to manage their copyright interests through open content licensing strategies (such as CC licences), to create what amounts to a "commons" of PSI that can be readily accessed, used and reused by individuals, not for profit organisations and businesses.

While permitting a broad range of uses of PSI, government may often, justifiably, want to continue to be able to control the use of its material, even though that power may only rarely be exercised. This is especially the case where PSI takes the form of materials that are part of the official record or have authoritative status. An integral aspect of governmental responsibility is ensuring that important records and documents are distributed in an accurate and reliable form. For such materials, the continued recognition of copyright is regarded as central to ensuring the integrity and authenticity of PSI, so that the public can be aware of the status of each publication.[27] Distribution of PSI under copyright licensing conditions provides governments with a means of ensuring the integrity and authenticity of their materials, whether by terminating the licence and/or bringing an action for copyright infringement if materials are misused or misrepresented.[28]

---

[27]   See CLRC, *Crown Copyright,* 2005, footnote 93, para 4.66 at p 53 and para 4.68, at p 53, referring to Submission 64 (Victorian Government) at p 1.

[28]   See J Gilchrist, *The role of government as proprietor and disseminator of information,* (1996) Vol. 7, No. 1, Australian Journal of Corporate Law pp 62-79, at p 79. On this point, see also J Bannister, *Open Access to Legal Sources in Australasia: Current Debate on Crown Copyright and the Case of the Anthropomorphic Postbox* (1996) 3 Journal of Information, Law and Technology (JILT), available at http://www2.warwick.ac.uk/fac/soc/law/elj/jilt/1996_3/bannister (accessed 9 November 2009), commenting on *Baillieu and Poggioli (of and on behalf of the Liberal Party of Australia, Victorian Division) v Australian Electoral Commission and Commonwealth of Australia* [1996] FCA 1202.

4.2 PROVENANCE AND ATTRIBUTION

For much PSI, it is important that information about its origin, quality, currency and significance continues to be displayed on or in association with it, for example, by means of a metadata description accompanying the document or accessible via hyperlink. The credibility a user gives to information (whether generated by the public sector or otherwise) relates directly to who has created it and how, and what it represents. Ensuring that the provenance of PSI is properly documented is even more important for authoritative or official materials and in circumstances where correct attribution of ideas and information is a prerequisite to its public release, such as with scientific research results.[29] Using copyright-based licence conditions to ensure that provenance and attribution information is retained with PSI not only enhances its reliability but also significantly improves its discoverability by search engines. Where PSI represents the findings of scientific research, the inclusion of an attribution requirement in a copyright-based open content licence provides formal legal expression of the well-established normative practice of attribution that is central to "the traditional system under which [scientific] ideas and research output are shared".[30]

4.3 AVOIDS FINANCIAL AND TECHNICAL LOCK-UP OF TAXPAYER-FUNDED MATERIALS

In the absence of copyright protection for PSI, any recipient of PSI that is distributed without restrictions as to its reuse[31] is free to incorporate it into a new work. The newly created independent work may consist primarily of PSI which has been value added, for example, through features which better organise the base material and make it more easily searchable, or may consist largely of new materials produced by third parties. In either situation, the creator of the new work will own copyright and may assert their rights against all other parties, including the government, notwithstanding that the work has been produced by drawing on, and incorporates, PSI.[32] PSI is produced at taxpayers' expense. Yet, if PSI is distributed without copyright-based or other obligations designed to ensure

---

[29]   See V Stodden, *Enabling Reproducible Research: Licensing for Scientific Innovation* (2009) 13 International J of Communications Law & Policy at pp 18-19.

[30]   V Stodden, *Enabling Reproducible Research: Licensing for Scientific Innovation* (2009) 13 International J of Communications Law & Policy at p 18.

[31]   Such restrictions could apply under a contract between the government and a particular recipient or could apply generally under legislative provisions.

[32]   David Bollier, *Viral Spiral: How the Commoners Built a Digital Republic of Their Own,* The New Press, New York, 2008 at pp 192-193, available at http://www.viralspiral.cc/download-book (accessed 10 December 2009).

that it continues to be freely accessible and reusable, there is nothing to prevent a private entity from including it in a new, copyright-protected work access to which is restricted by legal and technological controls. Retaining copyright in PSI and distributing it under open content licences such as CC ensures that PSI released by the government continues to be freely available for access and reuse, even where it has been included in a value added commercial product or locked up behind technological measures. Importantly, copyright preserves the openness of PSI and avoids the situation which would see governments and citizens alike having to obtain permission and pay for the pleasure of using their publicly funded democratic and cultural heritage. [33]

5. Government ("Crown") Copyright

Under Australian law, copyright protects much of the creative, cultural, educational, scientific and informational material generated by federal, State/Territory and local governments and their constituent departments and agencies. Ownership of copyright by the government agencies is dealt with in Part VII of the *Copyright Act* 1968 (the "Crown copyright" provisions). Sections 176 and 178 of the *Copyright Act* 1968 provide that the government owns copyright in literary, dramatic, musical and artistic works, sound recordings and films "made by, or under the direction or control of the Commonwealth or a State". Section 177 further provides that the government owns copyright in a literary, dramatic, musical or artistic work that is first published in Australia "by, or under the direction or control of, the Commonwealth or a State". [34]

The meaning of the phrase "by, or under the direction or control of, [the Crown]" was considered by the Full Federal Court in *Copyright Agency Limited v State of New South Wales* [2007] FCAFC 80, which made it clear that governments will own copyright not only in works produced by their employees but by a more extensive (but not clearly defined) group:

> [122] "By" is concerned with those circumstances where a servant or agent of the Crown brings the work into existence for and on behalf of the Crown. "Direction" and "control" are not concerned with the situation where the work is made by the Crown but with situations where the person making the work is subject to either the

---

[33]   See Copyright Law Review Committee, *Crown Copyright,* 2005 at p 81, para 5.66, quoting from the submission by the New South Wales Attorney General's Department. A similar concern was expressed by the Federal government's Department of Finance and Administration.

[34]   Sections 176-178 are subject to any agreement between the Crown and the maker of the work or subject matter under which it is agreed that copyright is to belong to the author or maker or some other specified person (s 179).

direction or control of the Crown as to how the work is to be made. In the copyright context, that may mean how the work is to be expressed in a material form.

......

[125] Thus, when the provisions refer to a work being made under the direction or control of the Crown, in contrast to being made by the Crown, the provisions must involve the concept of the Crown bringing about the making of the work. It does not extend to the Crown laying down how a work is to be made, if a citizen chooses to make a work, without having any obligation to do so.[35]

Governments own copyright in a vast range of written and other materials (including legislation, judgments, parliamentary materials and reports of government-commissioned review bodies).[36] As the *Copyright Act* 1968 does not generally differentiate between the rights of government as copyright owner and the rights of private parties who own copyright, government can exercise the same range of rights as non-government copyright owners.[37] Consequently, to give effect to their information access and reuse policies, governments need to develop and implement copyright management strategies to ensure that their exclusive rights are exercised consistently with their open access objectives.

The primary rights of copyright are the rights to reproduce (copy), first publish, publicly perform, make an adaptation[38] of the work and to communicate it to the public in digital form (e.g. on a website).[39] Other important rights of copyright owners in the digital era are the rights to ensure that electronic rights management information (ERMI) is not removed or altered and to prevent the circumvention of technological protection measures (TPM) they apply to their copyright materials to control access to or copying of it.

---

[35]   See *Copyright Agency Limited v State of New South Wales* [2007] FCAFC 80, paras 122 – 125, where the Full Federal Court considered the meaning of the phrase "by, or under the direction or control of, [the Crown]" .
[36]   For a listing of the various kinds of copyright materials produced by or for governments, see CLRC, *Crown Copyright,* 2005 at pp 10-11, available at http://www.clrc.gov.au/www/agd/agd.nsf/Page/RWPBB79ED8E4858F514CA25735100827 559 (accessed 9 November 2009). For discussion of copyright in judgments being owned by government, see pp 46-48.
[37]   Section 182 specifically states that, apart from the provisions in Part VII of the *Copyright Act* 1968 (in ss 176-181) relating to the subsistence, duration and ownership of copyright, the provisions of Part III and Part IV of the Act apply. One of the few points of difference is that the duration of copyright for materials within the scope of ss 176 – 178 is 50 years from the end of the calendar year in which the copyright item is first published or is made (ss 180, 181).
[38]   For literary, dramatic and musical works: *Copyright Act* 1968, s 31(1)(a)(vi).
[39]   *Copyright Act* 1968, ss 31, 85-88.

ERMI is electronic information (including numbers or codes representing such information) which is either attached to or embodied in the copyright material, or appears in connection with a communication or the making available of the copyright material.[40] It is an infringement of the copyright owner's rights to remove or alter ERMI relating to a copyright work or other subject matter without the permission of the copyright owner or exclusive licensee, if the person doing the act knows or ought reasonably to have known that the removal or alteration would induce, enable, facilitate or conceal an infringement of copyright.[41] The anti-circumvention provisions enable copyright owners to protect their materials by applying technical measures that control access to or copying of the work. It is an infringement to knowingly deal in devices designed to circumvent TPMs[42] and, where the TPM controls access to a copyright work, it is an infringement to knowingly circumvent the TPM.[43]

As well as the rights described above, individual authors of copyright works can also exercise moral rights, which are personal to the author and cannot be transferred. They are the right of attribution, the right against false attribution and the right of integrity. [44]

Although government does not, itself, have moral rights, government may own copyright in materials in respect of which individual authors can exercise moral rights. This situation can arise where copyright ownership vests in the government (including through an assignment of rights) but the individual creator of the materials has not consented that their moral rights will not be respected.[45] As moral rights are not transferred along with copyright, the individual creator will still be able to exercise their moral rights unless they have agreed not to exercise them.

While government, as copyright owner, enjoys the same exclusive economic rights as other copyright owners, the nature and purpose of

---

[40] The main provisions dealing with ERMI are set out in Division 2A, Subdivision B of the *Copyright Act* 1968. Section 116D sets out the legal remedies (including an injunction or damages) available for the removal of and interference with ERMI. See *Copyright Act* 1968, s10(1) for the definition of ERMI.

[41] *Copyright Act* 1968, ss 116B-116D. In certain circumstances the removal or alteration of ERMI relating to a copyright work may be a criminal offence under the *Copyright Act* (ss 132AQ-132AS).

[42] *Copyright Act* 1968, s 116AO(1).

[43] *Copyright Act* 1968, s 116AN(1). The meaning of the statutory definition "access control technological protection measure" (TPM), appearing in section 10(1) of the *Copyright Act* 1968, was considered by the High Court in *Stevens v Kabushiki Kaisha Sony Computer Entertainment* [2005] HCA 58. See B Fitzgerald, A Fitzgerald et al, *Internet and E-Commerce Law: Technology, Law, and Policy*, Lawbook Co/Thomson, Sydney, 2007, at pp 223-230.

[44] *Copyright Act* 1968, Part IX, ss 189-195AZR.

[45] Subject to their terms of employment, government employees may be entitled to moral rights in respect of copyright works which they authored.

government copyright means that these rights should not be exercised in a way that restricts the flow of PSI. It seems to be widely acknowledged, in Australia and other jurisdictions that at least part of the original rationale for government copyright ownership was to "promote the accuracy and integrity of official government publications".[46] Consequently, the exclusive rights to copy, publish, perform and distribute electronically to the public would not usually be exercised by governments to restrict the distribution of accurate and integral copies of the vast majority of government copyright materials. The exercise of these rights to prevent others from using government works would occur only in a narrow and distinct range of circumstances, such as to halt the circulation of erroneous or falsely attributed materials or where it is necessary for national security reasons.

Copyright should not, as a general practice, be relied upon by governments for secondary purposes not directly related to the exercise of Crown copyright (such as to restrict access to government documents containing confidential or otherwise sensitive information).[47] Where, under an open access policy, PSI has been identified as suitable to make available for access and reuse, the government should not rely on copyright to control use of the work, irrespective of the purpose for which the PSI is used.

6. Creative Commons Licences

Creative Commons (CC) licences are standardized, "open content" copyright licences which grant permission to use copyright works, in accordance with the terms of the particular set of template clauses applied by the licensor (who may be the copyright owner or another person who has the authority to license the material). "Open content" licences are based on copyright, with the copyright owner retaining ownership and exercising their rights liberally to ensure that the work can be accessed and used. While copyright is claimed in the work, under the terms of an open content licence, the copyright owner exercises their exclusive rights to permit the

---

[46]   See Copyright Law Review Committee, *Crown Copyright,* 2005 at p xxiv, available at
http://www.clrc.gov.au/www/agd/agd.nsf/Page/RWPBB79ED8E4858F514CA25735100827 559.

[47]   See CLRC, *Crown Copyright,* 2005 at p 39. See also J Gilchrist, *The role of government as proprietor and disseminator of information,* (1996) vol. 7, no. 1, Australian Journal of Corporate Law pp 62-79, at p 62 (criticising the use of copyright to preserve confidentiality of documents in in *Commonwealth v Fairfax* (1980) 147 CLR 39) .

copying, publication and distribution by users for a wide range of purposes, subject only to restrictions on certain kinds of reuse.[48]

The open content model of copyright licensing can be contrasted with traditional, "all rights reserved" copyright licensing practices in which the copyright owner exercises their rights by limiting the use of the copyright material to specified persons and purposes. The focus of traditional copyright licensing is on the exercise of the exclusive rights to reproduce and distribute copies of the work, with rights being granted to specific parties, on certain conditions and often for some economic return to the licensor. Open content licensing, by contrast, is predicated on the exercise of the exclusive rights to permit reproduction and distribution by all users, subject to specific conditions applying to use of the copyright work.[49]

As open content licensing starts from the premise that copyright will be exercised to permit reproduction and distribution of the copyright material by users (although there may be other conditions of use), it is particularly relevant in systems designed to facilitate access to and re-use of PSI, especially where material is distributed online in digital form. While acknowledging the government's ownership of copyright in the material, open content licences enable a government to give effect to its open access policy and to set the conditions on which PSI may be accessed and reused. Open access licences such as CC can be seen as both the legal expression of a policy supporting access and reuse and the means of implementing the policy. Although it was not initially envisaged or intended that CC licences would be used on government materials, their potential for use by governments and publicly funded research institutes was soon recognised, particularly in jurisdictions such as Australia where copyright subsists in a vast range of PSI.[50]

---

[48] See N Suzor and B Fitzgerald, "The Role of Open Content Licences in Building Open Content Communities: Creative Commons, GFDL and Other Licences", in C Kapitzke and M Peters (eds.) *Global knowledge cultures*, 2007, Sense Publishers, Rotterdam, Netherlands, pp 145-159.

[49] Whilst there are 6 types of Creative Commons licences, the most appropriate for use with most PSI in practice is the CC-BY (attribution) licence, with CC- BY- ND (no derivatives) being appropriate for a more limited segment of PSI. By contrast, the use by government of either of the Share Alike licences may in practice result in more restricted reuse than intended.

[50] An early Australian example of recognition of the potential for applying CC licences to PSI is the GILF project. See Queensland Government, Queensland Spatial Information Council, *Government Information and Open Content Licensing: An access and use strategy* (Government Information Licensing Framework Project Stage 2 Report), October 2006, (hereinafter referred to as "GILF Stage 2 Report") available at http://www.qsic.qld.gov.au/qsic/QSIC.nsf/CPByUNID/BFDC06236FADB6814A25727B00 13C7EE accessed 14 November 2009. See the submission by Professor Brian Fitzgerald to the Copyright Law Review Committee at http://www.ag.gov.au/agd/WWW/clrHome.nsf/Page/Present_Inquiries_Crown_copyright_S ubmissions_2004_Sub_No_17_-_Professor_Brian_Fitzgerald.

7. Creative Commons – Australian Licences

Creative Commons (CC) licences were devised from the outset to operate in both the digital, online and analog environments and aimed to be user friendly for non-lawyers.[51] Each of the CC licences contains standardised licensing terms describing user permissions in simple ("human readable") language, depicted by symbols (the "Licence Deed" or "Commons Deed"), a legally enforceable ("lawyer readable") licence (the "Legal Code"), and computer ("machine readable") code (the "Digital Code" or "Licence Metadata").

Australian versions of the CC licences were released in January 2005. They enable owners of materials that qualify for protection under the *Copyright Act* 1968 to license them in accordance with Australian law. The Australian CC licences contain the same basic elements as those found in the international CC licences, but in terms crafted to reflect Australian law.[52] The current version of the Australian CC licences is version 2.5; work on porting the updated version 3.0 of the licences is underway and version 3.0 of the Australian licences will be published in 2010. In Australia, the Creative Commons office is based at the Queensland University of Technology (QUT), in Brisbane, Queensland.[53]

Under each of the CC licences, users are expressly granted permission to do a range of specified acts in relation to the licensed material – these are referred to here as the "baseline rights". However, CC licences do not grant users the right to do everything within the scope of the copyright owner's rights but, rather, some of the rights are kept (or "reserved") by the owner. In reliance on the rights retained by the copyright owner, under CC licences the licensor – as well as granting rights to users – imposes restrictions (or conditions) on the use of the licensed material. The recipient of a CC-licensed work is permitted to exercise the rights granted, subject to respecting the restrictions (or conditions) imposed by the copyright owner. In practice, the user of a CC-licensed work will be required, depending on which CC licence has been selected by the licensor, to observe conditions

---

[51]   For the background to the Creative Commons licences, see David Bollier, *Viral Spiral: How the Commoners Built a Digital Republic of their Own*, The New Press, New York, 2008, available at http://www.viralspiral.cc/download-book (accessed 10 December 2009); B Fitzgerald, "Structuring open access to knowledge: The Creative Commons story", in C Kapitzke and B Bertram (eds), *Libraries: Changing information space and practice*, 2006, Lawrence Erlbaum Associates, pp 271-280.

[52]   The CC licences do not limit or remove statutory rights, such as "fair dealing", conferred under the *Copyright Act* 1968 (Cth).

[53]   The office was established under the terms of an Affiliation Agreement entered into between QUT and Creative Commons Corporation in 2004. The QUT Project leads are Professor Tom Cochrane and Professor Brian Fitzgerald. For more information on the CC licences see the Creative Commons Australia (CCau) website at http://www.creativecommons.org.au.

that range from simply acknowledging the author of the work (or the copyright owner as indicated), to refraining from using it for commercial purposes or from making any derivative works.

The baseline rights granted under the CC licences are:
- to reproduce the work;
- to incorporate the work into Collective Works;[54]
- to reproduce the work as incorporated in the Collective Works; and
- to publish, communicate to the public, distribute copies or records of, exhibit or display publicly or perform publicly the Work (including as incorporated in Collective Works).[55]

Each of the CC licences – other than those which include a "No Derivative Works" condition – also grant the user the rights:
- to create and reproduce Derivative Works;[56] and
- to publish, communicate to the public, distribute copies or records of, exhibit or display publicly or perform publicly the Derivative Works.[57]

There are four standardised sets of conditions which can be applied by copyright owners when licensing their materials under a CC licence:

 Attribution (BY): The work is made available to the public with the baseline rights, on condition that the work is distributed with the licensing information, the author or another specified person (e.g. the custodian) is attributed in the manner specified in the licence, the work is not falsely attributed to another person and the work is not distorted or altered to the prejudice of the author's reputation. The Attribution (BY) condition applies to each of the current Australian CC licences.

---

[54] As defined in Clause 1(a), Legal Code, Attribution 2.5 Australia to mean "a work, such as a periodical issue, anthology or encyclopedia, in which the Work in its entirety in its unmodified form, along with a number of other contributions, constituting separate and independent works in themselves, are assembled into a collective whole."

[55] Clause 3(a) – (d), Legal Code, Attribution 2.5 Australia.

[56] As defined in Clause 1(b), Legal Code, Attribution 2.5 Australia to mean "a work that reproduces a substantial part of the Work, or of the Work and other pre-existing works protected by copyright, or that is an adaptation of a Work that is a literary, dramatic, musical or artistic work…[but] a work that constitutes a Collective Work will not be considered a Derivative Work for the purpose of this Licence".

[57] Clause 3(a) – (d), Legal Code, Attribution 2.5 Australia.

Non-Commercial (NC): The work can be copied, displayed and distributed, provided any use of the material is for non-commercial purposes.[58]

 No Derivative Works (ND): This licence grants baseline rights, but it does not allow Derivative Works to be created from the original. A Derivative Work is one in which a substantial part of the licensed work is reproduced or an adaptation of the work (for example, a translation or dramatisation).

 Share Alike (SA): Derivative works based on the licensed work can be created, but the Derivative Work must be distributed under a Share Alike licence, creating a "viral" licence aimed at maintaining the openness of the original work.[59]

These four sets of conditions, together with the baseline permissions, can be combined to create six licences:

- Attribution 2.5 (BY)
- Attribution No Derivatives 2.5 (BY-ND)
- Attribution Non-Commercial 2.5 (BY-NC)
- Attribution Non-Commercial No Derivatives 2.5 (BY-NC-ND)
- Attribution Non-Commercial Share Alike 2.5 (BY-NC-SA)
- Attribution Share Alike 2.5 (BY-SA)[60]

8. Advantages of using Creative Commons Licences on Government Copyright Materials

CC licences have several advantages for governments in managing copyright to give effect to open access policy objectives. Where an open access policy has been adopted, CC licences provide a means of managing copyright to establish a commons of PSI in which the broadest possible rights of access and reuse are conferred on all users.

8.1 ENFORCEABILITY

---

[58] Creative Commons has conducted consultations around the meaning of the term "non-commercial". In September 2009, Creative Commons published the report, *Defining "Noncommercial": A Study of How the Online Population Understands "Noncommercial Use"*, See http://creativecommons.org/press-releases/entry/17721 and http://wiki.creativecommons.org/Defining_Noncommercial (accessed on 21 January 2010).
[59] It is important to note that a licence cannot feature both the Share Alike and No Derivative Works options. The Share Alike requirement applies only to derivative works.
[60] See http://creativecommons.org.au/licences (accessed on 24 May 2010).

It is not disputed that bare (non-contractual) licences applied to copyright materials distributed in digital form on the internet will be recognised and enforced by the Australian courts. This much was established in Australia as far back as 1996 in *Trumpet Software v OzEmail* [1996] FCA 560, a case involving shareware distributed on openly accessible FTP sites.[61] If a copyright owner grants a licence authorising the doing of certain of the acts within the owner's exclusive rights under s 31 of the Copyright Act, any such act will be deemed to have been done with the permission of the copyright owner. However, if the licensee does acts outside the scope of their licence, those acts may infringe copyright.[62]

Notwithstanding (or perhaps because of) the widespread use of CC and other open content and open source licences, there have been relatively few cases in which their validity and enforceability has been tested in court.[63] The most authoritative consideration to date of the effectiveness of open source licences is the decision of the United States Court of Appeals for the Federal Circuit in *Jacobsen v Katzer* in August 2008.[64] Although the licence at issue was an open source licence of computer programming code, the decision is of direct relevance to CC licences as Creative Commons intervened in the appeal as *amici curiae*. In this case, software was licensed for no fee under a copyright-based open source licence (the "Artistic License") which permitted users to modify and distribute the copyright material, subject to a requirement that certain attribution and identification information was distributed along with it. As the authorisation to modify and distribute the software was subject to the conditions expressly stated in the open source licence, by failing to include the copyright notices and the "copying" file, the defendant had gone beyond the scope of the licence and thereby infringed copyright. From the decision in *Jacobsen v Katzer* it is clear that open source and CC licences will be upheld by the courts, even though they are applied to copyright materials distributed for no financial reward, and that failure to comply with the licence conditions may be an infringement of copyright, for which the usual remedies will apply. CC

---

61   *Trumpet Software Pty Ltd & Anor v OzEmail Pty Ltd & Ors* [1996] FCA 560.
62   See: *Quanta Software International Pty Ltd v Computer Management Services Pty Ltd* [2001] FCA 1459 and *Sullivan v FNH Investments Pty Ltd* [2003] FCA 323.
63   L Rosen, *Bad facts make good law: The Jacobsen case and Open Source,* (2009) 1 International Free and Open Source Software Law Review 27.
64   *Jacobsen v. Katzer,* 535 F.3d 1373 (Fed.Cir. Aug 13, 2008), on remand, *Jacobsen v. Katzer,* 609 F.Supp.2d 925 (N.D.Cal. Jan 5, 2009), available at http://www.cafc.uscourts.gov/opinions/08-1001.pdf. For comment, see: B Fitzgerald and R Olwan, , "The Legality of Free and Open Source Software Licences: the case of *Jacobsen v. Katzer*" in M. Perry and B. Fitzgerald (eds.) *Knowledge Policy for the 21st Century*, Irwin Law Toronto, 2008, available at http://eprints.qut.edu.au/15148/ (accessed 29 January 2010).

licences have also been enforced in the Netherlands and Bulgaria,[65] treated as valid in court cases in Spain and enforced in Norway.[66]

8.2 EXPLICIT STATEMENT OF REUSE RIGHTS

Government agencies can use CC licences to clearly communicate to users just what they are permitted to do with the licensed PSI, without having to seek permission or to engage in time-consuming negotiation of licensing conditions.

Where a copyright notice is displayed on government websites and other materials, the statement typically addresses what the user cannot do and requires them to seek express permission (sometimes, in writing) to do anything beyond the very circumscribed range of permitted activities. [67] A very real advantage of using open content licences drafted along the model found in the CC licence suite is that they expressly tell users what they can do with the licensed material.[68] In keeping with the nature and purpose of government copyright, typically, the only restrictions imposed on users (where a CC BY licence is applied to PSI) will be a requirement to maintain the licensing information, to properly attribute the licensor, to not falsely attribute another party as licensor and to distribute accurate copies of the material.

8.3 CLEAR STATEMENT THAT INFORMATION IS SOURCED FROM GOVERNMENT – INCREASED USER CONFIDENCE

The amount of information accessible online is increasing exponentially, and is of variable quality and reliability. Importantly, all CC licences have a requirement that attribution be given to the author, or other party (e.g. the owner of copyright) designated for the purposes of attribution. In this way the source of the information is identified clearly to the user. Where the source is clear the user may make an informed decision about whether or not to use the information or the degree of credence to be given to it.

---

[65]   See "Creative Commons Bulgaria Licence upheld in court", Veni Markovski, 9 June 2008, at http://blog.veni.com/?p=494.
[66] See "Creative Commons License Honoured, US$ 2150 for Flickr Photo", on Gisele Hannemyr's "Trails" blog, 15 October 2006, at http://heim.ifi.uio.no/~gisle/blog/?p=92, accessed 14 November 2009.
[67]   See Catherine Bond, *The State of Licensing: Towards Reuse of NSW Government Information,* Unlocking IP Working Paper, [2006] AIPLRes 43, at http://www.austlii.edu.au/other/AIPLRes/2006/43.html.
[68]   Siu-Ming Tam, Australian Bureau of Statistics, *Informing the Nation – Open Access to Statistical Information in Australia,* paper presented to the United Nations Economic Commission for Europe (UNECE) Work Session on the Communication and Dissemination of Statistics, Poland, May 2009, at para 34, available http://www.unece.org/stats/documents/ece/ces/ge.45/2009/wp.11.e.pdf.

Conversely, if the provenance of information is not stated in clear and transparent terms, the degree of confidence a user may have in it will diminish, reducing the likelihood that - and the extent to which - the information will be used or relied upon.[69]

Another advantage of adopting a standard practice of applying CC licences to copyright material is that it prospectively avoids the problem of so-called "orphan" copyright works, for which it is not possible to identify or locate the copyright owner in order to obtain permission to use the material. With respect to PSI, the problems currently encountered with orphan works could be virtually eliminated in the future if metadata – including the name of the creator/s of the work, copyright owner/s and licensing permissions - were to be attached to or embedded in copyright works at the time they are created and before distribution.

8.4 UNIVERSAL RECOGNITION OF SYMBOLS

The symbols used to indicate the terms of CC licences have the advantage of being widely recognised and understood, irrespective of the language in which the Licence Deed or Legal Code is written, or the location of the licensor. This is a particularly important advantage for works distributed online in digital form. When a government agency applies a CC licence and related symbols to a public sector work, the terms on which the work can be used are readily apparent to users, independently of their jurisdiction or language.

8.5 DISCOVERABILITY OF DIGITAL OBJECTS

CC licences are designed for the web 2.0 environment. Each of the CC licences is expressed in machine readable Digital Code (or Licence Metadata) which is used to "tag" the digital object (or file), as well as the web page that links to it. Unlike the static copyright notices typically found on government websites, the Digital Code of CC licences travels with the digital object, facilitating the distribution and discoverability of CC licensed works. [70]

The machine-readable Digital Code enables CC-licensed materials to be indexed and retrieved by search engines such as Google, along with the licensing information. The inclusion of both the human-readable Licence

---

[69] See further Dr Prodromos Tsiavos, *Case Studies Mapping the Flows of Content, Value and Rights across the Public Sector*, March 2009, the Executive Summary, p 6, and p 40, para 5.4.1., available at www.jisc.ac.uk/contentalliance.

[70] New Zealand Government, State Services Commission, *Draft New Zealand Government Open Access and Licensing Framework* (NZGOAL), August 2009, at p 18, available at http://www.e.govt.nz/policy/information-data/nzgoalframework.html (accessed 25 January 2010).

Deed and the machine-readable Digital Code means that a user is immediately provided with information about what they can and cannot do with the material, which can be verified by checking with the licensor.

8.6 ENABLE LEGAL REMIXING OF COPYRIGHT MATERIALS

A significant impediment to the efficient sharing and reuse of PSI is the diversity of licensing practices and the lack of consistency or compatibility of the rights granted to users. Incompatibility of licence terms creates a legal logjam and presents a major obstacle to the ready flow of PSI. Although it may be possible, technologically, to obtain access to, and to mix and match (mash up or remix) various information inputs or products, this does not mean that such remixing or reuse of the information inputs or products is lawful.[71]

Open content licences such as CC are a legally effective and efficient way in which to promote globally compatible reuse rights for copyright material, including PSI. The Government Information Licensing Framework (GILF) project was instigated by QSIC specifically to address the recurring problems in accessing and sharing spatial information among government agencies and utility service providers during and after natural disasters,[72] due to the fragmented, inefficient and confusing arrangements for information access and reuse.[73] For the Australian Bureau of Statistics the recognition that, even after making much of its data freely available online, the potential remained for its licensing practices to form "an undesirable barrier to those wishing to reuse significant amounts of data" led to the decision to go a step further and adopt Creative Commons licensing for its online data.[74]

---

[71]   On the importance of being able to remix from among a wide range of existing materials, see Dr T Culter, *The Role of Cultural Collections in Australia's Innovation System*, keynote address presented at the State Library of Victoria, 23 October 2009, at pp 3-4. Dr Cutler introduces the term "combinatorial innovation" to refer to remix.

[72]   In Queensland, these problems were highlighted by destructive Cyclone Larry in 2005; in Victoria, the 2009 bushfires, in which many perished, demonstrated the criticality of real time, spatially-related information to enable effective emergency response management.

[73]   GILF Stage 2 Report, available at http://www.qsic.qld.gov.au/qsic/QSIC.nsf/CPByUNID/BFDC06236FADB6814A25727B00 13C7EE. See also http://www.gilf.gov.au.

[74]   Siu-Ming Tam, Australian Bureau of Statistics, *Informing the Nation – Open Access to Statistical Information in Australia,* paper presented to the United Nations Economic Commission for Europe (UNECE) Work Session on the Communication and Dissemination of Statistics, Poland, May 2009, at para 32, available at http://www.unece.org/stats/documents/ece/ces/ge.45/2009/wp.11.e.pdf.

8.7 MONITORING LEVELS OF USAGE

With the increasing sophistication of online search capabilities it is now practicable for licensors to monitor the level of usage of their material licensed in the online world. This ability largely removes the need for licensors to continue to seek to impose a reporting obligation on a licensee to record and report back on the number of licences granted over a specified period. Now, the licensor can simply do an internet search for the licensed material, largely eliminating the need for detailed reporting conditions.

9. Conclusion

How best to manage PSI to foster innovation is one of the most significant challenges faced by governments at the present time. Unlocking the potential of the huge amount of informational, creative, educational and scientific material produced or funded by government requires the development and implementation of copyright management and licensing strategies that facilitate access and reuse.[75] Recent Australian experience has shown that CC licences offer a legally and operationally effective means by which much copyright protected PSI may be unlocked for innovative reuse. Open content licensing supports the shift by government towards open access policies and practices. Initiatives by Australian governments at the Federal, State and local level have shown that CC licences provide the "simple, open and internationally recognised licensing framework" which is required in order to maximise the value of PSI in the web 2.0 era.[76] Governments are increasingly delivering information and services online with the increasing efficiencies that it brings. The adoption of CC licences by Australian governments is a logical step towards utilising

---

[75]   B Fitzgerald, "It's vital to sort out the ownership of ideas" February 27, 2008, The Australian (Higher Education Supplement)
http://www.theaustralian.news.com.au/story/0,25197,23280526-25192,00.html; B Fitzgerald and B Atkinson 'Third Party Copyright and Public Information Infrastructure/Registries: How much copyright tax must the public pay? in B Fitzgerald and M Perry (eds), *Knowledge Policy for the 21st Century* , 2008, available at
http://eprints.qut.edu.au/archive/000113627/; Tracey P. Lauriault and Hugh McGuire, "Data Access in Canada: CivicAccess.ca" (2008)
http://www.osbr.ca/ojs/index.php/osbr/article/view/514; M van Eechoud and B van der Wal, *Creative Commons Licensing for Public Sector Information: Opportunities and Pitfalls,* 2007, available at http://www.ivir.nl/creativecommons/index-en.html.
[76]   Siu-Ming Tam, Australian Bureau of Statistics, *Informing the Nation – Open Access to Statistical Information in Australia,* paper presented to the United Nations Economic Commission for Europe (UNECE) Work Session on the Communication and Dissemination of Statistics, Poland, May 2009, at para 33, available at
http://www.unece.org/stats/documents/ece/ces/ge.45/2009/wp.11.e.pdf.

the functionality available through web 2.0 technologies (and beyond) for the benefit of all sectors of the Australian community. The adoption of CC licences by all levels of government in the online environment will fuel the development of a vibrant global commons of PSI, the real value of which can only be realised when it is reused for social, economic and cultural benefit.

References

Australian Government, Department of Broadband, Communications and the Digital Economy, Australia's Digital Economy: Future Directions, July 2009, available at http://www.dbcde.gov.au/?a=117295.

Cutler & Company (for the Australian Government Department of Innovation, Industry, Science and Research), Venturous Australia - Building Strength in Innovation, report on the Review of the National Innovation System, 29 August 2008, available at http://www.innovation.gov.au/innovationreview/Pages/home.aspx.

Fitzgerald A, Open Access Policies, Practices and Licensing: A review of the literature in Australia and selected jurisdictions, QUT, July 2009, available at http://www.aupsi.org/news/CompiledLiteratureReviewnowavailableinhardcopy.jsp.

Fitzgerald, A.; Fitzgerald, B.; Hooper, N. (2010), Enabling open access to public sector information with Creative Commons Licences : the Australian experience, in 'Access to Public Sector Information : Law, Technology & Policy', Sydney University Press, Sydney, 2010, available at: http://eprints.qut.edu.au/29773/ (accessed 17 May 2010).

Fitzgerald, A, (2010) Open access and public sector information: policy developments in Australia and key jurisdictions in 'Access to Public Sector Information: Law, Technology and Policy', Sydney University Press, Sydney, 2010, available at: http://eprints.qut.edu.au/31024/ (accessed 17 May 2010).

Government 2.0 Taskforce, Engage: Getting on with Government 2.0 – Report of the Government 2.0 Taskforce, Department of Finance and Deregulation, 2009, available at http://gov2.net.au/report.

Queensland Spatial Information Office, Office of Economic and Statistical Research, Queensland Treasury, Government Information and Open Content Licensing: An Access and Use Strategy, Government Information Licensing Framework Project Stage 2 Report, October 2006, available at http://www.qsic.qld.gov.au/QSIC/QSIC.nsf/0/F82522D9F23F6F1C4A2572EA007D57A6/$FILE/Stage%202%20Final%20Report%20-%20PDF%20Format.pdf?openelement.

Victorian Parliament, Economic Development and Infrastructure Committee, Inquiry into Improving Access to Victorian Public Sector Information and Data (Final Report), June 2009, available at http://www.parliament.vic.gov.au/edic/inquiries/access_to_PSI/final_report.html.

Government of Victoria, Whole of Government Response to the Final Report of the Economic Development and Infrastructure Committee's Inquiry into

Improving Access to Victorian Public Sector Information and Data, February 2010, available at http://www.diird.vic.gov.au/diird-projects/access-to-public-sector-information.

Legal Commons and Social Commons
Creativity and Innovation in the Global Peripheries

Ronaldo Lemos
Center for Technology & Society (Fundacao Getulio Vargas), Law School, Rio de Janeiro

Abstract. This article describes the idea of legal commons in contrast with the idea of social commons. While the idea of legal commons can be understood as the voluntary use of licenses such as Creative Commons in order to create a "commons", the idea of social commons has to do with the tensions between legality and illegality in developing countries. These tensions appear prominently in the so-called global "peripheries", and often make the legal structure of intellectual property irrelevant, unfamiliar, or unenforceable for various reasons.

With the emergence of digital technology and the Internet, in many places and regions in developing countries (especially in the "peripheries"), technology ended up arriving earlier than the idea of intellectual property. Such a de facto situation propitiated the emergence of cultural industries that were not driven by intellectual property incentives. In these cultural businesses, the idea of "sharing" and of free dissemination of the content is intrinsic to the social circumstances taking place in these peripheries. Also, the appropriation of technology on the part of the "peripheries" ends up promoting autonomous forms of bridging the digital divide, such as the "LAN house" phenomenon discussed below. This paper proposes that many lessons can be learnt from the business models emerging from social commons practices in developing countries.

The tension between legality and illegality in "peripheral" areas in developing countries is not new. The work of Boaventura de Sousa Santos (1977) and others in the 1970s was paradigmatic for the discussion of legal pluralism regarding the occupation of land in Brazil. This paper aims to follow in that same pioneer tradition of studies about legal pluralism, and to apply those principles to the discussion of "intellectual property" rather than the ownership of land.

Keywords: Creative Commons, Social Commons, Legal pluralism, Intellectual Property, Global Peripheries,

1. Introduction

Chapter 2 of this paper describes two different phenomena. The first is the appropriation of technology on the part of the Brazilian "peripheries", i.e., the most marginalized and poor areas in the country. It describes, for instance, the emergence of bottom-up entrepreneurial initiatives that are bridging the digital divide in unexpected ways, such as the "lan-house" phenomenon. The second is the emergence of new business models in the global peripheries, such as the *tecnobrega* music scene in the North of Brazil, and the Nigerian film industry.

The third chapter discusses how the idea of "legal commons", such as the "creative commons" is transformed and acquires different meanings in developing countries such as Brazil.

2. Innovation Arising from the Global Peripheries

Access to computers is in many cases restricted in Brazil. In spite of the digital divide, the last few years have seen a profound change in the ways technology are being appropriated by different segments of the Brazilian society, including at the so-called "peripheries". This appropriation of technology by the poorest and most marginalized segments of the population is producing new types of bottom-up entrepreneurial activities. One of the most important is the emergence of the so-called "LAN houses", which have succeeded in bringing computers connected to the internet to some of the poorest regions in Brazil.

2.1. LAN HOUSES AS THE NEW TOOL FOR DIGITAL INCLUSION

There is a new center of digital convergence for youth in low-income Brazilian neighborhoods (and perhaps global ones). This point of convergence is represented by LAN houses[1], small businesses such as street stores or kiosks filled with computers where members of the community go to access the Internet and to play multiplayer games on a network. LAN houses are extremely popular among young people from all social backgrounds. Due to this popularity, the number of LAN houses has increased rapidly in Brazil in recent years. Today, the majority of poor neighborhoods in Brazil, even in smaller towns or in the favelas (shantytowns), now have at least one LAN house.

General initiatives for bridging the digital divide in developing countries always face at least two challenges: social efficacy and economic sustainability. The social efficacy problem arises in most cases in connection because of difficulties in the assimilation of the initiative on the part of the community. The possibility of burglary and robbery increases when, for instance, the digital inclusion initiative is regarded as an extraneous element to the community, a sort of external intervention in community life. This creates the perspective of "otherness" and prevents the integration of the project in the community, which in turn prevents a feeling of community responsibility for its maintenance. In addition, it is

---

[1]   The term LAN stands for "Local Area Network", meaning that all the computers in a LAN house are connected to each other, forming a network. This network allows the users to play games and interact with each other. Most of the LAN houses also have a connection between the entire network and the internet.

worth pointing out that many digital inclusion initiatives implemented in Brazil prohibit the use of electronic games in their computers. This policy neglects to consider the fact that many children, from all social classes, develop an interest in computers specifically because of videogames. As a result, a significant percentage of youth are drawn away from publicly funded telecenters, including some of those young people who would most benefit from familiarity with computers and the internet.

Economic sustainability problems are a significant challenge when funding for digital inclusion initiatives is available only for a limited period of time. After the exhaustion of the funds, many projects are left to their own fate to find ways to sustain themselves. In the short term, economic problems lead to technological obsolescence. In the mid-term, these problems often lead to the dismantling of the projects. The positive impact of the digital inclusion policies, accordingly, may unfortunately be small and limited in time.

The rise of LAN houses in poor areas, however, shows that digital inclusion can be achieved not only by public or semi-public efforts, but also through the private sector. The problems of social efficacy and economic sustainability that tend to plague large, publicly funded initiatives can be significantly mitigated within the LAN house model. The LAN houses are generally small enterprises, created with private funds and owned in most cases by a member of the community in which they are located. These community entrepreneurs have direct, local knowledge about the daily practices of the community that allows them to evaluate the best place to set up the store and the computers. Further, the owner of the LAN house is working for profit, and therefore attempts to maximize the number of customers that the store receives, usually by enabling the multiplayer games either on the local network or through the Internet. That has an impact on the economic sustainability: games tend to be extremely appealing for young people, and the relatively low prices (in general, approximately US$0.50 per hour) ensure that even lower-income citizens will have access to the internet and other LAN house facilities. If the enterprise is successful, the business owner can increase the number of computers or even open new stores.

A recent study by Ibope/Netratings2 found that more than 6 million people in Brazil (approximately one third of the online population) access the internet from a public place. Of those people, only 1.6 million access the internet from points of access provided by the government, such as telecenters and other digital inclusion initiatives. The absolute majority, 4.4 million people, access the internet through LAN houses and other paid

---

[2] http://idgnow.uol.com.br/internet/2006/10/02/idgnoticia.2006-10-02.6756378514/IDGNoticia_view

access points located, in many cases, in the poorest areas of the Brazilian cities. These numbers demonstrate the current importance of LAN houses in the country, and hint at their unexplored potential.

LAN houses represent a self-sustaining entrepreneurial initiative that is helping to bridge the digital divide, bringing technology and internet connectivity to those who need it the most. As with any other business, the revenues that LAN houses produce provide for their own sustainability and expansion. These entrepreneurial efforts can be a supplementary model to the digital inclusion initiatives that focus on government-funded telecenters, which can be vulnerable and difficult to sustain because of issues such as their dependence on continuous public funding.

Finally, it is important to consider the fact that LAN houses produce significant positive externalities for the community, especially because of the Internet connection they provide, and indications are that these positive effects can be developed even more fully with the right programs. In interviews conducted by the Center for Technology & Society in the communities of Rocinha[3] and Cidade de Deus[4] in Rio de Janeiro, it became clear from the statements made by the owners of the local LAN houses that the population frequently asks whether they also provide "courses" and other cultural and educational activities. Members of the community ask the owners, for instance, whether they provide courses for teaching people how to use computers. The owners themselves claim in the interviews that they have interest in providing these courses, but that they do not have the skills to do so. Owners also claim that these courses would be good for the business, especially in the morning period, when the LAN houses generally have a low attendance rate. In other words, there is an unexplored interest on the part of the small-scale entrepreneurs in implementing citizenship and cultural activities within the realm of activities of the LAN houses, making the model a feasible and promising one[5] for bridging the digital divide in developing countries.

---

[3] Rocinha is the largest favela in Rio de Janeiro. It is located in the city of Rio de Janeiro, between the neighborhoods of São Conrado and Leblon. In a preliminary research, more than 50 LAN Houses were counted at Rocinha, each one charging approximately US$0.30 for an hour of Internet access.

[4] Cidade de Deus is a community located in Rio de Janeiro, which was made famous by the film "City of God". It is a large community created by the government in the 1960s, and then turned into a very poor area, located in the Western areas of Rio de Janeiro. Even though the precise number could not be determined, it has more than 20 LAN Houses.

[5] A very important case demonstrating the potential and possibilities of this model has been documented throughout the website Overmundo, where the community of Ellery, in the Northeast outskirts of the city of Fortaleza, State of Ceará in Brazil is using LAN Houses to create a virtual community and even to engage in citizenship journalism, in the style of the so-called "web 2.0". See *Comunidade.com, at* http://www.overmundo.com.br/overblog/comunidadecom

In these circumstances, with the right incentives, LAN houses can eventually achieve the same objectives that other digital inclusion initiatives are expected to fulfill. In addition, LAN houses can go beyond simply offering internet connectivity and multiplayer games: and can develop and use social tools to promote and develop the cultural activities of their own communities, facilitate access to e-government and e-citizenship, and promote communication with communities in other areas of Brazil, exchanging social practices and cultural products. This could be an alternative paradigm that could influence future public policies regarding digital inclusion.

In short, there is an unexplored capacity of LAN houses to become places where citizenship can be put in practice and culture can be created and disseminated. The positive potential of LAN houses can be further developed by creating the right incentives and evaluating the effective importance of the LAN houses to the communities in which they are located. LAN houses are a perfect example of how peripheries are appropriating technology in order to provide solutions for their own problems, without any intervention from the state or from the third sector. They demonstrate that these initiatives should be investigated and taken seriously, inasmuch as they can offer clues about how technology will help in the near future to provide6 tools for access to information, citizenship and development.

2.2. SOCIAL COMMONS: CULTURAL INDUSTRIES EMERGING FROM THE PERIPHERIES.

Giorgio Agambem (2004) defines the idea of "state of exception" as follows:

> "It is a historical matter: the state of exception or state of emergency has become a paradigm of government today. Originally understood as something extraordinary, an exception, which should have validity only for a limited period of time, but a historical transformation has made it the normal form of governance. I wanted to show the consequence of this change for the state of the democracies in which we live. The second is of a philosophical nature and deals with the strange relationship of law and lawlessness, law and anomy. The state of exception establishes a hidden but fundamental relationship between law and the absence of law. It is a void, a blank and this empty space is constitutive of the legal system."

---

6   Cf. http://film.guardian.co.uk/features/featurepages/0,,1737425,00.html

The idea of "social commons" is connected with Agamben's "state of exception". It is the result of historical and social circumstances that generate a situation in which the very idea of intellectual property becomes inapplicable, irrelevant, unfamiliar or unenforceable. As de Souza Santos (1977) demonstrated in his studies about the illegal occupation of land in Brazil, two parallel legal realities could be detected. The first was the "official" legal system, regulated by the Brazilian Civil Code, which governed the acquisition and transfer of property. The other was a collection of social practices taking place in the *favelas* (shantytowns), which regulated the acquisition and transfer of "property" within that particular environment. These social rules were rooted in the ideas of illegality and informality: illegality because the occupation of land in the *favelas* was in the majority of cases the result of the illegal "squatter" settlements by migrants to large urban areas, and informality because due to this original illegality, the rules subsequently applicable to govern the acquisition, use, and transfer of the land were forged by the community itself, without any direct contact with the "official" legal system. De Sousa Santos points out in his work that the courts exercised basically no jurisdictional power over the land transactions taking place in the favelas, and that from the perspective of the favelas' inhabitants, the courts were seen as a "foreign" element, connected with the "official" legal system, that had no role to play in local disputes regarding the occupied land.

As with many developing and developed countries, the same social "state of exception" issues which lead to "illegality" and "informality" persist within the Brazilian society, not only at the peripheries but also elsewhere. At the peripheries these circumstances are especially visible. At the same time these peripheries deconstruct the idea of "rule of law", the fact that one simply cannot rely on the intellectual property system as a means of organizing a business leads to an interesting situation when digital technology comes into play. Digital technology makes fully apparent the non-competitive and non-rival characteristics of intellectual creations: unlike physical property, ideas and other intellectual creations can be simultaneously used by many people without reducing the value for any individual. In the digital environment, scarcity is longer a problem. Hence, the "official" legal system functions as a way of recreating scarcity by means of the law. But under the "state of exception", in places where intellectual property is simply not socially available, it is reasonable to expect that the recreation of scarcity by law will not be successful. Accordingly, when digital technologies start to be appropriated by the peripheries, the absence of the "official" intellectual property system creates a "social commons", a situation in which any cultural businesses emerging out of it has the characteristics of an "open business model"[7], in the sense that intellectual property does not play a significant role and content is regarded as part of a "commons".

Below is a description of some forms of cultural industries emerging out of "social commons" circumstances.

2.3. THE NIGERIAN FILM INDUSTRY

The most eloquent case for a cultural industry emerging out of the global peripheries is the Nigerian film scene. Nigeria features in the *2005 Atlas of World Cinema*, published by the French magazine *Cahiers du Cinema*, with an impressive amount of more than 1200 movies produced in that year. It is interesting to note that India produced some 911 films and the United States produced 611 in that same year, according to the magazine.

Both important newspapers such as *The Guardian* and business magazines such as *The Economist*[8] have recently been publishing articles describing the Nigerian phenomenon. According to the former, the Nigerian movie industry is the third industry in the world in terms of revenue, producing more than 200 million dollars per year. And according to the latter, the industry employs more that 1 million people, making it second only to agriculture as the largest source of employment in the country.

The interesting thing about the Nigerian market is that it emerged through an innovative business model. Instead of high-cost and high-profile films, a film in Nigeria costs between US$15,000 and 100,000 to produce. Movies are shot in most cases in digital video and distributed directly to the domestic market, in videocassettes or, in the last few years, DVDs. Charles Igwe,[9] a well-known producer in Nigeria, notes that contrary to other industries in the world, the Nigerian film industry is ready to absorb technology changes promptly. As an example, he cites the fact that the films are shot in high-definition format, a new trend in that market. Another remarkable element of the Nigerian market is that it emerged without the support of any strong intellectual property laws. Just like the majority of developing countries, Nigeria struggles to enforce the laws and even to

---

[7]   About the definition of Open Business, cf. the open business project at http://www.openbusiness.cc/

[8]   Cf. http://www.economist.com/displaystory.cfm?story_id=E1_SNNGDDJ

[9]   For a very comprehensive and interesting report on the Nigerian film industry, see the transcription of the conference given by Charles Igwe at the Center for Technology & Society at the FGV Law School in Brazil: http://www.culturalivre.org.br/index.php?option=com_content&task=view&id=80&Itemid=60

educate people about what the idea of intellectual property means. It is a case where culture lives in a state of "social commons", a commons that is generated not by the use of legal structures to create it, but by the absence of enforcement, cultural inadequacy, nonexistence, or other elements of an imperfect intellectual property regime. Regardless of whether this "social commons" is good or bad, or whether it should be fought or fostered, the fact is that if one considers intellectual property as the only, or even the primary, incentive for creative and for doing business out of cultural industries, the Nigerian case eloquently demonstrates that other incentives and other models are viable.

The Nigerian case is not alone. It is safe to assume that everywhere in the world, where there is a peripheral, marginalized area, this area is likely starting to produce some form of cultural expression, regardless of the intellectual property regime that applies. When technology is assimilated by these forms of cultural production emerging from the peripheries, autonomous industries can be generated. This is the case, for instance, for the "champeta" rhythm in Colombia, the different musical and economic scenes based on the "cumbia" rhythm throughout Latin America, and for the multitude of singers and composers in the Arab world who make a point of freely disseminating their songs online[10] because their source of revenue comes from live presentations such as performing at weddings (and being well-paid for that, sometimes more than US$20,000 for one performance). This phenomenon is not a privilege of developing countries, but it also takes place in the developed countries, especially in the poor areas of the biggest cities. As mentioned above, the "mix-tape" markets in New York and London follow the same patterns. Scenes like the "dubstep" and other rhythms in the peripheries of London emerged thanks to the dissemination of the music through pirate radios the mix tape market. In other words, the idea of "periphery", and consequently of "social commons", emerge regardless of any geographical or geopolitical status. It takes place both in the peripheries of the developing world and in the peripheries of the developed world.

2.4 THE TECNOBREGA INDUSTRY IN BELÉM DO PARÁ, BRAZIL

One of the most important examples of this new forms of industry based on the "social commons" is the *tecnobrega* scene in Belém do Pará, a city located at the Northern region of Brazil. While the "official" music industry in Brazil is struggling to produce a handful of CDs per year, the tecnobrega in Belém do Pará has generated a multi-million dollar industry releasing

---

[10]   Cf. Websites for freely disseminating music in the Arab world, such as Mazika (http://www.mazika.com/en/default.aspx) or 6arab (http://www.6arab.com) which calls itself "the Arabic music revolution".

numerous new CDs each year. There are no official statistics about how many CDs are released in the region, but the numbers obtained from the initial research undertaken by the Open Business project in the city of Belém indicate that more than 400 new CDs are released there every year.

If one tries to find any of these CDs in a traditional music store in Belém do Pará, the probability of success is close to none. Tecnobrega CDs are produced and recorded to be directly distributed throughout the street vendors, the same vendors that a few years ago sold only "pirated" content. In the case of tecnobrega, the CDs are deliberately delivered to the network of street vendors, so that they can disseminate them as much as they can. In other words, tecnobrega artists see the CDs as a form of advertising, rather than a source of revenue.

One might ask how a tecnobrega artist can make money in such circumstances. The answer to that question is complex, and is also the object of research of the Open Business project[11], which will be concluded by April 2007. An initial explanation is that the revenues at the tecnobrega scene are generated primarily by live concerts and presentations, which take place at the so-called *"aparelhagem"* (soundsystem) parties in the outskirts of Belém. These parties are big events, sometimes attracting 5,000 or more people. In some weekends, more than one aparelhagem party takes place, increasing the numbers of the tecnobrega fans attending different parties simultaneously in one single night to occasionally more than 20,000.

The aparelhagem parties are the focal point for generating revenues in the tecnobrega industry. The party organizers collect an entry fee from the tecnobrega fans, and receive other revenues for selling drinks and other tecnobrega-related products. The aparelhagem organization also pays the artists and DJs for their performances. Artists present their new songs at the tecnobrega party, and "test" the acceptance on the part of the public. An interesting aspect of the tecnobrega system is that concerts are occasionally recorded live, and a few CDs are produced to be sold at the exit of the aparelhagem parties when party is over. These few CDs are sold at a premium price (approximately R$15, corresponding to approximately U$7). Sometimes, the live recording produces material that is considered outstanding, for instance, when the DJs and artists present new songs that are well-received by the public and have not previously been distributed. In this case, the material recorded live is further replicated in the days following the party and the CDs are delivered to the street vendors, who disseminate them widely.

---

11   www.openbusiness.cc

The dissemination through the street vendors is the primary promotional tool for the artists and DJs. A popular DJ becomes, then, highly demanded by the aparelhagem party organizers, and then the circle is complete. Figure 1 show the basic economic cycle of the tecnobrega scene.

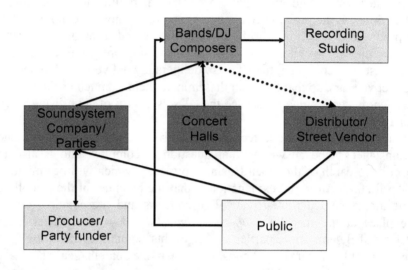

Figure 1. Linkages Among Economic Actors on the Tecnobrega Scene

The solid arrows depict the economic transactions between the various agents in the tecnobrega chain. At the beginning of the chain, one can find the bands, DJs, and composers. In many cases, the composer is the same person as the DJ or the performer, so in many instances the composer is not an autonomous figure in the graphic. Musicians and DJs record their tecnobrega songs at a recording studio, in many cases paying the studio a certain fee. The bands then disseminate the music through the distributors/street vendors (represented by the dotted arrow). There are also other modalities of dissemination. One of them is traditional radio, which in Belém, thanks to pressure from the public, reserves some airtime for locally produced music, including tecnobrega. Popular artists then perform live at the aparelhagem (soundsytem) parties, as well as at regular concert halls, receiving money in both cases. Another important ancillary link of the chain is the existence of intermediaries between the artists and the street vendors (distributors). These intermediaries are responsible in many cases for compiling the best songs, and for selecting the artists they think will best meet consumers' taste at that moment. The aparelhagem parties are also important taste-makers. A successful live performance at an aparelhagem party might be recorded and then sold, helping to improve the popularity of the artist.

The public purchases tickets from concert halls, and also from the aparelhagem parties. They also purchase CDs, either from the street vendors, or directly from the bands and artists at the end of the concerts. In the first case, when CDs are purchased from street vendors, the artists do not receive any royalties or revenue. When the purchase is made directly from the bands, that money goes to them. It is important to mention that the sales of CDs and DVDs by the street vendors do not compete with the direct sale of CDs and DVDs by the bands. The street vendor generally sells a poorer quality product, for a lower price. The CDs are generally plain CD-Rs, without any graphic material or pictures, and sometimes without even the tracklist. The bands selling CDs and DVDs directly at the concerts sell them for a higher price. These CDs come with graphic material, tracklist and better packaging. The direct sales of CDs and DVDs by the bands represent a significant source of income to the artists.

One last link of the tecnobrega chain is the producer or party sponsor. These are individuals or companies that are responsible for funding the aparelhagem parties. Sometimes they provide loans to the owners of the soundsystems, and sometimes the become partners in the parties. Accordingly, the both provide money to the aparelhagem parties, and can receive either interests over the loans provided, or a percentage of the profits earned.

Some critics have argued that the tecnobrega model is a "pre-industrial" form of organization of the music business. This argument, however, is not correct. The first element to consider is the fact that although the tecnobrega scene takes place in the poor areas of Belém, it is very intensive in its use of technology. The appropriation of technology, in fact, is what makes it possible for such an economically important scene to exist. Secondly, most artists on the tecnobrega scene actually make more money through the business organization of the current industry than they would make otherwise. An evidence of that is the fact that during the interviews conducted by the Open Business project, some artists mentioned that they had previously tried to market their music through traditional channels, and they know that it has become impossible to make money through recording contracts and CD sales in today's market. The Open Business tecnobrega research indicates that 88% of all artists on the scene have never had any contact with record companies.

The most successful artist arising from the tecnobrega scene, the band called Calypso, has been approached several times by traditional record labels, but has turned down all the offers. The reason is that they make more money by means of the existing business model. In an interview to the largest Brazilian newspaper, the singer of the band Calypso expressly said[12]: "We do not fight with the pirates. We have become big because of piracy, which has taken our music to cities where it would never have been". Calypso is well known for attracting huge crowds wherever they play in Brazil, not only in Belém but in any other city in the country. Sometimes they attract more than 50,000 people to one single concert. The *Folha de São Paulo* newspaper mentions that Calypso has sold more than 5 million albums in Brazil.

Finally, one might ask what would happen should broadband internet become widely available in Belém and in Brazil as a whole. How would this impact the tecnobrega business model? Considering that the tecnobrega cycle depends primarily on the broadest possible dissemination of content (i.e. making tecnobrega music freely available, so that more people go to the aparelhagem parties), it would be reasonable to assume that the model would actually become stronger, although the link represented by the street vendors would probably become less important. The internet would represent a more efficient way to make tecnobrega music broadly and freely available to audiences, which would increase even more the attendance at the tecnobrega parties and the popularity of the artists. As discussed in the next section, a transition from the "social commons" to the "legal commons" would then become necessary, and a legal structure such as the Creative Commons would have an important role to play in that transition.

Once again, the tecnobrega industry does not rely on intellectual property enforcement in the formation of its business model. It is a business model arising from the circumstances of "social commons". The corresponding elements of this particular "social commons" surrounding tecnobrega, i.e., the fact that the business model depends on the free and broad dissemination of content, can also be reproduced online, for instance by the adoption of Creative Commons licenses. This would be a perfect example of a case in which new technology would be in harmony, rather than competition, with a music business model.

3. The Legal Commons and Its Role in Developing Countries

This section focuses on how the legal commons, represented for instance by the Creative Commons licenses, can play an important role in the developing countries. The arguments here are based on the experience with the Creative Commons project in Brazil over the past three years.

---

[12]   Folha de São Paulo, November 29, 2005.

3.1 CREATIVE COMMONS – CRITICISM AND A DEVELOPING WORLD PERSPECTIVE

Criticism of the Creative Commons project can come not only from intellectual property constituencies and beneficiaries but also, for instance, from copyleft activists and copyleft enthusiasts. From the developing world perspective, especially based on the Brazilian experience, there are important elements that should be taken into account to rebut these critiques. There is no intention of being exhaustive in this paper, but some major critiques are singled out and addressed below:

a) Creative Commons is based on the copyright system

This is a critique coming especially from academic researchers and professors who would prefer that the intellectual property system be completely reformed or even suppressed. The point of the critique is that Creative Commons reinforces the current intellectual property system, rather than challenging it. The ambition of this criticism is that Creative Commons should engage in activism to reform or eliminate the copyright system, rather than in developing copyright-based licenses that allow creators to permit certain uses of their works.

It is curious to note that this criticism comes primarily from academics. One of the most important problems of the current intellectual property regime is the fact that is has been systematically changed in the past 20 years without any impact assessment. In other words, intellectual property law has been changed, or in some cases, changes have been proposed without any form of study or any empirical background that could support such change. Neither beneficiaries nor harmed groups are identified. The law is changing based on abstract assumptions.

Accordingly, accepting the criticism that Creative Commons should simply engage in activism against the intellectual property system would be to make the same mistake. One of the most important elements of the Creative Commons is that it provides a safe way to experiment with works that use a different form of intellectual protection regime. In March 2009, Creative Commons reached approximately 200 million link backs to the licenses (Boyle, 2009), indicating that there exists a significant universe of works free and available to be used and reused according to the permissions granted by the licenses. This number has grown even further since that time. Based on the various types of business models that are emerging from Creative Commons works, it will be soon possible to make an assessment of the real impact and benefits of intellectual property, and then propose a change to the law that is based on empirical evidence. These business models include well-respected projects such as the Public Library of Sciences (PLoS) for academic journals, the website Flickr for photos, and the record label Magnatune for music, among many others.

The problem of this criticism is that it is often mediated by a theoretical framework or theoretical assumptions that in their turn are not directly connected with empirical evidence or with problem-solving issues. Accordingly, it might work well from a theoretical point of view, but it fails to reach, for instance, the "disintermediation" of reality discussed by authors such as Gilles Deleuze, who is often quoted by the supporters of this particular criticism.

Another important aspect that this criticism fails to consider is the fact that the possibility of reforming the intellectual property system has been deeply limited by the adoption of the TRIPS agreement under the World Trade Organization. In other words, changes in the intellectual property system that conflict with the TRIPS agreement can imply commercial retaliations that developing countries simply cannot afford. From the point of view of a developing country as Brazil, being part of the WTO has brought significant trade benefits, which are put at risk by any modification to the Brazilian law that might conflict with the TRIPS agreement.

Not by coincidence, Brazil is one of the members of the group of countries called "Friends of Development". These 14 countries have proposed to the World Intellectual Property Organization the so-called "Development Agenda", a set of proposals aimed at promoting more equitable means for access to knowledge and culture. The Development Agenda argues that intellectual property should not be seen as an end in itself, but rather as a means to foster development. In this sense, the original Development Agenda document expressly mentions free software and the Creative Commons projects as important forms of experimentation that should be fostered, and that can indicate new possibilities of development in the near future.

Accordingly, the criticism that Creative Commons licenses support the legal status quo expressly rejects the present system in favor of an unknown future. The experience with the Creative Commons project in Brazil provides indicates that a more incremental and balanced path is possible.

Creative Commons has two important merits worth emphasizing. The first is that it puts into practice right here and right now a different model of intellectual property, a model that is compatible with business models that do not depend on the legal scarcity generated by the copyright regime. Conversely, it promotes business models where the economic impact of the cultural product increases the more this same product is shared and disseminated. Another important aspect of

Creative Commons is that it promotes an environment favorable to experimentation, avoiding any form of "social engineering", that is, changing the law without a prior assessment of the corresponding social impact.

Hence, Creative Commons allows experimenting in practice with the variables that might lead to a change in the intellectual property regime, based not on theory, but on empirical evidence. Creative Commons can be an important tool for "open business models" to develop and become economically sound. The more these business models emerge, the stronger will be the case to reform of the IP system.

b) Creative Commons has a "non-commercial' option

Another criticism that is presented against Creative Commons is that the project offers different "levels" of licenses. For instance, one of the most popular Creative Commons licenses allows the free dissemination of the intellectual or creative work, but not for commercial purposes. This "non-commercial" license has been criticized by different academics and activists, who would say the non-commercial clause makes the license not "free enough". This is a criticism that takes place, for instance, among the free software community, which adopts and defends one single model for licensing software, represented by the GNU General Public License[13].

However, the "non-commercial" license has proven very important in practice, especially in developing countries. The first element to be considered is the fact that cultural artifacts work differently than software. One might not use the same criteria for evaluating software licenses as for evaluating the licensing of a song, a film or a photograph. Additionally, if one agrees that an important public interest objective of discussing new intellectual property models is the goal of building a more open and decentralized society, where the barriers between producers and consumers of culture are irrelevant, and above all where everyone is invited to participate, than the non-commercial license becomes a very important step, especially in developing countries.

In developing countries such as Brazil, the "non-commercial" license is the type of license that actually empowers civil society to build channels for the dissemination and participatory building of information and culture. When an author chooses to license his or her works under a non-commercial license, what he or she is actually doing is allowing society at large to have free access to the work, with the exception of

---

[13]   http://www.gnu.org/copyleft/gpl.html

commercial institutions such as the traditional twentieth century media companies. In a developing country, this contrast and this particularity are important. As mentioned in the first portion of this paper, there are numerous symptoms of an ongoing crisis at the traditional twentieth century media in a developing country as Brazil. These media are failing to provide adequate channels for cultural dissemination and especially to provide adequate incentives for culture to be produced and circulated. The result is that cultural production is becoming increasingly disconnected from these traditional media forms. More than that, many traditional media companies are facing economic challenges in the twenty-first century, as they watch their business models transform dramatically.

At the same time, cultural production is migrating to civil society and/or the peripheries, which to a greater or lesser extent already operate in a "social commons" environment and do not depend on intellectual property within their business models. Accordingly, when an author licenses a work under a "non-commercial" license, important social players will be granted full access to the work: NGOs, schools, professors, telecenters, cultural hotspots, libraries, cell phone users, "web 2.0" users etc. However, industry players such as the broadcast TVs, multinational labels, and movie theaters owners will not have access to this body of free culture.

In the long run, what the non-commercial clause allows is the creation of a massive body of free culture available to society at large, but not available to the twentieth century media industry unless a specific permission is grated by each individual author. In the software realm, a "one-size-fits-all" license that includes the permission for commercially exploiting the software piece is adequate for the dissemination of the knowledge within the software and the emergence of corresponding business models. However, in the realm of culture, things are more complex and this single model does not work. If the goal of promoting new business models and disseminating culture and knowledge is shared, then the non-commercial clause performs an important function in developing countries.

The example of Trama Virtual, mentioned above, illustrates this fact. The largest local Brazilian recording label, Trama, announced at the 2006 iCommons Summit[14] that they will provide the option for TramaVirtual website users to use Creative Commons to license their works. TramaVirtual has more than 35,000 artists at the website. Certainly, Trama does not want a competitor, say, a multinational record

---

[14]   The iSummit Commons is the yearly Creative Commons community summit. The announcement was made at the iCommons Summit 2006, taking place in Rio de Janeiro. See www.icommons.org.

label to have access to this huge collection of recordings built in the past few years. Nonetheless, Trama does not care if society at large has access to this content. Accordingly, a "non-commercial" Creative Commons license is the model that allows a balance between the interests of Trama in receiving recognition for its efforts in building TramaVirtual, and the interests of society as whole in having flexible access to the content. At the same time, Trama is developing innovative business models around its open music catalog, which go beyond the sale of physical copies of the music to include sophisticated arrangements such as trademark licensing, as well as "wholesale" music licensing to cell phone companies, video-games, and other modalities that are benefited by the free availability of the content. The Creative Commons non-commercial clause is precisely the requisite necessary for Trama to allow experimentation with "free" models to distribute content, at the same time allowing it to innovate in terms of business models. The non-commercial license allows Trama to grant the at-large audience access to its content, online and without any form of technological protection, while ensuring that Trama's commercial competitors cannot use the content that results from its unrestricted infrastructure. Thus, Creative Commons legally protects Trama from the competition of other players in the market while allowing it to develop innovative new business models, which are beneficial to society inasmuch as they involve open and technologically unrestricted content. Accordingly, some criticism of the non-commercial licensing clause can be rebutted by practical examples taking place in Brazil. Criticizing this clause just for the sake of the "purity" of the copyleft movement would be an intellectual attitude similar to the positivist legal school thought at the end of the nineteenth century and first half of the twentieth century, which struggled for a "pure theory of law". The nefarious consequences of this legal school of thought that were seeking for "purity" through a mere formalistic fashion can even today be felt in the many Latin American countries, including Brazil, where positivism played an important role.

3.2 CREATIVE COMMONS – BENEFITS FROM A DEVELOPING WORLD PERSPECTIVE

Below I would like to highlight some of the benefits that the Creative Commons licenses can help to provide in developing countries, based on the experience with the project in Brazil.

a) Creative Commons has become a powerful brand

Creative Commons has become a powerful brand, supported by millions: more than 140 million link backs to the Creative Commons licenses are currently counted. Additionally, the Creative Commons project has been able to build partnerships worldwide with important institutions. There are more than 60 countries in which Creative Commons is now present, by means of partnerships with local institutions.

b) Creative Commons brings people together who share the same values

One of the most interesting aspects of Creative Commons in Brazil is the way it brings together different people, individuals, and institutions that share the same values in terms of promoting access to knowledge and access to culture.

As an example, the Creative Commons project in Brazil works in many instances with the Free Software movement, as well as hackers in general, lawyers, artists, journalists, bloggers, musicians, movie-makers, NGOs, and the government, to mention only a few. Traditional movements in the country, such as the consumer protection movement, have also begun to realize the impact that an unbalanced intellectual property regime has on consumer rights and consumer expectations toward cultural products.

c) Creative Commons promotes media decentralization

Another very important feature of Creative Commons is that it works as a tool for media decentralization. As in most places, media ownership and access in Brazil is very concentrated. One of the short-term possibilities for the scenario to change is the emergence of the cell phone networks, as well as the emergence of digital radio and digital television, but even these networks risk reproducing the concentration model and content structure of traditional twentieth century media. Nevertheless, the first steps are being taken toward the creation of a wireless broadband internet infrastructure that would be available to all. The year 2006 saw the beginning of discussions about opening public bidding for the construction of wireless broadband internet service countrywide.

If successful, this national internet infrastructure would make it possible for new media to emerge in a decentralized fashion. All this, considered alongside the fact that there is a huge interest in Brazil in collaboratively produced content, suggests a new possibility for culture and information dissemination in the country. By way of example, the social networking website called Orkut[15], operated by Google, has achieved tremendous success in the country (Orkut indicates that 49,82% of its users are Brazilians). A significant portion of all the time spent by Brazilians on the Internet is spent at Orkut. The popularity of the social networking site creates a favorable environment for collaborative business models to emerge.

It is interesting to note that Orkut has become a phenomenon not only throughout the richest segments of the Brazilian society, but also among the poor areas in Brazil. In other words, the same peripheries mentioned above as the focal point for the new cultural production in Brazil are also using Orkut as a tool for communication and for sharing information and other relevant social data. Orkut has become a reflection of the Brazilian society, one still distorted by digital divide factors but becoming more and more accurate.

Another important element for media decentralization in Brazil is the role that Creative Commons plays in terms of securing the so-called "interoperability" of cultural content. One of the most important worries of the present day is the fact that cultural artifacts being sold digitally are protected by the so-called "DRM" (Digital Rights Management) systems. In other words, a song bought a particular music store might not work with a particular music player device, because the device was not certified by the music store. This creates economic inefficiencies in the music market, harms competition, and above all, harms the consumers' interests in having flexible access to legally purchased digital content.

At the same time, Creative Commons-licensed materials can become a viable alternative for emerging media (such as cell phone companies, digital radio and digital TV), potentially making the adoption of DRM-based networks an inefficient decision. Creative Commons licenses include provisions that are violated if a DRM system is applied over CC licensed material, precluding the user from exercise all the freedoms guaranteed by the Creative Commons license. In other words, networks are compelled to technologically respect all the rights and freedoms established by the CC license: one can only use Creative Commons-licensed content if the DRM features do not conflict with the terms of the license.

Accordingly, Creative Commons licenses enable the creation of a catalog of free culture, which might then compete with the catalog of traditionally protected culture. This is important because one of the most powerful assets of the twentieth century media industries is their catalog

---

15   www.orkut.com

of content. One might ask what would be the consequences if a decentralized catalog licensed under a Creative Commons license emerges, competing with and becoming as relevant as the "old" catalog of the traditional media, but without all the sort of restrictions such as DRMs imposed by the traditional industry. Usually, the power of the catalog is used by the traditional media industries to shape how new networks must be built (i.e. allowing access to their content only if the network complies with their DRM standard). From the moment a competitive and interesting body of free culture is built, a body that can compete with the traditional catalog, all the conditions are in place for the building of a much freer and open structure for the media, especially in developing countries.

d) Creative Commons can help bridge the gap between the "social commons" and "legal commons"

As demonstrated above, the copyright-based industries in Brazil (and in many other countries) are failing to provide the adequate channels for promoting local content and for the dissemination of culture and knowledge as a whole. From the standpoint of a country with a thriving cultural scenario such as Brazil, this is a highly unsatisfactory situation. The result is the fact that many vibrant and important cultural scenes in the country are taking place in the peripheries, as described above with the tecnobrega case.

That is precisely where Creative Commons comes into play. There is an enormous demand for the dissemination of the culture being produced in Brazil in all fields. The majority of artists simply do not care about copyright protection, because their ultimate goal is to be seen, read, and heard. This explains, for instance, why Creative Commons has been significantly used in Brazil.

Additionally, this extreme situation in which the traditional cultural industry failed to provide adequate channels for cultural businesses has created an environment where "open business models" are becoming the standard business model for cultural production. The term "open" in this case refers to models in which copyright is not a factor, or plays a secondary role. This is the case for different forms of "brega" in the Northeast and North regions in Brazil (the brega in Pernambuco, the "cybertechnobrega" in Belém do Pará, the electronic forró in Ceará, the forró scene in Manaus, and so it goes).

Considering that one of the most important problems faced not only by Brazil but also by several other developing countries is how to bring "formal" business practices to the so-called "informal" economy, Creative Commons has a role to play in the process in regard to intellectual property practices. Creative Commons provides a simple, non-bureaucratic structure for intellectual property that might help to integrate the massive marginal culture that is arising in the peripheries with the "official", "formal" structures of the Brazilian economy. Even if this role is not important at present, because the majority of the peripheral cultural scenes operate at the margins of intellectual property (under a "social commons" regime), in the near future Creative Commons might provide the way for these emerging cultural forms to find their way online when broadband internet becomes widespread in the country.

4. Final Remarks

Developing countries are seeing their traditional twentieth century media fail in the promotion of viable incentives for cultural production and cultural dissemination. At the same time, two forms of cultural "commons" coexist in developing countries. The first is the "social commons", that is, social situations in which for numerous reasons intellectual property is not enforced, does not exist, is unfamiliar, or is irrelevant. Different business models are emerging from the "social commons", especially because the most marginalized populations in the developing countries (the "peripheries") are appropriating technology in order to produce their own cultural industries. In other words, in many places in the developing countries, technology, and its possibilities for sharing and freely disseminating content, has arrived earlier than intellectual property. More than that, the appropriation of technology on the part of the peripheries creates initiatives that end up helping to bridge the digital divide in an autonomous, bottom-up fashion, such as the LAN house phenomenon in Brazil.

It is important to mention that the idea of "social commons" is not a peculiarity of the developing world. It does not imply a dichotomy between the rich North and the poor South, or even between the idea of "center" and "periphery"[16]. The "social commons" exist in rich or poor countries, at the center or at the peripheries. For example, for many years in the beginning of the computer industry, software was held as a "commons". The transformation of software that was originally "free" into a proprietary good (as it happened to the UNIX operational system), as described by Lessig (2001), was perceived as an action of enclosure. The reaction was Richard Stallman's creation of the Free Software Foundation and the beginning of the free software movement, which aimed to reclaim the idea

---

[16]   For the discussion between "center" and "periphery" in Brazil, cf. Vianna (2006).

of "freedom" for software in an effort to bring it back to the commons realm.

At the same time, the "open" business practices emerging in the peripheries of the developing world's cities are similar to those taking place in the peripheries of the developed world cities. In this sense, the vibrant "mixtape"[17] markets in New York and London (Leeds, 2007) operate under fundamentally the same logic as the emerging markets in peripheries in Brazil and elsewhere. They both face the challenge of "informality" and "illegality", and circumstances where intellectual property is not expected to apply.

Finally, peer-to-peer file-sharing networks also contribute to the dissemination of "states of exception", rendering the enforcement of intellectual property difficult. Peer-to-peer networks can then be seen as one of the forces promoting the globalization of informality/illegality. In this sense, different forms of "social commons" can be increasingly found on a global scale. As the Brazilian anthropologist Viveiros de Castro points out in a recent interview, making reference to Stefan Zweig's book *Brazil, Land of the Future*:

> "Someone was talking the other day about how capitalism is changing in the whole word, changing the work force, eliminating social security, generating informality etc. Someone else then reminded that all that has always existed in Brazil. I thought with myself, there is a general belief that Brazil will be the land of the future. That is wrong, the future is becoming Brazil. The future has not arrived in Brazil, it is the opposite. Like it or not, now everything is Brazil." (Castro, 2007)

At the same time, the "legal commons" structure is beginning to play a prominent role in Brazil. An example of "legal commons" is the Creative Commons project, which allows creators of content to license their works so that society can have access to them, according to the terms and conditions defined by the licensor. These legal commons instruments use the legal system in order to create a body of content that is free for certain uses, and can work as building blocks for the emergence of a truly participatory culture. Both the "social commons" and the "legal commons" can learn from one another, as the "Open Business"[18] project demonstrates, and both, together, can also indicate important alternate paths to those of the traditional media industries, which are struggling to renovate their business models in the twenty-first century.

---

[17]   For more details, see Dames (2006).

[18]   www.openbusiness.cc

References

Agamben, G. (2004), *Interview with Giorgio Agamben Life, A Work of Art Without an Author: The State of Exception, the Administration of Disorder and Private Life*, German Law Journal, No. 5, available at: http://www.germanlawjournal.com/article.php?id=437 (accessed 5 May 2010).

Boyle, J. (2009), *CC By(e Bye)*, available at: http://www.thepublicdomain.org/2009/03/31/cc-bye-bye/ (accessed 3 May 2010).

Castro, E.V (2007), Saque/Dádiva Interview to *Azougue Magazine,* No. 11, January, available at: www.azougue.com.br. (accessed 3 May 2010).

Dames, M.K. (2006), *Mixtapes are no Longer Underground*, available at: http://www.copycense.com/2006/04/mixtapes_are_no.html (accessed 5 May 2010).

de Sousa Santos, B. (1977). *The Law of the Oppressed: The Construction and Reproduction of Legality in Pasargada,* Law & Society Review, Vol. 12, No. 1, pp. 5-126, available at http://www.jstor.org/view/00239216/sp020014/02x0165i/0 (accessed 5 May 2010).

Leeds, J. (2007), *Cracking Down on Mixtape CDs*, The New York Times, January 22, available at: http://www.nytimes.com/2007/01/22/business/22mixtape.html?ex=1327122000&en=c1b3c63511e8e3ed&ei=5088&partner=rssnyt&emc=rss (accessed 5 May 2010).

Lessig, L. (2001), *The Future of Ideas*, Random House, pp. 51-72.

Vianna, H. (2006), *Paradas do Sucesso Periférico*, Revista Sexta-Feira, No. 8, 34th ed., available at: http://overmundo.com.br/banco/paradas-do-sucesso-periferico (accessed 7 May 2010).

Collecting Societies and Creative Commons Licensing

Herkko Hietanen
Researcher Helsinki Institute for Information Technology,
Visiting Scientist, MIT,
Berkman Fellow, Harvard University

Abstract. Collecting society licensing is a successful method of garnering royalties from broadcasters and other licensees who use massive amounts of copyrighted works. However, the system is not optimal at supporting non-commercial or royalty-free licensing. The focus of this chapter is to describe the functions and the scope of collective licensing and to examine the overlap among the individual, collective and the Creative Commons ("CC") public licensing procedures, and to determine whether such institutions can coexist.

Just as collecting societies were solutions to the cultural and industrial revolutions of the past, the online licensing initiatives seem to provide answers to the post-industrial network economy. However, many rights owners are also interested to combine the two licensing models and this raises a question of in what ways do these systems cooperate? The CC licenses include a clause that clarifies that the rights owner reserves rights to collect royalties from the uses that the license does not cover. At the same time, the licenses also recognize that authors cannot waive the right to collect royalties in some jurisdictions.

Liberal thinkers like John Stuart Mill believe that the paternalistic approach to rights owners' creates a negative effect to their autonomy, while the societies see it as a bargaining position. The question of the interoperability of the two licensing models includes a bigger question: Can the collecting societies combine the collective and individual licensing, and in such a case, how does the market equilibrium change? Should we let authors manage their rights, even if it could lead to negative consequences?

Keywords
collecting society, collective management, copyright, licensing

1. Collecting Societies

The underlying idea of collective copyright management is widely shared, and collecting societies have a key role in all developed countries. In cases where the rights cannot be enforced vis-à-vis individual members of the public or where individual management would not be appropriate given the number and type of uses involved and the high transaction costs of individual licensing, rights owners are instead granted a remuneration right. Collecting societies manage these rights. The importance of collecting societies to rights owners is comparable to a banking institution. Collecting societies administer many of the rights owner's rights and the system enables industrial-scale licensing. The societies are an answer to industrial-age copyright markets, born in a time when the demand for sheet music and music records was growing (Ehrlich, 1989). The societies currently collect and distribute royalties for nearly every conceivable public performance and reproduction of creative works. In 2006, the royalty collections of collecting societies around the world equalled over 7 billion Euros.

Composers, performers, lyric writers, and arrangers were one of the first authors to use collective management. Authors also use collective management to collect royalties for photocopying and broadcast retransmission in many countries. Because of the historical, legal, economic, and cultural diversity among countries, regulation of collecting societies and the markets where they act varies from one country to another. At the international level, articles 11bis(2) and 13(1) of the Berne Convention and article 12 of the Rome Convention, lay out a very loose framework for collective management and state that Member States may determine the conditions under which certain rights may be exercised.

In Europe, collecting societies require their members to transfer *exclusive* administration rights of all of their works to them. United States antitrust law has placed restrictions on exclusive representation. Collecting societies in the U.S. and Canada have less restricting rules as members maintain their rights simultaneously with collecting societies (Katz 2005). Various U.S. courts have concluded that direct licensing is a realistic alternative for the users of musical works (Buffalo, 1985 and Columbia, 1981). For the past century, legislators in Europe have determined that the benefits of collecting societies outweighed the anticompetitive disadvantages they have created (e.g., Rigg, 2002). As technology has made it easier to distribute works online and license directly with the rights owners, collective licensing also has faced scrutiny.

Recently, the European Union Commission started an investigation into European copyright societies. Charlie McCreevy, the European Commissioner for Internal Market and Services, stated in his speech, *"Europe's model of copyright clearance belongs more to the nineteenth century than to the 21st. Once upon a time it may have made sense for the member state to be the basic unit of division. The internet overturns that premise"*. The Commission was worried, that national societies might stifle the online sale of music. In 2005, it issued a recommendation on cross-border management of copyrights. Its full impact to collective societies' competition is still unclear. However, it is apparent that European collecting societies are facing changes in the near future.

Individual management of copyrights can be costly for users and an inefficient way to generate significant revenues for rights owners. Individual transaction costs are often greater than the value of the rights in question. Collective management is justified as efficient mechanism to minimize searching and contracting transaction costs between intermediary distributors like online retailers or public broadcasters and copyright owners. Having a *one-stop-shop* that represents all rights owners eliminates the high transaction costs of clearing rights with every individual author, publisher, composer, lyricist, artist, performer and record company. Collective management is a practical way of administering high volume, low value usage of rights. Collective systems spread the cost of administration over all members of the collecting society. The societies cover the costs of administration by an overhead, typically between 12–20 percent of collected royalties.

Most of the collecting societies are associations or other societies. Societies' members give an annual mandate and approve the terms for licensing and administration. The members decide the content of the mandate and pass the resolutions by a simple majority.

Collecting society is effectively an organization handling the outsourced function of rights management. Rights owners transfer to collecting society rights to: 1) sell non-exclusive licenses; 2) collect royalties; 3) distribute collected royalties; 4) enter into reciprocal arrangements with other collecting societies; and to 5) enforce their rights. Collecting societies also negotiate license fees for public performance and reproduction, as well as act as lobbying interest groups.

Collecting societies sell blanket licenses, which grant the right to use their catalogue for a period. Such a license might for example provide a broadcaster with a single annual authorization encompassing thousands of songs owned by thousands of composers, lyricists and publishers. The societies also sell individual licenses for users who reproduce and distribute music. The larger individual and blanket licensees have to report their use of works for accurate royalty payments while the societies estimate the usage of the smaller users by occasional sampling.

The national copyright law often gives a special status to collecting societies. Compulsory licensing schemes broaden collecting societies' power from purely contractual limits. Compulsory licenses allow societies to represent non-members, unless they have specifically opted out. In Finland, for example, collecting societies collect non-member royalties for radio and TV broadcasting, but members also receive additional compensation for mechanical music played in bars from levies collected on some blank storage media.

2. Combination of the Two Systems

"Ideally, the management of copyrights should be exclusively individual, because it is a great freedom for all acting parties and specifically creators, who are individuals."

(Marc Guez, Managing Director of French collecting society of record companies, 2003).

The free and open source movement has shown that it is possible to find several distribution and business models to support the development of freely available content. Collecting societies have been slow in finding ways to foster this sort of innovative creativity and to serve their future customer base that is looking to use open licensing models.

The CC seems to be creating parallel open content markets where only "all rights reserved" markets used to exist. The quality, sophistication and number of open content works is nowhere close to the "all rights reserved" market, but as the strong adoption of open source software has shown the open production model may create a parallel open market to proprietary products. This development began to show in the software sector in early 1990 where free and open source software products started to compete for users. Just as the Free Software has captured some parts of the software market, it is possible that open content will compete with, replace, and complement commercial content.

No set of property rights work equivalently in all types of settings. Amateurs and professionals, including those who are in different stages of their careers, have different expectations for the protection that copyright provides. Using open content licenses may not be a wise decision for an established author, just as holding on to all rights is not necessarily the best business strategy for new and upcoming or long forgotten artists. Currently rights owners have to make decisions whether they want to use the individual, collective, or public licensing schemas. The CC licenses and website are instructing licensors and licensees about the potential incompatibility issues of the licensing systems.

> **"Non-waivable Compulsory License Schemes**. In those jurisdictions in which the right to collect royalties through any statutory or compulsory licensing scheme cannot be waived, the Licensor reserves the exclusive right to collect such royalties for any exercise by You of the rights granted under this License"

Only a few collecting societies have reacted to the CC licensing and most European collecting societies do not have any policy for CC-licensed material. A few collecting societies have started pilot projects to see how the two licensing systems could live side by side (Moeltke, 2008, Schröder, 2008). The goal is to give authors more control of their works in a non-commercial field, while at the same time, provide them with royalty collecting services. The results from these pilot projects are not available at the time. However, there are several concerns that collecting society executives have expressed before the pilot projects have started. The next section addresses these concerns in detail.

2.1. INTERPRETATION OF CC LICENSES

All the CC licenses grant royalty-free permission to copy and use the work for non-commercial use. Approximately two-thirds of the content licensed with a CC license has a clause that reserves commercial use: "4c You may not exercise any of the rights ... in any manner that is primarily intended for or directed toward commercial advantage or private monetary compensation." The non-commercial clause does not derive from the international copyright system and its interpretation might be different in every national legal system, individual cases, and individual circumstances (Hietanen, 2007). The clause may have different meanings in different cases even when interpreting the same license.

The problems arise when collecting societies enforce their rights to collect remuneration. They have to make decisions about whether the users of a work are using it under a relevant CC license or not. Collective systems rely on automated licensing practices, which guarantee low administrative overheads. The societies have a long history of selling licenses to a range of groups from muzak playing super markets to girl scouts singing songs around the campfire. Licensee need to buy a license to make the work available and for public performances. Collecting societies have objected to individual license terms because they cannot efficiently enforce licensing terms that require judgment, interpretation, and may discriminate a field of endeavour. The counter argument is that collecting societies have successfully interpreted the vague line between private use and public performances for decades. In the end, the licensee has the risk of showing that the license covers the use. In such a case, the licensee will have to show where he got the license and why the use of the work falls for example within the non-commercial license grant.

Collective licensing relies on transparency. The system can reduce transaction costs only if the licensees know what they are licensing. If the potential licensee does not have clear information about the conditions under which the rights owner is allowing them to use works, in this case the CC licenses, they would be more likely to pay the royalty fee rather that start a legal process to determine whether the CC license covers their use. In a sense, collecting societies might help to reduce problems of license interpretation. A licensee could simply avoid the problematic license interpretation by buying a license from a collecting society. Danish Koda, the only European collecting society that enables CC licensing, has created a document that their members must accept in order to use non-commercial CC licenses. The document specifies the meaning of the non-commercial clause. Authors are encouraged to link this document to the copyright licensing and information page.

2.2. DIVERSE LICENSE TERMS

Collecting societies typically represent both local and international authors and composers. The societies form a network that has reciprocal co-operation agreements. The agreements provide, for example, the German society GEMA a right to collect royalties and represent American composer Irving Berlin. In this sense, the catalogue of collecting societies is truly global.

The CC has six generic licenses and a few customized licenses that allow specific use such as sampling. As of January 2008, the licenses reached version 3.01. Forty-three countries have translated and adapted the licenses to their legal systems and several countries are in the process of localizing the licenses. There are currently over three hundred official CC licenses and the number is most likely to double in a year as the new 3.01 licenses are localized. While most of these licenses seem interoperable and have similar license terms, some contain unique clauses that are not in other licenses. The CC faces the problem of license proliferation (Elkin-Koren, 2006). While the goal of the CC in translating the licenses was to provide a set of licenses that have common terms, the devil, as always, hides in details. Licensees face dozens of licenses in languages they cannot understand. The licensees are not alone. Collecting societies who are in charge of enforcing the rights of their clients should at least understand the licenses. Elkin-Koren point that the multiplicity of the licenses does increase the external information cost is especially valid with collecting societies.

Most of the CC licenses do not have rules for international license selection. Unlike the rest of the licenses, "share alike" licenses have a clause allowing mixing of international licenses that have the same license elements. The rest of the licenses make no mention of the possibility of international license replacement. The rationale of international license adaptation was to adjust the licenses to suit the needs of local legal systems and to make them easier to understand. Although it seems that the objective would require the use of interchangeable licenses, this is not the case. One can only conclude that all the licenses are separate and non-interchangeable unless otherwise noted. Accordingly, a French court cannot use a French version of the license even for interpretation, if the licensor licensed it with a Swedish license. It would be a demanding task for a court to enforce the licenses according to international private law. It is difficult to see how collecting societies could manage a content pool licensed with over 100 licenses.

The CC has discussed of the possibility of including an international choice of law clause to its licenses. The CC anticipates that the clause would enable licensors to choose the applicable law. However, it also would be beneficial to have a clause allowing courts to interpret the nationally translated and localized license instead of the license originally chosen. A clause granting the licensors power to choose a local license instead of the original non-local license could alleviate the license proliferation problem and potentially limit the licenses from hundreds to just a few. The solution would significantly reduce the licenses, making international licensing manageable. However, the changes to the license should be done carefully while taking into account potential forum shopping and the minor differences in license translations.

Interchangeable licenses would also open the question of consent. Arguably, the licensor has not consented to use of foreign or future licenses and to interpretations that may diverge from the original license. The international choice of law clause may also mean that the license might turn into a contract that requires contractual formation from both parties.

2.3. SCOPE OF CC LICENSES

The CC licenses define licensed works very broadly: "Work means the copyrightable work of authorship offered under the terms of this License." This broad definition creates two problems. First, copyrightable works vary from country to country. The scope of copyright is different in different countries, which may lead to different outcomes in legal disputes even if the Berne and World Trade Organization's conventions have harmonized the basic principles. The U.S. has limited copyright protection for artists' rights to performance or so-called neighbouring rights. In Europe, copyright law offers protection for performances and other neighbouring rights and performers have their own collecting societies. It is unclear whether the neighbouring rights are included in the "copyrightable work." Many of the European localized CC licenses include neighbouring rights, which clarify the license scope.

Second, the licenses do not define the work offered under the license. For example, if a rights owner slaps a concert recording with a CC license link, it is unclear if the license applies to lyrics, underlying composition, performance, video, background art, or all of them. These problems occur because of the mass-market nature of the licenses. Making changes to the licenses is against the idea of standardization of open content licenses. Altering the licenses and labelling them as "creative commons" may also breach the trademark owned by CC (Välimäki & Hietanen, 2004).

The licenses have a requirement to "keep intact all copyright notices for the Work" and to provide a link that refers to "the copyright notice or licensing information. " The link can point to the CC web site, where the official licenses are stored, or to a web page where rights owners can provide additional information. This information provides clarification as to which elements of a recording are licensed and whether the licensor wants to license them as a set of indivisible rights or whether every element is individually licensed.

However, separate license information that is changeable by the licensor goes against the idea of perpetual, non-revocable license. The licensor could alter the copyright information and force the licensee to prove the existence of the license details and its scope in an infringement claim. The existence of a public registry of licensed works could help to reduce the legal uncertainty of the online CC licenses. A private company could offer the same function, or better yet, a collecting society.

2.4. AUTOMATED LICENSING

"No   one   should   let   artists   give   up   their   rights."
(*Andy Frazer, songwriter of "All Right Now"*).

Two lawyers of collecting societies, Péter Tóth and Emma Pike, have criticized the CC website and its licensing procedure. Pike is concerned that creators may not be aware that the CC licenses are "royalty free and offer no remuneration, run for the entire duration of copyright of the work, apply to the whole world and cannot be revoked." Tóth points out that, unlike collecting societies, the CC does not help rights owners to enforce their rights. Both Pike and Tóth criticize the ease with which enables right owners to grant rights away with CC licenses.

The concern of irrevocability may be justified. CC licenses are practically irrevocable and they terminate only if the licensee breaches the license. Even if the licensor decides to change his or her mind, courts have held that licenses are comparable to gifts and right owners cannot revoke them once they are available to public. In *Hadady v. Dean Witter Reynolds,* the court decided that: "abandonment of copyright can occur regardless of owner's intent to preserve copyright." Some CC licenses are comparable to the partial abandonment of copyrights because of the permanent and public nature of the licenses. From the collecting society's perspective, a public license that allows commercial use is effectively the same as releasing the work into the public domain. This critique about the lack of information has led the CC to modify its licensing web page. It now includes detailed information on the restrictions of CC licensing and of the possible incompatibility of the licenses and collecting societies.

Collecting societies' reluctance to act as administrative intermediaries for CC rights owners has opened a business window for new Internet companies. Online record companies, such as Magnatune, have found a place in the music business. Magnatune has made its repertoire available online at its webpage Magnatune.org with non-commercial CC licenses. It has managed to create a truly one-stop shop where licensing is made easy. Anyone can listen to the music before deciding to buy licenses and download hi-fi quality music instantaneously online.

Magnatune makes money by selling: download privileges, commercial licenses, records and "all you can eat" -subscription services. According to the Magnatune statistics, the company had in 2010 over 300 artists and almost 10,000 songs in its repertoire. Magnatune shares half of its income with artists. Even with the administrative overheads 30 percent higher than with collecting societies, the artists benefit greatly (Buckman, 2001). According to Buckman, the average annual royalty income (approximately $1,500) of a Magnatune artist equals the average royalty income (717€) (Teosto, 2005) of a member of a Finnish collecting society. While the income from Magnatune is not directly comparable to royalties provided by a collecting society, it provides a comparison of how private companies could take the role of collecting societies in niche markets. In fact, there is nothing preventing Apple from selling licenses to businesses through its iTunes store. It could truly provide a one-stop shop where licensees could obtain both songs and the public performance licenses to them. Combined with subscription service, Apple could even consider selling blanket licenses to its catalogue.

2.5. LICENSE MONITORING

Unlike their European counterparts, U.S. collecting societies' members can license their works with CC licenses because they retain the right to grant individual licenses to users. Some major U.S. artists have used CC licenses to distribute their songs. On a CD distributed by the Wired-magazine in 2004, artists such as the Beastie Boys, David Byrne, and Chuck D used CC sampling licenses to allow the public to remix their songs. Several front row artists like Pearl Jam, Nine Inch Nails, and Radiohead have also experimented with CC distribution. The U.S. societies are not alone in providing CC-licensed material in their catalogues. Reciprocity agreements oblige European collecting societies to enforce and license member rights of sister organizations. Globally granted CC licenses have found their way into the catalogues of all collecting societies, which are hardly aware what content is CC-licensed. However, CC licenses act as an estoppels document. The licensee can state that the license covers his non-commercial use and refuse to pay for the license.

There are two cases from Spain where a bar refused to pay royalties because the rights owners of the music it played had licensed the music with CC licenses, which granted the bar a royalty-free permission to publicly perform the work. In *SGAE v. Luis,* the Spanish collecting society SGAE managed to convince the court that their employee had heard the defendant playing non-CC licensed works in a bar. In another similar case *SGAE v. Fernández,* the court held that the defendant had the personal and technical ability to find royalty-free music and play it in his establishment and, in fact, had done so. The court dismissed the case.

Eventually collecting societies will have local CC content in their catalogues, and right owners, who have CC licensed works, will become their members. CC licenses are perpetual for the duration of copyright in the work and no one can revoke the license. Rights owner can also evade the licensing ban by resigning, licensing and then rejoining. For example, Finnish Teosto's termination of the customer account comes in force from the beginning of a year. This means that the termination period can be from one to 365 days long. The requirement of resignation and rejoining seems an unfair and non-economic way to administer rights.

In *BRT/SABAM II,* the court held that societies could not impose quarantine periods after member withdrawal. As explained by the court:

> "A compulsory assignment of all copyrights, both present and future, no distinction being drawn between the different generally accepted types of exploitation, may appear an unfair condition, especially if such assignment is required for an extended period after the member's withdrawal."

The European Commission has accepted the detachment of some rights from collective administration. In the *Daft Punk* case (Banghalter), the Commission decided that a collecting society could retain its rules against individual management provided they grant derogations. Any refusal by a collecting society to grant such derogation would have to be exceptional and based on objective reasons. The Commission considered it legitimate for a collecting society to retain the means to monitor artists wishing to manage certain rights individually and the reasons behind it. Having a public trusted registry would offer safeguards for the potential licensees against fraudulent licensing.

Many collecting societies have the authority to collect royalties also for non-members. If non-members want to relinquish royalties, they have to submit a written form to each collecting society. Collecting societies are collecting also royalties for non-member CC licensors against the CC license agreement. A registry of individually managed works and rights could solve the collision problem. Collecting societies could well operate the registry. The voluntary registry would include global licensing information and it would have a guarantee function by authenticating licensors and their works.

2.6. ADMINISTRATION COSTS

Author/composer members run most of the copyright societies in Europe. Only the members who receive royalties have a right to vote. At first, it would look like that accepting CC licensors as members would not generate income to the collective, but on the contrary, it would burden societies' administrative systems. There is a risk that the members perceive CC as a burden and useless expenditure to revenue-generating right owners. Rochelandet (2002) describes the problem:

> "Beyond their common goal of individual revenues maximization, all members have not the same interest: from the large members' viewpoint, CCS [copyright collecting society] have to specialize on the collection of the most valuable rights, i.e. those that are the less costly to administrate, whereas less important members expect their organization to collect any right, even if it proves to be costly for a CCS to adopt such a development strategy. In fact, the conflict here is centred on the cross-subsidies between highly valuable copyrights and costly-to-collect copyrights. However, in the spirit of the copyright law, copyright is not aimed to favour some copyright holders to the detriment of others. So copyrights should tend to their social value for all kind of copyrighted uses and CCS should maximize the sums they collect and distribute."

Obtaining voting members' approval for policy changes that might decrease their royalties or even placing the matter on the agenda might turn out to be impossible. The administration system is rigged in a way that the decisions are made by established creators who are more likely to oppose disruptive business models.

Because of recent mergers, the broadcast and record industries are concentrated among a few companies. If there are no benefits, but only higher administrative costs, there is a risk that the biggest names and users may start their own collecting body that better serves their needs. Such a new and exclusive copyright society could cover the majority of music played on commercial radio and TV. This was one the motivations when American collecting society BMI was formed. In 1941, American broadcast companies started their own collecting society after a dispute with artist run ASCAP society (e.g., Besen, 1992).

After the Commission started examining the cross border licensing, the European collecting societies expressed fear of a race to bottom (Gesac, 2005). Their fear scenario is more than likely as there are over fifty music-collecting societies in Europe for a population that is roughly twice as big as in U.S. One concern is that the major record companies and music publishers will find a common licensing and collection body that would not accept "small" unprofitable authors as clients or at least that their special needs would not be viewed as important. Big organizations might be able to utilize the economies of scale and reduce the administrative overhead. However, a central exclusive licensing organization might mean that licensing the long tail of non-hit music would be more difficult and expensive. The small collecting societies also fear that big inter-European collecting societies would not take into account the special national circumstances and would eventually impoverish the supply of national music.

The biggest cost incurred by collecting societies from CC licensing probably would be to implement a registry of CC-licensed works. It is hard to argue why rights owners who do not use CC licenses should subsidize the members who do use them.

One solution would be to introduce higher administrative overheads for CC licensed works. However, the cost of CC-licensed content should really fall on licensees who get the benefit of the license. Users are in best position to assess if they need to buy a separate license or pay royalties. They also carry the liability of possible infringement which creates incentive to do copyright due diligence thoroughly. Licensing lawyers would ultimately determinate whether to buy a license and case law interpretation of the licenses would eventually be developed. Leaving the enforcement of the CC licenses out of collecting societies' assignments would be both practical and cost saving. Free and open source licensing has shown that the community is successful in finding infringers and that peer pressure can force infringers to respect open licenses. Typically, the open license breaches are clear and they do not proceed to courts. There are only a few examples of open licensing where the licenses were part of litigation.

By shifting the risk of license assessments to licensees and enforcement to rights owners and the community, the CC licensors would not create extra administration costs for other members of the collecting society. Granting a license for performing rights involves some fixed costs and proposed licensing of CC material would mean almost no cost for each additional song.

2.7. THE PROBLEM OF CHERRY-PICKING

A one-stop shop depends on collecting societies' ability to provide every user a license with predefined terms. In *BRT v SABAM,* the European Court of Justice stated that there must be "a balance between the requirement of maximum freedom for authors, composers, and publishers to dispose of their works and that of the effective management of their rights by an undertaking which in practice they avoid joining."

Members who could manage lucrative licensing deals and leave the rest to collecting societies would undermine the delicate balance. It is hard to argue why societies should limit individual licensing to just one group, *i.e.,* users of CC licenses. Opening the individual licensing floodgate would change the very nature of collective licensing and might lead to a situation economists refer as adverse selection. Artists would manage lucrative deals themselves, leaving low-income rights to collecting societies. Societies would collect fewer royalties and their overheads would grow. This would make the societies even less appealing and more authors would handle licensing and collecting themselves.

Transferring all rights exclusively limits rights owners' ability to use and invest their intellectual property. Sometimes rights owners can make better deals directly with users. The model has worked in the U.S. where it has not diluted collecting societies' ability to work and it has ensured that rights owners have the ability to invest their intellectual property the way they choose. It is somewhat perverse that the European copyright system, which is based on the idea of authors' sovereignty, is limiting authors' power to administer their rights.

The European Court of Justice has considered collecting societies' rights to limit competition and the free flow of the creative works of its members in several cases. In *BRT v. SABAM* (1974), the court concluded that:

> "The fact that an undertaking entrusted with the exploitation of copyrights and occupying a dominant position within the meaning of article 86 *[abuse of dominant position]* imposes on its members obligations which are not absolutely necessary for the attainment of its object and which thus encroach unfairly upon a member's freedom to exercise his copyright can constitute an abuse."

The court reached the same conclusion in two other cases, *Ministere Public v. Tournier* and *Lucazeau v. Sacem*. In *Tournier*, the court ruled that copyright management societies pursued a legitimate aim when they endeavoured to safeguard the rights and interests of their members vis-à-vis the users of recorded music. The court also held that the action was legitimate unless the practice exceeded the limit of what was necessary for the attainment of that aim. *Tournier* and *Sacem* both stand for the proposition that monopoly in principle is not a problem for competition, as long as collecting societies do not impose unreasonable restrictions on their members or on access to rights by prospective clients.

National antitrust bodies have gone even further. In 1995, the Irish pop group U2 and its publisher wanted the right to administer U2's live concerts themselves, which the Performing Rights Society (PRS) rejected on the grounds of its statutes (Evans, 2002, Lawson 2002). U2 claimed that the assignment of all categories of performing rights was not necessary for the PRS's operations and objectives. They also claimed that rights owners obtained more money more quickly when they exercised these rights themselves. The British Monopolies and Mergers Commission investigated the claims and stated:

> "We were not persuaded that the PRS's present practice of exclusivity was so essential that no further exceptions could be allowed. Nor were we convinced that any considerable additional costs would necessarily fall on the PRS. If members consider that they can administer live performances themselves at least as effectively as the PRS then they should be free to choose, but should bear any reasonable additional costs caused to the PRS."

The parties settled the U2 case and as a result, PRS amended its statutes and introduced a general policy under which it would grant each member a license for live performances upon request.

It may be that the concerns of collecting societies are overstated. In the American collective management system, rights owners can individually license their rights in conjunction with membership of collecting societies. There is no evidence that the delicate balance in the U.S. has tilted or suffered increased costs. However, it is hard to say if the individual licensing has had positive financial effect on American music industry. Nevertheless, it has offered rights owners a choice to test new licensing models.

2.8. NO BENEFIT FOR BLANKET LICENSEES

Collecting societies achieve a further reduction of bargaining costs with "blanket licenses". The societies grant blanket licensees as "bundle" of rights. The license includes the right to use the entire repertoire. Blanket licensees usually pay a certain percentage of their profits. For example, a radio station might pay 20 percent of its advertising income to collecting society if it plays over seven hours of music daily. The station is also obliged to report the use of licensed music to collecting societies. These reports enable fair distribution of royalties to right owners. A majority of collecting societies' royalty income comes from blanket licenses.

Introducing CC-licensed music to collecting societies would require users to get discounts for the royalty-free music they play. Collecting societies could implement this by creating a new license fee category for the free music. For example, a radio channel could obtain its annual license

20 percent cheaper if a minimum of 15 percent of its music was royalty-free. Having to categorize played works might sound cumbersome, but radio stations already fill out detailed reports of the music they play.

The royalty system serves another goal as well. Tax funded public broadcasters have a duty to support local arts and culture. The public broadcasters can distribute the support for culture more accurately to authors through collective licensing than with a general grant system. Thus, in many European countries where public broadcast radio is strong, "discount CC radio" is unnecessary. The argument does not take into account the commercial and small amateur broad- and webcasters who have hard time living with the license fees (E.g. Fisher, 2004). The question boils down to whether the copyright system should serve big users, small users, or individuals. Finding a balance that serves them all is harder than it looks at first glance.

2.9. COMPETITION

European competition law has three policies that affect collective management of copyrights (Wood, 2002). First, community competition recognizes the need to promote creativity and cultural diversity. Second, the EU is based on a Europe without internal frontiers. The artists and services should be able to move freely and there should be no discrimination on grounds of nationality. Third, the EU is developing a European information society that stimulates Internet services and e-commerce.

The strong role of collecting societies as the protectors of authors' interests has been easy to defend in the past. The collecting society institution is comparable to labour trade agreements and labour unions. Collecting societies justify their position with a need to negotiate the best possible contract for their members. The joint administration of copyrights by collecting societies is a counterweight to the market power of the users of works. The mergers that have led to the concentration of the media industry emphasize the need for stronger collecting societies, which can negotiate balanced deals. Collecting societies like to pose as institutions that create balance, cut extravagance, guard against exploitative terms, and lower transaction costs. However, outsourcing and a flexible work force have replaced the era of strong trade unions. Collecting societies are relics from the bygone days of strong industry cartels. In a world where dynamic companies move their factories and work force from country to country to satisfy consumers' need for cheap goods, the creative sector has managed to protect itself against global competition rather well. This is partly because of the local nature of cultural goods. Nevertheless, the cultural sector is starting to face the realities of the digital revolution. Consumers demand new services that provide more freedoms than local record stores. Legal online services have found it hard to compete with illegal file sharing services, as online licensing practices are still developing. The monopoly position that collecting societies have enjoyed has also meant that there have been few incentives to develop their services which has hampered the development of new digital services. The collecting societies shift from the industrial age institution to information age institution is still very much in progress.

The music industry is one of the few industries where a legal horizontal venture of producers (*i.e.,* cartel) exists and there is virtually no price competition among producers, as they usually have only one common sales agency selling their licenses. Posner (2001) uses collecting societies as an example of a few cases of "benign cartels" and concludes that: "So high are those [transaction] costs that it is nearly certain that the output of the song industry is greater than it would be if the BMI and ASCAP cartels were outlawed." In general, each national collecting society for authors' rights enjoys *de jure* and *de facto* monopoly in its territory, where practically all significant composers' and songwriters' are members of the organization (Vinje et. al., 2003).

As in all intellectual property rights regulation, antitrust and competition law control is present. Competition law partly ties collecting societies' hands. For example, they must license domestic music with the same terms as foreign music. Societies cannot have price discrimination, which means that they have to sell the hit music for the same price as any other music.

The regulator has to take into account several factors. The regulators will not intervene to licensing if it raises the overall cost of licensing. On the other hand, the low cost of licensing alone should not justify anticompetitive behaviour. The regulation of the collecting societies is not purely utilitarian. Regulators may tolerate some otherwise anticompetitive actions and policies if they progress cultural diversity.

In many cases, the law requires efficient administration in order to obtain authorization for the society, which has caused a barrier for entry and the societies have enjoyed their natural monopoly status. Many natural monopolies have disappeared because of technology. Landlines and long distance phone calls face competition from mobile phones and voice over IP telephony. While technology has changed natural monopolies, consumers have typically benefited from the competition and new services.

The competition law is relevant in three cases: 1) the level of fees that societies collect; 2) the relationship between collecting societies; and 3) the relationship between members and their collecting society. The Commission has acted lately in the second category in so-called Santiago Agreement case. The Santiago Agreement, signed by several collecting societies, provides that users of online services should obtain a license for the music repertoire of all collecting societies participating in the Agreement from the collecting society of their member state. The license would be valid all over Europe. However, since the Santiago Agreement insisted that an entity wishing to purchase music rights must buy them from a collecting society in their own country, the European Commission saw the system as anti-competitive. The central problem was that online users wanted more choices as to which collective rights manager can grant a multi-territorial licenses.

In 2004, the Commission opened proceedings against sixteen European collecting societies as another measure to break down the monopolies of national collecting societies and to create competition in the field of collective management of copyrights. The Commission considered that online-related activities should be accompanied by an increasing freedom of choice by consumers and commercial users throughout Europe as regards their service providers, such as to achieve a genuine European single market. With the implementation of a true European one-stop shop, the collecting societies could compete with online licensing terms and policies. The lack of competition between national collecting societies in Europe may be one reason for the inefficiencies of European online music services. The Commission recommended that: "right-holders should be able to determine the online rights to be entrusted for collective management."

Collecting societies opposed the Commission's recommendation. They felt that there were insufficient justifications leading to the recommendation. CISAC modified its model contract in 2004. New provisions remove restrictions for rights holders to join the society of their choice. The Commission's recommendation follows the lines of the previous court decisions of *GEMA I* and *U2* with an added Internet twist. At first glance, the recommendation seems to make little change to the current situation. Yet, as the Commission reduces the cost of changing collecting society to few mouse clicks, the globalization and competition in the cultural field might suddenly become reality. At best, the competitive advantage could include lower administrative overhead and creator-friendly licensing such as CC licenses. The second option is a race to the bottom, where collecting societies compete with low administrative overhead by trimming all extra services. Such development could lead to few large central licensing societies and boutique societies that would cater with innovative services. The small collecting societies fear that their most productive members would flee to large, low-overhead societies. Such development would lead to small societies combining their force as joint ventures. The need for national societies would not disappear, as the effective enforcement of members' rights requires national presence. The Commission's recommendation may have far-reaching impacts to

European online licensing including the CC licensing. The change is present as European societies are in the process of reforming their policies and rules. Whether the societies see CC as competitive advantage or hindrance remains to be seen. Considering that the ultimate goal of the Commission was to increase the competition at the level of the rights holders, it is not impossible that the Commission would intervene again if it believed that societies' discrimination of CC licensing is anti-competitive.

2.10. ENDORSEMENT

It can be hard to argue why the collecting societies should paternalistically guard its members from using the Internet as a marketing and distributing medium. Nadel (2004) states that "copyright law's prohibition against unauthorized copying and sales may, counter to the law's purported goal, have an overall negative impact on the production and dissemination of creative content." One may disagree with Nadel, but it is hard to deny that prohibiting rights owners from authoring copying on their own terms has a negative effect on our culture.

The music business is like the movie business; both are superstar economies (Rosen 1981). Success depends heavily of the amount of advertising invested in the product. The CC may enable Internet marketing for new artists who do not have the resources for promotion. Additionally, use for the licenses is a loss leader approach, where rights owners reintroduce works that have passed the high point of their product life cycle to the public with CC license terms in the hope of rediscovery. For example, rights owners could use non-commercial licenses to generate demand for commercial licenses. Online distribution could also boost the sales of concerts, products, and records. Through this process, rights owner may extend the commercial lifespan of their protected works.

3. The Future Role of the Collecting Society Institution

While the CC licenses are permissive, as compared to traditional copyright licenses, rights owners reserve some rights that they could transfer to societies' administration. It is notable that the majority of the CC-licensed works are reserving rights for commercial use. Below is Table 1 showing the tasks that collecting societies would manage and the rights they could sell if they adopt CC-licensed content. There are three categories. Selling licenses that enable:
1. Commercial use
2. Making derivative works
3. Creation of derivative works without share-alike terms (dual licensing).

Most of the works licensed with CC licenses have a non-commercial clause that reserves the commercial use of the work. All the commercial users need to buy a separate license in order to use the work. Having one common location where the works are for sale would benefit the rights owner and the buyer as well. CC licenses also enable dual licensing. Duality means that the rights owner combines both CC distribution mechanism and traditional content production. There is technically only one core product but two licenses: one for the free distribution and share-alike modifications, and another with terms that are more traditional. Because of the viral nature of the share-alike license, some users might find it compelling to buy a separate license that does not pose restrictions for distribution of derivative works.

Consider a film production that would want to use non-commercial, share-alike licensed music. If the production is commercial, they would have to get a separate license that permits the commercial use of music. If the production is non-commercial but they do not want to license the final movie with the CC license, they would need to get a separate license that does not include the share-alike term. The collecting societies would be a natural institution to sell the licenses to users willing to pay for them. Having a one place to clear the rights of the whole movie and its songs would benefit the producers.

Table 1. Creative Commons version 3.0 Licenses

Licenses	Synchronization	Derivative works	Reproduction	Public performance
①	No license	No license	No license	No license
①⊜	Separate license	Separate license	No license	No license
①⊜⑤	Separate license	Separate license	License for commercial use	License for commercial use
①⑤	License for commercial use	License for commercial use	License for commercial use	License for commercial use
①⑤⊙	Commercial use & dual licensing	Commercial use & dual licensing	Commercial use & dual licensing	Commercial use & dual licensing
①⊙	Dual licensing	Dual licensing	No license	No license

Licenses symbols: **⊜**   **⑤**   **⊙**   **①**

4. Conclusions

This chapter has examined the collective copyright management institute. The institute was born, just like CC licensing, to solve market inefficiencies. Traditionally collecting societies have served authors by collecting royalties, acting as negotiators and as a lobbying power for strong author's rights. The collective management is an industrial age's answer to market demand. However, the needs of the post-industrial network society have changed. The societies have had hard time understanding the shift to a world where rights owners want to share their works in non-commercial markets. This is visible with some of the societies' attitudes to the CC licensing.

While the CC relies on a strong copyright system, it is not compatible with collecting societies' licensing structures. There are two major incompatibilities:

1. Problems with the CC licenses and the licensing system
2. General problems related to combining individual and collective administration of copyrights.

The changed needs of the creators of copyrighted works call for changes in the ways we administer copyrights. By limiting their clients' licensing power, collecting societies are using their legal cartel position in a way that may require action from legislators. We must reconsider the role of the collecting societies. This paper has lead us to the practical question of how one could apply more liberal licenses such as those provided by the CC to works governed by collecting societies. Three options arise.

The first option would be for publishers and collecting societies to change their policies. Such a change would require thorough economic research of the benefits and costs of allowing member to use CC licensing. Reducing collecting societies' role to bare license collection would eliminate some of the costs related to interpretation and enforcement of the licenses. The cost of licensing would be on licensee and the cost of enforcement on the licensor.

According to Landes and Posner (2003), given today's technology, the creation of a "universal" copyright registry in exchange for incremental benefits to authors would be highly attractive. The burden on authors is minor in exchange for what is likely to be a very substantial benefit to those who seek to republish that author's work. Licensees could check from the registry whether the rights owners have legally licensed the content by verifying rights owner's permissions. Users would eventually get used to legal metadata and learn to respect copyrights. A verification server could also include pricing information of the commercial rights, peer evaluation of the music, links to similar music and an e-commerce site where commercial rights and fan products would be for sale. A registry would dramatically reduce the transactions costs of licensing. It would also serve users who could verify that content is legally distributed and thus reduce risk of infringement.

A second option would be to force reforms on collecting societies. The European Commission has lately shown interest in dismantling all barriers to competition for copyright societies. The Commissions' decisions have not had the desired effect on competition and legislation seems inevitable. The European Parliament (2003) has started to recognize that: "The freedom of creators to decide for themselves which rights they wish to confer on collective management societies, and which rights they wish to manage individually must also be safeguarded by legislation."

The third option would be to develop copyright law in a way that gives the author the ability to get his copyright back in limited cases for re-licensing under reasonable circumstances. Germany has recently enacted a law on copyright contracts with the intention of balancing the negotiation power of individual authors with publishers. Under certain conditions, it is even possible for an author to terminate the publishing contract and republish the work under new terms. Such an exception in copyright law might hurt liberal licensing systems if it was possible to withhold from CC licenses because the public had too much power over the work and because the license was perpetual (Välimäki & Hietanen, 2004).

The collecting societies as well as the open content licenses serve the public by lowering transaction costs. Finding a way to combine the two institutions could mean all the artists receiving payments for the use of their works, and at the same time, consumers would have more culture available on creators' terms. In order to reach the goal, both institutions must make changes. The CC must clarify its licenses and modify them to fit to the automatic licensing scheme of the collecting societies. The collecting societies on their behalf have to open their paternalistic administration systems to reflect the changed motivations of rights owners and the new business models they are using. With few simple changes, it is possible that centralized intermediaries can operate side-by-side with amateurs, and both can profit from the experience.

References

Besen, S.; Kirby, S. and Salop, S. (1992), *An Economic Analysis of Copyright Collectives*, Virginia Law Review, Vol. 78, No. 1, Symposium on the Law and Economics of Intellectual Property February 1992, pp. 383 - 411.

Buckman, J. (2004), *Magnatune, an Open Music Experiment*, Linux Journal, Vol 118, available at: http://new.linuxjournal.com/article/7220 (accessed 3 may 2010).

Ehrlich, C. (1989), *Harmonious Alliance, A History of the Performing Right Society*, Oxford University Press.

Elkin-Koren, N. (2006), *Creative Commons: A Skeptical View of a Worthy Pursuit, in the future of the public domain,* in Hugenholtz, P. B.; Guibault, L. (Eds.), Kluwer Law International, available at: http://ssrn.com/abstract=885466 (accessed 3 May 2010).

European parliament (2003), *Report by the European Parliament on a Community Framework for Collecting Societies for Authors' Rights, 2002/2274(INI),* Committee on Legal Affairs and the Internal Market.

Evans, C.; Larrieu, N. (2002), *Collective Licensing Today (non digital media) Performing Rights: The Licensor Experience – Live Performances: the PRS Experience,* in Kendrick, J. (Ed.), "International Association of Entertainment Lawyers, Collective Licensing: Past, Present and Future", I.A.E.L. pp. 61.

Fisher, W. (2004), *Promises to Keep, Technology, Law, and the Future of Entertainment,* Stanford University Press.

Gesac (2005), *Working document of 7 july 2005 from the directorate-general for the internal market on a community initiative on the cross-border collective management of copyright – Gesac's Preliminary Comments,* July 2005, available at: http://www.gesac.org/eng/positions/download/GCOLLECT094ipen05.doc (accessed 3 May 2010).

Guez, M. (2003), *Hearing on Collecting Societies European Parliament,* available at: http://www.europarl.europa.eu/hearings/20031007/juri/guez.pdf (accessed 3 May 2010).

Hess, C. and Ostrom, E. (2003), *Ideas, Artifacts, and Facilities: Information as a Common-Pool Resource,* Law and Contemporary Problems, Vol. 66, pp. 111 – 146.

Hietanen, H. (2007), *Analyzing the Nature of Creative Commons Licenses,* Nordiskt Immateriellt Rättsskydd, Vol. 6, pp. 517 - 535.

Katz, A. (2005), *The Potential Demise of Another Natural Monopoly: Rethinking the Collective Administration of Performing Rights,* Journal of Competition Law and Economics, Vol. 1, pp. 541 – 593.

Lawson, E. (2002), *Collective Licensing Today (non digital media) – Performing Rights: The Licensee Experience – Live Performances: Collecting Societies and the Public Performance Right,* in Kendrick, J. (Ed.) "International Association of Entertainment Lawyers, Collective Licensing: Past, Present and Future", I.A.E.L., pp. 89.

Landes, W. and Posner, R. (2003), *The Economic Structure of Intellectual Property Law,* Harvard University Press.

Magnatune Statistics: what sells?, available at: http://magnatune.com/info/stats/ (accessed 1 May 2010).

Moeltke, H. (2008) *KODA-medlemmer kan nu bruge Creative Commons,* available at: http://creativecommons.dk/?p=11 (accessed 3 May 2010).

Monopolies and Mergers Commission (1996), *Performing Rights: A Report on the Supply in the UK of the Services of Administering Performing Rights and Film Synchronisation Right,* summary, available at: www.competition-commission.org.uk/rep_pub/reports/1996/378 performing.htm (accessed 3 May 2010).

Nadel, M. (2004), *How Current Copyright Law Discourages Creative Output: the Overlooked Impact of Marketing*, Berkeley Technology Law Journal, Vol. 19, pp. 785 – 856.

Pike, E. (2005), *What You Need to Know about Creative Commons,* issue 15.

Posner, R. (2001), *Antitrust Law*, University of Chicago Press.

Rigg, N. (2002), *The European Perspective,* in Kendrick, J. (Ed.) "International Association of Entertainment Lawyers, Collective Licensing: Past, Present and Future", I.A.E.L. pp. 18 – 30.

Rochelandet, F. (2002), *Are Copyright Collecting Societies Efficient? An Evaluation of Collective Administration of Copyright in Europe,* available at: http://www.serci.org/2002/rochelandet.pdf (accessed 3 May 2010).

Rosen, S. (1981), *The Economics of Superstars*, The American Economics Review, Vol. 71, pp. 845 - 858.

Schrøder, A. (2008), *KODA og Creative Commons*, available at: http://koda.dk/medlemmer/musikverker/creative-commons/koda-og-creative-commons (accessed 3 May 2010).

Tóth, P. (2005), *Creative Humbug;Personal Feelings About the Creative Commons Licenses,* available at: http://www.indicare.org/tiki-read_article.php?article=118 (accessed 3 May 2010).

Vinje, T.; Paemen, D. and Romelsjö, J. (2003), *Collecting society practices retard development of online music market: a European perspective*, Computer and Internet Lawyer, Vol. 20, No. 12.

Välimäki, M. and Hietanen, H. (2004), *Challenges of Open Content Licensing in Europe: What are the legal implications when the principles of open source software licensing are applied to other copyrighted works on the Internet?*, Computer Law Review International, Issue 6, pp. 173 – 178.

Wood, D. (2002), *Collective Management and EU Competition Law*, in Kendrick, J. (Ed.), "International Association of Entertainment Lawyers, Collective Licensing: Past, Present and Future", I.A.E.L.

Cases
BRT/SABAM II, 1973 ECR.

Buffalo Broadcasting Co. v. ASCAP, 744 F.2d 917, 928-29, cert. denied, 469 U.S. 1311 (1985).

Columbia Broadcasting Sys. v. ASCAP, 620 F.2d 930, 937, cert. denied, 450 U.S. 970 (1981).

"*Daft Punk*" Banghalter et Homem Christo v Sacem COMP/C2/37.219.

Hadady Corp. v. Dean Witter Reynolds, Inc., 739 F. Supp. 1392 (C.D. Cal. 1990)

Lucazeau v Sacem, Joined cases 110/88, 241/88 and 242/88, 1989 E.C.R. 2811.

Ministere Public v Tournier, Case 395/87, 1989 E.C.R 2521.

SGAE v. Luis, Spanish Provincial Court of Pontevedra, (3008/2005).

SGAE v. Fernández, Badajoz Sixth court of First instance (15/2.006.).

The SeLiLi Project: Free Advice on Free Licenses

Juan Carlos De Martín, Andrea Glorioso
Politecnico di Torino, NEXA Center for Internet and Society

Abstract. Although reliable figures have so far proven difficult to obtain, it is undeniable that social practices of sharing informational and information-based goods have become a substantial part of our world. Since the seminal work of the Free Software Foundation in the early '80s, these social practices continue to be based upon a set of legal instruments: copyright licenses. Free/Open Source licenses, such as the GNU General Public License, and licenses for other forms of creative works, such as the Creative Commons Public Licenses, have become much more than a mere curiosity for legal scholars: they are used day after day by persons from all backgrounds, who often do not have the necessary skills to properly understand either the legal meaning of these licenses, or the specific ways to use these licenses in their ordinary activities in a given legal system. Recognizing the cultural and economic value of encouraging new forms of creativity, based upon a "some rights reserved" principle that permits a more liberal and pervasive sharing of informational goods than allowed by "standard" copyright, the Government of the Piedmont Region has teamed with the Politecnico of Torino to create SeLiLi – Servizio Licenze Libere (Libre Licenses Service): a project based in Torino (Italy) and aimed at providing private persons, public institutions and small businesses with information and, when necessary, consulting services on these licenses, with a multi-disciplinar perspective that draws upon law, economics and computer science. This chapter describes the main characteristics of SeLiLi and summarizes the results of its first year of activities.

Keywords: Creative Commons, Free Licenses, Licencing Services

1. Introduction

SeLiLi[1] – the acronym of "SErvizio LIcenze LIbere", or "Libre Licenses Services" – is a project launched by the Polytechnic of Turin and the Piedmont Regional Government in 2006, with the goal to provide the public with professional, up-to-date information and consulting services on copyright licensing; more specifically, on those licenses[2] whose terms are inspired to principles of knowledge and information sharing – termed

---

[1]   See http://selili.polito.it/.

[2]   In this contribution we will use the generic term "licenses" without taking a position on the discussion whether licenses such as the GNU General Public License or Creative Commons Public Licenses are to be considered contracts, obligations, or something else altogether. For a discussion based on the Italian law system, see C. Piana (2006).

"licenze libere" in Italian and roughly translatable as "libre licenses"[3] in English.[4]

2. Why SeLiLi is needed

Although research is still trying to find satisfactory answers to the methodological challenges that must be solved before being able to provide some empirically-sound numbers on the actual usage rate of "libre licenses" by the world population[5] – a first precondition to evaluate the economic value of the transactions that are based upon such licenses[6] – it can be argued that the number of people or organizations wishing to use

---

[3]   The French/Spanish term "libre" has been used with some success in Europe, originally as an alternative to "free" in "free software". The term has the obvious advantage of clarifying the ambiguous meaning of "free", i.e. free as in "gratis" or free as in "freedom", the latter being the correct one in this context.

[4]   The founders of SeLiLi were well aware of the debates on the usage of the term "libero" in the context of licensing practices, as well as of the fact that the Free Software Foundation does not consider a large subset of the Creative Commons licenses as "libre licenses"   or   "licenze   libere"   (see   *inter   alia* http://www.chander.com/2006/03/richard_stallma.html, last visited on 27/03/2008). Nonetheless, it was decided to focus on the practical goals of the project, for which a catchy name and mission would have been arguably more useful than lengthy discussions on terminology.

[5]   See *inter alia* C. Waelde et al. (2005), G. Cheliotis et al. (2007), B. Bildstein (2007).

[6]   See *inter alia* R. Pollock, *The Value of the Public Domain*, IPPR, 2006, available at: http://www.ippr.org.uk/publicationsandreports/publication.asp?id=482, chapter 6 of P. Aigrain (2005), and the recent call for tenders of the European Commission (INFSO/2007/0043, " Assessment of the economic and social impacts of the public domain in the Information Society", which, on the basis of a broad definition of public domain which encompassed "content is material that is not or no longer protected by intellectual property rights", but also "material that, although strictly speaking copyright protected, is generally available for all, as the copyright holder has waived part of his rights allowing for its use and re-use ", requested "to estimate the number of works in the public domain in the EU [...] for published works, such as literary or artistic works, music and audiovisual material, to calculate approximately the levels and ways of use of the public domain material and to highlight the main users in the above mentioned sectors, [...] [t]o estimate the current economic value of public domain works and estimate the value of the works that in the next 10-20 years are to be released into the public domain and determine any change in its value whilst under copyright and once it is on the public domain, [...] [t]o identify and analyze the current practices for re-use of public domain content held by European cultural institutions and assess their capacity to implement the principles for re-use as established in the Public Sector Information (PSI) Directive, [...] [t]o identify and analyze current available mechanisms for voluntary sharing of content and to ascertain the pro's and cons of each mechanism, highlighting the degree of use of the most successful ones and their impact based   on   relevant   indicators".   The   study,   led   by   Rightscom   (see http://www.rightscom.co.uk/) is currently undergoing.

"libre licenses" on their intellectual output is significant. It is certainly so in Italy, judging from the number of blogs and institutional newspapers[7] that are using Creative Commons licenses, from the experiments of public administrations with FLOSS,[8] and from the anecdotal experiences of the members of the Creative Commons Italia working group.[9]

However, the desire to employ "libre licenses" does not necessarily go hand in hand with all the knowledge that is necessary to understand how to properly use them. This is particularly true for private users, who often do not have expertise in law, technology or economics: the emergence of phenomena variously labeled as "commons-based peer production",[10]

---

[7]   For example, the tech-centered online newspaper Punto Informatico (http://www.punto-informatico.it/) or La Stampa (http://www.lastampa.it/), which has licensed two of its major editorial products, TuttoLibri and TuttoScience, using Creative Commons licenses.

[8]   FLOSS – "Free, Libre, Open Source Software" – can be briefly described as the set of all computer programs (software) whose licensing terms grant licensees the rights (a) to use the program for whatever purpose, (b) to study how the program works (having access to the source code of the program – meaning the preferred form of modification, usually consisting in a complex and large series of statements in a specific formal language – is a logical and practical precondition for this right to be exercised), (c) to copy the program and redistribute such copies, (d) to modify the program and redistribute such modified versions (here again as in point (b), access to the source code is a logical and practical precondition for this right to be exercised). We use the term FLOSS, proposed by Rishab Ghosh, to avoid any discussion on which term – "free", "open source", "libre" – is preferable.

[9]   In Italy, the translation/porting of CC licenses have been conducted since version 2.0, by the "Creative Commons Italia" working group (http://creativecommons.it), chaired by Prof. Marco Ricolfi of the Dipartimento di Scienze Giuridiche (DSG) of the University of Torino. Creative Commons Italia is not a formal association, but rather a "variable geometry" group of people interested in the Italian porting of the CCPL. The Istituto di Elettronica e di Ingegneria dell'Informazione e delle Telecomunicazioni of the CNR (IEIIT-CNR) provided help and information on the computer-related aspects of the CC licenses. Nowadays, the Italian adaptation of the CCPL, as well as their dissemination, is managed by the Politecnico di Torino, which hosts a multi-disciplinary working group chaired by Prof. Juan Carlos De Martin.

[10]   See Y. Benkler (2002, 2004, 2007). This model, proposed by Benkler as an alternative to the Coasean dichotomy between the market and the firm (Coase, 1937) can be basically summarized as a mode of economic production in which the horizontal efforts of large numbers of coordinated   volunteers result in the production of complex innovation, given a certain number of *ex ante* (namely that (1) information is "quirky" (sic), i.e. purely non-rival and characterized by the fact that the primary non-human input of information-based activities are the same as its output; (2) physical capital costs of information production have declined; (3) the primary human input in the process – talent – is highly variable and individuals have the best knowledge on how to allocate it, whether themselves or thanks to distributed peer reviewing of each other's talent; (4) information exchange is particularly cheap today) and *ex post* (that no "reduction of [the] intrinsic benefits of participation" to the peer production takes place; this could happen in Benkler's model when behaviours that affects contributor's valuation of the value of participation, such as an

"user-centered innovation",[11] "pro-am revolution",[12] "user-generated content",[13] coupled with the overarching importance that copyright and other policies on "intellectual property"[14] have acquired in recent years – in terms of legal regulations, technological innovations and new business models – puts a large burden on the shoulders of creators and innovators. Even small and medium businesses (which in Europe constitute a large part of the economic landscape[15] and in Italy often take the form of "micro

---

unilateral appropriation by a member of the project, take place, or when the provisioning of the integration function fails) conditions. Benkler, in *Coase's Penguin*, cites the Linux kernel (see http://www.kernel.org/), the online discussion forum Slashdot (see http://www.slashdot.org/) and the online collaborative encyclopaedia Wikipedia (see http://www.wikipedia.org/) among other, as examples of complex innovations that were produced through peer production.

[11] The concept, proposed by Eric Von Hippel (1998, 2005), is based on the assumption that modern-day economic entities do not necessarily own all body of knowledge, whether formalized or not, that is needed in order to produce innovation. Consequently, the attention shifts towards what lies outside the web of entities that are normally understood as being part of the innovation process, i.e. the users. In this model users, rather than the original creators, will be under certain conditions more efficient in innovating a certain product/process.

[12] See Leadbeater and Miller (2004).

[13] See Organisation for Economic Co-operation and Development, *Participative Web: User-Created Content*, Report DSTI/ICCP/IE(2006)7/FINAL, 2007, which define User-Generated or User-Created Content as "i) content made publicly available over the Interent, ii) which reflects a "certain amonut of creative effort", and iii) which is "created outside of professional routines and practices".

[14] We tend to agree with the view that the laws and policies coalesced under the term "intellectual property" are so different from one another that it may be difficult to engage in meaningful discussions. See F.M. Scherer (2007) and R.M.Stallman (2004): for this reason, we will use the term in quotes throughout this contribution. On the other hand, and relevant for the goals of SeLiLi, we notice that defining "intellectual property" as property can produce nice "side effects" in some countries, such as Italy, where property is explicitly supposed to serve a "social function" (Italian Constitution, art. 42(2): "Private property is recognized and guaranteed by the law, which determines the ways it can be acquired, used and its limits, with the goal of ensuring its social functions and making it available for everybody", English translation by the authors, emphasis added). For a thorough review of this argument, see M.A. Carrier (2004): "[c]ourts, commentators, and companies describe IP as a type of absolute property, bereft of any restraints. Examples even make their way into public discourse, as revealed by debates on copyrights that essentially last forever. But astonishingly, some of the most important consequences of this revolution have gone unnoticed. Although scholars have lamented the propertization of IP, they have failed to recognize a hidden promise of the transformation: the narrowing of IP").

[15] According to the European Commission, DG Enterprise and Industry, 99% of all enterprises in the European Union are Small and Medium Enterprises, for a total of 23 million businesses (see http://ec.europa.eu/enterprise/smes/facts_figures_en.htm).

enterprises"[16] with a very limited staff) can have a hard time finding all the necessary know-how "in house."

On the other hand, the government of the Piedmont region has been recently focusing a significant part of its budgetary and human resources for the promotion of the "creative economy",[17] on the assumptions – shared by other major institutional actors, including the European Union[18] – that

---

[16]   "The average firm in the EU employs just seven people, even though it's true that the figures vary greatly from country to country. Micro-businesses dominate employment in countries **such as Italy (48%)** and Greece (57%), whilst the share of large enterprises in total employment in the United Kingdom is over 45%". Micro-businesses are defined as enterprises having 1 to 9 employees" (European Commission, DG Enterprise and Industry, *supra* n. 15, emphasis added).

[17]   *Programma Triennale della Ricerca 2007/2009 (legge regionale 4/2006, art. 5),* http://www.regione.piemonte.it/ricerca/dwd/progr_trien.pdf.

[18]   The European Union has embraced the "i2010 strategy", which is the "policy framework for the information society and media. It promotes the positive contribution that information and communication technologies (ICT) can make to the economy, society and personal quality of life. The i2010 strategy has three aims: to create a Single European Information Space, which promotes an open and competitive internal market for information society and media services, to strengthen innovation and investment in ICT research, to support inclusion, better public services and quality of life through the use of ICT" (http://ec.europa.eu/information_society/eeurope/i2010/index_en.htm). In the context of the i2010 strategy, see in particular Communication COM/2007/0146 final from the Commission to the European Parliament, the Council, the European Economic and Social Committee and the Committee of the Regions - i2010 - Annual Information Society Report 2007, where a significant part is devoted to the explosion of "user-created content" (see *supra* n. 13), the Decision No 456/2005/EC of the European Parliament and of the Council of 9 March 2005 establishing a multiannual Community programme to make digital content in Europe more accessible, usable and exploitable ("The 4-year programme (2005–08), proposed by the European Commission, will have a budget of € 149 million to tackle organisational barriers and promote take up of leading-edge technical solutions to improve accessibility and usability of digital material in a multilingual environment. The Programme addresses specific market areas where development has been slow: geographic content (as a key constituent of public sector content), educational content, cultural, scientific and scholarly content. The Programme also supports EU-wide co-ordination of collections in libraries, museums and archives and the preservation of digital collections so as to ensure availability of cultural, scholarly and scientific assets for future use. **The programme aims at facilitating access to digital content, its use and exploitation, enhancing quality of content with well-defined metadata, and reinforcing cooperation between digital content stakeholders**. It will tackle multilingual and multicultural barriers", http://ec.europa.eu/information_society/activities/econtentplus/, emphasis added) and the eContent+ Work Programme 2006 ("[f]or the purposes of this work programme, public domain refers to content that is not or no longer protected by copyright, for example because it is not entitled to copyright protection or the copyright has been waived or has expired. Related issues that also require examination include material that is protected by copyright, but can be accessed and used by all, e.g. through open access, under Creative Commons licences or as orphan works, i.e. works protected by copyright but where it is impossible to identify the person entitled to exercise the rights", http://ec.europa.eu/information_society/activities/econtentplus/docs/call_2006/ecp_work_pr ogramme_2006.pdf).

a) the knowledge-based economy is a key asset in ensuring competitiveness and growth for society and that b) a more liberal approach to "intellectual property" can be beneficial in achieving both economic efficiency for private actors and public policy goals, some of which are clearly prescribed by the Italian Constitution.[19] Providing practical instruments that could ease the uptake of knowledge-related activities is a natural consequence of this approach. The convergence of the above dynamics resulted – among others initiative – in the creation of SeLiLi.

3. Institutional structure

From an institutional point of view, SeLiLi was founded and is currently hosted at the Department of Automation and Computer Engineering of the Politecnico of Torino; more specifically, SeLiLi is a project of the NEXA Center for Internet & Society, a research center for multidisciplinary Internet studies. The key expertise of its relevant members in the fields under consideration, as testified by previous and ongoing activities in the Italian porting of Creative Commons licenses,[20] was considered a basic asset for the success of the project. The Piedmont Region provides the financial resources that are used to cover the costs of second-level consulting services,[21] while the costs incurred for the day-to-day management of the project and for handling first-level cases are covered by the Politecnico of Torino.

4. Operational structure

Similar to the dynamics that "libre licenses" try to promote, SeLiLi is structured in a decentralized way and tries to use as much as practically possible and useful the "wisdom of the crowd".[22] Out of metaphor, the main actors of SeLiLi are the head of operations,[23] the scientific director,[24] and the technical manager. Besides these roles, a number of external auditors participate, on a volunteer basis, in the discussion of some of the cases submitted to SeLiLi. External consultants, specialized in different

---

[19]   For example, article 9(1) of the Italian Constitution states that "the [Italian] Republic promotes the development of culture and of scientific and technical research"; art. 33(1) states that "art and science, as well as their teaching, are free [as in freedom]". See also n. 14 *supra*.

[20]   See *supra* n. 9.

[21]   For a description of the different "levels", see the section "Operational structure".

[22]   See J. Surowiecki (2004).

[23]   Dr Andrea Glorioso took this role from the start of the project until February 2008, when he was replaced by Dr Thomas Margoni.

[24]   Prof. Juan Carlos De Martin is the scientific director of SeLiLi.

fields, are hired whenever a case seems to be particularly complex. It is worth stressing – since SeLiLi was criticized by some parties based on a wrong understanding of this specific point – that the activities of external consultants are the only one which draw upon the budget allocated by the Piedmont Region to SeLiLi.

A brief work flow of a typical request to SeLiLi will help clarify the role of the above actors and their relationships.

A typical requestor might want to clarify her doubts – of a legal, technological or economic nature – related to "libre licenses". She visits the SeLiLi website and finds references to a number of Frequently Asked Questions that might already provide an answer to her questions. Otherwise, she can contact the "front desk" of SeLiLi via a phone number or using a web-based form.[25]

Either way, the request is handled by the head of operations who will collect as much data as possible on the case. This is often one of the most difficult and most delicate steps of the whole process: a thorough understanding of what exactly is being asked is a precondition for choosing the most appropriate response, but at the same time most requestors pose very generic questions and/or use a "non technical" language that needs further clarifications. The head of operations does not have a mere "book keeping" role to play, but acts as an interface between two worlds: the one of requestors that are often amateurs, if not necessarily in their field, certainly in the field of copyright licensing, and the one of the auditors and of external consultants who are instead highly specialized in their respective fields, but not necessarily in interacting with end-users. This task might require at times scheduling a conference call or a face-to-face meeting in order to clarify any unclear issues. Another parallel task of the head of operations is to filter the requests in order to make sure that certain substantial and procedural requirements are satisfied, i.e. that the request deals with the topics on which SeLiLi provides its services,[26] and that the request comes from a person or from a small business.[27]

---

25   http://selili.polito.it/contact.

26   For example, a request to provide assistance for "copyright clearance" activities, even though they might necessary in order to license a particular work under a "libre license", would arguably be only tangential to the institutional goals of SeLiLi. There are obviously many "gray zones" in which a certain degree of elasticity is needed, since only extremely simple requests are exclusively focused on copyright licensing, and even more so on "libre licenses". See also the section "The road ahead".

27   The internal regulation of SeLiLi, on the basis of which the Piedmont Region agreed to provide funding to the project, explicitly limits the provision of information and consulting services to "private persons that wish to use 'libre licenses' outside their professional activities; public organisations (including schools and universities); not-for-profit organisations; professional users and enterprises [...] with less than fifteen employees"

Once the head of operations has duly understood the request and is satisfied that it passes the relevant substantial and procedural requirements, he produces a brief summary of the case which is sent to an internal, private mailing list. A number of external auditors – with expertise in law, computer science, economics – are subscribed to this mailing list and can thus read the summary posted by the head of operations: if any of them feels so inclined, he can provide his own opinion on the best way to answer the specific request. A strict adherence to the "Chatham house" principle, according to which opinions of the auditors, but not their names, can be quoted in the response, has allowed the flow of contributions to flourish, providing a significant added value to the activities of SeLiLi. Again, for the sake of clarity, it is worth repeating that all the external auditors participate strictly on a volunteer, unpaid basis.

At this point, the head of operations might come to the conclusion that a direct answer to the request, possibly with the help of the auditors, can be provided. The case is then classified as a "first-level case" and no further action is required.

However, in some cases the request might be too complex for the head of operations or the auditors to provide a satisfying answer. If this is the case, the request is classified as a "second-level case": the scientific director will contact an external consultant and ask her to provide the necessary consulting services. This activity is paid on the basis of a fixed fee and the relevant budget is provided by the Piedmont Region. Once the external consultant and the requestor have been put in contact – often through a meeting which is attended by the head of operations to facilitate information exchange – the whole process "moves out" of SeLiLi. In many cases – for example, when legal counseling is requested – this is necessary in order to ensure that all the relevant regulations on privacy and professional ethics are respected. The head of operations continues to interact on a rolling basis with the external consultant to keep track of the status of open requests, but will not be provided any further information on the substance of the case. At the end of the consulting activity, the external consultant provides SeLiLi with a report on her activities, with personal or other sensitive data duly omitted when necessary.

However, some cases might be too complex even for the "second-level" procedure to prove effective, especially considering the fixed fee that SeLiLi is able to provide, which might be too low for an external consultant to devote all the necessary resources for the problem at hand. To overcome this problem a special category of projects – the so-called "third-level cases" or "special projects" – have been devised. In this case all the terms of the consulting activity, including the duration, the cost and the desired

---

(unofficial English translation of the general bylaws of SeLiLi, available in Italian at http://selili.polito.it/node/38).

output, is negotiated on an "ad hoc" basis between the requestor, which is often a large organization, and SeLiLi. External consultants might be used as well for "special projects", but the nature and characteristics of their involvement, including the financial details, will also be negotiated by SeLiLi.

Until the end of 2007, SeLiLi has received twenty-nine requests that have been handled as "first-level cases", three requests handled as "second-level cases" and two requests that led to the creation of "special projects". The following section reports and discusses some of these requests/cases.

5. Some cases

5.1. FIRST-LEVEL CASES

As was explained in the previous section, many requests that are classified as "first-level cases" tend to be simple. They can often be answered by pointing the requestor to a list of Frequently Asked Questions or via a semi-automated response that is "cut and pasted" by the head of operations from previous responses to similar requests. Only in a minor number of cases was the intervention of the auditors necessary in order to answer – although the head of operations often asked for comments in order to stimulate internal debate and to have a second opinion on the request.

Common cases of "first-level" requests that were handled by SeLiLi included questions on which kind of works could the Creative Commons licenses be applied to (all works that are statutorily protected by Italian copyright law); how to correctly use material taken from Wikipedia (the answer pointed to the relevant passages of the GNU Free Documentation License, reminding the requestor that different resources used by Wikipedia, for example the media repository, could be licensed under different terms, and stressing that in any case the relevant statutory provisions on "exceptions and limitations" to copyright would apply, e.g. use for criticism and discussion); how to implement a web form for selecting a particular Creative Commons license while uploading a digital music file to a website (the requestor was given technical references by the technical manager of SeLiLi); whether Creative Commons licenses permitted synchronization of video and audio pieces to obtain a final product (the answer pointed at the relevant text of Creative Commons licensed that define "derivative work");[28] whether it was possible to use

---

28   Namely, art. 1(b) of the Creative Commons licenses, which define a Derivative Work as "a work based upon the Work or upon the Work and other pre-existing works, such as a translation, musical arrangement, dramatization, fictionalization, motion picture version, sound recording, art reproduction, abridgment, condensation, or any other form in which the Work may be recast, transformed, or adapted, except that a work that constitutes a

"the Creative Commons license" for various activities, including playing music in a cinema or licensing the contents of a database of images which would be used for an advertisement banner exchanges between not-for-profit organizations (in this and similar cases the standard answer was that, since there is not only one "Creative Commons license", the requestor had to select a CC license based upon the intended usage – basic directions to choose were provided and further information requested, but in most cases the requestor did not follow up).

Besides these fairly simple cases – which, at least when it is necessary to choose a particular Creative Commons license and especially whether the "Non Commercial" option[29] used to license a certain work would impede actual usage of that work in a specific situation, were not so trivial after all, but were anyway not turned into "second-level cases" because of an apparent lack of interest by the requestors – there are at least two categories of "first-level requests" that stood out and deserve a fuller treatment.

The first category is conceptual and refers to various questions which, at their core, were all based on the wrong assumption that "Creative Commons licenses" (or, by analogy, other licenses) "protected" the licensor's copyright over his/her work or were in any way or form the "source" of such rights. In all these cases the standard answer was that it was statutory law that granted the relevant rights, defined the ways in which these rights "came into life", and protected them – or rather, protected the legitimate holder of these rights. While this might seem absolutely obvious to a person with a legal background, the number of requests on this topic suggest a very limited understanding by "common people" of the basics of copyright law. While this is not by itself a surprise, this might play a role in evaluating the mission of SeLiLi: more specifically, whether SeLiLi should extend its core mission to providing information and consulting services simply on copyright law in general, rather than simply on "libre licenses".

The second category of requests that stood out among all the "first-level cases" is substantial and refers to the relationship between Creative

---

Collective Work will not be considered a Derivative Work for the purpose of this License. *For the avoidance of doubt, where the Work is a musical composition or sound recording, the synchronization of the Work in timed-relation with a moving image ("synching") will be considered a Derivative Work for the purpose of this License"* (emphasis added).

[29]   According to the provisions of Creative Commons licenses which include the NC options, the rights conferred to the licensee cannot be exercised "in any manner that is primarily intended for or directed toward commercial advantage or private monetary compensation. The exchange of the Work for other copyrighted works by means of digital file-sharing or otherwise shall not be considered to be intended for or directed toward commercial advantage or private monetary compensation, provided there is no payment of any monetary compensation in connection with the exchange of copyrighted works".

Commons licenses and the Italian collecting society, SIAE.[30] Reasons of space do not allow a full treatment of the issues involved, but the basic issue that was raised again and again is the possibility for creators, who mandated SIAE to handle their rights – in particular the collection and redistribution of royalties arising from the usage of their works – to use a Creative Commons license on works which SIAE is managing or on other works for which an explicit mandate to SIAE was not given. Given the current legal landscape in Italy, the standard answer to this kind of questions is, unfortunately, that there is a basic, structural incompatibility between licensing using Creative Commons licenses and mandating SIAE to manage one's own rights, because such mandate is exclusive and applies to every single work of the author, including future ones.[31]

Text is displayed by indenting it from the left margin. Quotations are commonly displayed. There are short quotations

5.2. SECOND-LEVEL CASES

As has been discussed above, "second-level cases" stem from requests that are deemed to be particularly complex and to deserve the intervention of an

---

[30]   See http://www.siae.it/ and art. 180 of Italian copyright law ("The right to act as an intermediary in any manner whether by direct or indirect intervention, mediation, agency or representation, or by assignment of the exercise of the rights of performance, recitation, broadcasting, including communication to the public by satellite, and mechanical and cinematographic reproduction of protected works, shall belong exclusively to the SIAE. It shall pursue the following activities: 1. the granting of licenses and authorizations for the exploitation of protected works, for the account of and in the interests of the right holders; 2. the collection of the revenue from the licenses and authorizations; 3. the distribution of that revenue among the right holders. The SIAE shall also pursue its activities, in accordance with the provisions of the regulations, in those foreign countries in which it possesses organized representation. These exclusive powers shall not prejudice the right of the author or his successors in title to exercise directly the rights afforded them by this Law. In the distribution of the proceeds referred to in item 3 of the second paragraph, a share shall be reserved for the author in all cases. The limits and the methods of distribution shall be determined by the regulations. However, if the exploitation rights in a work may give rise to the collection of funds abroad on behalf of Italian citizens domiciled or resident within the State territory and the owners of such rights do not, for any reason, collect those funds, the SIAE shall be empowered, after the lapse of one year from the date on which liability for payment arose, to exercise the rights for the account and in the interests of the author or his successors in title. The funds mentioned in the preceding paragraph which are collected by SIAE shall be held, after deduction of the expenses of collection, at the disposal of claimants for a period of three years. If this period elapses without such funds being claimed, they shall be paid to the National Federation of Professional Artists [Confederazione nazionale professionisti ed artisti] for the purposes of providing aid to authors, writers and musicians" – unofficial English translation of Italian Law n. 633 of 1941, as amended by subsequent laws, available at http://www.wipo.int/clea/docs_new/en/it/it112en.html).

[31]   For a thorough analysis of this issue, see A.M. Ricci (2006a, 2006b).

external consultant, paid with the funds provided by the Piedmont Region. SeLiLi has been handling three second-level cases so far.

The first case was based on a project to create static DVD versions of Wikipedia,[32] the online collaborative encyclopedia, and distribute them, either for a fee or for free over the Internet. The requestor was specifically interested to understand which kind of legal responsibility, if any, would be incurred by redistributing information taken from Wikipedia which might potentially infringe third parties' rights.[33] An external consultant – a lawyer – provided an opinion, advising the project from pursuing its objectives without a clear agreement with the Wikimedia Foundation.[34]

The second case was prompted by a request of a local public administration, which was providing funds to produce a video with and by school pupils, to be released under a Creative Commons license, to help in the "rights clearance" processes for third parties' material. The case was assigned to an external consultant – again, a lawyer – and is still under examination at the time of writing.

The third case originated from a project aimed at collecting Italian traditional cultural expressions, in particular traditional music pieces, and catalog them in an online database, to be released under some form of "libre license" for the public at large. The requestor asked for help in clarifying the legal implications of the project – which were numerous, including the identification of copyright holders, whether the works being recorded could be considered in the "public domain", how the neighboring rights of performers should be managed, how the *sui generis* right over the database[35] could be handled using a Creative Commons license – and the technical strategies do adopt, such as the compression techniques to use to save online the music recordings, most of which resulted in very big files, which kind of database platform to use to handle all the data, and others. The case was assigned to an external consultant for the legal questions (obviously a lawyer) and is pending assignment to another external

---

[32]   See http://www.wikipedia.org/.

[33]   In particular, the requestor wanted to know whether it might possible to use as a defense against third parties' claims the exemptions that EU law grants to "information society providers" *ex* articles 12, 13 and 14 of Directive 2000/31/EC of the European Parliament and of the Council of 8 June 2000 on certain legal aspects of information society services, in particular electronic commerce, in the Internal Market.

[34]   See http://wikimediafoundation.org/: "the Wikimedia Foundation, Inc., is a nonprofit charitable organization dedicated to encouraging the growth, development and distribution of free, multilingual content, and to providing the full content of these wiki-based projects to the public free of charge. The Wikimedia Foundation operates some of the largest collaboratively edited reference projects in the world, including Wikipedia, one of the 10 most visited websites in the world".

[35]   *Ex* Directive 96/9/EC of the European Parliament and of the Council of 11 March 1996 on the legal protection of databases.

consultants for the technical questions. This case, too, is still under examination at the time of writing.

5.3. THIRD-LEVEL CASES ("SPECIAL PROJECTS")

So far, there were two "special projects" in process of being activated through SeLiLi: in one case, the goal was to help a large Italian regional administration to license its digital archives, containing an impressive wealth of resources – books, pictures, videos – related to the local culture of that part of Italy. The regional administration wanted to use a Creative Commons license, but needed help both for the "rights clearance" processes and to ensure that the provisions of Creative Commons licenses were indeed appropriate, legally, economically and politically, for the regional policy on this matter. There was also a strong interest in supporting the use of free and open source licenses.

The second case involved a legal analysis on the usage of "libre licenses" for the firmware[36] and the hardware (such as electronic, electric and mechanical designs) that are often used in industrial and engineering activities in the electromechanical field. As most "libre licenses" have been designed on the basis of copyright law, which does not necessarily apply for the aforementioned sectors, a "second level case" was not considered sufficient – in light of the timing and budgetary constraints discussed above – to conduct a proper analysis.

Both these "special projects" are still ongoing at the time of writing.

6. Lessons learned

First of all, after one year of activity the need for a service such as SeLiLi is clearly confirmed. The number, variety and interest of the requests, in fact, went beyond the original expectations of the founders, making the project worth confirming and, if possible, worth expanding. The demand also shows that there is probably ample room to create other similar centers elsewhere in Italy.

The implementation of the basic service was rather straightforward, given the pre-existence of a group of experts on the SeLiLi subject field and some seed money to finance the service itself. It took some time,

---

[36] "In computing, firmware is a computer program that is embedded in a hardware device, for example a microcontroller. It can also be provided on flash ROMs or as a binary image file that can be uploaded onto existing hardware by a user. As its name suggests, firmware is somewhere between hardware and software. Like software, it is a computer program which is executed by a microprocessor or a microcontroller. But it is also tightly linked to a piece of hardware, and has little meaning outside of it" (see http://en.wikipedia.org/w/index.php?title=Firmware&oldid=200669567).

however, to understand on the precise role of SeLiLi in the free licenses ecosystem: SeLiLi, in fact, was not meant to substitute traditional instruments such as mailing lists, which have the great advantage of building knowledge in a transparent and searchable way (e.g., via mailing list archives). Therefore, now SeLiLi staff directs requesters to existing mailing lists whenever it is clear that privacy or other legitimate concerns do not apply, acting as a fall-back solution if the mailing lists fail (as they sometime do.)

Less satisfactory are the results regarding making the SeLiLi website into a knowledge-base. A collection of links, pointers, documents, etc, about free licenses could have certainly been created had the SeLiLi staff not been busy with other tasks. There are, however, great obstacles regarding the creation of official, original material advising about free licenses, e.g., Frequently Asked Questions. Given the legal implications, in fact, of any such public document, the drafting requires a very substantial amount of highly skilled labor. Such material, however, is crucial if the community at large is to be enabled to self clarify many basic issues regarding free licenses.

Another lesson learned is that the broad scope of the requests seems to express the need for advice on something more than simply "free copyright licenses." The interest on free trademark or design licenses is an example of such broader requests. Or the area of exceptions and limitations, all the way to the public domain. It is, therefore, not unconceivable that SeLiLi might need to expand its official scope.

Finally, in the field of free culture it is clear that the interaction with collecting societies is inescapable. However, what is now an often difficult relationship could easily -at least, in principle- become a collaboration, when the use of free licenses by established players will become more widespread.

7. The road ahead

Besides the straightforward aim of bettering of the existing SeLiLi set-up, there are three potential directions that could be pursued in the near future.

The first direction consists in the creation of a network of SeLiLi-like centers in Italy and throughout Europe. There are many potential reasons for that, including a common regional copyright law, geographical proximity, and a common market (see also the example of IPR-Europe, the helpdesk for European projects.) But, also, more practically, the structure of SeLiLi clearly lends itself to economies of scale: the online knowledge base could be just one for each nation; the large resources needed to create original material could be found pooling national (if not European) resources; experts, too, could be pooled using a centralized database and electronic media. A network of regional SeLiLi could then offer physical meetings, which sometimes are needed, and, more crucially, the financial resources to pay for professional advice, on the assumption that each region would like to give precedence to its local citizens, institutions and companies.

The second direction consists in establishing links with institutional IP offices, e.g., university technology transfer offices, government legal departments, companies IP offices, etc. This is already happening, to some extent, but it could be done on a more systematic way, with the aim of including, with full dignity, the free incenses approach in the standard roster of instruments offered by IP offices, particularly in the public sector.

Finally, the third direction could be to enlarge the goals of SeLiLi, moving from licensing to a more general "commons" approach to intellectual property. The free licenses, in fact, are a means, not an end in themselves: continuing thinking is, therefore, needed to identify what are the best instruments to support free culture and free software at any given time and in any given set of circumstances – local, national, macro-regional and global.

References

Aigrain, P. (2005), *Cause Commune – L'Information entre Bien Commune et Proprieté*, Fayard, Paris.

Benkler, Y. (2002), *Coase's Penguin, or Linux and the Nature of the Firm*, Yale Law Journal, Vol. 112 No.3.

Benkler, Y. (2004), *Sharing Nicely: On Shareable Goods and the Emergence of Sharing as a Modality of Economic Production*, Yale Law Journal, Vol. 114, No. 273.

Benkler, Y. (2007), *The Wealth of Networks*, Yale University Press.

Bildstein, B. (2007), *Finding and Quantifying Australia's Online Commons*, in Script (Ed.), Vol. 4, No.1.

Carrier, M.A. (2004), *Cabining Intellectual Property through a Property Paradigm*, Duke Law Journal, Vol.54, No. 1.

Coase, R.H. (1937), *The Nature of the Firm*, Economica, Vol. 4.

Cheliotis, G.; Chik, W.; Guglani, A. and Taki, G.K. (2007), *Taking stock of the Creative Commons experiment – Monitoring the use of Creative Commons licenses and evaluating its implications for the Future of Creative Commons and for copyright law*, paper presented at the 35th Research Conference on Communication, Information and Internet Policy, 28-30 September, National Center for Technology and Law, George Mason University, August.

Leadbeater, C. and Miller, P. (2004), *The Pro-Am Revolution – How enthusiasts are changing our economy and society*, Demos.

Piana, C. (2006), *Licenze pubbliche di software e contratto*, Contratti, Vol.7, No. 1.

Pollock, R. (2006), *The Value of the Public Domain*, IPPR, available at: http://www.ippr.org.uk/publicationsandreports/publication.asp?id=482 (accessed 3 May 2010).

Ricci, A.M. (2006a), *Problematiche sottese all?impiego di licenze Creative Commons da parte di autori associati e mandanti non associati alla S.I.A.E. e quesiti*, available at: http://www.notelegali.it/page.asp?mode=Assolo (accessed 3 May 2010).

Ricci, A.M. (2006b), *Utilizzare le licenze Creative Commons (CC) per la diffusione di musica: alcune considerazioni generali*, available at: http://www.musicaedischi.it/musicaediritto.php (accessed 3 May 2010).

Scherer, F.M. (2007), *The Political Economy of Patent Policy Reform in The Unites States*, available at: http://www.researchoninnovation.org/scherer/patpolic.pdf (accessed 3 May 2010).

Surowiecki, J. (2004), *The Wisdom of Crowds: why the many are smarter than the few and how collective wisdom shapes business, economies, societies and nations*, Doubleday Books.

Stallman, R.M. (2004), *Did You Say "Intellectual Property"? It's a Seductive Mirage*, available at: http://www.gnu.org/philosophy/not-ipr.xhtml (accessed 3 May 2010).

von Hippel, E. (1998), *The Sources of Innovation*, Oxford University Press.

von Hippel, E. (2005), *Democratizing Innovation*, MIT Press.

Waelde, C.; Guadamuz, A. and Duncan, C. (2005), *The Common Information Environment and Creative Commons*, Common Information Environment.

SECTION II

Multimedia and Law: Managing Digital Contents

Virtual Culture and the Public Space (Position Paper)

Victòria Camps
Autonomous University of Barcelona

Abstract. This chapter deals with some ethic and political questions arisen in the new audiovisual space, where the internet plays the main role. Firstly, some of the fundamental rights have to be re-thought taking into account the features of the communication through the net. Specially, two rights so essential for democracy such us the freedom of speech and the right to be informed, and the right of intellectual property which is so intrinsically joint to the market relations, have to be guaranteed and the measures to do it must not damage other fundamental values of democracy. Since limiting the internet is a difficult and almost impossible task, the fact that the public authorities provide for the adoption of particular supervisory measures is not enough. Therefore, at the same time there should be model of citizen capable of self-regulating and orienting himself on the basis of some ethic and aesthetic values instead of exclusively economic values.

Keywords: Virtual culture, public space, rights, freedom of speech, right to be informed, intellectual property

1. The Internet and cyberspace: a different form of life

My aim in these pages it to analyse, firstly, the most prominent changes that the Internet and what is known as "cyberspace" are introducing into our lives. An initial terminological precision must be made to explain why I am referring to the Internet and cyberspace as two different realities. My starting point is the meaning conferred to both realities by one of the most recognised experts on the subject, Lawrence Lessig. In his book entitled Code 2.2, Lessig defines the "Internet" as a medium of communication: a fast an easy way to access information, purchase items and send messages. In sum, a different means of communicating and even of mobilising communities and depoliticizing bureaucratic centralism. The cyberspace, on the other hand, goes further than just facilitating communication. It introduces us into virtual worlds which allow us to adopt different personalities and discover what others are producing in a specific field. Second World and You Tube are examples of what can happen in cyberspace. In contrast with the Internet, cyberspace "is not just about making life easier. It is about making life different, or perhaps better. It is about making a different (or second) life. It evokes, or calls to life, ways of interacting that were not possible before" (Lessig, 2006).

In what sense does cyberspace make our lives different? And what requirements does the internet introduce into this new form of communication? I will limit these considerations to summarising the most prominent of these changes, those which are considered in the majority of the studies on the subject.

1. Individuals who circulate and communicate on the net are anonymous; they have no need to reveal their identity. Nobody knows who is using the internet. The cartoon that appeared some years ago in the New Yorker is well known: two dogs, one white and one black, are in front of a PC, and the black says to the white: On the internet, nobody knows you are a dog. Indeed, on the internet, one's identity, and the stereotypes linked to it, can remain unknown.

2. Thanks to the possible anonymity granted by the net, and that the technique it provides for communication is different, the discriminations of the real world cease to exist. Cyberspace even changes the meaning of the concepts of enabled and disabled. Not only can people with disabilities have an easier access to cyberspace, but individuals of a virtual community can appear with invented attributes, which differ from those in real life. Second Life is the example. And the negative reaction the program generated is a sign of the perversions that the transformation of real life into a virtual life, detached from the social norms to which we are accustomed, can reach.

3. Geographical references disappear with relation to the net. The internet user does not reside in any locatable place. The logic followed by email addresses is not spatial; it is not the logic of a postal address.

4. Traditional and canonical knowledge centres have been stripped of their sacred nature. Knowledge – or mere information, as being knowledgeable about something implies more than just being informed – is transmitted through other means, which reach further than books, the press, radio or television. Academies and libraries have been relegated to a second place as sources from which knowledge is transmitted or for where it is searched. Books have not been replaced, but they have lost the ordering centrality they had in other times.

5. It seems that the net favours a new communitarian spirit, a new form of community detached from geographical references or traditional identities. There has been talk of a "hacker ethic", based on solidarity and the abandonment of the idea of property, the basic "right" of the Western world (Himanen, 2001). A new human being appears, a "being on the net", whose most outstanding feature is his communitarian sensitivity.[1]

---

[1]   David Weinberg, as referred to by José Luis Molinuelo (2006).

2. Rethinking human rights

Not only is this spirit of solidarity calling into question, for example, the right to intellectual property, but the new virtual reality affects, in one way or another, rights as fundamental as the freedom of expression or the right to information. Some people are convinced that the net will contribute to enhancing free speech, as it opens the possibilities for communication and information to the whole world. There are, no doubt, economic disadvantages which result in what is known as the "digital divide": not everyone has the same access to the net. But, if we are able to eliminate these dangers, it is true that we are offered a much wider scope of freedoms. However, will these new forms of communication really mean a progress for freedom of expression? And in what will this progress consist? On the other hand, there is no doubt that the amount of information circulating on the web is excessive. We are more informed than when our sources of information were the press, radio and television in their classic forms. But it is also true that a larger amount of information does not mean that it is better or more useful, or that it increases the knowledge of those who access it. ¿Is the right to information more protected, or, is it actually endangered by elements which did not use to exist? I propose that, in order to take these considerations a step further, we pause briefly to analyse three fundamental rights: the right to freedom of speech, the right to property and the right to information.

2.1. FREEDOM OF SPEECH

As any other fundamental right, freedom of speech is not an absolute right. It has limits. The ethical problem which generally appears, with relation to freedom of expression, is that of establishing those limits and to whom this power can be conferred. The ideal situation, no doubt, is that it be each citizen who establishes such limits and imposes them on himself. But this does not usually happen, and therefore, as with the rest of basic rights, it falls on the state to guarantee that, at least, freedom of expression is not used to violate other rights or to hinder the right to liberty of others.

The characteristics highlighted above are indicators of the changes introduced in our lives by communication on the net and highlight, at the same time, two aspects to take in to account with relation to the limits of freedom of expression. One of them is that, via the web, the individual has much more liberty to do what she wants, to invent her life, to intimidate others, to violate the respect for private life, than through the more traditional means of communication. On the other hand, and this is the second aspect, precisely because the web favours a greater freedom of action, establishing limits to this freedom seems technically unviable. Not only technically unviable, but any attempt at control is immediately interpreted as a moral impropriety. Cyberspace is identified with liberty in such a way that limitations in this area are difficult to justify.

The above-mentioned Lawrence Lessing, who has studied the regulation of cyberspace in depth, affirms that it can be regulated. For a start, cyberspace is not and can not be detached from the rules of the market, and this is already a regulation. In addition, cyberspace has its own code or architecture thanks to which it functions in a certain way and not in another. This architecture of the net, made up of a certain physical and logical design, a specific configuration, a set of operative procedures and other various conditions, constitutes the peculiar regulation of the net. It is a code which is intrinsic to the systems or to each programme, which imposes its own rules of the game, such as the use of a password, the encryption of certain data, or having to follow a pre-established order. What is obvious is that cyberspace is not governed by anarchy. Movement and circulation happen in accordance with pre-established rules in the operative system.

Lessig highlights that this code or architecture of cyberspace is not untouchable. Some architectures, although not all, can be regulated. And in any case, governments can alter them directly or indirectly. One way of doing this, for example, is introducing a chip so that children can not access certain programmes. What is obvious is that the new forms of intervention on the part of the public authorities in order to preserve and guarantee citizen's rights to freedom of expression have to be really new. Ordinary forms of proceeding with relation to traditional means of communication are obsolete and inoperative, and thus of no use. I will illustrate this with three examples.

The Pentagon Papers in the United States were a classic case of defence of freedom of expression. These documents contained a very negative evaluation of US policy during the Vietnam War. Someone working in the Pentagon leaked the documents to the New York Times, and a first excerpt was published on the 13th June 1971.This publication caused the immediate alarm and reaction of the Attorney General, requesting the Supreme Court to exercise its power of prior restraint prohibiting the progressive publication of the papers. As is logical under the rule of law, the Supreme Court refused to do so, arguing that it contravened the First Amendment which protects the freedom of speech. With the internet, the process would have been different. Instead of sending the papers to a newspaper, these would have been published on any of the millions of existing blogs, preserving the anonymity of those responsible for the leak. It would be useless, and counter-productive, to try and prevent this from happening.

A similar example, although of more comical nature, occurred more or less a year ago in Spain with the magazine *El Jueves*. The classical procedure of ordering the seizure of all copies of the magazine for publishing bad taste images of the Princes of Asturias only resulted in a faster diffusion of what it was trying to hide. The same thing had happened shortly before with the ridiculing caricatures of Mahomet that appeared in a Danish publication. Their criticism generated the widest diffusion that could have been expected. In other words, if there has to be a way of controlling certain forms of expression, we need to think about more efficient means that obtain the desired results and not precisely the opposite.

To end these examples, the electoral law in Spain prohibits newspapers from publishing the polls with the predication of election results in the five last days of the campaign. What happened in the last general elections? A digital newspaper from Andorra published these polls and anyone in Spain who wanted to could consult them online.

We could multiply these examples which speak for themselves. They all highlight that we have effectively gained in liberty. And also that liberty remains more out of our control. This would be perfect if liberty was always used for good, and without contravening other rights or norms. But then, it probably would not be liberty. The human condition – as Socrates already warned us, and Pico Della Mirandola followed – is constituted in such a way that it can use liberty to enhance o degrade itself. This is then where the problem lies, and, the more the liberty, its dimensions increase.

2.2. INTELLECTUAL PROPERTY RIGHTS

We have all heard of the "digital canon", an attempt to limit the free circulation of works of art (music, especially) and to guarantee that the artists do not stop being the beneficiaries of what is acquired freely and with no cost on the net. Intellectual property rights could be on the road to extinction, due to the facility of obtaining all kinds of films and music, without the bothersome obligation of paying a toll, offered by the net.

The fact is that this communitarian spirit generated by cyberspace has resulted in a movement that has taken up the extreme defence of "free software". This Copyleft movement is opposed to the copyright, which wants to continue protecting the rights of the artists. As defenders of absolute liberty on the Internet, they claim that everything should be free to be used, copied, studied and redistributed without obstacles. Their starting point is that, on the Internet, the copy is the rule and not the exception. For example, to tell a joke on the Internet is to send it. Because of this, they consider existence of intellectual property rights in this new world and ask the revolutionary question: why should all forms of creative expression be subject to the law of copyright?

Richard Stallman is the founder of the Free Software Foundation against "proprietor software". He defends it with all his ability for argument and eloquence. Its objective is to avoid the control of computers, that code or internal architecture that conditions us when we use it, remaining in the hands of a few large corporations, the usual centres of power. Software should not be the object of private property; it should be free so that anyone can manipulate it.

This changed a lot of other things. Without going any further, it changes hierarchical structures. In a net structure everyone is on the same level. "Consumers" of information are not just that, but "pro-consumers": they produce while they consume. Wikipedia is the model: an encyclopaedia created with the collaboration of all those who want to participate. In fact, all technologies have been altering the invasion of private property. Tapping a telephone, for example, is not the same as kicking down a door. It is maybe more delicate, but it can be more invasive.

3. THE RIGHT TO INFORMATION

Information is a basic good for many areas, also for the development and progress of democracy. People can not be asked to participate in decision-making if they have not been correctly informed previously of what is at stake in each case. In principle, these new forms of communication favour information, at least in its range and immediacy. But two issues must not be ignored.

The first is the already mentioned "digital divide". Democratic governments should be concerned about information not reaching everyone, as access to internet is a privilege of the few who have the means to procure it for themselves. There are two causes of this discrimination: an economic cause and a chronological cause. Sometimes these coincide. In any case, people with scarce economic resources and those who, having the resources lack the necessary skills to do so, do not have access to the internet. We all know that currently this lack of skills has a generational explanation. New generations seem to be born with the ability to use the Internet and to adapt to digital communication. The same can not be said about those generations of a more advanced age. And there will continue to be a fracture or discrimination if the necessary technology is not at everyone's disposal, as it was in the times of television. Because of this, access to digital technology is part of what is called "fourth generation rights", which respond to the discovery of new problems or to the consequences of technological development.

The second issue to be considered regarding the right to information is the credibility of the information itself. The novelty, today, lies on the quantity and immediacy of information. We have access to much more information and we can access it in real time. But, can we trust the information we receive? What substitutes the credibility of the best newspapers or the radio stations of reference on the Internet? In 1996, a TWA plane crashed close to New York. There were 200 victims. Rumours of a conspiracy started circulating on the internet immediately, and before the corresponding investigation could be carried out: the accident had been the consequence of a missile attack with involvement of the US government. The attempts by the government to refute these rumours only resulted in the appearance of more proof in favour of the conspiracy theory on the web. Even a report from someone inside the government appeared backing the conspiracy. And there was no way to stop the dynamic started, highlighting the difficulty of halting rumours which circulate on the net. The more they are denied, the larger they grow. And, when it can be proved that the rumours were false, the damage caused is of a dimension which is difficult to repair.

This new kind of power resulting from new technologies has been called "netocracy". Power networks are distortioned and manipulated with false information which hinders and blocs the access to real knowledge (Alonso, 2007). Needless to say, the fight against this whirlpool of confusing and on many occasions erroneous data is not only an impossible task, but it always generates the opposition of those who have conferred on themselves the role of guardians of freedom of expression. Blogs and the competition among bloggers, they claim, is the best way to cooperate in the discovery of the truth. There is no better way forward for progress than information in free competition.[2]

3. The construction of a public cyberspace

The well-known communication scholar, Jesus Martin Barbero, has written that "the transformations in the circulation of knowledge constitute one of the most profound mutations a society can suffer" (Barbero, 2001). Mutations for the good or for the bad? My specific question now is: how will the new virtual environment affect the citizens? So far I have referred

---

[2]   To avoid the accumulation of erroneous data, the exemplary Wikipedia has had to establish something similar to what scientific publications have: peer review as a guarantee of the quality of the contents it includes. However, this guarantee is not always complete nor can it beat certain powerful and dominating interests. Let us just remember the case of the Korean scientist Woo-Suk who managed to fool all his colleagues, national and international, regarding the supposed success of a technique for cloning stem cells. These loopholes in the control system will continue to occur, but there will be fewer if certain safeguards are introduced to prevent them.

a series of rights, rights of the citizen, that can be threatened, enhanced, or both, in this new culture. But the citizen is, at the same time, the subject of duties: duties of participation, cooperation in the common interest, solidarity and tolerance; duties for which the consumer economy is more of an obstacle than an aid. Political theories that are more critical of liberalism, like communitarianism or republicanism, challenge liberal politics for their inability to construct citizenship. At the same time, enthusiasts of the electronic era tend to see ideal instruments and scenarios in it to recover the citizenship lost. Will it be as they say? Will the individual in the new society loose the vices of the "consumer man"? Will he feel closer to those that are different and more committed to democracy? Let us analyse again some of the features of the society on the net.

3.1. CITIZENS OR CONSUMERS?

I must note from the start that both aspects are not incompatible. The citizenship of our times corresponds to the "liberty of the modern", the liberty to focus on oneself and to work for one's own affairs. Selfishness is the premise of the conception of modern man. A premise, however, that politics, democratic life, should, at least partially, correct. The citizen of today does not live, and should not live, for politics – he is not the Aristotelic *zoon politikon* -, but he lives in a democracy and under the rule of law, and it is part of his obligations to contribute to preserving and improving both of these realities.

Let us return to the new communication technologies. In principle, as I have mentioned, they are usually celebrated as an opening to liberty, information and citizen participation. But these technologies also exist in a "consumer society", or better said, are possible thanks to this consumer economy. They are, as a result, susceptible to yielding to the interests of capital and of the large corporations that promote them, ignoring the issue of citizenship completely. The citizen and the consumer live together in a same individual, but they adopt different and very often contradictory roles. In his most recent books, Cass Sunstein (2001, 2006) has noted the disproportionate growth of the ".com sites". These were not, on the other hand, the first to exist. The first sites on the internet did not respond to commercial interests but to educational or organisational ones (.edu and .org). But the individual has ended up embracing new technologies, especially because they facilitate consumption. What we must ask ourselves is if these unlimited options for consumption do not but limit and darken the horizons of citizenship. We must inquire what gives content to and establish objectives for this "liberty of the modern", which is the most fundamental individual right. What do we want liberty for? What is really governing us, our own selves or certain higher interests that lead us in their direction?

Sunstein himself confirms that, in the United States, the celebrated First Amendment is usually defended, in practice, in the name of "the sovereignty of the consumer". The consumer has a right to liberty, and to a liberty with no more limits than those imposed by his own pocket. This idea, which is strongly rooted in the mind of any contemporary individual, rules out, from the start, any discussion relating to the limits of freedom of expression. Should everything be permitted? Should, for example, excessive violence or other forms of expression which damage democracy or the values it proclaims be permitted?

3.2. FREEDOM AND THE "DEMOS"

I believe it is valid to state that, in a democracy, freedom of expression should not be an end in itself. It should be more a means to promote democratic values; with liberty, of course. In the background of this idea is the concept of moral autonomy, especially in its Kantian version. According to Kant, the rational being is autonomous, free, but he is so to do his duty. He can, of course, not do it, and act against his duty or ignore it. In that case, he will act freely but not rationally. If we substitute the rational being for the democratic being, we can make the same statement. In a democracy not all expressions of liberty are permitted. Those that are susceptible of seriously damaging others are punished and penalised by the law. While this is valid for the more serious cases, living in a community requires something more than not killing or not stealing. The duties of a citizen are the result of these requirements which, undoubtedly, limit his liberty in some way.

One of the issues that liberal societies do not manage to resolve, to the point that many times they do not even consider it as a problem, is the following: to what extent should governments do something to promote the adherence of freedom of expression to democratic values? How far can they reach in this task without incurring in censorship and in practices conflicting with democracy itself?

Republican theorists tackle this question directly and answer referring to the need for democracies to be effectively constructed as a public domain, in which a wide number of people, with a variety of points of view, can express themselves. A domain which itself promotes tolerance, respect, reasonableness and civility. In other words, for democracy to function, a set of more or less efficient public institutions is not enough, there also needs to be a framework of common reference for all the members of the democracy. This is the demos in which the democratic regime is founded.

3.3. THE "DAILY ME" AND THE HERD

Maintaining a demos becomes difficult because, to the contrary of what one would expect from means that communicate everyone with everyone, reality indicates that there is more of a tendency towards fragmentation than a desire to learn about what does not affect one's own interests or does not agree with one's own sensitivities. The fact is that, in spite of new technologies, or thanks to these, more and more, people tend to make themselves a communication to measure. Years ago Nikolas Negroponte predicted the Daily Me, the personalised newspaper. Currently this does not only apply to newspapers, there is a tendency for all communication to become personalised, as everyone looks for and reads exclusively what matches their own way of thinking. There are webs and digital newspapers for all kinds of tastes and sensitivities. The result is the fragmentation of the population and its polarisation in different directions. The result is the appearance of ghettos which see one another as enemies.

In a similar sense, Dany Robert Dafour, in an article entitled "Living in the herd and believing oneself free", refers to the formation of a new social conglomerate: ego-gregarism.[3] Individuals live apart but are linked together in the virtual sphere in order to be driven to where higher interests lead them. In other words, new forms of domination, to use the terminology of Philip Pettit, are stalking the individual who believes himself progressively gaining in liberty.

The well-known Judge Brandeis, in the Nineteenth Century and concerned about the meaning the First Amendment, wrote that the greatest threat for liberty is "an inert people". John Stuart Mill had said something similar when expressing his fears that liberty would stop being promoted individually and give way to the force of customs and different social dominations. New republicanism also attempts to fight against this, against all dominations no legitimised by law, but existing, and, frequently, without the awareness of their victims. The inert people allows itself to be swept along, without arguing or being concerned with what is public, except if it interferes directly with one of its interests. This is not, without doubt, the best breeding ground for the construction of citizenship.

3.4. PARTICIPATION AND DELIBERATION

Tocqueville had also warned that the "democratic passion" for equality can "reduce each nation to nothing more than a herd of timid and industrious animals" liberated from "the bother of thinking" (Tocqueville, [1835-40] 1980). The pragmatist philosopher John Dewey also saw a contradiction

---

[3]   Le Monde Diplomatique, January, 2008.

between the ideal of citizenship and what he called "the eclipse of the public".

Habermas has been expressing his opinion in the same sense since he published his book on the difficulties of forming a public opinion in societies colonised by the economy and by administrative bureaucracy. In a recent article, he insists on the same idea, highlighting that the institutional design of a liberal democracy should guarantee, together with the security of the people and political participation of citizens, a public sphere capable of contribution to the formation of public opinion (Habermas, 2006). The objective of democratic institutions has to be to effectively guarantee rights of communication and association, the independence of the media and access to it by everyone. Habermas' fear is that the "structure of power of the public sphere" distorts communication, politicising the media and preventing the existence of real and effective feedback between it and civil society, due to, on the one hand, social inequalities, and on the other, the colonisation of the market. What is more, the reduction of communication to entertainment, the simplification of information and the polarisation of conflicts may seemingly attract the immediate curiosity of people, but, in the long run, they only frighten off the citizens and generate distrust.

A good synthesis of what I have been saying is put forward by the Portuguese journalist Mário Mesquita (2007): "Politically mediated communication in the public sphere can facilitate deliberative legitimising processes in complex societies only if a self-regulatory media system becomes independent from its social environment, and if the anonymous audiences guarantee a feedback between the discourse of an informed elite and a responsible civil society". The journalist refers to the opinion of Elihu Katz, according to which, in the information society there is "more communication than information". In other words, we have abandoned the requirements we demand from information in benefit of being more communicated. A practice which in reality is no sufficiently demanding to guarantee the conditions for a democracy of citizens, and not just a club of friends who share the same interests.

What results from this analysis is that the construction of a public sphere that responds to the characteristics of the demos as a constitutive element of democracy requires something more than technological changes brought by means through which reality and information can be accessed more efficiently, communication is easier and faster and the individual feels more in control of his abilities. Certain issues do not change, in spite of the transformations in their surroundings. One of these is the moral enabling of a person in order for him to learn to interact, not at his discretion, but fairly and democratically in the new reality. Nowadays we highlight the need, for example, of a more deliberative democracy, and we argue that the new means of communication can facilitate this. But we have to ask ourselves if the blogosphere, this gigantic assembly of many minds, is sufficient to obtain better decisions. Or if actual deliberation takes place in the blogosphere or simply more noise is made. When everyone is speaking at the same time it is hard for people to understand each other. One of the classical examples referred to repeatedly in these pages, Wikipedia, highlights the fact that the sum of different knowledge and contributions only favours the whole to a certain point. Someone finally has to establish order in the submissions and filter out the false information and the stupidities. Citizenship, like any other moral enterprise, depends on the will and the character of people, not on certain means of communication which, as such, can be but at the service of noble and not so noble ends.

References

Alonso, A. (2001), *Acerca del software y del conocimiento libres. Una guía para el filósofo*, Argumentos de Razón Técnica: Revista española de Ciencia, Tecnología y Sociedad y Filosofía de la Tecnología, No. 10, Sevilla, pp. 181-197.

Barbero, J. M. (2001), *Transformaciones del saber en la 'sociedad del conocimiento' y del 'mercado'*, Pasajes: Revista de pensamiento contemporáneo, No. 7, pp. 7-13.

Habermas, J. (2006), *Political Communication in Media Society*, Communication Theory, No. 16, pp. 411-426.

Himanen, P. (2001), *The hacker ethic and the spirit of the information age*, Trade Publishing.

Lessig, L. (2006), *Code 2.0*, Basic Books, N.Y.

Mesquita, M. (2007), *El cuarto equívoco. El poder de los medios en la sociedad contemporánea*, Ed. Fragua, Madrid.

Molinuelo, J. L. (2006), *La vida en tiempo real*, Biblioteca Nueva, Madrid.

Sunstein, C. (2001), *Republic.com*, Princeton University Press.

Sunstein, C. (2006), *Infotopia* Oxford University Press.

Tocqueville, A. de [1835-40] (1980), *La democracia en América*, Alianza Editorial, Madrid.

Regulation and Co-Regulation in the 2.0 Public Space (Position Paper)

Joan Barata
Consell de l'Audiovisual de Catalunya

Abstract. Convergence is the capacity to access services and diverse contents from the same receiver or terminal, as well as the possibility to enjoy the same service or content from different terminals. The modernization of the telecommunication networks has transformed the classical value chain in the provision of audiovisual services introducing elements that increase the complexity of the applicable regulatory framework. So it seems we are moving in a field where the traditional mechanisms of regulation and exercise of public legal powers by the relevant regulators will have to let the place to alternative modalities of intervention.

Keywords: Convergence, Regulation, Audiovisual, Electronic communications

The so-called technological convergence is a phenomenon directly linked to the possibilities that the digitalization technique or the digital compression offer. These techniques facilitate and transform the way in which information circulates through the diverse networks of electronic communications.

The changes associated to the fact that the above mentioned technological innovations appear, fall into four standing domains which explain the interest aroused within the field of the social sciences:

1. The value chain of the provision of audiovisual services and the respective market/s.
2. The definition and application of the notion of public interest from the perspective of the different regulators.
3. The new modalities to consume which derive from the technological changes, in particular from the point of view of the consumers' control and decision capacity.
4. The transformations that take place strictly in the communicative domain as a consequence of the progressive blurring of the border which separates the public and private spaces of communication.

In this brief analysis, I will try to explain in a concrete way the fundamental elements related to the second of these domains. I will specially take into account the new regulatory contexts and the difficulties and uncertainties that the current regulatory authorities start facing at the moment.

The notion of convergence can be delimited from different approaches. However, bearing in mind the point of view of the final user, we can define convergence as the capacity to access services and diverse contents from the same receiver or terminal, as well as the possibility to enjoy the same service or content from different terminals.

As I have pointed out, one of the consequences of convergence seems to be the appearance of new actors in the so-called value chain of audiovisual services.

In the traditional schema, this chain was essentially composed by three subjects, but public intervention was only focused on the last one: producers, rights managers and broadcasters. Traditional over-the-air broadcaster, as the subject in charge of packing a sequential offer of audiovisual contents previously acquired or entrusted to third persons –or produced by itself—, and as the subject legally authorized to, precisely, *disseminate* those contents or programs through a terrestrial network of electronic communications, has been historically put under a direct public control. This control derives from the usage of a limited good such as the airwave spectrum. In brief, the broadcasters that use the mentioned transmission system have only been able to render their services when the relevant public power –most of the cases, at the national level— has granted the access to a specific portion of the radio-electric spectrum. This has traditionally been subject to the accomplishment of a potentially wide range of conditions.

The modernization of the telecommunication networks has transformed this basic schema introducing elements that increase the complexity of the regulatory framework of the audiovisual services' provision. In this sense, considering new links in the value chain before mentioned becomes necessary. These new links are placed in a *later* moment or position with regard to the traditional broadcasters. In this field, we can include audiovisual services distributors (in other words, those actors that offer a set of *channels* or programs previously *packed* by a third subject, in other words, platforms of cable or satellite audiovisual services), Internet service providers (operators which facilitate the access to any kind of contents, even audiovisual, which are at the public's disposal through the Internet platform), *portals* or search engines (those actors that play an *active* role within the Internet in the selection and offer of contents generally facilitated by third parties); and network operators (those actors that *regulate* the flow of bits that circulate through the net and make possible the distribution and reception of contents by the different Internet users).

It is obvious that not only do these actors condition and alter from an economic point of view the classic schema of the provision of audiovisual services (adding a higher degree of complexity, for instance, to the analysis and detection of relevant markets in this field), but they also have a direct influence on the way the public is going to access the contents. Several examples draw a clear picture in this field.

A first example of this influence is the capacity of the distributors to choose the different TV channels which are going to constitute the commercial offer that their platform will provide. It is clear that the distributor decides the contents that its subscribers will be able to access, bearing in mind that the access to the traditional television service generally only takes place through a single platform or access system in each household. In this context, the fact that a lot of these distributors may present a *triple-play* offer (giving access to audiovisual, Internet and phone services at the same time) to their users has to be taken into account. This position gives to these actors a special economic capacity and negotiation power in the acquisition of premium contents (that is, feature films' premieres and sports rights). This acquisition has conferred them a particularly prevailing and control role over the activities and even over the decisions of the traditional broadcasters.

On the basis of these special circumstances and power position that hold the distributors, regulatory measures such as the so-called *must carry* and *must offer* norms have been created, as well as other kind of norms, such as those which regulate the conditions of the independent broadcasters' access to this sort of distribution platforms.

Within a different order of considerations, the Internet portals and search engines are also invested with a special influence and play an important role in the value chain of the audiovisual communication. In short, it is obvious that these subjects may accomplish a mission especially outstanding in terms of *gate keeping* concerning access to Internet audiovisual contents by end users. In this sense, and despite the arguments of neutrality that in general are put forward by these subjects, they have a clear function of content selection and prioritization. It is true that we cannot place all the portals and search engines under the same consideration. It is very clear that while in some cases the prioritization of content offer is the result of a marked and confessed *editorial* decision; in other cases, the presentation of the corresponding offer would depend exclusively on the strict application of computer logarithms and merely *organic* criteria. Nevertheless, the discussion about the neutrality, as well as the reproaches about the lack of transparency or *public disclosure* of these criteria, formulated from different academic sectors and users, also feed with special intensity the debate about the position and the power of such operators. However, there has been no regulatory intervention in this field up to now and, in any case, its hypothetical modality and instance of application is far from being peaceful.

Finally, I should make some comments on the position of the net operators, as far as they make possible the access and consumption of

Internet content. This has mostly to do with the widely extended discussion (especially in the United States) about the requirement for net operators to manage the traffic in the net in a neutral way. This debate is generally known under the denomination of *net neutrality*. It is obvious that I cannot deal now with this matter with the extension it deserves. Nonetheless, it is an especially illustrative case of the emergence of new actors which have a particular power within the chain of elaboration and distribution of contents (audiovisual contents, too). In this field, the need to set regulatory measures different from the traditional ones arises.

In brief, the concept of *net neutrality* means that each Internet user would have the right to access in equal conditions and not being subject to unjustified discriminations to the available applications, services and contents through the Internet platform. Nevertheless, it is an evolutive concept: when Professor Tim Wu –who is considered to be the author— created it, he started from a conception of strict equalitarianism in the Internet (which means that all users should have access to all the contents at identical speed). At present, almost nobody defends this conception yet. A discrimination strictly based on providing a larger band width with a higher final price is considered to be a non-neutral management of the network. This idea of neutrality would neither be altered by the net operator's management and prioritization of the traffic of contents on the basis of the need to avoid damaging contents such as viruses or spam.

On the contrary, much more controversial is the possibility of the operators to give priority to certain contents, applications and services before others when managing traffic in the net, on the basis of certain economic agreements with their providers or just because the contents, applications and services were offered by the same operator, or even with the intention to *diminish* the quality of those provided by third parties. The issue of the *net neutrality* focuses the debate on the need to set regulatory measures which guarantee a neutral and transparent management of the net in the fields lastly referred. The considerations that the Federal Communications Commission (FCC) has given in its decision *FCC vs. Comcast*, 1st August 2008, are especially illustrative. However, in this debate there are still a lot of things to clarify, in particular the peculiar nature of the norms that should guarantee the neutral management of the net. In this sense, it is not clear if a mere adaptation of the antitrust regime is enough, if the already existing norms can still be valid, or if it will be necessary to set a completely newly-coined regulatory intervention. In any case, it is worth to warn that the debate about the need of the regulatory intervention has placed some activists who, in the origins of the Internet were against any kind public intervention in the net, now in favour of it.

Taking into account the abovementioned considerations, some problems will probably focus the future discussions about the role and the regulatory instruments at the disposal of the regulators in the new technological environment.

Firstly, we have to warn about the progressive dilution of a key concept in this field, such as the editorial responsibility.

The legal regime of audiovisuals communications was based on the existence of a broadcaster, which had the editorial responsibility of the contents at the disposal of an, essentially, passive public. This is the basic schema which constitutes the bedrock of the regulatory system established by the Directive 89/552/CEE, known as the *Directive on the television without frontiers*. The European legislator keeps this schema on the occasion of the reform of 1997 and adapts it, without altering its essence, in the new and current Directive 2007/65/CE, known as the *Directive on audiovisual media services*. The new directive introduces the audiovisual services provided under demand within the traditional regulatory schema, widening the application domain in other fields different from the traditional television. Nonetheless, the idea of the editorial responsibility is clearly kept as central notion or regulatory criterion, since the services under demand are within the field of application of the rules (specific for them, and less interventionist than those which apply to traditional television), as far as the existence of a subject in charge of configuring and deciding the effective way of the catalogue of contents offered to the public can be identified. So the European legislator, after long negotiations in which the position and influence of the Member States such as the United Kingdom have been quite relevant and influent, declines covering with its rules the formats and models of provision of audiovisual contents in which the individual initiative of users plays a central role and consequently it cannot be attributed a direct responsibility for the configuration of the catalogue corresponding to the holder of the web or application, who finally makes possible the access (in other words and briefly, the *Youtube* model).

Nevertheless, this model focused on an idea of typical editorial responsibility within a public sphere controlled by the broadcasters is nowadays going through a crisis. The broadcasters have not disappeared (because, as everybody knows, and to say it in a way, video has not been able to kill the radio star), but it is true that in our days this crisis is a real fact shored up by two key factors:

1. The fact that most of the available audiovisual contents for the public in general (and for this reason with the capacity to overwhelm the strictly private communication and move in the field of the formation of the public opinion) are not any more elaborated and supplied in the heart of the traditional value chain. The audiovisual contents are created and

actively disseminated by subjects placed in any point of the planet who are reasonably able escape from any traditional regulatory practice.

2. Since in the distribution of audiovisual contents or any other kind of content, the role of the broadcasters is complemented or even circumvented by the new actors we have referred to (search engines, portals, distributors and even net operators), these last subjects do not have, in most of the legal systems, a legally attributed responsibility which can be compared to the traditional responsibility that used to belong to the broadcasters (we have to warn that the traditional responsibility is directly conditioned by the fact that in most cases the provision of their services is subject to a licence previously obtained).

In this sense, the option of placing the above mentioned subjects in a similar position to the traditional broadcasters could be suggested from a regulatory point of view. In some cases this would even be reasonably practicable since subjects such as the net operators need at last a physical infrastructure, a *last mile*, which would allow an intervention by the specific relevant authority with regard to the territory and an effective application of the corresponding norm. Nonetheless, should it be noticed that this discussion is clearly linked to the abovementioned debate about the need to introduce regulatory elements that guarantee the objective, transparent or neutral behaviour of most of these last actors. However, if we accepted this need, it would be impossible, from a regulatory point of view, to go further than that, particularly imposing requirements directly related to the *active* idea of the exercise of editorial responsibility as far as this would contradict the later requirement of objective and neutral behaviour when managing the distribution of audiovisual content.

In any case, and no matter which the result of this debate is, the role of the *gatekeepers* cannot be denied. These actors are in charge to play an important role in the heart of the new digital culture, and therefore their collaboration and intervention within any future regulatory framework is fundamental.

In this sense, and according to the current debates, two ideas seem to build the basis on which the regulatory policies of the future will be built:

1. It does not seem proportioned, no matter which their role and their effective capacity of intervention or management of the bits' flow and/or contents is, to impose to certain gatekeepers or network operators the same regulatory rules which apply to the traditional broadcasters, concerning the selection and offer of contents, services and application whose access is facilitated. Despite the fact that the regulators can have the temptation to adopt this position in *possibilist* terms, this approach

would be completely far away from reality and would mean giving them a responsibility that does not correspond with their real role.

2. The effective regulation or, at least, the guarantee of the effectiveness of certain values, principles and rights in the heart of the public audiovisual sphere will require the necessary collaboration of these actors. In several cases, they will be the only subject to whom the regulators will have reasonably access or will be able to have a minimum degree of influence.

So it seems we are moving in a field where the traditional mechanisms of regulation and exercise of public legal powers by the relevant regulators will have to let the place to alternative modalities of intervention. Whether these modalities may be based on the mere promotion of the auto-regulation or more sophisticated mechanisms of co-regulation it is an issue still to be deeply discussed within the academia and regulators' forums. These new mechanisms will probably require the collaboration between public and private subjects, moving from traditional imperative rules. In any case new rules should be particularly transparent and satisfy the expectations of regulatory protection and *accountability* (of both the regulator and the regulated actors) that in any moment can have the citizens.

In any case, and to sum up, it seems clear that the technological changes are giving rise to a deep transformation process of the mechanisms of public regulatory intervention in the guarantee of an open, diverse free and transparent public audiovisual space. This space has to go on allowing a free formation of the citizens' opinions within the democratic process. Any reflection and any change in the mentioned mechanisms of intervention will only be legitimate and proportioned as far as the effective validity and realization of those principles is guaranteed.

References

Ariño, M. (2007), *Content Regulation and New Media. A case study of online video portals*. Communications & Strategies, France, IDATE, pp. 115-135.

Barata Mir, J. (2006), *Democracia y audiovisual. Fundamentos normativos para la reforma del régimen español*, Madrid, Marcial Pons.

Consell de l'Audiovisual de Catalunya, (2009), *Technological and audiovisual convergente*, Quaderns del CAC, No. 31-32, Barcelona.

Gardam, T. and Levi, D.A. (2008), *The price of plurality. Choice, Diversity and Broadcasting Institutions in the Digital Age*, Londres, Reuter Institute.

Richards, E.; Foster, R. and Kiedrowski, T. (2006), *Communications. The next decade*. OFCOM, Londres.

A Catalan Code of Best Practices for the Audiovisual Sector

Emma Teodoro, Núria Galera, Jorge González-Conejero, Pompeu Casanovas
UAB-Institute of Law and Technology (IDT), Universitat Autònoma de Barcelona, Spain

Abstract. In spite of a new general law regarding Audiovisual Communication, the regulatory framework of the audiovisual sector in Spain can still be defined as huge, disperse and obsolete. The first part of this paper provides an overview of the major challenges of the Spanish audiovisual sector as a result of the convergence of platforms, services and operators, paying especial attention to the Audiovisual Sector in Catalonia. In the second part, we will present an example of self-regulation through the previous research work done for the future Code of Best Professional Practices of the Catalan Audiovisual Union. Some issues regarding protection of minors and youth, privacy, general public right of access to digital content on line, intellectual property, pluralism, harm and offence content are examined in the light of self-regulation instruments.

Keywords: Self-regulation, audiovisual media, digital content online, intellectual property, code of best practices, ethical media.

1. Introduction

The emergence of new technological changes resulting from the digitization process and the convergence of information technologies and telecommunications in connection with the storage, processing and distribution of information are creating new challenges within the audiovisual sector.

In this context of digital convergence, there is an international uncertainty with regard to new digital business models in the future as it is unpredictable to determine how patterns of use and consume will be, specially when linked to the use of the Internet. Self-regulation codes applied with the right instruments could be useful for professionals to respond rapidly than state regulations to the functional and technological transformations occurred as a result of the convergence of the activity of different industries (content production, telecommunications, media, Internet and services of the Information Society).

Consequently, it is difficult to clearly identify which ethical values and good professional practices should be preserved and defended as a professional group.

The Catalan Union of Audiovisual Professionals has started a research project on the drafting and adopting a code of best practices. This project implies as we will see later on, the examination of emerging issues as such as enforcement, procedures, content issues, government legislation, and child/consumer protection regarding the audiovisual sector.

2. The regulatory framework of the Spanish Audiovisual Sector

The value chain of the Audiovisual Services has been affected by the so-called technological convergence phenomenon. The convergence of platforms, services and operators increase the complexity of the regulatory framework of the audiovisual services' provision. The EU Audiovisual Media Services Directive (AVMSD)[1], as the main instrument of the European audiovisual regulatory policy, calls on Member States to reform their legislation on this field with the aim of harmonizing and reforming the different regulations covering the audiovisual sector. The Audiovisual Media Services Directive provides a more general but flexible regulation in comparison with the Television without Frontiers Directive (TWF)[2]. The new rules respond to technological developments and represent the opportunity to improve common minimum standards in Europe for traditional broadcasting[3] and emerging on-demand audiovisual media services. It is crucial, specially in order to avoid distortions of competition, to improve legal certainty, help the internal market and also safeguard certain public interest. In this respect, the Directive attempts to preserve cultural diversity, protect children and consumers, safeguard media pluralism, fight racial and religious hatred and guarantee the independence of national media regulators.

In sum, the AVMSD Directive provides the key concepts on audiovisual regulation based on the objective of convergence of technologies, businesses, contents and services.

In Spain, with the exceptions[4] considered below, there was not a general law regulating audiovisual communication services. To avoid this situation,

---

[1] Directive 2007/65/EC of the European Parliament and of the Council of 11 December 2007 amending Council Directive 89/552/EEC on the coordination of certain provisions laid down by law, regulation or administrative action in Member States concerning the pursuit of television broadcasting activities.

[2] Council Directive 89/552/EEC of 3 October 1989 on the coordination of certain provisions laid down by law, regulation or administrative action in Member States concerning the pursuit of television broadcasting activities (updated in 1997 and 2007).

[3] Television broadcasting includes: analogue and digital television, live streaming, web casting and near-video-on-demand.

[4] The most important Spanish Acts covering the audiovisual sector are: Act 25/94 of 7 June modifying law 22/1999 on the implementation of the TVWF Directive; Act 10/2005, on urgent measures for the promotion of digital terrestrial TV, liberalization of cable and promotion of media pluralism; Act 22/2005, on Catalan Audiovisual Communication; Act 17/2006, on national public radio and TV; Act 55/2007, on the Cinema Law; Decree 1/2009, on urgent measures for the telecommunications sector.

the Spanish government drafted a general legislative proposal regulating this field[5] and during the month of March 2010, the Spanish Parliament passed the General Law of Audiovisual Communication.[6] The audiovisual sectors as well as consumer's organizations have been requiring this specific regulation in different occasions and for the last six years some different legislative proposals have been discussed in the Spanish Parliament without success. The principal issues addressed by this New General Law are:

- It determines which are the rights concerning on the one hand, consumers[7] and, on the other hand, media service providers[8].
- It fixes several rules regarding content and mode of operation for the players in the sectors.
- It creates a new supervisory body called National Council for Audiovisual Media. There are in Spain at the Autonomous Region level some regulatory bodies with similar functions[9], so it could be very possible that competence conflicts arise between them; that is, the National Council and the Autonomous Audiovisual Councils.
- It sets out some rules with regard to advertisement, sponsorship and product placement.
- It proposes to take into account the percentage of the population who speak secondary official languages (Basque, Catalan and Galician) in the different Autonomous Regions for financial purposes regarding film productions and other audiovisual works.

---

[5] The new legislative proposal focuses on the following aspects: reformulating public service broadcasting and its adequate funding; licensing procedures for broadcasters (automatic renovation of licenses after 15 years); private broadcasters may sell o lease their licenses (only 50%); fines around 1 million € when: (1) public or private channels do not comply with the economic obligation to support cinema without justification, (2) channels exceed the period of time established for advertising (no more than twelve minutes per hour), (3) channels modify their TV program schedule without a clear justification to do it (three days before, they should communicate TV programming changes to the public); and the creation of an independent regulatory authority to govern the audiovisual area.

[6] Act 7/2010, of 31st March 2010 on General Audiovisual Communication. Available at: http://noticias.juridicas.com/base_datos/Vacatio/l7-2010.html#

[7] These rights are: the right to receive a plural and transparent audiovisual communication, the right to get cultural and linguistic diversity and the right to participate to the control on the audiovisual content. The Act also stresses the rights protecting minors and person's disability.

[8] The new Spanish Audiovisual Law recognizes for the media service providers the following rights: freedom regarding editorial management, the right of access and self regulation, the right to do commercial communications, and exclusivity over certain audiovisual content for broadcasters.

[9] Autonomous Communities such as Navarra (CAN), Catalonia (CAC), and Andalucía (CAA) have their Audiovisual Councils.

- It states that private broadcasters have the right to negotiate remuneration with satellite or cable platforms in exchange for their free-to-air channels. By way of compensation, public broadcasters will do it without any type of remuneration.
- It will promote own productions by public service channels guarantying linguistic and cultural diversity in broadcasters (either national or from the Autonomous Regions). Broadcasters will be on the alert concerning this issue with regards to their broadcasts.

Moreover, the regulatory framework of the audiovisual sector in Spain has been defined as huge, disperse and obsolete. Regulations concerning broadcasting have been produced under governmental control and it is almost impossible to obtain agreements from all the stakeholders involved in order to pass a general law for the audiovisual sector.

On 29th May 2009, the Spanish government approved a bill law on the funding scheme of RTVE. Nowadays, this is raising a wide debate within the broadcasting sector because of the new rules concerning: (1) choosing a dual funding scheme: suppression of advertising spaces on public service broadcasting and establishing economic contributions for free-to view TV (3%), Pay TV and conditional access TV (1, 5%); and (2) avoiding TV operators to lose their license if they do not contribute with their taxes. They will be punished with general sanctions according to the tax system established in Spain.

Looking at this broad picture, we can conclude that successive governments have approved different regulations to face concrete situations as a consequence of new technological changes occurred during the past years. It seems to be clear the need to design Spanish audiovisual and media regulations. However, as we will state later, regulation does not involve mainly legislative drafting. We cannot forget the importance of this sector for societies, democracy, education and culture.

2.1. THE CATALAN AUDIOVISUAL LEGAL FRAMEWORK

At the autonomous regions level, Catalonia has done its homework in terms of regulating the audiovisual sector by proposing a mixed model of public service broadcasting (public and private broadcasters coexist). Firstly, broadcasters develop their activity under provisions made by art. 20 of the Spanish Constitution (audiovisual communication freedom) and not for being concessionaire of a public service mandate. Secondly, the legislation designed a public broadcasting sector based on the general interest and on common values such as freedom of expression and information, the right of reply, pluralism, protection of copyright, promotion of cultural and human diversity, minors and consumers.

The Catalan Communication legal framework is constituted by the Act 2/2000, of May 4, on the Audiovisual Council of Catalonia[10], the Act 22/2005, of December 29, on the Audiovisual Communication in Catalonia[11], and the Act 11/2007, of October 11, on Catalan Broadcasting Corporation[12]. This legislative package should be implemented with the Spanish legislation on the audiovisual matter according to the European Audiovisual policies.

As we pointed out above, the European Audiovisual Policy tries to establish and guarantee a minimum of uniformity regarding audiovisual content within the European Union. It recognizes certain discretional activity on behalf of Member States in relation with national audiovisual regulations.

The brief description presented concerning the audiovisual legal framework at different legislative levels is necessary to understand the legal constraints that audiovisual professionals must take into account in order to develop their professional activity. Even if audiovisual professionals are working under the umbrella of public or commercial broadcasters, they are limited by these regulations. It seems clear what Catalan and Spanish regulations concerning audiovisual communication have in common: both regulations have the same receiver, traditional broadcasters.   Other important agents who are part of the value chain of the audiovisual are not under the legal umbrella of these regulations (e.g. creators, producers, Internet Service Providers…). It must be understood as they are not compelled by these specific regulations as legal subjects; however, they are obliged to respect others legal regimes (Criminal Law, Intellectual Property Law, the Information Society Service and Electronic Commerce Act…etc) by law. There is a public debate concerning the possibility to share the regulatory weight between traditional broadcasters and the others subjects implied in the audiovisual value chain (Barata, 2009).

All the relevant actors are concerned: consumers, customers, citizens, broadcasters and service servers alike. But the most sensitive areas are to be found among professional associations, namely the official guilds or unions known in Spain as Colegios profesionales.

3. Self-regulation and co-regulation under a professional user perspective

Self-regulation and co-regulation could be presented as two forms to assume professional responsibilities. These mechanisms are not used to

---

[10] Available at: http://noticias.juridicas.com/base_datos/CCAA/ca-l2-2000.html

[11] Available at: http://noticias.juridicas.com/base_datos/CCAA/ca-l22-2005.html

[12] Available at: http://noticias.juridicas.com/base_datos/CCAA/ca-l11-2007.html

avoid regulatory constraints by the audiovisual professionals. On the contrary, these regulatory resources have been used by professionals in order to exercise their moral autonomy within their professional arena (Camps, 2009). The difference between them consists of which sectors take part in the regulatory task: if we consider self-regulation, a professional sector is the one to establish a set of rules. On the other hand, co-regulation implies that more than one sector is concerned with the professional activity. Therefore, these sectors should reach an agreement regarding a set of rules acceptable for each of them concerned.

Within the communication arena, these self-regulation instruments may be shaped in different ways:

- Deontological Codes (normally adopted by professional associations[13]).
- Internal Codes adopted by broadcasters or media corporations, for example, with the aim to regulate a set of professional conducts with respect to editorial principles.[14]
- Codes of conduct adopted by some of the audiovisual companies as a consequence of audience pressures with regard to certain contents or even to avoid state regulations on those issues.[15] At the same time, we can include in this paragraph those recommendations adopted by official regulatory bodies addressed not only to professionals, but also to media.[16]

4. Self-regulation and professional best practices

One year ago, the Union of Audiovisual Professionals of Catalonia[17] decided to provide a code of best practices. Provisions from its General Rules include as an important professional obligation "to exercise the

---

[13] Deontogical Code. Federation of the Spanish Press Association, 1993. Available   at: http://www.fape.es/index.php?option=com_content&task=view&id=101&Itemid=120

[14] See for example, the editorial principles of Sogecable (one of the most important pay television media group in Spain). Available at: http://www.sogecable.es/noticias.html?id=555719&item=1160&lang=ES

[15] Código de Autorregulación sobre contenidos televisivos e infancia, 2004 (TVE, Antena3, Telecinco, Sogecable). Available at: http://www.tvinfancia.es/Textos/CodigoAutorregulacion/Codigo.htm

[16] For example, in CAC 2007 Report, there are two specific actions regarding self-regulation: Recommendations on the coverage of Anorexia and Bulimia and Recommendations on media coverage concerning drugs information. Available at: http://www.cac.cat/web/actuacions/index.jsp?MjI%3D&MQ%3D%3D&L3dlYi9hY3R1YW Npb25zL2xsaXN0YXRDb250ZW50#

[17] http://cpac.cat/

profession in accordance with the professional ethics needed and respecting the fundamental rights of the citizens".

Some recent studies[18] agree with detailing some transformations which have an impact concerning working conditions on the communicative domain. These transformations could be defined as technological and functional (Scolari et al. 2008). Firstly, technological transformation implies that professionals should incorporate new expert knowledge in order to deal with digital instruments. On the other hand, functional transformations mean that professionals should carry out new tasks normally developed by other professionals as a result of the so-called convergence phenomenon. New working places have been created under a crisis situation within the communicative domain as consequence of:

- chaotic growth of the most important agents of the sector (media groups)
- dependence of most of these agents (broadcasters, production companies...etc).
- there are no strong barriers to access within the profession. Different professionals coming from other disciplines such as photography, printing, web design, etc. without specific knowledge on audiovisual communication have been accessing the profession. Some reasons could explain this trend: the poor value assigned to the professional results with regard to audiovisual professionals and the growth of amateur contents which frequently blur the difference between both professional content and amateur content.

In general terms, codes are basically adopted to meet different objectives: (1) avoiding liability; (2) protecting users; (3) imposing professional standards; (4) preventing or commanding control regulation; (5) building trust among users, audiences, readers, etc and; (6) raising the public image of a company.

We may concede that growing proliferation of codes of best practices within professional groups is due to the important value of freedom in our liberal societies (respecting the right of people to their own privacy and public image), and to the development of the information society

---

[18] See the detailed report with regard to the research *"El sector de la comunicació a Barcelona: 15 Perfils Professionals"*, Barcelona, 2009. It is a research carried out by the Employment Agency of the Communication Faculty (Blanquerna University). See also the study "Nous perfils professionals de l'actual panorama informatiu audiovisual i multimèdia de Catalunya" by the Group of Research of Digital Interactions (http://www.uvic.cat/showrecerca/11) at the Business and Communication Faculty (University of Vic), September 2006.

technologies (Camps, 2009). This soft-regulation form of government has been adopted by the EU policies since 2000 along with target development and benchmarking (implementation by publication /monitoring /learning), voluntary accords and procedural norms (Héritier, 2002).

Self-regulations codes applied with the right instruments could be useful to order the sector. Nevertheless, professionals concerned should have an incentive (fear towards a public mandatory regulation or to gain citizens' confidence) in order to respect self-regulation codes (Barata, 2009).

In Spain, self-regulation in the audiovisual sector offers the following features:

- Journalism: Codes of Journalists[19] are opened to any professional media.
- Radio: only some editorial principles can be found in the sphere of Public Regional Broadcasters (Canal Sur Radio, Radio Castilla la Mancha, Catalunya Radio and Canal Nou Radio). The common values collected by these editorial principles are: respect for constitutional principles; truthfulness of information, respect towards the principles of freedom of speech, protection and privacy; respect towards political and social pluralism; protection of minors and promoting identity and regional values.
- Television: public and commercial broadcasters have ombudsmen to protect the audience (Televisión Española, Televisió de Catalunya[20]...). With regard to content (especially minors, education, violence and fiction, anorexia, racism and immigration, human tragedies and trash TV, to mention some of the most important ones), self-regulation initiatives are taking place involving both public and commercial broadcasters.
- Cinema and Video: none
- The Internet: three initiatives can be found corresponding to: the code of best practices of ASIMILEC[21]; the cluster of companies dedicated to electronics, communications and information technologies, and the Internet Users Association (they do not have a code of conduct although they use to promote good use of the

---

[19] See for instance, the Declaration of Principles of the Journalistic Profession in Catalonia. The Deontological Code of the Catalan Journalists was approved by the Union of Journalists of Catalonia on 22 October 1992.
Available at: http://www.periodistes.org/documents_codi_deontologic
[20] As an example of ombudsman protecting the audience, see the official
web of the Spanish Television : http://www.rtve.es/television/20090326/cual-papel-defensora-delespectador/254209.shtml
[21] ASIMILEC Code of Good Practices is available at: http://www.asimelec.es/

Internet); the Spanish Internet Observatory (it was created to study and disseminate issues regarding the Internet).
-   Videogames: the Pan European Game Information Code, 2003.
-   Quite surprisingly, there is nothing regarding cinema and video. It seems difficult to find how to regulate the audiovisual sector without damaging the right of freedom of speech. We believe that we should review the relationship between the future content of the code of conduct and the existing regulations regarding that content.
-   The schedule of the future code for the audiovisual will contain five parts such as constitution, coverage, content, compliance and communications, following the 5C+ approach (Tambini et al. 2008).
-   In particular, the content of the code should cover the following domains:
-   Audiovisual content: this part will focus on establishing best practices linked with human dignity, respect towards human rights, protection of minors and youth, deontological norms, protection of pluralism and norms concerning truthfulness of information.
-   Labour relationships
-   Compliance of the code
-   Editorial relationships.

For instance, if we pay attention to the production of digital contents, we observe that, in Spain, almost two thirds of the population currently accesses it, as stated by the White Paper on Digital Content in Spain 2008. New ways of using network contents are performing new business opportunities beyond the traditional models.

In 2009, the Ministry of Industry, Tourism and Commerce published an update of the tendencies with regard to this industry. Following the official data, the growth of the digital content industries in Spain is positive. They have experienced an annual growth of 3% between 2004 and 2008, as Figure 1 shows. This result demonstrates as well as consolidates the vitality of the digital dimension. Two causes are mentioned as a key factors for the advancement of this industry in Spain: on the one hand, the continuous improvement of Internet access (fixed and mobile broadband) and, on the other hand, the increased broadband coverage.

Digital content production industries in Spain: evolution of turnover, 2003-2008 (€M)

	2003	2004	2005	2006	2007	2008	CAGR 2004-2008
Publications	6,965	7,286	7,377	7,722	7,997	7,864	2.5%
Audio-visual	4,677	4,532	5,028	5,346	5,767	5,526	3.4%
Video games	465	500	537	576	719	744	10%
Music	457	406	399	368	284	254	-11%
Cinema	1,052	1,096	927	911	916	860	-4%
Online advertising	75	94	121	160	482	610	52%
Total	13,691	13,914	14,389	15,083	16,165	15,858	3%

Source: ONTSI, 2009

Figure 1. Digital content production industries in Spain: evolution of turnover, 2003-2008 (€M). Source: White Paper on Digital Content in Spain 2009.

In general, foreign multinational companies are dominating the digital content industry in Spain. There is an international uncertainty with regard to new digital business models in the future as it is unpredictable to determine how patterns of use and consume will take place, specially linked with the use of the Internet. As a consequence, it is difficult to identify clearly which ethical values and good professional practices should be preserved and defended as a professional group.

It seems clear, following the conclusions of this report concerning the audiovisual sector that "new opportunities are opening up with the development of infrastructures, the sale of new devices and the growing number of services and subscribers"(ibid.p.25) New services of interactive content and its digital derivatives are building up new and interesting business opportunities within the sector.

Another example of the new challenges of audiovisual sector is peer-to-peer technology. For the last years, file sharing of copyright protected material, particularly peer-to-peer networks, has been an important threat to the established business models of the content industry. An increasing civil and criminal pressure against users of the Internet seems to be the strategy of the traditional content industry to face copyright issues as a consequence of new technological changes resulting from the digitization process and the convergence of information technologies and telecommunications.

Peer-to-peer networks allow millions of users to share their music and film files through the Internet. Most of these files are copyright protected material and their authors (music and film creators, software developers, publishers…) cannot protect their property from piracy.

Governments from several countries have taken different types of measures in order to fight piracy[22]. The US Congress Committee included Spain in its 2009 Piracy Watchlist of countries with "alarming" levels of illegal file-sharing[23]. The Spanish Courts have ruled repeatedly that free music and film downloading is not illegal if it is not for commercial use. Music downloads for personal uses are permitted. Spaniards pay special taxes on CDs, DVDs and memory cards to compensate the music industry for its losses. The debate on that issue is performed by powerful collecting societies led by the *Sociedad General de Autores* (SGAE) or PROMUSICAE, and service providers (Telefónica, Vodafone…). Spanish collecting societies keep asking for a set of measures related to the effective protection of the intellectual property. They specially claim for:

- legislative changes to protect intellectual property against piracy;
- an agreement with service providers to fight piracy;
- respect for intellectual property from users using media educational campaigns;
- and governmental action leading piracy fight.

On the other side, interesting questions regarding the neutrality of the Internet and privacy are pointed out by users in order to preserve freedom. The perception that all the information available in the Internet is in the public domain and that everyone should be allowed to copy and use these materials —even when they are copyright protected— is a well known challenge. To deal with it and other similar situations, professionals would need to define the content of their best practices. However, the first obstacle comes from the heterogeneity of the target itself: cinema directors, producers, scriptwriters, camera operators, actors, makeup artists and other professional people belong to the same union.

5. The future Code of Best Practices

The UAB Institute of Law and Technology (IDT)[24] is the research centre that carries out the research on this project.[25] From an interdisciplinary

---

[22] In Spain, the government worked out a code of good practices regarding piracy in the Internet and offenses against intellectual property.
Available at: http://www.mcu.es/propiedadInt/MC/Mbp/index.html
[23] Available at: http://schiff.house.gov/antipiracycaucus/pdf/IAPC_2009_Watch_List.pdf
[24] http://idt.uab.es/

perspective, the research team puts together professional researchers, legal experts, audiovisual professionals and associations of users related to audiovisual issues.[26]

The project is divided into three phases. The first stage consists of producing three technical reports addressed to obtain:

- comparative studies regarding ethical media codes in Europe and the United States;
- identification of the key aspects of the European and Spanish intellectual property law;
- a concluding report.

The second stage focuses on collecting qualitative and quantitative data on members' profiles, experiences and needs. A *SNAP* questionnaire is being distributed among the Union's members. In parallel, a preliminary map of problems and functional domains has been already obtained from the first exchanges between professionals and researchers (vid. Fig. 2). Dissemination of the final results will come at the end.

We are confident that the future code will help to achieve ethical values within the profession. But, according to the work already done, the first effect being produced is adding some internal consistency to the profession itself. The main purpose is favouring a stakeholders' identity (members and representatives of the union) that could be able to deal with new forms of governance and law based on dialogue and a relational way to deal with problems; that is to say, putting aside traditional corporative values and favouring a more open attitude.

---

[25] http://www.codibonespractiquescpac.com/
[26] http://www.cpaudiovisual.cat

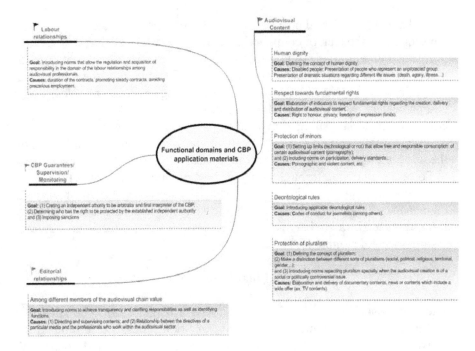

Figure 2. Mapping of functional domains of the Code of Best Practices.

Especially Internet users are not only consumers, but prosumers of audiovisual content. This means that conflict scenarios and working frameworks are not only defined by governments, institutions, companies and professionals but by a multitude of stakeholders (Casanovas, 2009)[27]. Web 2.0 and Web 3.0 links allow new kinds of communication that the existing codes in the broadcasting field do not take into account yet[28]. The so-called "social web" and the emerging "web of contents" (the Semantic Web) are interwoven, and allow users to move from traditional roles to more complex ones (Hendler, 2009).

Some countries such as Sweden, France and UK have reinforced their legislations to pursue the exchange of files protected by copyright. However, downloading files protected by copyright is allowed in Spain.

---

[27] *Relational Justice* may be defined as the substantive and formal structure that allows end users, in the broader sense (as citizens, consumers, customers, clients, managers, officials…), to participate in the making of their own regulation and legal outcomes through all the mixed and plural strategies that the Semantic Web framework allows (ibid.).

[28] British Broadcasting Corporation: Producer's Guidelines
http://www.bbc.co.uk/info/editorial/prodgl/index.shtmlhttp://www.google.es/
CBC Radio-Canada Journalistic Standards and Practices
http://www.cbc.radio-canada.ca/accountability/journalistic/conflict.shtml

This happens under the legal umbrella of the "private copy" and, consequently, the lack of commercial profit.

Spanish entertainment and telecommunication industries are not close to reach an agreement concerning the users' claims. On the one hand, entertainment industries warn about the growing decrease of sales. Some companies are asking for penalties for those users who download protected copyright material, suing downloaders and blocking websites.[29] On the other hand, telecommunication industries are against penalties and focus on the need of data protection and privacy issues[30].

Fostering dialogue through codes of best practices will not solve all the problems that the audiovisual sector shows. But it may help to reshaping them and enlarging the field to all the stakeholders involved, including Internet users' associations, service providers, professional unions, institutions and companies.

6. Final Remarks

The audiovisual sector in Spain continues reshaping public broadcasting and it is also implementing the digital transition process according to the convergence of technologies, platforms and services (traditional TV, internet TV, IPTV, web TV, TV on mobile phones and other mobile devices).

A strong control exerted by the state or government alone on the audiovisual sector will not work. Moreover, we should keep in mind that the system of public broadcasting is directly related to democratic, social and cultural needs, and to the need to preserve media pluralism.

As regards digital content, the main issue is the lower cost of online distribution. Hard copy distribution, management of copyright online, piracy, protection of minors and cultural diversity are some of the main challenges of the sector, especially for the professionals.

Internet has become the meeting point where the net users are fighting for their civil rights. Protection of privacy, free software, suppression of patents, exchange of files through the net, and the opposition to the current ruling copyright laws are the most common users' claims[31].

---

[29] Creators and Content Industry Coalition *(Coalición de Creadores e Industrias de Contenido)* is a lobby formed by cultural industries, specially collecting societies (EGEDA, SGAE, FAP, ADIVAN, Promusicae and ADICAN) in 2008.

[30] Redtel (http://www.redtel.es) is the association of the most important mobile industries (ONO, Orange, Telefónica and Vodafone).

[31] The Pirate Party, with representation in the European Parliament, has on its agenda these claims. See the Pirate Party Declaration of Principles 3.2, available at: http://www.piratpartiet.se/international/english

We are confident that the future code will help to achieve ethical values within the profession. But, according to the work already done, the first effect being produced is adding some internal consistency to the profession itself.

Acknowledgements

The research presented in this paper has been developed within the framework of the project *Projecte de Codi de Bones Pràctiques del Col.legi Professional de l'Audiovisual a Catalunya* (number of contract 11123), the Spanish Ministry of Science and Innovation (CSO-2008-05536-SOCI), and the Spanish Ministry of Industry (TSI-020501-2008-131).

References

Agejas, J.A.; Serrano, J.F. (2002), *Ética de la comunicación y de la información*, Ariel, Barcelona.

Aznar, H. (1999), *Comunicación responsable: Deontología y autorregulación de los medios*, Ariel, Barcelona.

Barata, J. (2009), *Regulation and Co-regulation in the 2.0 Public Space* in Bourcier, D.; Casanovas, P.; Maracke, C. and Dulong de Resnay, M. (Eds.), Intelligent Multimedia. Managing Creative Works in a Digital World. Florence: European Publishing Academic Press.

Boix, A. (2007), *Transformacions en l'ecosistema mediàtic i noves pautes de regulació administrativa del fet audiovisual*, in Quaderns del CAC, 29, pp. 8-40. Consell Audiovisual de Catalunya, Barcelona .

Bonete, E. (Ed.) (1999), *Ética de la comunicación audiovisual: materiales para una ética mediática*, Tecnos, Madrid.

Campos, F. (2007), *La nueva directiva europea sobre los medios audiovisuales remueve el mapa de la television*, in ICONO 14, 9, pp. 5-9. Revista de Comunicación y Nuevas Tecnologías, Madrid.

Camps, V. (2009), *Virtual culture and the Public Space*, in Bourcier, D; Casanovas, P.; Maracke, C. and Dulong de Resnay, M. (Eds.), Intelligent Multimedia. Managing Creative Works in a Digital World. Florence: European Publishing Academic Press.

Casanovas, P. (2009), *The Future of Law: Relational Justice and Next Generation of Web Services*, in M. Fernández-Barrera, N. Nunes Gomes de Andrade, P. de Filippi, M. Viola de Azevedo Cunha, G. Sartor, P. Casanovas (Eds.), European Press Academic Publishing, Florence, pp. 137-156.

Cuenca, J. (Coord.) (2009), *"El sector de la comunicació a Barcelona: 15 Perfils Professionals"*, Barcelona, 2009. It is a research carried out by the Employment Agency of the Communication Faculty (Blanquerna University).

Foster, I.; Kesselman, C.; Nick, J. and Tuecke, S. (2002), *The Physiology of the Grid: an Open Grid Services Architecture for Distributed Systems Integration.*

Technical report, Global Grid Forum, European Commission, available at: http://ec.europa.eu/avpolicy/reg/avms/index_en (accessed 3 May 2010).

Hendler, J. (2009), *Web 3.0 emerging, IEEE Intelligent Systems*, January 2009, pp. 88-90.

Héritier, A. (2002), *New Modes of Governance in Europe: Policy-Making without Legislating?*, in Héritier, A. (Ed.) Common Goods: Reinventing European and International Governance, Lanham, Maryland: Boulder, CO, Rowman & Littlefield.

Informe GRETEL (2005), *El sector audiovisual y su evolución. La televisión: retos y oportunidades*, Colegio Oficial de Ingenieros de Telecomunicaciones, Madrid.

Mayoral, R. (2006), *El sector audiovisual: Derecho Comparado, los Estados de la Unión Europea*, Diario La Ley, n. 3, Sección Temas de Hoy. La Ley, Madrid.

Red.es, (2008), White Paper on Digital Content in Spain, available at: http://www.ontsi.red.es/articles/detail.action%3bjsessionid=7%20CCA3334D8 6C83D2028AFE815C4C93DA.vertebra_dni02?id=2662&request_locale=en (accessed May 2010).

Red.es, (2009), Main Figures for Digital Content in Spain 2009.

Scolari, C; Navarro, H; Pardo, H; Micó, J.L. (2007), *Nous perfils professionals i polivalència periodística a Catalunya*, in Quaderns del CAC, No.27, pp. 115-118. Consell Audiovisual de Catalunya, Barcelona .

Tambini, D; Danilo, L. and Marsden, C. (2008), *Codifying Cyberspace: Communications ,Selfregulation in the Age of Internet Convergence*, Abingdon: Routledge.

Zallo, R. (2010), *The audiovisual communications policy of the PSOE Government (2004-2009): A neoliberal Turn.l*, Revista Latina de Comunicación Social, No. 65, pp. 14-29, available at: http://www.revistalatinacs.org/10/art/880_UPV/02_ZalloIng.html (accessed 8 May 2010).

Privacy-Preserving Digital Rights Management

Antoni Roig

UAB Institute of Law and Technology (IDT), Universitat Autònoma de Barcelona, Spain

Abstract. Digital Rights Management (DRM) is a technology that provides content protection by enforcing the use of digital content according to granted rights. DRM can be privacy-invasive due to many reasons. The solution is not easy: there are economic and legitimate reasons for distributors and network operators to collect data about users and their activities, such as traffic modelling for infrastructure planning or statistical sampling. Furthermore, traditional PET – such as encryption, anonymity and pseudonymity– cannot solve all the privacy problems raised by DRM, even if they can help. Privacy and security considerations should be included in the design of DRM from the beginning, and they should not be considered as a property that can be added on. PET is considered as technology for privacy protection, in different fields. However, PET solutions are not the only ones to be considered useful to complement DRM systems. The contrary is also true: DRM systems are adapted as technical platforms for privacy. In short, there is a deep change in PET related to the web 2.0, and it is also true for P2DRM: transparency and other new techniques are preferred, or at least added, to anonymity, authentication and other traditional protections.

Keywords: Privacy Enhancing Technology (PET), Digital Rights Managements (DRM), Privacy-Preserving Digital Rights Management (P2DRM), Privacy-Friendly Design.

1. DRM has the potential for threatening privacy

Digital Rights Management (DRM) is a technology that provides content protection by enforcing the use of digital content according to granted rights (Conrado et al. 2004). A DRM system normally includes content protection, rights creation and enforcement, identification of users and usage of content monitoring:

-   Security and integrity features of computer operating systems, for instance, file-access privileges.
-   Rights-management languages that determine whether requested uses should be allowed.
-   Encryption
-   Digital signatures provide assured provenance of digital content and non repudiation of transactions.

– Fingerprinting and other "marking" technology so as to facilitate copy tracking, distribution or usage. User tracking or network control of users' computers are potentially destructive for user privacy. Data collection by distributors and network operators can be a real problem for user's privacy.

– Thus, DRM can be privacy-invasive due to many reasons (Feigenbaum et al. 2002):

– DRM does not support anonymous or unlinkability, so it is quite different from buying a CD paying cash.
– DRM content acquisition is also privacy-invasive. A distributor may use complete DRM metadata with digital content. Each file downloaded by a user from the distributor's web would include both the content and the metadata with the "rights" that the user has acquired. So the user could only access the content as specified by the metadata. And the rights' metadata are minable as user information.
– The device uploaded can also be privacy-invasive. The download could be oriented to a specific device with a serial number. The device is then the user's information that can be collected and mined. The upload of the device, due to malfunctioning or purchase of a new one, also offers the possibility of tracking user's information.
– Another DRM privacy problem is the usage track. The downloaded content of the user can also be mined and collected. The potential tracking of a concrete user's information includes all its listening, viewing and reading.
– Finally, there are economic reasons for collecting user's data. For instance, DRM data networks should provide usage tracking for efficient management and artists' compensation, but should not provide user tracking. Personal Identifying Information (PII) such as names, addresses and telephones should be preserved; for example, using anonymous payment.

2. Traditional Privacy Enhancing Technologies (PET) cannot solve all problems

2.1. LIMITS

The solution is not easy. There are economic and legitimate reasons for distributors and network operators to collect data about users and their activities; for example, traffic modelling for infrastructure planning or statistical sampling. Furthermore, traditional PET, like encryption, anonymity and pseudonymity cannot solve all the privacy problems raised by DRM, even if they may help (Feigenbaum et al., 2002).

2.2. CRYPTOGRAPHY

While cryptography is useful for the Trusted Computing Base (TCB), it is considered inadequate for commercial content distribution (Feigenbaum *et al.*, 2002). Cryptography needs to define exactly whether there is legitimate use of data or not and what the single relationship between two identified persons or institutions is. Another difficulty with cryptography is that public-key cryptography is slow, so if privacy in DRM uses this possibility, it will reduce considerably the rate of simultaneous connections. On the other hand, DRM will not generally accept cryptographic e-cash but it will rather continue with credit cards. As a result, vendors will have the possibility of learning how much is paying someone.

2.3. AUTHENTICATION

Traditional authentication can also be criticized. The management of users' identity should be based on recognition rather than authentication (Seigneur, 2009). As Seigneur says, in an authentication process there is:

-   Enrolment: generally involves an administrator or human intervention.
-   Triggering: someone clicks on a web link to a resource that requires authentication to be downloaded.
-   Detective work: the main task is to verify that the entity's claimed identity is correct.
-   Action: the identification is subsequently used in some ways.
-   On the other hand, recognition consists of:
-   Triggering (passive and active sense): the recognising user can trigger itself.
-   Detective work: recognising the user.
-   Upper-level action (optional): the outcome of the recognition is subsequently used in some ways.

The recognition process is an example of a more general replacement for authentication that does not necessarily bind an identity to the recognised identity. On the contrary, authentication is a recognition process that binds a real-world identity to the virtual identity. The possibility of recognising a user, analysing some of its attributes, is sufficient to establish trust based on past experience. One way of preserving both privacy and trust is using pseudonyms. Nevertheless, traffic analysis, data triangulation and data-mining can also associate a pseudonym with the real user. That is the reason why it is important that multiple pseudonyms are provided.

Technical solutions, such as a trust transfer, can be adopted then to avoid the misuse of multiple pseudonyms (Seigneur, 2009). Another example is the EU-funded FP6 project PRIME (Privacy and Identity Management for Europe), whose approach uses "private credentials". This private credentials enable proving one's authorization (e.g., to be over 18 years old) without identifying the individual. They are derived from certificates issued on different pseudonyms of the same person, and they are neither linkable to each other nor to the issuance interaction. Only in the case of misuse, the user's anonymity can be revoked (Hansen, 2008).

2.4. FUTURE TRENDS

Consumers are largely unable to differentiate between privacy options: "Best practices" for privacy engineering have not yet been standardized. Even if businesses decide to offer privacy, like Earthlink and its "totally anonymous Internet" or Zero-Knowledge Freedom network with its pseudonymity, this consumer inability to differentiate motivates companies not to invest in expensive technological options (Feigenbaum *et al.*, 2002).

Indeed, the desire for preserving user's privacy in DRM may not be enough motivation to force an infrastructural change. Some interim steps are needed in today's infrastructure. Even if consumers seem more and more concerned about privacy, they do not use at the moment significant privacy-preserving tools. New PET and privacy design principles are needed for this purpose, at every stage of DRM-system design, development and deployment, as can be seen later. Let's begin with design and then see implementations of Privacy-Preserving Digital Rights Management (P2DRM).

3. Privacy-friendly Design (or Engineering) for DRM

3.1. PRINCIPLES

Privacy and security considerations should be included in the design of DRM from the beginning and they should not be considered as a property that can be added on. In fact, integrating privacy tools in legacy systems poses many problems (Feigenbaum *et al.*, 2002). First, dual operation due to compatibility of two designs is easy to attack. Second, legacy systems might expect more information than the information provided by the privacy device. Third, legacy systems might expect different performance than the one offered by the privacy protocol. Finally, there may be a congestive collapse of networking in the legacy system.

Some guidelines of privacy protection, the so-called Fair Information Principles (FIP) or general principles of the E. U. Data Protection Directive, may be useful as practical privacy engineering. Below there is a list with general goals which are not concrete technological options:

- Collection limitation
- Data accuracy
- Purpose disclosure
- Use limits
- Security
- Openness
- Participation
- Organizational accountability

3.1.1. *Collection Limitation*
A system should work with *minimal data exchanges* and PII should not be included by default. A first design decision is to analyze the need for information and to determine how the information flow can be minimized. Most of the system applications will only need pseudonyms instead of PII. Proxies can help a collection-limitation approach. Indeed, a trusted third party that provides some seal of approval may be preferable than an audit that happens after data collection.

3.1.2. *Data Accuracy*
If PII is necessary, then it should be erased after its immediate need has been fulfilled.

3.1.3. *Purpose Disclosure*
Notices should be easily understandable.

3.1.4. *Openness*
The idea is to combine notice and auditability. A company will not want to be exposed by violating its advertised privacy policy.

3.1.5. *Low cost solutions*
The advantage of such general goals or FIPs is that it allows us to consider low-cost solutions for privacy-preserving electronic commerce technologies. Technological solutions are not always necessary or useful for each problem. Some of these low-cost solutions might be (Feigenbaum *et al.*, 2002):

- Privacy enhancement should be built directly into the DRM technology that powers consumer applications. No additional steps to protect their privacy should be necessary.
- The business costs of introducing privacy enhancement into DRM should be low.
- The consumer costs, including "user experience", of using privacy-enhanced DRM should also be low.

3.2. TECHNIQUES

On the other hand, some authors consider that it is time to not only include privacy goals, but also concrete privacy preserving techniques to help engineering designers from the beginning. For instance, *PriS* is an engineering method which incorporates privacy requirements early in the system development process (Kalloniatis et al., 2008). Privacy requirements are considered as organisational goals that need to be satisfied. *PriS* provides a description of the effect of privacy requirements on business processes, and it allows the identification of the best privacy-preserving system architecture.

PriS conceptual model is based on the Enterprise Knowledge Development (EKD) framework (Kavakli and Loucopoulos, 1999), which develops organisational knowledge. It models the organisational goals of the enterprise, the processes and the software systems that support the above mentioned processes. As a result, a connection is established between system purpose and system structure. Privacy requirements are a special type of goal, privacy goals, which constraint the causal transformation of organisational goals into processes. One relevant aspect of *PriS* is that it indicates the concrete technique available to the designer for a goal, once adapted to respect a privacy requirement. So, it's useful during the design, and it helps to bridge the gap between design and implementation.

4. New PET for DRM (P2DRM)

4.1. LICENCES

PET is usually considered technology for privacy protection in different fields. Nonetheless, Korba and Kenny have observed that the interests a service user has in dealing with sensitive data are similar to those of providers of copyrighted digital contents (Korba, 2002). Thus, not only are PET solutions considered useful to complement DRM systems, but the contrary is also true: DRM systems are adapted as technical platforms for privacy.

For instance, this happens for data protection. One of the aims of data protection regulation is control over ones' data. Furthermore, data protection is known in Germany as the so-called self-determination of personal data right. Users need more control over their transmitted data, or during the use of a service (Hohl, 2007). If we consider sensitive personal data, it is sent in a protected way to the service provider. This encrypted data has a license attached to it when communicated to the service providers. The license limits the use of this personal data. It uses then classical anonymization techniques and the concepts of data minimality and data obfuscation (Hohl, Zugenmaier, 2007).

Privacy-preserving DRM system, or P2DRM, should also allow a user to interact with the system in an anonymous/pseudonymous way while buying and consuming digital content. On the other hand, this has to be done in a way that content is going to be used according to issued licenses and cannot be illegally copied (Conrado *et al.*, 2004).

We have already said that some authors consider cryptography inadequate for DRM. For others P2DRM can be based on cryptography. The idea is that a possible disclosure of the association between the user who transfers and the user who receives a given license is a privacy concern. This can be avoided with revocation lists and generic (or anonymous) licenses issued by the content provider (Claudine Conrado *et al.*, 2004). The licenses are anonymous in the sense that they do not include any identifier of the user who bought or exchanged his old license for the anonymous license. However, they include a unique identifier to prevent that an anonymous license is copied and redeemed multiple times. In the case of licenses in an authorized domain, the solution proposed is private creation and functioning, preventing the content provider from learning which domain members composes a domain (Koster, 2006). A domain manager device, trusted by the content provider, is introduced to solve privacy problems within the domain.

Personalized restrictions in specific domains are also a proposed solution (Petkovic, 2006). One possibility for a user to protect his interest and privacy is to apply some access control on licenses or content that he obtains from the content provider. However, access control only offers a limited functionality. Therefore a solution is a DRM system that allows the user to set further restrictions on the licenses obtained from the content provider. The proposed method is based on a specific form of a delegation license, called star-license, and an activation mechanism. The star-licenses allow adding further restricting rights-expressions by indicating who may define further restrictions and activate the license (Petkovic *et al*, 2006.).

4.2. DISTRIBUTED DRM

Another PETDRM or P2DRM solution can be a distributed DRM (Abie, 2004). The design of this system is based on trusted systems (Sadeghi, 2007). In the core of the system, a Privacy Enforcement Module (PEM) allows the privacy officer to define and update privacy policy. On the basis of this policy, it will allow or disallow actions. When a request is made for access to certain privacy sensitive elements or operations on an information object, the request is sent to the PEM. The PEM then decides whether the operation is to be permitted or not (Abie *et al*, 2004).

4.3. MOBILE DRM

Mobile DRM needs also new technical solutions. Even if it is not strictly a PET, the guaranty of non-repudiation is perhaps not only useful for DRM, but also for P2DRM. Non-repudiation is in charge of ensuring that no party can deny having participated in a transaction (Onieva, 2007). So having evidences of malicious activities by any of the peers may help. This service has not been included so far in DRM specifications due to practical issues and the type of content distributed. Non-repudiation can also protect privacy, and more precisely "sensitive information" such as financial statement, medical records, and contracts available in digital form. If we want to securely store this sensitive information, share it or distribute it within and between organizations, non-repudiation is an adequate technical solution. A non-repudiation protocol must generate cryptographic evidence to support eventual dispute resolution. A *trusted third party* (TTP) usually helps entities to accomplish their goals. One interesting aspect of the protocol of non-repudiation proposed by Onieva *et al.* (2007) is that anonymity could be preserved. In that sense, neither the content provider nor the user needs any knowledge (i.e., digital certificates) about each other in order to reach a successful protocol end.

4.4. DRM FOR PRIVACY INFORMATION RETRIEVAL (PIR)

Another P2DRM to consider is DRM for PIR (Asonov, 2004). PIR provides such an execution of user queries over a database of digital goods that no information about user queries is revealed, even to the server that actually accesses the digital goods. All a provider can do is to count the number of queries issued by a single user, and to charge it on a pay-per-query basis. In a strict version of PIR, DRM cannot be managed. Asonov's (2004) idea is to eliminate this conflict between DRM and user privacy relaxing the privacy constraint of PIR. He considers the possibility of revealing some information about user queries in order to be able to perform the distribution of interests of DRM. Indeed, users should be able to deny any claims about their queries. This repudiation capacity transforms PIR in Repudiative Information Retrieval (RIR). Furthermore, the precision of the DRM system depends on the robustness of the repudiation provided.

4.5. LOCATION BASED SERVICES

Location Based Services (LBS), like PDA, will also generate a wide range of DRM-privacy issues. Gunter *et al.* describe an architecture based on Personal Digital Rights Management (PDRM), which uses DRM concepts as a foundation for the specification and negotiation of privacy rights (Gunter, 2005). Their prototype, *AdLoc*, manages advertising interrupts on PDA based on location determined by WiFi sightings in accordance with contracts written in the DRM language XrML. PDRM uses the same DRM mechanisms to enable individuals to license their private data. Indeed, PDRM can specify that a private telephone number can only be used once for a specific purpose. The prototype approach, as stated before, is based on the use of the XrML digital rights language with negotiated privacy rights derived from specific sectors.

4.6. PLATFORMS

Multilateral-secure platforms can also offer P2DRM solutions. Sadeghi *et al.* describe a multilateral-secure DRM platform that can preserve some aspects of privacy (Sadeghi, 2005). The platform can be realized based on existing open platform technologies and trusted computing hardware like a Trusted Platform Module (TPM). An interesting aspect is that discrimination of open-source software due to TPM can be solved by a property-based attestation described by the authors.

4.7. SITDRM

Sheppard *et al.* (2006) have implemented a privacy protection system (SITDRM Enterprise) based on the Intellectual Property Management and Protection (IPMP) components of the MPEG-21 multimedia framework (Sheppard, 2006). This seems better than using the P3P policy language for expressing the privacy preferences of data subjects. P3P is adequate to inform data subjects of the global privacy practices of Internet service providers. However, users have to specify their preferences regarding a particular item of data in DRM. Nevertheless, P3P is used more recently in a complementary way with SITDRM to communicate enterprise privacy policies to consumers, and enable them to easily construct data licenses

(Salim, 2007). SITDRM required the design of an extension to the MPEG Rights Expression Language (MPEG-REL) to cater for privacy applications, and the development of software that allowed individuals' information and privacy preferences to be securely collected, stored and interpreted. The possibility of a future grand unified DRM system seems technically feasible, but the authors doubt about the utility of such a non-specific tool.

5. Conclusions

In 2002, Feigenbaum *et al.*, were convinced that a *practical methodology for privacy engineering* was necessary, involving procedures for the analysis of privacy-relevant aspects of a system. Nevertheless, they advise that developing such a methodology even for the problem of DRM systems would be quite challenging. Has the situation changed from 2002?

Every new PET seems to have difficulties to be implemented after its theoretical formulation. This is also true with respect to DRM. But there is a new element that can make the difference in this case: DRM systems are also adapted in a way to protect privacy. So PET for DRM and DRM adapted to privacy are converging in P2DRM. This can be useful for designing and implementing P2DRM from the PET perspective, or from the DRM one. So PET and DRM specialists should consider the new field an opportunity for respecting both DRM and privacy goals.

We have seen that authentication can adapt to a non-identification version, more flexible and less dangerous for privacy. Nonetheless, there is a deep change in PET related to the web 2.0 which is also true for P2DRM: transparency and other new techniques are preferred to anonymity, authentication and other traditional protections. Old PET are still useful, but they do not give enough guaranty to new privacy threatens. The value of transparency tools depends on how precise and understandable the information is. Standardization could help humans to understand and machines to interpret the information made transparent. Another challenge is that a transparency process can be also privacy-invasive. So data minimization with minimal disclosure of personal information is usually more effective than relying on "notice and choice" (Hansen, 2008). Context and purpose limitation attach to the identifiable data is also a new PET tool useful with web 2.0, the participatory Web (Weiss, 2008).

References

Abie H., Spilling P., and Bent F. (2004), *A distributed digital rights management model for secure information-distribution systems*, International Journal of Information and Security num. 3, pp. 113–128.

Asonov D. (2004), *Querying Databases Privately*, LNCS 3128, Springer, Heidelberg, Berlin, pp. 77–97.

Conrado C., Petkovic M., and Jonker W. (2004), in Jonker W. and Petkovic M. (Eds.)," SDM 2004", Springer, Heidelberg, Berlin, pp. 83–99.

Feigenbaum J., Freedman M.J., Sander T., and Shostack A.(2002), in Sander T. (Ed.), "DRM 2001", Springer, Heildelberg, Berlin, pp. 76–105.

Gunter C.A., May M.J., and Stubblebine S.G. (2005), *A Formal Privacy System and Its Application to Location Based Services*, in D. Martin and A. Serjantov (Eds.), "PET 2004", Springer, Berlin, New York, pp. 256–282.

Hansen, M., (2008), in Simone Fischer-Hübner, Penny Duquenoy, Albin Zuccato, Leonardo Martucci (Eds), *The Future of Identity in the Information Society*, IFIP International Federation for Information Processing, Volume 262, Springer, Boston, pp. 199–220.

Hohl, A. and Zugenmaier, A. (2007), in Venter, H., Eloff, M., Labuschagne, L., Eloff, J., and Von Solms, R. (Eds.), *New Approaches for Security, Privacy and Trust in Complex Environments*, IFIP International Federation for Information Processing, Volume 232, Springer, Boston, pp. 449-456.

Kalloniatis C., Kavakli E. and Gritzalis S. (2008), *Addressing Privacy Requirements in System Design: the PriS Method*, Requirements Engineering 13, pp. 241–255.

Kavakli V. (1999), *Enterprise knowledge management and conceptual modelling*, LNCS, vol. 1565, Springer, Berlin, pp 123–143.

Kavakli, V. and Loucopoulos, P. (1999), *Modelling of Organisational Change Using the EKD Framework*, Communications of the Association for Information Systems (CAIS), Vol 2.

Korba, L., and Kenny, S. (2003), *Towards Meeting the Privacy Challenge: Adapting DRM*, ACM Workshop on Digital Rights Management, Springer, Berlin.

Onieva J.A., López J., Román R., Zhou J., and Gritzalis S. (2007), *Integration of non-repudiation services in mobile DRM scenarios*, Telecommun Syst, 35, pp. 161–176.

Sadeghi A.-R., Wolf M., Stüble C., Asokan N., and Ekberg J.-E. (2007), *Enabling Fairer Digital Rights Management with Trusted Computing*, in Garay J. et al. (Eds.), ISC 2007, LNCS 4779, pp. 53–70.

Sadeghi A.-R. and Stüble C. (2005), *Towards Multilateral-Secure DRM Platforms*, in Deng, R. H. et al. (Eds.), ISPEC 2005, LNCS 3439, pp. 326–337.

Salim F., Sheppard N.P., and Safavi-Naini R. (2007), *Enforcing P3P Policies Using a Digital Rights Management System*, in Borisov N. and Golle P. (Eds.), PET 2007, LNCS 4776, pp. 200–217.

Seigneur J.M. (2009), *Social Trust of Virtual Identities,* in Golbeck J. (ed.), Computing with Social Trust, Human-Computer Interaction Series, Springer-Verlag, London.

Sheppard N.P. and Safavi-Naini R. (2006), *Protecting Privacy with the MPEG-21 IPMP Framework*, in Danezis G. and Golle P. (Eds.), PET 2006, LNCS 4258, pp. 152–171.

Weiss S., (2008), in Fischer-Hübner, S., Duquenoy, P., Zuccato, A., and Martucci, L. (Eds.), The Future of Identity in the Information Society, IFIP International Federation for Information Processing, Volume 262, Springer, Boston, pp. 161–171.

Petković M., and Koster, R.P. (2006), *User-Attributed Rights in DRM*, in Safavi-Naini R. and Yung M. (Eds.), DRMTICS 2005, LNCS 3919, pp. 75 – 89.

Enhancing Electronic Contracts with Semantics. The Case of Multimedia Content Distribution

Víctor Rodríguez Doncel, Jaime Delgado
Distributed Multimedia Applications Group
Universitat Politècnica de Catalunya

Abstract. Multimedia content can be digitally distributed to end users or in B2B transactions. While B2C distribution has been extensively carried out by digital platforms governed by digital licenses, B2B multimedia content exchange has received less attention. The digital licenses for end users have been expressed either in proprietary formats or in standard Rights Expression Languages and they can be seen as the electronic replacement of distribution contracts and end user licenses. However RELs fail to replace the rest of the contracts agreed along the complete Intellectual Property value chain. To represent their corresponding electronic counterpart licenses, an schema based on the Media Value Chain Ontology is presented here. It has been conceived to deal with a broader set of parties, to handle typical clauses found in the audiovisual market contracts, and to govern every transaction performed on IP objects. Contract clauses are modelled as deontic logic propositions, and an event-based system is described to allow a DRM system the execution of the contract.

Keywords: Contract, license, DRM, Intellectual Property, Ontology, MPEG-21, REL, ODRL, Semantic Web.

1. Introduction

DRM (Digital Rights Management) systems for the distribution of multimedia content have been present since the last decade. On despite of the controversy arisen around its mere existence, DRM systems have striven to preserve the Intellectual Property (IP) of artistic creations in digital format.

However, consumers have been reluctant to accept the restrictions imposed by these DRM systems, and content distribution has been diverted to a large extent in alternative channels where Intellectual Property rights have been ignored. Nevertheless, although DRM systems for distribution of multimedia content to the end user may have failed to prevent illegal copies, they have proved to be a technological success and they have provided solid channels for a fair trade. On despite of the folk conceptions, '*DRM*' is not only protection, but also, and essentially, management.

The market of audiovisual content is a complex ecosystem with many different players and commercial interests besides the B2C segment. From the very original idea in an author's mind until the final product, there have been some other intermediate IP objects along this process (this process is called *value chain*), and they are subject to possible trade too. It is the case of the B2B trading of rights on compositions, concerts, editions, broadcastings, etc. In this B2B sector the regulations and commercial agreements have remained largely up to date in the analogue world. These contracts include author contracts, performance contracts, synchronization contracts and edition contracts among others and all of them revolve around the idea of IP.

For the case of B2B commerce of multimedia content, the need for controlled trade under the terms of the law has been undisputed, but only timid ecommerce platforms have been deployed. When multimedia material is purchased not for venial leisure time but for business, formal written contracts are offered, agreed and observed. These contracts are paper contracts (often referred as *narrative contracts*) and they are signed personally. Their negotiation, management and execution rely in the traditional methods, and its expression is not substituted at all by digital licenses.

Lack of trust on electronic transactions is not the only reason explaining the disappointing spread of DRM systems in the B2B transactions of multimedia material. We can find the reasons in the insufficient scope of current Right Expression Languages (REL) and the lack of formalism in electronic contract representations among other problems.

RELs allow the specification of licenses in digital files, usually as XML, in which one party gives another party certain rights over a resource given that certain conditions are satisfied. However, current RELs are not expressive enough to model the agreements arranged along the Intellectual Property Value Chain, and this chapter gives an overview of new more expressive representations based on the Web 3.0 technologies.

On the other hand, the existing electronic contract representations lack the required formalism for ecommerce platforms to be governed.

This chapter will show how to integrate the most prominent electronic contract format (OASIS eContracts) with formalised expressions able to run B2B DRM platforms. The Media Value Chain Ontology (MVCO), a domain ontology of the IP value chain, will serve as a basis model to represent the core information of the agreements and eventually govern a DRM system. This representation will be able to express contract clauses (obligations, permissions or prohibitions) appearing in typical contracts.

2. Overview of electronic contracts formats

This section reviews the existing electronic contract formats and studies their ability to govern a DRM system.

Contracts are legally binding agreements and they are made of mutual promises between two or more parties to do (or refrain from doing) something. The terms of a contract may be expressed written or orally, implied by conduct, industry custom, and law or by a combination of these things. Contracts can also be digitally represented: a contract whose representation can be understood by computers is called *electronic contract*, and it may allow DRM systems to control it and execute it or enforce it automatically.

Narrative contracts are passive in the sense that once they are signed, their prominence only arises in case of dispute. Electronic contracts in a DRM system are active as they play an important role in the execution of the contract.

The earliest electronic contract representations were born together with the electronic commerce and the first Electronic Data Interchange (EDI) standards. EDI has been of huge importance in the industry, and comprises a set of standards for structuring information to be electronically exchanged between and within businesses, organizations, government entities and other groups.

COSMOS (Kobryn, 1998) was an e-commerce architecture supporting catalogue browsing, contract negotiation and contract execution. It defined a contract model in UML and proposed a CORBA-based software architecture in a coherent manner. UML is a highly expressive language, but its representation cannot be directly mapped to a formal system.

DocLog (Yao, 2000) was an electronic contract representation language introduced in the 2000 with a 'XML like' structure, which anticipated the next generation of XML-based contract representations. When XML was mature enough it was seen as a good container of contract clauses, and thus the new format specifications came under the form of a XML Schema or a DTD. An effort to achieve a common XML contract representation was the Contract Expression Language (CEL) (CRF, 2002), developed by the Content Reference Forum. It formalized a language that enabled machine-readable representation of typical terms found in content distribution contracts and was compliant with the Business Collaboration Framework (Hofreiter, 2004), but it was not finally standardized.

In the following years, the advent of the Semantic Web reached the contract expression formats, and new representations evolved from the syntactic representation level to the semantic one (Kabilan, 2003; Llorente, 2005; Yan, 2006) being developed domain ontologies in the KIF or OWL languages.

Still climbing levels in the Semantic Web layered model, RuleML first and SWRL after were enacted as the new model container for electronic contracts, given that a contract declares a set of rules (Paschke, 2005). SWRL provides a Web-oriented abstract syntax and declarative knowledge representation semantics for rules; but the concrete syntax can have the form of a RDF schema, thus providing a seamless integration with OWL ontologies. Some of these contract models have been aimed also at governing Information Technology systems (Morciniec, 2001; Krishna 2005).

However, the ultimate technology on contract representation has given a step backwards in this evolution line and banks on XML again. We are referring to "eContracts", the new OASIS standard. In 2002 OASIS established the LegalXML eContracts Technical Committee to evaluate a possible eContracts Schema, and its first version of the standard has been approved during 2007 (Leff, 2007). This seems to be the most promising of all the aforementioned and the current reference format.

The model proposed in this chapter does not rely either on a SWRL-based schema, but still adheres to the ontology representation. It considers that the Intellectual Property model lacks a simple model representing the universal know-how on the field, and this model has to be established first before the rules are described. Also, the models reviewed in this section are general oriented, excepting CEL, while this work is only interested on specific contracts in the multimedia content sector.

The work presented in this chapter aims at representing the B2B contracts in the multimedia market, and at using this representation as the governing steer of the DRM system.

3. Analysis of real contracts in the market of multimedia material

Among the different parties and interests in the value chain, we may find creators, adaptors, performers, producers, distributors or broadcasters, all of them adding value to the product, and all of them tied by agreements in which Intellectual Property rights are handed over in exchange of economic compensations.

If every contract represents an agreement between two parties who belong to the value chain, contracts can be classified according to the signing parties. Figure 1 shows the typical name of the contract types and relates them with the parties, including the contract between End User and Distributor (usually an oral contract).

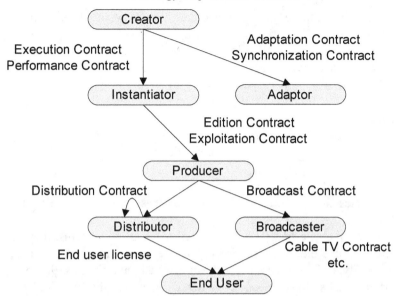

Figure 1. Most common contracts along the value chain

These kinds of contracts follow common patterns, which have been thoroughly analyzed for this study. Narrative paper contracts vary in extension and contents for each particular case, but usually account for a dozen or two of clauses, comprising less than ten pages (Rodríguez, 2007a, Rodríguez, 2008). Although clauses are representative as units of information, a single clause sometimes represented several complex ideas, and conversely, sometimes just one idea is spanned in several clauses. In the simplest case, clauses are sentences, and each of them can be classified according to the deontic logic, in terms of what can be done, must be done and is forbidden.

The most common clauses found in the multimedia contents contracts are the following:

- *Metadata clauses*. Title, declaration of the involved parties, date and place, signature.
- *Rights*. The licensee can exercise certain rights. This is usually the first and main clause.
- *Resource*. The referenced resource is either mentioned in the first clause as well, or detailed as an appendix when it is a list of items.
- *Report*. and Auditing In distribution contracts where benefits have to be distributed according to the sales, these sales have to be reported.
- *Fee*. The licensee must pay a fee with the described conditions
- *Territory*. The licensee must exercise the right (if he/she does) in the given location.

- *Term.* The licensee must exercise the right (if he/she does) in the given time
- *Confidentiality.* In B2B relations there is usually a clause banning the public issue of information.
- *Disclaimer.* To deny responsibilities on certain issues etc.
- *Jurisdiction.* In case of dispute, the agreed jurisdiction and court is agreed.
- *Breach and termination.* These clauses provision the end of the contract in normal or abnormal conditions.

4. Assessment of current RELs to express narrative contracts

Considering the role that REL licenses play on DRM systems, they can be seen as effective electronic contracts that are being enforced. As such, this section analyzes how well they perform this task, and for this, the two most important RELs have been considered, namely the MPEG-21 REL (ISO/IEC 2004) and the Open Digital Rights Language (ODRL) (Ianella, 2002). The later has additional importance considering that the Open Mobile Alliance (OMA) has developed its OMA DRM Rights Expression Language based on ODRL.

Both RELs were developed in the late 1990s, but none can be considered fully deployed up to this date. On July 2003, parts 5 and 6 of MPEG-21 were approved as Final Draft International Standards; they described the Rights Expression Language and the Rights Data Dictionary (ISO/IEC, 2004b) respectively. Previously, in 2000, the first version of the ODRL had been proposed as an open standard language for expressing rights information over content (it largely matches the objectives of the MPEG RDD too). In both cases, the incarnation of a REL expression is a XML file called *license*. This license is what we pretend to see and evaluate as an electronic contract.

In ODRL, the license pretends to express not only agreements, but also offers, what can be seen as simply potential contracts.

4.1 CONTRACT PARTIES IN THE LICENSE

Licenses refer always to two parties (actually an MPEG-21 license may content several grants each of them with a different party, but then we can consider the grant as the basic license unit). In MPEG-21 language, parties are called *issuer* and *principal*, while in ODRL they are directly referred as *parties*, classified as *end users* and *right holders*.

No more information is given about who might be these parties, excepting that they are uniquely identified, and that one of them (the rights issuer) electronically signs the document. In the framework of MPEG-21, users include *"individuals, consumers, communities, organizations, corporations, consortia, governments and other standards bodies and initiatives around the world"* (Bormans, 2002). In ODRL, *"parties can be humans, organizations, and defined roles"*. According to the standards, users are only defined by the actions they perform, but if we attend to the expressivity of both RELs, in the licenses there can be only end users and distributors (see Table I and Table II).

Table I. Rights defined by MPEG-21 REL in its core and multimedia extension

Right	Party	Right	Party
Issue	distributor	Extract	end-user
Revoke	distributor	embed	end-user
possessproperty	end-user	play	end-user
Obtain	distributor	print	end-user
Modify	end-user	execute	end-user
Enlarge	end-user	install	end-user
Reduce	end-user	uninstall	end-user
Move	end-user	delete	end-user
Adapt	end-user		

Table II Permissions defined by ODRL. Transfer actions belong to distributors

Usage	Reuse	Asset Management	Transfer
	End-user		Distributor
Display	Modify	Move	Sell
Print	Excerpt	Duplicate	Lend
Play	Annotate	Delete	Give
Execute	Aggregate	Verify	Lease
		Backup/Restore	
		Install/Uninstall	

Both MPEG-21 and REL do not characterize in depth more kind of users than End Users and Distributor but a contract model should consider all the user roles appearing in Figure 1.

4.2 RIGHTS EXPRESSED IN THE LICENSE

The rights defined by MPEG-21 REL and ODRL are those shown in Table I and Table II. They have to be compared with the real necessities detected in the analysis of the contracts performed in the previous section, and they have to be compared with the basic action defined along the IP Value Chain. The new list of actions and rights needed to express the contract information are listed in Table III.

Table III Main actions and rights to be considered in a contract representation

Most common rights appeared in contracts			
Reproduce	Broadcast	Adapt	Lease
Download	Copy	Convert	License
Upload	Print	Transcode	Promote
MakeAvailable	Record	Remix	Stream
PubliclyPerform	Modify	Distribute	
Exhibit	Translate	Sell	
Transmit	Dub	Advertise	

Actions and rights in Table II do not take into account the REL rights, and the latter can be evaluated about how well they match the contract-extracted rights. The comparison shows that MPEG-21 rights and ODRL permissions do not completely represent the information expressed in the contracts, and although RELs foresee mechanisms for the extension of the rights list, the main unaddressed issue is that they were not B2B conceived.

5. The Media Value Chain Ontology

XML representation of contracts, under the form of REL licenses is of limited expressivity compared to the ontology-based contracts presented in Section 2. However none of the domain ontologies in Section 2 has been applied in the context of a content distribution system or a DRM system.

The Media Value Chain Ontology (MPEG-21, 2008) is a semantic representation of the Intellectual Property along the Value Chain conceived in the framework of the MPEG-21 standard. This model defines the minimal set of kinds of Intellectual Property, the roles of the users interacting with them, and the relevant actions regarding the Intellectual Property law. Besides this, a basis for authorizations along the chain is been laid out, and the model is ready for managing class instances representing real objects and users. The MVCO is based on work by the authors (Rodríguez, 2007b) and from an ontology that is part of the Interoperable DRM Platform (IDP), published by the Digital Media Project (Gauvin, 2007).

The Media Value Chain Ontology also provides a Java reference API in order to build practical applications whose management is based on handling ontology individuals. An example of such an application has been implemented in the context of the AXMEDIS[1] project (AXMEDIS, 2007).

The Media Value Chain Ontology is represented using the expressivity of OWL-DL, and thus each class is well defined and related to a set of attributes and to other classes in a very precise way. In practice, applications can be deployed where the particular users, IP entities, actions etc. are instances of the ontology.

Three of the main classes in MVCO are "Action", "User" and "IP Entity", whose class relationship is shown in Figure 2. Users act Actions over IP entities, over which they have the IP rights. The execution of these actions may create in turn new derived IP entities.

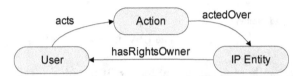

Figure 2 Three main classes and their relationships of the ontology

Table IV lists some of the derived classes, consisting of the main IP entities (Work, Product etc.), the main roles (Creator, Producer etc.) and the main actions, subdivided between transforming actions (creating new IP Entities) and end user actions focused to the end user.

Table IV. Main classes of the ontology

Root classes	Subclasses
IP Entities	Work, Adaptation, Manifestation, Instance, Copy, Product
Roles	Creator, Adaptor, Instantiator, Producer, Distributor, EndUser
Actions	TransformingActions (adapt, perform, etc.), EndUserActions (play etc)

Figure 3 shows the IP entities along the value chain, starting from *work* as the original abstract conception of an artist and finishing in the *product* as the most elaborate IP entity ready to be enjoyed by the end user.

---

[1] AXMEDIS Automating Production of Cross Media Content for Multi-channel Distribution, EU 6th Framework Program, IST-2-511299, available at http://www.axmedis.org

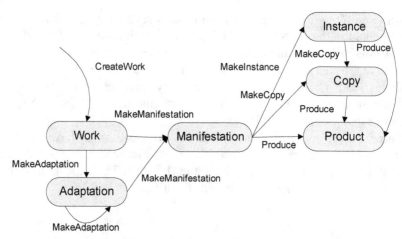

Figure 3. The IP Value Chain

Rights can be handed over users by means of permissions. The Permission class is related to the user who issues it and to the action that is permitted: "who acts which over what" (see Figure 4). The actions that are permitted allow the transformation of the object in other IP entities or its final consumtion. Permissions are subject to the satisfaction of requirements expressed as facts with a truth value.

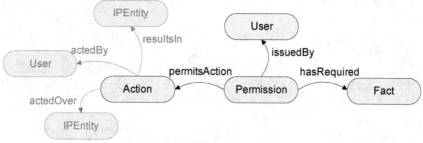

Figure 4. Permission class

The Permission class lays down the entry point for an extension of the MVCO to represent contracts. Thus, if a contract is seen as set of permissions and obligations, etc., instances of this class may represent the term of a contract.

6. Semantic Representation of Contracts

The XML contract represented in the eContracts format has the top elements shown in Figure 5.

The ec:metadata element includes elementary metadata information like date, contract author etc. The ec:contract-front describes the

parties, lists the terminology to be used along the contract, etc. The
`ec:body` element is a sequence of `ec:items`, which can be
`ec:chapters`, `ec:parts`, `ec:sections`, `ec:clauses` or
`ec:subclauses`.

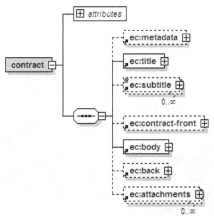

Figure 5. Top elements in the eContracts XML contract

However, the content of these items or clauses is no further refined, and it
can be as simple as English text. The structure is good but unable to
represent a computer enforceable contract *per se*, therefore the content of
these eContracts elements has to be more precise so that computers can
interpret it. To do this in the framework of multimedia contracts, the
MVCO elements can perform well: MVCO is an OWL ontology and as
such it is XML-serializable and its elements easily integrated within an
XML eContract.

OWL-DL is a Description Logics knowledge representation language,
whose expression can be mapped to a first order predicate logic system.
Predicates are verb phrase templates that describe properties of objects, or a
relationship among objects represented by the variables (e.g. "Bob is a
Creator"). As the given statements representing the domain knowledge
constitute a formal deductive system, the ontology can be queried (e.g. "has
Bob created any Work?"). For each syntactically correct expression, the
OWL-DL ontology is able to assert its truth value: either true, false or
unkown (for the latter case, note that that OWL uses the open world
assumption).

All the above makes OWL an ideal mean to handle the truthness of
propositions. However, not all the propositions in the English language (or
human thinking) convey a truth value. Commands, questions or deontic
expressions cannot be said to be true or false, and contracts carry its most
valuable information in sentences like these (e.g. "Party A must pay party

B in a yearly base"). This kind of expressions lies in the field of deontic logic (Rodríguez, 1978).

Modal logics are concerned with other modalities of existence (usually necessity or possibility), and introduce two new monadic operators related like this:

$$\Diamond P \leftrightarrow \neg\Box\neg P$$

and

$$\Box P \leftrightarrow \neg\Diamond\neg P$$

The deontic logic is a kind of modal logic of the highest interest to represent contracts, and in place of the operators $\Box$, $\Diamond$ we can interpret "Obligation", and "Permission" (in the above expressions, it can be read that "P is obligatory" is equivalent to "it is not permitted not P"). Actually only one of both operators is strictly necessary, as the second one can be deduced from the first, but for readability, usually both are kept. In these expressions, P is no more than an alethic (with a truth value, from the Greek αλήθεια, truth) proposition.

The MVCO defines a class "Fact" with a definite truth value (overcoming the open world assumption which enabled an unkown state), and an object property "hasRequired" which linked to a Permission enables the expression of obligations.

The most important clauses found in multimedia content contracts, as they were defined in Section 3 are either alethic sentences (we call them *Claims*) or deontic expressions, the latter being either *Permisison*, *Prohibition* or *Obligation* (see Table V). Similar approaches in the treatment of contracts can also be found in the literature (Prisacariu, 2007)

Table V. Classification of contract clauses according to their deontic nature

Kind of Clause	Logic expression	Typical clauses
Claim *Something is*	P	Jurisdiction, Disclaimer, Breach Termination
Permission *The licensee can*	$\neg\Diamond\neg P$	Rights-Resource
Obligation *The licensee must*	$\Diamond P$	Fee, Territory, Term, Report
Prohibition *The licensee must not*	$\Diamond\neg P$	Confidentiality

Some of these clauses may be interesting to be electronically enforced in a content distribution system while others can be discarded. An example of the latter can be seen in Figure 6. While the MVCO defines a Permission class, it does include neither the Prohibition nor the Obligation, but its inclusion as an extension in terms of the former is a trivial task.

```
00<ec:item>
01 <mvco:Prohibition rdf:ID="12">
02  <rdfs:comment> The Program(s) may not be shown at festivals,
03 conventions and markets without Licensor's prior consent.
04  </rdfs:comment>
05 </mvco:Prohibition>
06</ec:item>
```

Figure 6. eContracts clause with a narrative content

Those clauses which are liable to be enforced can have a more precise representation. For example, if the parties declaration take the form shown in Figure 7, individuals are uniquely identified (lines 03 and 04) and can be related to those of a larger Information System.

```
00<ec:contract xmlns="urn:oasis:names:tc:eContracts:1:0">
01 <ec:contract-front>
02  <ec:parties>
03   <ec:party><mvco:User rdf:about="#Alice"/></ec:party>
04   <ec:party><mvco:User rdf:about="#Bob"/></ec:party>
05 </ec:parties>
06</ec:contract-front>
```

Figure 7. eContracts parties declaration using the MVCO expressions

A real eContract clause carrying RDF triples of the MVCO can take the form shown in Figure 8.

```
00<ec:body>
01 <ec:item>
02  <mvco:Permission rdf:about="#Permission000">
03   <mvco:permitsAction rdf:resource="#Action000"/>
04   <mvco:issuedBy rdf:resource="#Alice"/>
05   <mvco:hasRequired rdf:resource="#Germany"/>
06  </mvco:Permission>
07  <mvco:MakeAdaptation rdf:about="#Action000">
08   <mvco:actedBy rdf:resource="#Bob"/>
09   <mvco:actedOver rdf:resource="#Obra1"/>
10  </mvco:MakeAdaptation>
11  <mvco:Territory rdf:about="#Germany">
12   <mvco:hasCountry>DE</mvco:hasCountry>
13  </mvco:Territory>
14  <mvco:Work rdf:about="#Obra1">
15   <mvco:hasRightsOwner rdf:resource="#Alice"/>
16  </mvco:Work>
17 </ec:item>
18</ec:body>
```

Figure 8. eContracts clause integrated with a MVCO Permission

A permission is expressed (lines 02-06 in Figure 8) in which Alice grants a right to make an adaptation (lines 07-10), over the work "obra1" (line 09) to Bob (line 08), once proved that it is executed in Germany (lines 11-13).

7. Conclusions

This work acknowledges REL licenses as the governing element in DRM systems for B2C distribution of multimedia content, and declared licenses as the digital version of end user or distributor contracts. However, after an analysis of real contracts in the IP contents B2B market, it was observed that more flexibility was required to cope with the complexity of those narrative contracts.

On the other hand, other electronic contract representations lack the needed formalism to steer content distribution systems. The MVCO, a recently presented ontology of the IP value chain model, may overcome the limitations of the existing RELs and may merge well into the OASIS eContract structure.

This combination can govern a content distribution system with all the value chain players if some additions are made. In particular, an event description system is needed, and an authorisation mechanism too, capable of processing the dynamic events, the current context and these MVCO-extended eContracts. The execution of SWRL rules can determine this authorisation and make the electronic contracts to be truly semantic containers.

References

AXMEDIS (2007), *Specification of Axmedis, AX4HOME Architecture*, Automatic Production of Cross Media Content for Multi-Channel Distribution, DE12.1.3.1, July.

Bormans, J. and Keith Hill, K. (2002), *MPEG-21 Overview v.5*, ISO/IEC JTC1/SC29/WG11/N5231, October.

CRF Content Reference Forum (2002), *CEL: Contract Expression Language*, available at: http://www.crforum.org/candidate/CELWG002_celspec.doc (accessed 3 May 2010).

Gauvin, M.; Delgado, J., and Rodriguez-Doncel, V. (2007), *Proposed RRD Text for Approved Document No 2 – Technical Reference: Architecture*, v. 2.1, Digital Media Project DMP0952/AHG40, July.

Hofreiter, B. and Huemer, C. (2004), *UN/CEFACT's Business Collaboration Framework - Motivation and Basic Concepts*, Proceedings of the Multi-Konferenz Wirtschaftsinformatik, Germany, March.

Ianella, R. (2002), *Open Digital Rights Language (ODRL) Version 1.1*, W3C, September, available at: http://www.w3.org/TR/odrl/ (accessed 5 May 2010).

ISO/IEC (2004), *ISO/IEC International Standard 21000-5 - Rights Expression Language.*

ISO/IEC (2004b), *ISO/IEC International Standard 21000-6 - Rights Data Dictionary.*

Kabilan, V. and Johannesson, P. (2003), *Semantic Representation of Contract Knowledge using Multi Tier Ontology*, Proceedings of the First International Workshop on Semantic Web and Databases, Germany, June.

Kobryn, C.; Atkinson, C. and Milosevic, Z. (1998), *Electronic Contracting with COSMOS - How to Establish, Negotiate and Execute Electronic Contracts on the Internet*, in "2nd Int. Enterprise Distributed Object Computing Workshop" (EDOC '98), CA, USA.

Krishna, P.R.; Karlapaplem, K. and Dani. A.R. (2005), *From Contracts to E-Contracts: Modeling and Enactment*, Information Technology and Management, Vol. 6, No. 4, pp. 363-387.

Leff, L. and Meyer, P. (2007), *OASIS LegalXML eContracts Version 1.0 Committee Specification*, available at: http://docs.oasis-open.org/legalxml-econtracts/CS01/legalxml-econtracts-specification-1.0.pdf (accessed 2 May 2010).

Llorente, S.; Delgado, J.; Rodríguez, E.; Barrio, R.; Longo, I. and Bixio, F. (2005), *Generation of Standardised Rights Expressions from Contracts: An Ontology Approach?*, Proceedings of the On the Move to Meaningful Internet Systems, Cyprus, November.

Morciniec, M.; Salle, M. and Monahan, B. (2001), *Towards Regulating Electronic Communities with Contracts*, Proceedings of the 2nd Workshop on Norms and Institution in Multi-agent Systems, Canada, June.

MPEG-21 (2008), *Media Value Chain Ontology, Committee Draft*, ISO/IEC JTC1/SC29/WG11 N10264, Busan, South Korea, October.

Paschke, A.; Bichler, M. and Dietrich, J. (2005), *ContractLog: An Approach to Rule Based Monitoring and Execution of Service Level Agreements*, Proceedings of the Rules and rule markup languages for the semantic web, pp. 209-217, Ireland, November.

Prisacariu, C. and Schneider, G. (2007), *A Formal Language for Electronic Contracts*, Proceedings of the 9th IFIP International Conference on Formal Methods for Open Object-Based Distributed Systems (FMOODS'07), Cyprus, June.

Rodríguez, J. (1978), *Lógica deóntica: Concepto y Sistemas*, Universidad de Valencia, Secretariado de Publicaciones, Valencia.

Rodríguez, V.; Delgado, J. and Rodríguez, E. (2007), *From Narrative Contracts to Electronic Licenses: A Guided Translation Process for the Case of Audiovisual Content Management*, Proceedings of the 3rd International Conference on Automated Production of Cross Media Content for Multi-Channel Distribution, Spain, November.

Rodríguez, V.; Gauvin, M. and Delgado, J. (2007), *An Ontology for the Expression of Intellectual Property Entities and Relations*, Proceedings of the 5th International Workshop on Security in Information Systems (WOSIS 2007), Portugal, April.

Rodríguez, V. and Delgado, J. (2008), *Multimedia Content Distribution Governed by Ontology-Represented Contracts*, Workshop on Multimedia Ontologies and Artificial Intelligence Techniques in Law, Netherlands, December.

Yan, Y.; Zhang, J. and Yan, M. (2006), *Ontology Modeling for Contract: Using OWL to Express Semantic Relations,* Proceedings of the 10th IEEE International Enterprise Distributed Object Computing Conference, IEEE Computer Society, pp. 409-412.

Yao Hua, T. and Thoen, W. (2000), *DocLog: an electronic contract representation language*, Proceedings of the 11th International Workshop on Database and Expert Systems Applications, September.

Natural Language Oriented Engineering of a Copyright Ontology for Controlled Natural Language Presentation

Roberto García, Rosa Gil
Universitat de Lleida, Jaume II, 69. Lleida, Spain

Abstract. Existing ontology engineering methodologies concentrate on proposing development process and support activities but place less effort on providing some guidance for how to structure the ontology content. Moreover, knowledge based systems find great difficulties when they reach end-users, which are usually not formal language experts. The ontology engineering pattern proposed in this paper tries to face both issues from a natural language oriented perspective. It is applied during the development of a Copyright Ontology, in order to facilitate its development but also in order to facilitate rendering expressions based on the ontology, mainly licenses, as Controlled Natural Language. This rendering has proved to be more appealing for end-users and the expressions build from the proposed pattern more usable for them.

Keywords: Ontology, engineering, controlled natural language, copyright, digital rights management, usability.

1. Introduction

Formal knowledge facilitates the use of computerised means for information processing. However, at the endpoint of information processes there are human users, for which formal languages are not intended. These are users that are not experts in formal languages so they find very difficult to deal with logic or diagrammatic expressions.

Formal knowledge facilitates the use of computerised means for information processing. However, at the endpoint of information processes there are human users, for which formal languages are not intended. These are users that are not experts in formal languages so they find very difficult to deal with logic or diagrammatic expressions.

Therefore, there is the need for some layer that isolates end-users from the knowledge representation language complexities. On one hand, these tend to be some kind of natural language processing or specific input forms in the knowledge acquisition end-point. On the other hand, there are specific graphical user interfaces in the knowledge presentation end-point.

In both end-points there is the need for a lot of work as these are the steps of information processing flux that require more ad-hoc development. Therefore, they constitute the bottlenecks of the whole process during the daily exploitation of knowledge-based systems.

An alternative to make knowledge arrive to end-users is to use controlled natural languages (Schwitter, 2004). Controlled natural languages (CNL) make information more usable and facilitate the development of knowledge systems (Kuhn, Royer, Fuchs, & Schroeder, 2006). The need for ad-hoc knowledge acquisition and presentation means is mitigated as the acquisition and presentation functionalities are inherent to them.

This is especially relevant in the motivating scenario of this work, the development of a Digital Rights Management (DRM) system that facilitates users deal with copyright. In this application scenario, users have extensively adopted Creative Commons licenses (Lessig, 2003) showing that they prefer approaches based on a natural language rendering instead of those based on other approaches. However, Creative Commons lacks a computer-friendlier version that facilitates the automation of advanced DRM.

Therefore, the objective of an advanced and usable DRM system motivated the development of a pattern for natural language oriented ontology engineering. This pattern was employed to develop the Copyright Ontology[1] (García & Gil, 2008), the core of the Semantic DRM System[2]. This pattern, as it is exemplified by the Copyright Ontology and the CNL-based licenses it supports, facilitates the generation of usable CNL expressions.

This works relies on existing CNL initiatives as it does not propose any new alternative. On the other hand, it proposes a pattern oriented towards engineering ontologies that make CNL more natural and usable for end-users. The main contribution is instead in the ontology engineering domain, where it proposes some guidelines geared towards producing ontologies that facilitate the generation of more usable CNL renderings.

The rest of this paper is organised as follows. The following subsection introduces the copyright ontology engineering scenario that motivated the development of the proposed pattern and that is used as a way to illustrate its features through this paper. Then, Section 2 presents the ontology pattern and how it is applied in order to build the Copyright Ontology. Next, Section 3 shows how the pattern facilitates the production of more usable CNL expressions and some examples from the copyright domain. Finally, the conclusions and future work are presented in Section 4.

---

[1]   Copyright Ontology, http://rhizomik.net/ontologies/copyrightonto

[2]   Semantic Digital Rights Management System, http://rhizomik.net/semdrms

1.1. APPLICATION SCENARIO

Recently, there have been great changes in the copyright market motivated by the digital and Internet revolutions. First, these revolutions have introduced new risks in the classical market, which was basically based on the distribution of physical instances of content. Second, they have opened opportunities to create new markets based on digital creations and the Internet distribution medium.

In order to manage this new situation, the main approach is to take profit from the new technological opportunities in order to develop systems to manage and protect digital works. This is referred to as Digital Rights Management, or DRM. A DRM system (DRMS) is build from IT components and services along with the corresponding law, policies and business models.

Due to the globalisation of the digital content market, different DRMSs are being forced to interoperate. One of the main initiatives for DRM interoperability is the ISO/IEC MPEG-21 (De Walle & Burnett, 2005) standardisation effort. The main interoperability facilitation component is the Rights Expression Language (REL), which is based on a XML grammar. Therefore, it is syntax-based. There is also the MPEG-21 Rights Data Dictionary (RDD) that captures the semantics of the terms employed in the REL (Wang, DeMartini, Wragg, Paramasivam, & Barlas 2005). However, it does so without defining formal semantics (García & Delgado, 2005).

The limitations of a purely syntactic approach and the lack of formal semantics can be overcome using a formal semantics approach based on ontologies. They have been used, for instance, to validate and correct inconsistencies in MPEG-21 RDD (García, Delgado, & Rodríguez, 2005). Another MPEG-21 RDD formalisation is OREL (Qu, Zhang, & Li, 2004). In any case, these initiatives focus on the RDD semantics that are too specific to facilitate interoperability.

In order to build a generic ontological framework that facilitates interoperability, the focus must be placed on the underlying legal, commercial and technical copyright aspects. This is the approach for the Copyright Ontology, which constitutes the scenario for illustrating the ontology engineering pattern throughout this paper.

However, the use of a formal language for DRM faces a great problem of usability. Users prefer DRM licenses in natural language form like the ones proposed by the Creative Commons (CC) initiative (Lessig, 2003). Despite the CC approach is not formal and is constrained to a set of predefined licenses, it is currently the more extensively used DRM system nowadays. The preferred and mandatory form of CC licenses is natural language in simplified or full-legal form, while there is a simple formal licenses version intended for archiving purposes. An example of CC license is shown in Table I.

Table I. Creative Commons Attribution license version 2.5 3

You are free:
–   to copy, distribute, display, and perform the work
–   to make derivative works
–   to make commercial use of the work
Under the following conditions:
–   Attribution. You must attribute the work in the manner specified by the author or licensor.
–   For any reuse or distribution, you must make clear to others the license terms of this work.

Therefore, there is a trade-off between more or less formalised DRM languages, which facilitate automated DRM systems but are less usable by end-users, and informal DRM languages, which are preferred by end users due to their usability but make automation a very complicated issue, basically license archiving.

The Copyright Ontology project, which is used as the illustrating example through this paper, motivated the development of an ontology engineering pattern more suited to the requirements at hand.

On one hand, it should produce a formalisation of the copyright domain for automated DRM and provide some guidance for ontology creation. On the other hand, it should facilitate generating a controlled natural language rendering that, while keeping its formal foundations, makes it easier to end-user to interact with licenses. This pattern is described in Section 2, together with how it was applied to the Copyright Ontology development.

2.   A NL-Oriented Ontology Engineering Pattern

As it has been pointed out in the related work section, this work proposes an ontology creation pattern. This pattern must be complemented with an ontology development process and other support activities in order to guarantee that ontologies are engineered in a proper way.

Consequently, there is the need to select one of the existing ontology engineering methodologies in order to put the NL oriented pattern into practice. The Methontology methodology has been chosen because it provides guidance for ontology development process but also for other

---

3   Creative   Commons   Attribution   license   version   2.5,
http://creativecommons.org/licenses/by/2.5/deed.en

support and management activities. Moreover, it is extensively based on "classical" software engineering methodologies and this fact makes it easier to learn and apply for people with some software engineering experience.

Methontology proposes some ontology management activities, which include scheduling, control and quality assurance. There are also ontology support activities, which are performed at the same time as the development-oriented activities, namely: knowledge acquisition, evaluation, reuse (merging or aligning other ontologies), documentation and configuration management. These are all support activities while the main ontology creation work is performed in development process.

Consequently, the NL-Oriented pattern is integrated into an ontology developing process composed by the following phases: specification, conceptualisation, formalization, implementation and maintenance.

The specification phase corresponds to the pre-development aspects, where the development requirements are identified. The maintenance phase is a post-development activity, it is performed once the ontology is developed. During the conceptualisation activity, the domain knowledge is structured as meaningful models. This is the point where the proposed pattern is applied.

Moreover, if a formal language is used to build the model, it is possible to automate the formalisation and implementation activities so all the pattern work is applied just in this phase and its benefits automatically propagated though the other development activities.

Therefore, the pattern is applied during the conceptualisation activity, when the domain models are built. The pattern is applied starting with the static part of the domain at hand and applying a classical methodology (bottom-up, up-bottom or middle out) in order to identify and structure the concepts corresponding to the static aspects. The static part corresponds to the concepts called continuants or endurants (Gangemi, Guarino, Masolo, Oltramari, & Schneider, 2002).

Then it is time to the dynamic part, which corresponds to the concepts called ocurrents or perdurants (Gangemi et al., 2002). The dynamic part is the part for which there is less proposed work in the ontology engineering area and where a greater contribution can be made in order to make the resulting knowledge structures more usable.

The objective is to facilitate the process of building a model for the dynamic ontology aspects and guarantee that this model can be translated to CNL in a more natural way, i.e. the resulting CNL expressions are more usable for users that are not formal languages experts.

The proposed pattern is inspired by the way we actually model the dynamic aspects of the world using our main knowledge representation tools, i.e. natural language. Our tool for this is the verb, which models the dynamic aspects and constitutes the central point of sentences.

The objective is to apply this same pattern when modelling the dynamic aspects of an ontology. The first step is to identify the verb concepts corresponding to the ocurrents in the domain at hand, i.e. processes, situations, events, etc. These concepts will constitute the main part of the model for the dynamic part, just the same role verbs play in NL sentences.

This first step just identifies some concepts that are not enough to build complex knowledge expressions. In order to do that, the inspiration is also from how NL sentences work. In NL sentences, the verb is connected to other sentence constituents, i.e. participants, in order to build expressions that model processes, events, situations, etc. This kind of connection has been studied for long in the NL domain and a characterisation of them has been made. These connections are characterised as verb fillers called case roles or thematic roles (McRae, Ferretti, & Amyote, 1997).

This approach has been extensively used in the NL research domain but there is little work about applying case roles for ontology engineering. There is the FrameNet (Fillmore, Johnson, & Petruck, 2003) initiative but it is mainly oriented towards knowledge acquisition from NL sources by semi-automatic annotation.

Two of the main proposals about the application of case roles for knowledge representation are those for Sowa (2000) and Dick (1991). From these sources, a selection of case roles that can be extensively used to model the dynamic part of ontologies has been build. The contribution of this selection is that it is specially tailored to be integrated as pattern for ontology engineering.

Table II shows this case roles selection, which is organised in four classes of generic case roles, which are shown at the top, and six categories, which are shown at the right. These categories correspond to verb semantic facets, not disjoint classes of verbs. Therefore, the same verb concept can present one or more of these facets. For instance, the play verb can show the action, temporal and spatial facets in a particular sentence.

Table II. Case roles for the NL-Oriented Pattern

	initiator	resource	goal	essence
Action	agent, effector	instrument	result, recipient	patient, theme
Process	agent, origin	matter	result, recipient	patient, theme
Transfer	agent, origin	instrument, medium	experiencer, recipient	theme
Spatial	origin	path	destination	location
Temporal	start	duration	completion	pointInTime
Ambient	reason	manner	aim, consequence	condition

Consequently, once the verb concepts have been identified, the second step of the proposed pattern corresponds to the process of determining the case roles that are necessary to build the dynamic model. Formal methods can be employed to constraint how the verb concept and the case roles are related. Therefore, this pattern allows a great range of model detail levels. Moreover, it is a very complete set of case roles. It includes all the case roles identified in the refereed bibliography and, as it is shown in the next section, it has been used during the Copyright Ontology development. During this development process no case role lack was detected and all the verb models could be built with just the case roles in Table II.

2.1. THE COPYRIGHT ONTOLOGY SCENARIO

This section details the Copyright Ontology conceptualisation activity. This activity is used as an illustrative example of the pattern presented in the previous section, which was employed in the Copyright Ontology engineering process.

The copyright domain is a complex one and conceptualising it is a very challenging task. The conceptualisation process, as it has been shown in the pattern description, is divided into two phases. The first one concentrates on the static aspects of the domain. The static aspects are divided into two different submodels due to its complexity.

First, there is the creation submodel. This model is the basis for building the conceptual models of the rest of the parts. It defines the different forms a creation can take, which are classified following the three main points of view as proposed by many upper ontologies, e.g. the Suggested Upper Merged Ontology) (Niles & Pease, 2001):

- **Abstract**: Work.
- **Object**: Manifestation, Fixation and Instance.
- **Process**: Performance and Communication.

A part from identifying the key concepts in the creation submodel, it also includes some relations among them and a set of constraints on how they are interrelated. More details for this point and the following steps in the conceptualisation process are available from[4].

Second, there is the rights submodel, which is also part of the static part model. The Rights Model follows the World Intellectual Property Organisation (WIPO[5]) recommendations in order to define the rights

---

[4]   A   Semantic   Web   approach   to   Digital   Rights   Management,
http://rhizomik.net/~roberto/thesis
[5]   WIPO, http://www.wipo.int

hierarchy. The most relevant rights in the DRM context are economic rights as they are related to productive and commercial aspects of copyright. All the specific rights in copyright law are modelled as concepts. For the economic aspects of copyright there are the following rights: Reproduction, Distribution, Public Performance, Fixation, Communication and Transformation Right.

Each right governs a set of actions, i.e. things that the actors participating in the copyright life cycle can perform on the entities in the creation model. Therefore, it is time to move to the dynamic aspects of the domain. The model for the dynamic part is called the Action Model and it is built on the roots of the two previous ones.

Actions correspond to the primitive actions that can be performed on the concepts defined in the creation submodel and which are regulated by the rights in the rights submodel. For the economic rights, these are the actions:

- **Reproduction Right**: *reproduce*, commonly speaking *copy*.
- **Distribution Right**: *distribute*. More specifically *sell*, *rent* and *lend*.
- **Public Performance Right**: *perform*; it is regulated by copyright when it is a public performance and not a private one.
- **Fixation Right**: *fix*, or *record*.
- **Communication Right**: *communicate* when the subject is an object or *retransmit* when communicating a performance or previous communication, e.g. a re-broadcast. Other related actions, which depend on the intended audience, are *broadcast* or *make available*.
- **Transformation Right**: *derive*. Some specialisations are *adapt* or *translate*.

At this point we have completed the first phase of the dynamic model part, i.e. the verb concepts have been identified. They constitute the key elements in order to build knowledge expressions that represent the processes, events and situations that occur in the copyright domain.

In order to build this expression and relate the verb concepts to the other participants, i.e. concepts in the creation submodel or reused from other ontologies, it is time to complete the dynamic model and detail for each verb concept the corresponding case roles.

Due to space limitations, this section includes just the detailed model for the *Copy* action, which is formally known as *Reproduce*. However, it is commonly referred to as *Copy* and this term is the one that is going to be used in the ontology in order to improve its usability. Copies have been traditionally the basic medium for *Work* commercialisation. They are produced from a *Manifestation,* from a *Fixation* of a *Performance* or from another *Instance*. Therefore, these are the *theme* of the *Copy* verb.

The result is an *Instance* that is the item employed for the physical commercialisation of works, i.e. when a physical item is used as the vehicle to make the *Work* arrive to its consumers. For example, the making of copies of a protected work is the act performed by a publisher who wishes to distribute copies of a text-based work to the public, whether in the form of printed copies or digital media such as CD-ROMs.

Fig. 1 shows at the centre an example model for expression build using the proposed pattern as it is applied to the Copy verb concept. This kind of action patterns are also used to model licenses. Therefore, two additional verb concepts are identified and detailed using case roles: *Agree* and *Disagree*.

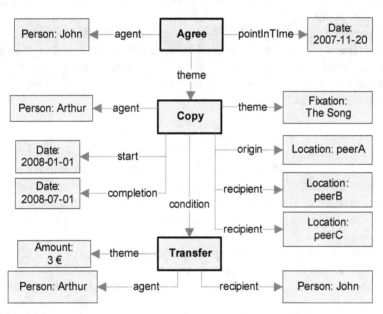

Fig. 1. Model for an agreement on a copy action pattern plus a condition

They are the building block of any license. Fig. 1 shows a license for the *Copy* action previously shown in Fig. 1. As it is shown, the *condition* case role is used in order to introduce a compensation for the agent that grants the copy action, a 3€ transfer from the granted agent.

As it can be observed in the figure, the *condition* case role is used to model the obligation deontic aspect inherent in copyright licenses. The permission and prohibition deontic aspects also present in licenses are captured by the *Agree* and *Disagree* verb concepts and their corresponding *theme* case roles.

The agreement *theme* corresponds to an implicit permission, i.e. the theme of an agreement is permitted. The *condition* on the agreement theme correspond to an obligation, i.e. in order to fulfil the theme action it is necessary to satisfy the pattern defined by the condition property object. Finally, it is also possible to model prohibitions using the *Disagree* verb concept and placing the prohibited action in the corresponding *theme*.

As a result of the Copyright Ontology development process, it has been possible to test the first objective of the proposed ontology engineering pattern. It facilitates the ontology conceptualisation because it provides a predefined pattern to face the conceptualisation process and a predefined set of constructs, the proposed case roles, which facilitate building a detailed model for the dynamic model aspects.

The other objective is to improve the usability of the expression build from the engineered ontology. This objective is based on a CNL rendering for these expressions, which is also facilitated by this pattern as it is shown in the following section.

A part from the Copyright Ontology conceptualisation presented in this section, there is an implementation[6] based on the Web Ontology Language (OWL), concretely on the Description Logic (DL) variant. This implementation can be used to develop a Semantic DRM System based on DL reasoning (García & Gil, 2006).

3.   Mapping to Controlled NL

This section details how the pattern presented in the previous section facilitates rendering knowledge representation expressions as controlled natural language. As the expressions are based on an ontology modelled from the previous NL-oriented pattern, it is easier to perform this rendering.

The mapping to CNL is simplified because it is possible to take profit from the sentence structure already present in the knowledge expression. The key point is how to render the case roles. Depending on the case role, the role filler can become the subject, the object or other component usually attached to the sentence by a preposition.

However, this is not a direct mapping between the case roles representation an NL. This would force a very detailed case by case procedure that would make the rendering very complicated to implement. Therefore, the approach we have undertaken is to stress the fact that we are generating CNL, which is a relaxed version of NL.

Consequently, many choices are removed and, although there is the possibility that the generated sentences are not grammatically correct. On the other hand, these limitations make the mapping much simpler.

---

[6]   Copyright Ontology, http://rhizomik.net/ontologies/copyrightonto

Table III shows a summary of the mapping that has been currently implemented in order to perform the translation to CNL. For each case role, there are the CNL particles used to attach it to the sentence. If there is more than one choice, the table specifies the condition under with that choice is made.

Table III. Mapping case roles to CNL

Case Role	Mapping Condition	CNL
agent		(subject)
effector		(subject)
experiencer	there is not agent/effector	(subject)
instrument	there is not agent/effector/experiencer	(subject)
	otherwise	with
theme	range is verb	that (end of sentence)
	range is not verb	(object)
patient		(object)
matter		of
medium		by
pointInTime		at
location		at
path		through
duration		for
origin		from
start		from
origin		from
destination		to
recipient		to
result		resulting
completion		until
reason		with reason
manner		with manner
aim		with aim
consequence		with consequence
condition		with condition

First, the objective of the mapping is to get the subject from the "agent", "effector", "experiencer" or "instrument" case roles. The preference is placed in the first two and the later are chosen when none of the previous is available in the expression being rendered as CNL. If "instrument" is not performing the subject role, it is attached to the sentence using the *with* particle.

Once the subject has been placed, it is time to place the concept for the verb, just considering the concordance with the subject number, singular or plural. It is important to note that, for any case role, if there are multiple instances of the case role they are rendered together using the *and* or *or* connectives as defined in the underlying formal expression being translated to CNL.

Then it is time for the "theme" and "patient" case roles, which perform the object role in the sentence. The *that* particle is used if the theme is a subordinate sentence, i.e. the theme point to a whole sentence pattern with its own verb concept. In this case the *that* particle and the case role filler are place at the end of the current sentence, once all the other case roles have been processed. If the theme is not a verb concept, then the case role filler is directly placed after the verb.

For the rest of the case roles, the mapping choices try to consider the more common particle used to build the corresponding case role in NL. In some cases this leads to some grammatical errors for some specific verbs. Additionally, if the choice was not clear, the alternative is to use a short sentence that generalises the meaning of the corresponding case role. This is the case for the case roles in the ambient group, e.g. the "condition" case role is mapped to the connective "with condition" in the CNL sentence.

It might be the case that these choices generate sentences that are not grammatically correct and, what is more important for the work at hand, are hardly usable for end-users. In order to try to minimise this problem, a usability test has been performed. However, due to resource and time limitations, the test has concentrated on the copyright domain. Moreover, this is the scenario where this procedure is intended to be applied first.

The usability test is based on a comparative study with NL sentences capturing the intended semantics of the corresponding Copyright Ontology expressions, like the ones shown in the following examples. The comparative study is between NL and CNL sentences because the test users are not logic experts and, therefore, are not used to logic notations.

The study is based on a correlation exercise between NL sentences and the corresponding CNL ones. The latter are generated from the formal expressions corresponding to the semantics of the NL sentences. From user exercise responses it was possible to detect some problematic problems and to find more appropriate alternatives. For instance, for the case roles in the ambient group many alternatives were tested and the only solution for a direct and usable mapping was to use the connective formed by the world with and the case role name, for instance *with manner* for the "manner" case role.

In any case, in order to mitigate the user sensibility to grammatical errors and the limitations of a CNL rendering, the approach has been also to render CNL sentences in a schematic way. Instead of building a normal sentence, the CNL sentence is split up into its particles and each case role is shown in a new line. This approach has been adopted because user tests have shown that users are less sensible to grammatical errors when they face a text shown in a schematic way.

3.1. COPYRIGHT ONTOLOGY CNL EXPRESSIONS EXAMPLES

The previous procedure is illustrated with the following example. All of them are from the copyright domain because this has been the kind of expressions that have been more extensively used to test the procedure.

In this example, the objective is to represent a full license using CNL from it model based on the Copyright Ontology. The original model is shown here using the N3[7] syntax and the concepts in the Copyright Ontology, using the "co" namespace. The CNL rendering for this expression is shown using the mappings in Table III.

```
[a   co:Agree;   co:agent   :John;   co:pointInTime   "2007-11-20";
   co:theme
   [a   co:Copy;   co:agent   :Arthur;   co:theme   :The   Song;
      co:origin       :peerA;       co:destination:peerB, :peerC;
      co:start
      co:start   "2008-01-01";   co:completion   "2008-07-01";
      co:condition
      [a   co:Transfer;   co:agent   :Peter;   co:recipient   :John;
         co:theme   [a   co:Amount;   rdf:value   3;   cr:currency
         cr:Euro]
      ]]].
```

"John agrees
  at 2007-11-20
  that Arthur cop*ies* The Song
    from peerA
    to peerB *or* peerC
    from 2008-01-01
    until 2008-07-01
    with condition Peter transfer*s* amount 3 Euro
      to John".

4. Conclusions and Future Work

As it has been shown through this paper, it is possible to reuse concepts from the natural language processing field in order to build an ontology engineering pattern with two direct benefits.

---

[7] Notation3 (N3) A readable RDF syntax, http://www.w3.org/DesignIssues/Notation3.html

First, this pattern provides some guidance during the ontology engineering process, especially during what is commonly called the conceptualisation activity. This is an aspect that is not usually included in existing ontology engineering methodologies, which concentrate on proposing ontology engineering processes and the kind of activities to be carried out during the process.

The pattern guidance is mainly useful while the model for the dynamic aspects of the ontology is being built. This is also an aspect that has received little attention from ontology engineering methodologies, which concentrate more on the static aspects of the domain at hand.

The pattern is inspired by how dynamic knowledge is modelled in natural language. The key issue is to use verb concepts to model processes, events, situations, etc. Additionally, case roles are also used as a knowledge representation pattern, which are used in natural language processing in order to analyse how verbs are related to the other participants in sentences.

The proposed set of case roles can be applied in most situations as a way to build detailed dynamic models starting from the identified verb concepts. These models provide a polyvalent way to model expression that captures the dynamic aspects of the domain knowledge being engineered.

The second benefit is a consequence of the pattern NL-oriented nature. Due to this fact, it is very easy to generate controlled natural language rendering for expressions build from ontologies based on this pattern. Moreover, these CNL expressions have proved to be very usable for end-users that are not logic experts.

All this features have been illustrated through the Copyright Ontology engineering scenario, which motivated the development of this pattern. The future work concentrates now on performing more detailed end-user test in order to improve the usability of the CNL rendering. There is also the need to test if both benefits are also achievable in other application scenarios and how well does the current CNL mappings perform in domains different from the copyright one.

Another interesting aspect to explore is the performance of an ontology engineered using the NL-oriented pattern for knowledge acquisition tasks from natural language sources. At a first glance, it seems easy to reverse the CNL to case roles mapping, which might make the mapping from natural language to formal expressions based on case roles and verbs concept quite natural and direct.

Acknowledgements

The work described in this paper has been partially supported by Spanish Ministry of Science and Innovation through the Open Platform for

Multichannel Content Distribution Management (OMediaDis) research project (TIN2008-06228).

References

de Walle, R.V. and Burnett, I. (2005), *The MPEG-21 Book,* Wiley & Sons.

Dick, J.P. (1991), *A conceptual, case-relation representation of text for intelligent retrieval,* PhD Thesis; University of Toronto, Canada.

Fillmore, C.J.; Johnson, C.R and Petruck, M.R.L. (2003), *Background to FrameNet,* International Journal of Lexicography, Vol.16 No.3, pp. 235-250.

Gangemi, A.; Guarino, N.; Masolo, C.; Oltramari, A. and Schneider, L. (2002), *Sweetening Ontologies with DOLCE,* in Gómez-Pérez, A. and Benjamins, R. (Eds.) "Knowledge Engineering and Knowledge Management", Springer; pp. 166-181.

García, R. and Delgado, J. (2005), *An Ontological Approach for the Management of Rights Data Dictionaries,* in Moens, M. and Spyns, P. (Eds.), "Frontiers in Artificial Intelligence and Applications", Vol. 134, proceeding of the 2005 conference on Legal Knowledge and Information Systems: JURIX 2005: The Eighteenth Annual Conference, IOS, Amsterdam.

García, R.; Delgado, J. and Rodríguez, E. (2005), *Ontological Analysis of the MPEG-21 Rights Data Dictionary (RDD),* Input document M12495, ISO/IEC JTC1 SC29 WG11 Meeting, Nice, France.

García, R. and Gil, R. (2006), *An OWL copyright ontology for semantic digital rights management,* in Meersman, R; Tari, Z. and Herrero, P. (Eds.), "OTM Workshops 2006", LNCS; Springer; Vol. 4278, pp. 1745-1754.

García, R. and Gil, R. (2008), *A web ontology for copyright contracts management,* International Journal of Electronic Commerce, Vol. 12, No.2.

Kuhn, T.; Royer, L.; Fuchs, N.E. and Schroeder, M. (2006), *Improving Text Mining with Controlled Natural Language: A Case Study for Protein Interactions,* Proceedings of 3rd International Workshop, "Data Integration in the Life Sciences" (DILS'06), Springer, LNBI, Vol. 4075, pp. 66-81.

Lessig, L. (2003), *The Creative Commons,* Tokyo, JP: RBL.

McRae, K.; Ferretti, T.R. and Amyote, L. (1997), *Thematic Roles as Verb-specific Concepts,* Language and Cognitive Processes Journal, Vol. 12, No. 2, pp.137-176.

Niles, I. and Pease, A. (2001), *Towards a Standard Upper Ontology,* in Welty, C. and Smith, B. (Eds.), "Proceedings of the 2nd International Conference on Formal Ontology in Information Systems", FOIS; Maine, USA; pp. 2-9.

Qu Y.; Zhang, X. and Li, H. (2004), *OREL: an ontology-based rights expression language,* "Proceedings of the 13th international World Wide Web Conference", New York, NY, ACM, pp. 324-325.

Schwitter, R. (2004), *Representing Knowledge in Controlled Natural Language: A Case Study,* in Negoita, M.G.; Howlett, R.J. and Jain L.C. (Eds.), "Knowledge-Based Intelligent Information and Engineering Systems Proceedings", Part I, Springer, LNAI, Vol. 3213, pp. 711-717.

Sowa, J.F. (2000), *Knowledge Representation, Logical, philosophical and computational foundations,* Brooks Cole Publishing Co. Pacific Grove, CA, USA.

Wang, X.; DeMartini, T.; Wragg, B.; Paramasivam, M.and Barlas, C. (2005), *The MPEG-21 rights expression language and rights data dictionary,* IEEE Transactions on Multimedia, Vol. 7, No. 3, pp. 408-417.

LiquidPublications and its Technical and Legal Challenges

Nardine Osman, Carles Sierra, Jordi Sabater-Mir
Artificial Intelligence Research Institute (IIIA-CSIC), Barcelona, Spain

Joseph R. Wakeling, Judith Simon, Gloria Origgi, Roberto Casati
Institut Jean Nicod (CNRS), École Normale Supérieure, 29 rue d'Ulm, F-75005 Paris, France

Abstract. This paper proposes a new paradigm for dealing with scientific knowledge in general, and publications in particular. The paradigm aims at changing the way in which knowledge is produced, disseminated, evaluated, and consumed. A formal model is proposed and the issues of credit attribution, copyrights and licensing, which are crucial for the success of any new model, are addressed.

Keywords: publications, credit attribution, copyrights and licensing

1. Introduction

The current publication model is based on promoting quality research by relying on peer review for selecting publishable papers, i.e. papers to be accepted by the community. This model requires a lot of effort and time from the authors, reviewers, editors, etc. Authors tend to waste a lot of effort and time on repackaging already existing ideas for the sole purpose of increasing their number of publications, and hence, their reputation. This results in a dissemination overhead for the community. Reviewers are subsequently affected by this overhead, and are also required to spend more and more time on reviewing papers. Additionally, peer review is not always fair: it sometimes results in the rejection of good papers; and if a paper is accepted, a long time (typically months) passes before the paper appears in a published outlet.

In this paper, we propose a new paradigm that aims at changing the way in which knowledge is produced, disseminated, evaluated, and consumed. Although this paper does not focus on the technical implementation details, it does provide a general overview of the proposed LiquidPub (LP) model, its implications on the life-cycle of scientific knowledge, and it addresses the crucial issues of credit attribution, copyrights and licensing that are key to the success of such systems.

Section 2 of this paper formally defines the proposed model. Section 3 illustrates how this model addresses the pitfalls of the existing one. Sections 4 and 5 address the crucial issues of credit attribution and copyrights and licensing, respectively. A motivating example is presented by Section 6. And conclusions are drawn by Section 7.

2. The LiquidPub Model

The more generic, yet expressive, a framework is, the more useful it would be for a large variety of audiences (or applications). For the world of publications, we propose a simple framework built on two main building blocks: the scientific knowledge objects (SKOs) and the researchers, or the users. We then propose a set of relations for linking these types of elements (which are, formally, nodes in a graph), based on the current needs of the publications field. Note that we avoid padding the system with extra rules on who can perform what action, since we believe this is generally context dependent and is the responsibility of the user; nevertheless, a minimum set of integrity constraints is needed to preserve the robustness of the system. Due to the lack of space, we refer the interested reader to Section 2.3.2 of Giunchiglia et al. (2009) for more information on the LP system's integrity constraints. The LP model is then defined as follows.

Definition 1. An LP system is defined as the tuple specified by a set of nodes and relations, accordingly:

$$LP = \langle N, G, O, P, V, S, C, R \rangle$$

where,

- N represents the set of SKOs (or research items),

- G represents the set of users (or researchers),

- $O \subseteq N \times G$ represents the *owns* relation that describes which user is the owner of which node,

- $P \subseteq G \times G$ represents the *part of* relation that describes which SKO constitutes a part of which other,

- $V \subseteq G \times G$ represents the *version of* relation that describes which SKO is considered to be a version of which other,

- $S \subseteq G \times G$ represents the *submitted to* relation that describes which SKO has been submitted to join which other,

- $C \subseteq G \times G$ represents the *cites* relation that describes which SKO cites which other, and

- $R \subseteq G \times G$ represents the *reviews* relation that describes which SKO is a review of which other.

The LP system may be viewed as being composed of different layers of networks and graphs. For instance, the *cites* relation helps build a citation network; the *part of* relation results in an SKO structural graph; co-authorship networks may be deduced; and so on. We note that the proposed model of this paper is a formal high level model. Implementation choices are better described by Section 1 of Giunchiglia et al. (2009). For additional and more technical details on the proposed LiquidPub model, we refer the interested reader to Section 2 of Giunchiglia et al. (2009).

The LP system distinguishes between various researcher roles. Mainly, the owner of a node plays different roles based on the type of this node. For example, if the node represented a conference, then the owner is viewed as the chair; if it represented a conference proceedings, then the owner is viewed as the editor; if it represented a paper, then the owner is viewed as an author; if it represented a review, then the owner is viewed as a reviewer; and so on.

A bunch of additional relations may be deduced from the information provided by the LP system. For example, the collaboration of authors may be defined as a relation that may be inferred, the reviewers of a given paper may also be defined as an inferred relation, etc. Such inferred relations can be specified by organisational charters, which may be viewed as a layer that lies on top of the LP system and provides additional definitions and constraints by making use of LP data. Organisational charters may also choose to define relations that are based on data not provided by the LP system, such as the degree of dependency between researchers, their degree of collaboration, etc. In such cases, the charter should also provide the means for obtaining this data. Section 6 provides a brief introduction to organisational charters through our motivating example.

Each node in the LP system should be defined through a set of attributes. Table I provides a sample of these attributes, which we believe are self-explanatory.

Table I. The attributes of LP nodes

Researchers (Users)	Research Work (SKOs)
First name	Title
Family name	Date
Primary affiliation	URI
Primary address	Type
Primary email	Access rights
...	...

Naturally, some of these attributes will be mandatory, such as the email address of a researcher, which could be used as his/her ID. These provide one example of the constraints essential for maintaining the integrity of the system: the integrity constraints described by Section 2.3.2 of Giunchiglia et al. (2009).

3. The LiquidPub Contribution

What changes does the proposed LP model bring to the publications world? LiquidPub aims at advancing the entire life-cycle of knowledge by improving the way knowledge is produced, disseminated, evaluated, and consumed. In what follows, we discuss how the proposed model influences these stages:

- **Production.** The LP model allows users to divide their work into chunks, linking them through the *part of* relation. This helps promote reuse. For example, in the case of writing papers, authors no longer need to spend too much time on re-writing and re-packaging already existing ideas; they could simply re-use existing sections. This also results in reducing the dissemination overhead of current publications. The ease of reusing and linking to others' work also promotes collaboration. A document can easily be constructed by combining several SKOs, where the owners vary for each SKO. Of course, maintaining a fair credit attribution (which we discuss shortly) is also crucial for promoting reuse and collaboration.

- **Dissemination.** The system promotes early sharing. With the existence of the *version of* relation, researchers may now share their initial developing research ideas with the community, without the fear of losing credit. Furthermore, early sharing helps in finding potential collaborators, getting the community feedback from an early stage, etc. As the work matures, later and more stable versions may be adopted by more reputable journals, conferences, etc. This essentially implies that the chances for good quality work to be brought to light is much higher than in the current system, where good papers can sometimes be rejected depending on the luck of who gets to review them. This system allows the community to judge and promote interesting ideas. Again, a fair credit attribution is crucial for the success of such a scenario.

- **Evaluation.** The LP model preserves the authorship of researchers on bits and pieces of a larger research work; hence, each author will be given credit based on what exactly s/he has contributed. Publishing papers which are different versions of each other, or that reuse a lot of existing material, could now be differentiated from publishing distinct novel ideas (to some extent, of course). All of this, along with the numerous information sources made available by the system (such as the social relations between researchers that could affect the reliability of reviews, the citations network, the co-authorship network, the structural graphs of SKOs, etc.) helps achieve a fairer credit attribution.

- **Consumption.** As illustrated above, research work does not need to be published to be brought to light. It is now the community that decides what is interesting, and hence, what receives higher credit and may then be published. The LP system facilitates sharing, finding, and publishing interesting research work. This becomes even more concrete with the introduction of the concept of Liquid Journals (Baez and Casati, 2009), which provide means based on social networking for sharing and promoting interesting work.

In addition to the technological challenges in building such a system, two crucial challenges confront the success of the proposed LP model: (1) to provide an incentive for researchers to use the system by providing fair credit attribution, and (2) to address the legal issues. These challenges are addressed by the following two sections, respectively.

4. The Issue of Credit Attribution

Credit attribution in the LP model is mainly concerned with computing the reputation of research and researchers. It is a common understanding that reputation represents group opinion. As such, we say that any available information that should influence reputation may be viewed as opinions. For instance, the LP system will contain direct opinions provided by reviews. Additionally, citations may also be viewed as an indication of how good a given research work is.[1] Hence, we first provide the following definition for opinions.

Definition 2. The opinion that a person β holds about an entity α concerning the attribute a at time t is defined as:

$$o(\beta, \alpha, a, t) = \{e_1 \mapsto v_1, ..., e_n \mapsto v_n\}$$

where,

- $\beta \in G$,

- $\alpha \in N$,

---

[1] In this paper, we assume that the functions that translate the information provided by the LP model into opinions are already provided. The *cites* relation provides one example of such information. Each citation may be viewed as an opinion being formed about the cited entity, whose value is equivalent to the reputation of the citing entity (which could be, for instance, an aggregation of the authors' *h*-index).

- $t \in T$, and T represents calendar time,

- $a \in A$, and A is the set of attributes that opinions may address (e.g. $A = \{quality, novelty, \ldots\}$),

- $\{e_1, \ldots, e_n\} = E$, and E is the evaluation space over which opinions are defined (e.g. $E = \{bad, good, v.good\}$), and

- $v_i \in [0,1]$ represents the value assigned to each element $e_i \in E$, with the condition that $\sum_i v_i = 1$

In other words, the opinion is specified as a probability distribution over the evaluation space E. We note that the opinion one holds about an SKO may change with time, hence various instances of $o(\beta, \alpha, a, t)$ may exist for the same α, β, and a, but with distinct ts.

We say, the reputation of an SKO should not only be influenced by the opinions it receives, but by its position in the SKO structural graph as well. For instance, a conference is reputable if it accepts high quality papers only. Similarly, people usually assume that in the absence of any information about a given paper, the fact that the paper has been accepted by a highly reputable journal implies that the paper should be of good quality. Hence, there is a notion of propagation of opinions along the *part of* relation of the structural SKO graphs.

The direction of propagation is crucial, so we differentiate between the opinion that propagates from parent to child and that which propagates from child to parent. We say that the *intrinsic* opinion about an SKO is either the result of direct opinions it has received or the aggregation of the opinions about its children SKOs:

$$\mathbb{P}_n^t = \frac{1}{\sum\limits_{(c,n) \in \mathcal{P}} \pi_c^t} \cdot \sum\limits_{(c,n) \in \mathcal{P}} \pi_c^t \cdot \mathbb{P}_c^t \tag{1}$$

where, $\mathbb{P}_x^t$ is the intrinsic opinion about the SKO x at time t, π_x^t represents the reliability of an intrinsic opinion and is defined as the proportion of nodes that have received a direct opinion in the structural sub-tree whose root node is x, and $(c,n) \in \mathcal{P}$ specifies that the SKO c is a child of (part of) n.

We then say the default opinion about an SKO, in the absence of any information about it or the parts that compose it, may be inherited from its parent SKOs. We call this the *extrinsic* opinion about an SKO, which we define accordingly:

$$\mathbb{D}_n^t = \frac{1}{\sum\limits_{(n,p) \in \mathcal{P}} \pi_p^t} \cdot \sum\limits_{(n,p) \in \mathcal{P}} \pi_p^t \cdot \mathbb{P}_p^t \tag{2}$$

The basic idea is that initially $\mathbb{P}_n^t = \mathbb{D}_n^t = \mathbb{F} = \frac{1}{|E|}$, i.e. the values of both the intrinsic and extrinsic opinions are equal to the flat (uniform) distribution $\mathbb{F}$. As times goes by, and as opinions start to be formed about parent or children nodes, the intrinsic and extrinsic opinions start to shape up.

With time, the intrinsic opinion loses its value. Technically speaking, this means the intrinsic opinions starts decaying towards its default $\mathbb{D}$, following the equation presented below:

$$\mathbb{P}_n^t = \Lambda(\mathbb{D}_n^t, \mathbb{P}_n^{t-1}) \tag{3}$$

where Λ is a *decay function* satisfying the property: $\lim_{t \to \infty} \mathbb{P}_n^t = \mathbb{D}_n^t$. In other words, Λ is a function that makes $\mathbb{P}_n^t$ converge to $\mathbb{D}_n^t$ with time.

And since all information loses its value with time, we say the default opinion $\mathbb{D}$ also decays, but towards the flat distribution $\mathbb{F}$ and presumably at a much slower pace than the decay of $\mathbb{P}$:

$$\mathbb{D}_n^t = \Lambda(\mathbb{F}, \mathbb{D}_n^{t-1}) \tag{4}$$

Interested readers may refer to Osman et al. (2010a, 2010b) for the technical details of our proposed propagation algorithm. Ongoing work investigates the calculation of researchers' reputation. In a similarly manner to computing the reputation of SKOs, the reputation of an author may be computed through the propagation of the reputation of the author's research work (SKOs) along the *owns* relation. However, when computing the reputation of authors, it is important to consider which SKOs are versions of which other. For instance, we say an author who has two highly reputable SKOs that are different versions of each other should have a lower reputation than an author who has two highly reputable novel SKOs that are independent of each other. In other words, it is crucial to consider the *version of* relation when computing the reputation of authors.

Existing mechanisms have addressed the issue of using citations for calculating the reputation of an author (Radicchi et al., 2009) or the reputation of a paper (Walker et al., 2007). Aggregating individual opinions to obtain the group opinion has been addressed by Sierra and Debenham (2009). Calculating the reliability of reviewers has been addressed by Sabater-Mir and Sierra (2002), Sabater-Mir et al. (2006), and Kuter and Golbeck (2007). In summary, existing research has already proposed numerous methods for calculating the reputation of isolated entities. And these are all useful and complementary methods to our proposed algorithm. However, what is novel in the LP model is the introduction of the notion of the SKO structural graphs: SKOs are linked to each other through the *part of* relation resulting in possible large structural graphs.

Our propagation mechanism allows one to deduce opinions about new entities by propagating opinions from other related entities. Additionally, the presented mechanism is highly customisable. For instance, a user may choose to run the propagation algorithm over a certain type of information, say its personal direct opinions only. In such a case, given one person's opinions on a set of nodes of a structural graph, the algorithm aids this person in deducing its opinion concerning the remaining nodes.

5. The Issue of Copyrights and Licensing

The LiquidPub project envisions a variety of different innovations in publishing and research dissemination. Among the concrete paradigms under development are liquid extensions of journals (Baez and Casati, 2009), books (Casati and Ragone, 2009) and conferences (Origgi and Schneider, 2009). In each of these cases it is possible to envision many different licensing practices that could be applied. However, it is important not just that there be innovation in individual areas of research dissemination but also that each of these innovations should complement the other. Therefore the principal focus needs to be on licensing models which enhance the interoperability and potential for exchange between these different liquid publishing paradigms, and which enhance the possibilities for further user-initiated innovations. As PLoS editor Fiona MacCallum notes of open access (MacCallum, 2007),

> [T]he beauty ... is not just that you can download and read an article for personal use. You can also redistribute it, make derivative copies of it ..., use it for educational purposes ..., or, most importantly, for purposes that we can't yet envisage.

Such potential for 'purposes that we can't yet envisage' needs to be firmly embedded into the licensing framework of LiquidPub.

If such a thought sounds scary—many researchers are understandably concerned about others re-using their articles in inappropriate or abusive ways—it is worthwhile to remember that copyright and licensing *per se* plays little part in determining what is acceptable practice in academia. Community norms and institutional constraints play a far larger role, as acknowledged for example in the Bethesda declaration on open access:

> Community standards, rather than copyright law, will continue to provide the mechanism for enforcement of proper attribution and responsible use of the published work, *as they do now* [our emphasis].

The extremely permissive licensing terms of many open access articles (MacCallum, 2007) have not so far resulted in obvious abuse; in fact if anything they have served primarily to pre-emptively avoid the potential for copyright holders to constrain what most academics would consider fair use (Zimmer, 2007). Even non-open access publishers grant many permissions for use of their content—such as author or institutional self-archiving (Harnad et al. 2004, 2008)—primarily in response to community demand.

Where licensing factors *can* play a role is in those circumstances where we want to *change* the community norms. For example, the free/open source software communities have been able to foster norms of sharing and re-using computer code through so-called 'copyleft' licensing, which constrains distributors of code to grant recipients key freedoms to use and modify the software (Stallman 1996, 1998, 2004; O'Mahony, 2003). One obvious parallel is that researchers might be much more willing to share datasets if there were a constraint that whoever used that data in a publication had to make available on similar terms any extra data they employed or created in that work.

With these factors in mind we can articulate a number of general principles for any LiquidPub licensing framework to bear in mind:

1. The licensing forms for different liquid publishing paradigms should complement and facilitate each other.

2. Licenses should encourage and facilitate independent innovation for 'purposes we can't yet envisage'.

3. Licenses should not result in *greater* restriction of dissemination than exists at present.

4. Community norms, rather than copyright restrictions, should be the principal source of *constraints* on use. The main use of legal constraints should be where it can *facilitate the emergence of new desirable norms.*

5. Licensing, and rights, need to be accorded to factors other than scientific texts—to things such as identity, reputation and so on.

As an example, we present the draft licensing framework being developed for *Liquid Conferences*. These are virtual 'meetings' in an online environment, where articles take the place of presentations, and discourse follows in the form of (usually moderated) comments from system users. This enables many of the key features of 'real' conferences—detailed presentation of ideas, focused discussion and exchange—while avoiding the costs and constraints associated with bringing many people together in the same place at the same time. The main working example,[2] is the website Interdisciplines (www.interdisciplines.org), which has been running such online events very successfully over a period of more than 10 years, and is now being significantly updated and expanded as part of the LiquidPub project.

---

[2] We are not aware of any other websites deliberately *designed* to be Liquid Conference platforms. However, as we note later, various other websites or publications can be seen as fitting closely with the Liquid Conference paradigm.

Interdisciplines operates an invitation-based system where conference organisers commission original articles from specially-chosen authors. All articles are subject to review prior to being publicly displayed on the website, although the details of the review process may vary from conference to conference. Once an article goes 'live', any reader of the website can post comments and feedback, subject to moderation in order to sustain the quality of the discussion.

Despite its various processes of selection and review, which grant its contents an academic validity at least equal to peer-reviewed conference proceedings, Interdisciplines is not a serial or other registered publication venue,[3] and so in distribution terms it occupies a middle ground not dissimilar to a preprint archive. From a licensing point of view, this system presents a number of challenges.

First, if the proceedings of a meeting are intended to be published in a book or journal special issue, the copies archived on Interdisciplines must be distributed according to terms that do not violate the publisher's rules on distribution (in particular, many publishers request an exclusive right to commercial distribution of content). If the proceedings are not intended to be published in a particular venue, authors must be able to individually seek publication for their articles, as long as this does not affect the ability of Interdisciplines to archive and distribute copies.

Secondly, wherever articles are eventually published, it should be possible for their accompanying commentary to be published with them: the carefully-cultivated discourse is often the most interesting part of an Interdisciplines conference, and is what sets Interdisciplines apart from other comment forums. At the same time, for this very reason, interaction with and re-use of the comments and discussion needs to be maximised.

Finally, since Interdisciplines content is intended to be freely available to all, it is desirable where possible to go beyond this to full or 'libre' open access where redistribution and re-use are widely encouraged (MacCallum, 2007; Suber, 2008).

The Interdisciplines licensing structure is designed to resolve these problems while still providing as much leeway as possible for authors and conference organisers to determine for themselves the distribution terms of their work. First, conference organisers must determine the range of acceptable licensing options for articles, selecting from a range of predetermined options: a basic non-exclusive and irrevocable license for Interdisciplines to distribute the article, plus a range of Creative Commons licenses (the four—CC-BY, CC-BY-SA, CC-BY-NC and CC-BY-NC-SA—that do not contain a 'no derivatives' clause). Authors submitting to the conference can then

---

[3] Depending on academic discipline, inclusion in conference proceedings may in any case not be considered as 'publication', whether the conference is a liquid one on Interdisciplines or a regular scientific meeting.

select from any of the licenses the organisers have deemed acceptable. In this way, conference organisers can weed out any license incompatible with a preselected publication venue, while permitting authors maximum possible choice where possible.

Comments and feedback technically fall under the same considerations. However, Interdisciplines has an interest in promoting interaction and dialogue around articles: conversely, from a publisher's point of view, comments are likely to only be of value when attached to their parent article. We therefore choose to mandate the permissive Creative Commons Attribution (CC-BY) license for comments, allowing maximum re-use while not touching the licensing status of articles.

This is a relatively conservative licensing framework, designed to create minimum conflict with current publishing norms. Much more radical frameworks are possible if we are willing to abandon such compatibility. One option is to share the research and writing process in a project setup similar to free and open source software projects (Wakeling et al., 2009), with copyleft-style licensing to ensure freedoms to access and use data, analyses and so on. The micro-structure of SKOs described in this article offers plentiful opportunities for frameworks based on re-use and reincorporation of others' work. Extended proposals for such fine-grained processes of sharing and credit attribution are the subject of ongoing research in the LiquidPub project.

6. Motivating Example

The LiquidPub system may be used for any process that deals with the creation of knowledge objects, collaboration between researchers, sharing with the community, evaluation by the community, publishing, etc. As an example, in this section we illustrate how a more traditional conference may be created, managed, and maintained through the proposed LiquidPub system. The (simplified) steps that need to followed by the conference chair to achieve this are:

1. **Create your conference SKO:**
   The SKO will be empty at this stage, but will later represent the conference proceedings. Later on, accepted papers (or SKOs) will be appended to this SKO through the *part of* relation.

2. **Invite reputable SKOs / Place a call for papers**:
   The chair here may decide either to invite papers, place a call for papers, or both.

3. **Collect submitted papers:**

At this stage authors will link their papers (SKOs) to the conference's SKO via the *submitted to* relation.

4. **Review submitted SKOs:**

The chair (or the conference SKO's owner) will assign reviewers for each SKO and provide them with the right to link their reviews to the appropriate SKO via the *reviews* relation. We note that access rights and constraints that deal with who can perform what action are dealt with by the LP system's integrity constraints, which is outside the scope of this paper.

5. **Select accepted SKOs:**

After the reviews are written, the chair checks the reputation of each submitted paper (SKOs) by using the systems' reputation module of Section 4 along with its own additional constraints on the selection criteria. Accepted SKOs are then linked to the main conference SKO via the *part of* relation.

Note that not all of the above steps have an immediate effect on the LiquidPub system. For example, inviting SKOs or placing a call for papers does not imply the addition, modification, or deletion of some nodes or relations. It simply requires the transmission of messages.

A process model, defined by the conference's organisational charter, may be used to drive these six steps. The process model, when initiated, will then control the flow of various actions. Some of these actions will have a direct effect on the LiquidPub system, such as the creation of a conference SKO, while others will be non-LiquidPub actions, such as message passing actions.

We note that the organisational charter may specify additional details that are related to the process model in general, such as the deadline for submission, the topics of the conference, the licensing constraints, the acceptance rate, how the reputation and reliability of reviewers is computed, how reputable SKOs are selected, the details of the process model, etc.

We use Electronic Institutions (EI) (Arcos et al., 2005) for the specification of organisational charters. Undergoing work[4] is being carried out to permit the automated generation and update of a web-based user interface, eliminating the need for manual modifications every time an EI specification is created or modified.

An example of a basic and generic process model that automates the entire process of a conference is provided by Figure 1. The actions in bold are the actions that require the use of our reputation module. This illustrates how the reputation module may also be invoked from within the interaction model. The actions in italic address the issues of copyrights and licensing.

---

[4] Interested readers may follow this work at http://project.liquidpub.org/lpms/

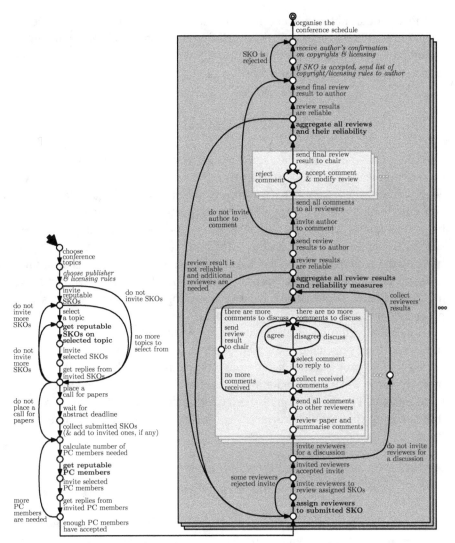

Figure 1. The state graph of a conference management process model

Note that the interaction could be made flexible enough to accommodate the various decisions of conference chairs. For example, the chair may decide whether or not to invite reputable SKOs, whether or not to invite reviewers for a discussion, whether or not to allow authors to defend their work by replying to reviewers' comments, and so on.

The sub-interaction model specified within the dark grey box represents the parallel instances of this sub-interaction, where each instance deals with a different SKO. As for the sub-interaction models specified within the light grey boxes, these represent parallel instances run by the various reviewers of a given SKO.

Finally, note that reviewers may discuss issues infinitely often; however, an author may only reply to a reviewer's comment once. Of course, the interaction model may easily be modified to allow authors to reply to reviewers' comments more than once, if needed.

7. Conclusion

The paper proposes a new paradigm that addresses some of the pitfalls of the current publication process by changing the way in which scientific knowledge is produced, disseminated, evaluated, and consumed. In summary, re-use and collaboration is encouraged by the structural SKO graph, which also helps maintain a 'fairer' credit attribution. Peer-review is no longer a necessity for dissemination. The system helps promote interesting research by relying on the community's feedback (either through direct opinions or indirect ones, such as measuring the traffic, subscriptions, citations, etc.). Nevertheless, peer review could still be used for selecting future publications, which provides some sort of official certification.

Additionally, the issue of credit attribution and the legal issues of copyrights and licensing have been addressed. A propagation algorithm is suggested for the propagation of opinions in structural graphs, which provides more dynamic and liquid reputations measures that are influenced by changes in the system. The system can also offer authors a wider and much more flexible licensing rules, which currently are focused on the Liquid Conferences use case.

Acknowledgements

This work is part of the Liquid Publications Project (http://project.LiquidPub.org/). The LiquidPub project acknowledges the financial support of the Future and Emerging Technologies (FET) programme within the Seventh Framework Programme for Research of the European Commission, under FET-Open grant number: 213360.

References

Arcos, J.L., Esteva, M., Noriega, P., Rodríguez-Aguilar, J.A., and Sierra, C. (2005), *Engineering open environments with electronic institutions*, Engineering applications of artificial intelligence, Vol. 18 No. 2, pp. 191-204.

Baez, M. and Casati, F. (2009), *Liquid Journals: knowledge dissemination in the web era*, technical document, LiquidPublications project, available at: http://project.liquidpub.org/solid-documents.

Casati, F. and Ragone, A. (2009), *Liquid Book: reuse and sharing of multifacet content for evolving books*, technical document, LiquidPublications project, available at: http://project.liquidpub.org/research-areas/liquid-book.

Giunchiglia, F., Chenu-Abente, R., Osman, N.Z., Sabater-Mir, J., Sierra, C., Xu, H., Babenko, D., and Schneider, L. (2009), *Design of the SKO structural model and evolution*, Project deliverable D1.2v1, LiquidPublications Project, available at: http://project.liquidpub.org/solid-documents.

Harnad, S., Brody, T., Vallières, F., Carr, L., Hitchcock, S. Gingras, Y., Oppenheim, C., Hajjem, C., and Hilf, E.R. (2008), *The access/impact problem and the green and gold roads to open access: an update*, Serials Review, Vol. 34 No. 1, pp. 36-40.

Harnad, S., Brody, T., Vallières, F., Carr, L., Hitchcock, S., Gingras, Y., Oppenheim, C., Stamerjohans, H., and Hilf, E.R. (2004), *The access/impact problem and the green and gold roads to open access*, Serials Review, Vol. 30 No. 4, pp. 310-314.

Kuter, U. and Golbeck, J. (2007), *SUNNY: A new algorithm for trust inference in social networks using probabilistic confidence models*, In proceedings of the 22nd national conference on artificial intelligence (AAAI'07), pp. 1377-1382, AAAI Press.

MacCallum, C.J. (2007), *When is open access not open access?*, PLoS Biology, Vol. 5 No. 10, pp. e285.

O'Mahony, S. (2003), *Guarding the commons: how community managed software projects protect their work*, Research Policy, Vol. 32 No. 7, pp. 1179-1198.

Origgi, G. and Schneider, L. (2009), *Liquid Conferences use case*, technical document, LiquidPublications project, available at: http://project.liquidpub.org/research-areas/liquid-conferences.

Osman, N.Z., Sierra, C., and Fabregues, A. (2010) *A propagation and aggregation algorithm for inferring opinions in structural graphs*, In proceedings of the 13th international workshop on Trust in Agent Societies, Toronto, Canada.

Osman, N.Z., Sierra, C., and Sabater-Mir, J. (2010) *Propagation of opinions in structural graphs*, technical document, LiquidPublications Project, available at: http://project.liquidpub.org/solid-documents.

Radicchi, F., Fortunato, S., Markines, B., and Vespignani, A. (2009), *Diffusion of scientific credits and the ranking of scientists*, e-Print archive, arXiv:0907.1050v2, available at: http://arxiv.org/abs/0907.1050.

Sabater-Mir, J. and Sierra, C. (2002), *Social ReGreT, a reputation model based on social relations*, ACM, SIGecom Exchanges, Vol. 3 No. 1, pp. 44-56.

Sabater-Mir, J., Paolucci, M., and Conte, R. (2006), *Repage: REPutation and imAGE among limited autonomous partners*, Journal of Artificial Societies and Social Simulation, Vol. 9 No. 2, pp. 3.

Sierra, C. and Debenham, J. (2009), *Information-based reputation*, In proceedings of the first international conference on reputation: theory and technology (ICORE'09), pp. 5-19, Gargonza, Italy.

Stallman, R.M. (1996), *What is copyleft?*, reprinted as Chapter 14 of Stallman (2004), updated version available at: http://www.gnu.org/copyleft/copyleft.html.

Stallman, R.M. (1998), *Copyleft: pragmatic idealism*, reprinted as Chapter 15 of Stallman (2004), updated version available at: http://www.gnu.org/philosophy/pragmatic.html.

Stallman, R.M. (2004), *Free Software, Free Society: selected essays of Richard M. Stallman*. GNU Press, Boston, MA, 2nd edition.

Suber, P. (2008), *Gratis and libre open access*, SPARC Open Access Newsletter, 2 August, No. 124, available at: http://www.earlham.edu/~peters/fos/newsletter/08-02-08.htm#gratis-libre.

Wakeling, J.R., Medo, M., Turrini, M., Birukou, A., Law, J., Marchese, M., Zhang, Y.C., and the LiquidPub-PEER community (2009-2010). *Peer review and quality promotion in science*, technical document, LiquidPublications project, available at: http://launchpad.net/liquidpub/peer/.

Walker, D., Xie, H., Yan, K.K., and Maslov, S. (2007), *Ranking scientific publications using a simple model of network traffic*, Journal of Statistical Mechanics: Theory and Experiment, Vol. 2007 No. 06, pp. P06010.

Zimmer, C. (2007) *An open mouse*, Scitizen, 29 May, available at: http://scitizen.com/science-policy/an-open-mouse_a-31-652.html.

Intelligent Multimedia Content Retrieval in Parliaments

Elena Sánchez-Nielsen[*], Francisco Chávez-Gutiérrez[°]
[*]Dpto. E.I.O. y Computación. *Universidad de La Laguna, 38271 La Laguna, Spain*
[°]*Parlamento de Canarias, Teobaldo Power 7, 38002 S/C de Tenerife, Spain*

Abstract. Intelligent representation and retrieval of multimedia content is vital for enabling personalized information and increasing coverage of parliamentary activities. However, it is becoming harder to access, manage and transmit multimedia content according to the meaning it embodies. This paper explores the challenges of: (1) personalizing and adapting multimedia parliamentary content to the preferences and needs of citizens according to daily life technologies, and (2) promoting to citizens a sense of ownerships of the political and democratic process. This approach is being developed for plenary sessions in the context of the Parliament of Canary Islands.

Keywords: Retrieval of multimedia legal information, dissemination of multimedia legal information, personalized multimedia legal information, MPEG-7.

1. Introduction

In any democracy, the parliament must be transparent and accountable to the citizens, two characteristics that intelligent multimedia retrieval of legal information can help foster. At the same time that people interact with multimedia every day: reading books, watching television, listening to music, etc; recent technologies and social media are emerging as a way of disseminating and sharing relevant information. This has opened up new opportunities for parliaments in order to people to be better informed about what parliament is doing. In this context, personalizing and adapting parliamentary content to the preferences and needs of citizens and allowing them to transmit their opinions plays two important roles. On the one hand, personalizing and adapting parliamentary multimedia content to the preferences and needs of citizens is focused on creating multimedia content for audiences that want to listen/view when they want, where they want and how they want with effective usage of multimedia content. On the other hand, allowing citizens to transmit their opinions to elective representatives in parliaments enables parliaments to become more sensitive to the needs and preferences of citizens and at the same time allowing the increase of public participation in the democratic process.

In the legislative domain, the most important task of parliamentary activity is the plenary session where the parliament formally sits to vote legislation and adopt its position on political issues by means of the elected representatives who are our agents in the parliament. Increasing transparency about what is debated in plenary sessions is an important priority for parliaments in order to foster the relationships between citizens and parliament and at the same time is an important priority for citizens in order they can access to information about what decisions are being taken which affect their lives. At the present, the flow of information from elected representatives is only in one sense: from politicians to citizens.

In this paper, we focus on meeting three important challenges: (1) how to access, manage and transmit parliamentary multimedia content that takes place in plenary sessions according to the meaning it embodies, (2) how to personalize and adapt parliamentary content to the preferences and needs of citizens using daily life technologies and, (3) how to reconnect people with the policy-making and making the decision-making processes easier to understand and follow through the use of daily life technologies.

In the next section, we examine the key features in realizing efficient access, management and transmission of multimedia contents. Section 3 then considers personalizing and adapting content to the preferences and needs of citizens for intelligent and efficient multimedia content retrieval. Section 4 focus on increasing public participation by means of transmitting public opinion to elected representatives. Section 5 describes how to meeting these challenges in the development of an information system that is being developed in the context of the parliament of Canary Islands. Section 5 summarizes and concludes this paper.

2. Challenges of Multimedia Content

Multimedia content encompasses a broad range of topics of interests to the research community from which the following key challenges areas may be identified:

- **The semantic gap in multimedia information retrieval:** the first critical point in the advancement of multimedia content-based retrieval is the semantic gap, where the meaning of an image is rarely self-evident. The concept of semantic gap can be understood according to Smeulders et al. (Smeulders, 2005) as: "...*the lack of coincidence between the information that one can extract from the visual data and the interpretation that the same data have for a user in a give situation.*" In this context, the aim of multimedia content-based retrieval must be to provide maximum support in bridging the semantic gap between the simplicity of available visual features and the richness of the user semantics.
- **Multimedia content description:** semantic representation of multimedia information is vital for enabling indexing, search and

retrieval capabilities. Metadata definition is the base for multimedia content description which is used to describe and store characteristics of multimedia resources and is used to decide how can be processed the multimedia content.

– **Multimedia content retrieval:** the aim of a good retrieval system is its ability to respond to a user's queries and present results in a desired fashion.

The most interesting topics related to these challenges are described in more detail in the following sections.

2.1. MULTIMEDIA CONTENT DESCRIPTION

Different standards and research projects have as a goal the definition of metadata for multimedia content description such as: Dublin Core, Resource Description Framework (RDF), Web Ontology Language (OWL) and MPEG-7 standard.

2.1.1. *Dublin Core (DC)*
The Dublin Core is a framework for descriptive metadata. It was developed to be simple, concise, extensible and semantically interoperable for cross-domain information resource description. It is widely used in applications such as video editors, content management systems and word processors. The Dublin Core metadata element set has 15 core elements (DCMI, 2000).

2.1.2. *Resource Description Framework (RDF)*
RDF is a family of World-Wide Web Consortium (W3C) which includes the RDF schema language RDFS (W3C, 2004) to represent metadata.

2.1.3. *Web Ontology Language (OWL)*
The Web Ontology Language (OWL) is a dominating standard in ontology definition. OWL has been developed according the description logic paradigm and uses RDF(S) syntax.

2.1.4. *MPEG-7 Standard*
MPEG-7 (Ana Benitez, 2002) is a standard for the description of multimedia content using machine-consumable metadata descriptors providing a standardized set of XML schemas for describing multimedia content richly and in a structured fashion. The MPEG-7 framework consists of Descriptors (Ds), Description Schemes (DSs) and a Description Definition Language (DDL). The data types needed for the semantic description of audiovisual content are defined in a set of Description Schemes rooted in the SemanticBase DS (Chang, 2001). As a result, the

MPEG-7 standard in addition to providing metadata descriptors for structural and low-level aspects of multimedia content also provides a set of tools to model the semantics in narrative worlds like events, objects, agents and places.

2.1.5. *Integrating Multimedia and Semantic Web Vocabularies*

The MPEG-7 standard provides important functionalities for manipulation and management of multimedia content and its associated metadata. The extraction of semantic description and annotation of the content with the corresponding metadata though, is out of the scope of the standard, thus motivating heavy research efforts in the direction of automatic annotation of multimedia content. In order to make MPEG-7 accessible, re-usable and interoperable with many domains, the semantics of the MPEG-7 metadata terms need to be expressed in an ontology using a machine-understable language. To this end, a number of attempts that stress the importance of complementing the MPEG-7 standard with domain-specific ontologies for multimedia annotation have been seen (Bloehdorn, 2004), (Tsinaraki, 2004) and (Hunter, 2004).

Different techniques based on manual and automatic annotations in order to generate semantics for multimedia content can be seen in (Jonathon, 2006).

3. Challenges of Personalizing Content to Citizens

Personalizing and adapting content to the preferences and needs of citizens require processing of the content, on the one hand, and recognizing patterns in citizens' behaviour, on the other. The former involves stages such as extraction and analysis of content semantics and structure, modelling of the resulting content metadata, filtering of content metadata through citizen profiles, and adaption of the content to suit the usage environment or adaption of the usage environment to suit the content. Recognizing citizen behaviour requires the construction of user models that record usage history and citizen preferences for types of content and interface modalities in order to tailor content to cater to these preferences and to predict future usage behaviour.

3.1. PERSONALIZED MULTIMEDIA CLIP GENERATION FROM AUDIOVISUAL CONTENT

All the audiovisual content recorded in a digital format from plenary sessions is not disseminated to citizens, because of two reasons: (1) the time consumed by plenary sessions, generally they take place about more than four hours; in this situation citizens need to download masses of data and (2) the development of an easy-to-use retrieval system answering the current information need with customized multimedia clips is a challenging goal. In the practice, real-streaming of video (Dapeng, 2001) and podcasting technology (Patterson, 2006) are being used by parliaments as communication tools to distribute legislative information from plenary sessions and parliamentary committees. The disadvantages of the use of these daily life technologies are: (1) the citizens cannot specify their preferences about what information they have interest and therefore they need to view/listen the disseminated content until the desired information is located and (2) no possibility of interaction between citizens and parliament about the outcomes of plenary sessions is achieved.

The scenario described above faces the following challenges: (1) recovery of legislative information from plenary sessions that best fit citizens' preferences with easy retrieval of audio/video clips of customized interest, and (2) the use of social-based filtering techniques in order to recommend legislative items between citizens with similar taste.

4. Public Participation

In the legislative domain, the most important task of parliamentary activity is the plenary session, which plays an important role in the process of a bill. On one hand, the parliament debates the bills where new changes can be introduced and on the other hand, the parliament sits to vote legislation and adopt its position on political issues by means of the elected representatives. However, the political debate in parliaments, instead of being a channel of communication between citizens and their elected representatives, tends to be monological and released for public consumption mainly based to a large extent on marketing criteria. For most citizens, political debate has come to be perceived as something to watch – or to switch off (Euripidis, 2007). As a result, the flow of communication is in only one sense: from politicians to citizens, where citizens cannot detail what are their preferences and needs about the decisions that are being taken in parliaments. In this context, the key problem to promote and enhance public participation could be summarized with a simple question: *"Why should I participate?"*.

Based on the above consideration, it is evident that there is a strong need to provide more sophisticated directions and solutions, in order to find the right conditions and incentives for public participation in the legislative process in the parliaments in the preparatory stages (such as debate processes). The incentive problem can be improved by two ways: (1) taking really into account the citizens' needs and debating, and translating these one to legal contents; and (2) encouraging more pro-social behaviour through group identity or other social process. The former stage can be computed by means of connecting citizens to elected representatives using feedback processes about the multimedia content that has been retrieved from citizens and introducing the use of clustering techniques in order to describe the different groupos of citizens with similar patterns.

4.1. CITIZENS INTERACTION

Two important types of citizens' interactions can be differentiated: (1) the citizens' interactions with the parliamentary multimedia content system and (2) the citizens' interactions with the elected representatives in parliaments.

An important challenge in the domain of citizen interaction with parliamentary multimedia content is helping citizens express what they need. Citizens often have a fuzzy understanding of what they are looking. Generally, it is hard for a citizen to express their information needs in a clear and precise way in a language required by the parliamentary website and/or application. The ways of citizen can interact with parliamentary multimedia systems vary from one in which the citizen can ask complex questions, to one in which the citizen does not have to ask anything but where the system pushes interesting content to the citizen. Four different ways of citizens' interactions with multimedia content systems are possible: (1) retrieval content focused on concept-based queries or content-based queries, (2) dynamic query interaction, (3) browsing and (4) recommendation interaction model where the system itself takes the initiative.

In order to foster the interaction between citizens and elected representatives and to give voice to the citizens as a means of participating in the parliamentary work, citizens must be able to interact to politicians by means of feedback processes.

5. Legislative Application Scenario for Intelligent Retrieval and Suggestions about Parliamentary Proceedings

The key challenges which have been explored in above sections are being devoloped by means of a legislative application scenario in the parliament of Canary Islands. This application scenario consist of an information system which aims at the creation of an intelligent multimedia content production support system for accessing, managing and distributing parliamentary proceedings according to customized needs of the citizens in a dynamic way using daily life technologies. At the same time, the multimedia content retrieved by citizens is used as a useful instrument that informs politicians about the audience profile. Based on these functionalities, the system aims to bring the following main services to the parliament:

- **Multimedia legislative content management and retrieval:** different functionalities are provided related to automatic and manual annotation of audiovisual content of plenary sessions for multimedia content description. Multimedia content retrieval is provided through the use of podcasting technology where automatic fragmentation of audiovisual content and customized feeds generation in a dynamic way from citizens' customized are computed.
- **Automated reports to elected representatives in parliaments:** are generated from the citizens' feedback after they have listened/viewed the content requested on-demand.

The system aims to bring the following services to citizens, business and other parliaments:

- **On-demand and personalized information:** legislative information of plenary sessions are provided as multimedia clips to citizens and businesses registered to the parliamentary website in an on-demand and customized way, answering to their preferences. As a result, some customized requests demanded by citizens about initiatives that have been debated in plenary sessions could be: "provide me a feed with all the grants about education", and "provide me a feed with all the intervention of the president of the government".
- **Interaction to elected representatives in parliaments:** once the citizens have listened/viewed the requested content, they can tell to their elected representatives their opinions about their outcomes and evaluate them in different dimensions. Then each elected representative receives an automated report with different details about their interventions.

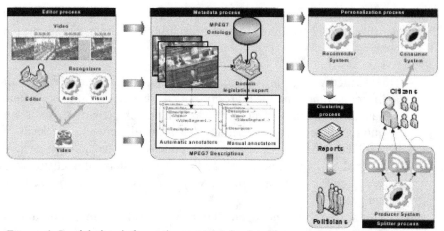

Figure 1. Legislative information system for intelligent multimedia management, retrieval and suggestions from citizens to elected representatives

Figure 1 shows an overview of the basic system processes for the legislative application scenario. The processes of the system are the following:

- **Personalization Process:** personalization permits citizens to adapt multimedia parliamentary content to individual goals. In our context, personalization means filtering information in such way that a citizen only receives relevant information, targeted at the person's unique and individual needs. The basic steps in the personalization process include: (i) building a citizen profile through the consumer system provided by the parliamentary website and (ii) content filtering by means of retrieving results to be relevant to that specific citizen. The different options of the citizen profile are expressed by means of a structural list that comprises the different preferences that can initially be selected about legislative content. The structural list is based on the main components of an ontology that follows MPEG-7 MDS specification (Elena, 2007) (i) agents, (ii) objects and (iii) events (interventions) that relate agents with objects. Additional information about genre, age, working conditions and civil status are requested for the production of automated reports in the clustering process. A personal user account with his/her customized feeds is associated to each citizen. The citizens can interact with the system through feedback processes in order to give their opinions after they have finished of listening/viewing the customized content. The feedback possibilities can be used in the system in two ways: (i) in the recommender system and (ii) in the report system.The recommender system uses the user profile with the following purposes: (i) to generate podcast feeds in a dynamic way according to the specific preferences of the citizen about legislative information of plenary sessions and (ii) to recommend the subscription to new feeds according to the taste of similar citizens.

- **Editor and Metadata Processes:** using visual/audio recognizers and semantic technologies based on MPEG-7 ontologies (Ana, 2002) automatic and manual annotations of audiovisual content of plenary sessions are computed. As a result of these processes, the audiovisual content of plenary sessions is annotated with marks that identify the start and end of the different interventions of politicians and the diverse subjects debated.

- **Splitter Process:** this process is responsible of customized feeds generation in a dynamic way using podcasting technology as an instrument of retrieval information. The producer system transforms the customized preferences computed from the consumer system to a query. The result of processing the query is the creation of a new feed in RSS format.

- **Clustering Process and production of automated reports to elected representatives:** in order to give voice to the citizens as a means of participating in the parliamentary work, citizens are able to interact to politicians by means of feedback processes. The feedback functionalises are: (i) to collect and store user's actions or implicit feedback (subscription feeds demanded/cancelled) and (ii) to collect and store the explicit user's feedback (rating the content of plenary sessions and the interventions of elected representatives). Automated reports are periodically generated by the report system and sent to the corresponding elected representatives with different charts which show diverse histograms of ratings. The histograms are classified according to users' profiles. This implicit feedback is an instrument that allows politicians to know if there are people with some interest about his/her appearance and if this interest is maintained along the time, that is, the audience profile. The explicit feedback gives users a change to rate the content of the episodes of podcast after users have listened/viewed the content. Three modalities of survey questions are provided through the user account in the consumer system: (i) technical quality of the service, (ii) subjects debated and (iii) evaluation of politicians' interventions. Questions about the technical quality of the service include a good image quality, a good audio quality and precision of the information provided as podcast episode. Questions about the subjects debated are related to the perception of importance of that subject and if that subject must be reconsidered for a posterior debate. The politicians' interventions are evaluated in the following dimensions: (i) the political speech (dialectical skill), (ii) the political proposal (if it is adequate or not), and (iii) the degree of trust to that politician.

6. Conclusions

Multimedia content is growing rapidly in parliamentary environments of plenary sessions and parliamentary committees. Intelligent multimedia content retrieval is vital for enabling personalized information to citizens, to foster public participation and, to report to elected representatives about the needs and preferences of citizens. In this paper, we have examined the different topics and meeting the key challenges in order to design a retrieval multimedia information system to respond to citizens' queries about what is happening in parliaments in the context of plenary sessions and present the results in a desired fashion using the daily life technologies.

The different stages involve: bridging the semantic gap, multimedia content description, multimedia content retrieval using podcast technology in a customized way, public participation and citizens' interaction. Our information system approach differs from previous solutions implemented in parliaments (real-time streaming and podcast technology) in several key ways. First, our solution aims at the creation of an intelligent and automated content production methods and tools using semantic technologies for personalized podcast publishing of plenary sessions at real-time. Second, the citizens can receive plausible recommendations of new feeds subscriptions from other citizens with similar taste by means of a collaborative recommender system. Third, the citizen interaction is integrated by means of a feedback process from citizens to elected representatives. Fourth, the elected representatives can be informed of the different groups of citizens with different needs and their opinions about them.

Acknowledgements

This work has been partially supported by the Spanish Government under the project TIN2008-06570-C04-03 and the Consellería de Innovación e Industria - Xunta de Galicia under the project 08SIN06322PR.

References

Benitez B.A. et al, (2002), *Semantics of multimedia in MPEG-7*. IEEE International Conference on Image Processing , Vol. 1, pp. 137 -140.

Bloehdorn, S.; Simou, N.; Tzouvaras, V.; Petridis, K.; Handschuh, S.; Avrithis, Y.; Kompatsiaris, I.; Staab, S. and Strintzis, M.G. (2004), *Knowledge representation for semantic multimedia content analysis and reasoning*, proceedings of the European Workshop on the Integration of Knowledge, Semantics and Digital Media Technology, London, U.K.

Chang, S. F.; Sikora T. and Puri A. (2001), *Overview of the MPEG-7 standard*, IEEE Transactions on Circuits and Systems for Video Technology, Vol. 11, No.6, pp. 688-695.

Dapeng, Wu.; Yiwei, T. H. and Wenwu, Zhu. (2001), *Streaming Video over the Internet: Approaches and Directions*. IEEE Transactions on Circuits and Systems for Video Technology, Vol. 11, No. 3.

DCMI. Dublin Core Metadata Initiative (2000), *Dublin core qualifiers*, available at: http://dublincore.org/documents/2000/07/11/dcmes-qualifiers (accessed 3 May 2010).

Sánchez, N.E. and Chávez, G.F. (2007), *Description and Annotation of Legislative Multimedia Content using MPEG-7 Tools for Podcast Environments*, 1st International Conference on Methodologies, Technologies and Tools enabling e-Government (MeTTeG07), Camerino, Italy.

Loukis, E.; Wimmer, M.; Triantafillou, A.; Charalabidis, Y.; Gionis, G. and Gatautis, R. (2007), *A development of legislation through electronic support of participation: LEX-IS Proyect*, eChallenges 2007 Conference, European Commission, The Hague.

Hunter, J.; Drennan, J. and Little, S. (2004), *Realizing the hydrogen economy through semantic web technologies*, IEEE Intelligent Systems – special eScience issue.

Hare, J.S.; Sinclair, P.A.S.; Lewis, P.H.; Martinez, K.; Enser, P.G.B. and Sandom, C.J. (2006), *Bridging the Semantic Gap in Multimedia Information Retrieval: Top-down and Bottom-up approaches*, Mastering the Gap: From Information Extraction to Semantic Representation / 3rd European Semantic Web Conference, Budva, Montenegro.

Patterson, L.J. (2006), *The Technology Underlying Podcasts*. IEEE Computer, Vol. 39, No. 10, pp. 103-105.

Smeulders, A.W.M.; Worring, M.; Santini, S.; Gupta, A. and Jain, R. (2000), *Content-based image retrieval at the end of the early years*, Journal of IEEE Trans. Pattern Anal. Mach. Intell., Vol. 22, pp. 1349-1380.

Tsinaraki, C.; Polydoros, P. and Christodoloulakis, S. (2004), *Interoperability support for ontology-based video retrieval applications*, Proceedings of the Third International Conference on Image and Video Retrieval, Dublin, Ireland.

W3C (2004), *Resource Description Framework (RDF): Concepts and abstract syntax*, available at: http://www.w3.org/TR/rdf-concepts (accessed 3 May 2010).

The Ontomedia Project: ODR, Relational Justice, Multimedia

Marta Poblet[*], Pompeu Casanovas[°], José Manuel López-Cobo[#], Álvaro Cabrerizo[+],
Juan Antonio Prieto[+]

[*]UAB-Institute of Law and Technology-ICREA, Barcelona,
Spain
[°]UAB Institute of Law and Technology, Barcelona, Spain
[#]Playence KG, Innsbruck, Austria
[+]XimetriX Network Thoughts, Sevilla, Spain

Abstract. More than ever, the Web is a space of social interaction. Recent trends reveal that Internet users spend more time interacting within online communities than in checking and replying to e-mail. Online communities and institutions create new spaces for interaction, but also open new avenues for the emergence of grievances, claims, and disputes. Consequently, online dispute resolution (ODR) procedures are core to these new online worlds. But can ODR mechanisms provide sufficient levels of reputation, trust, and enforceability so as to become mainstream? This contribution introduces the new approaches to ODR with an emphasis on the Ontomedia Project, which is currently developing a web-based platform to facilitate online mediation in different domains

Keywords: Semantic Web, Online Dispute Resolution, ODR, Web 3.0, Web Services, Web-based platforms

1. Introduction: Relational Justice and ODR

Technology both fosters and participates actively in the process of transformation of law. Drafting, contracting, sentencing and administrative management have been enlarged with all the Online Dispute Resolution (ODR) initiatives and new forms of self-regulation and access to justice. Besides, the web fosters personalization. Citizens require a greater participation and faster and more effective ways of facing their legal activities. We will refer to these legal forms as *relational justice*.

In a broad sense, relational justice (RJ) may be defined first as the justice produced through cooperative behavior, agreement, negotiation, or dialogue among natural or artificial actors. The RJ field includes Alternative Dispute Resolution (ADR) and ODR, all forms of mediation (in commerce, labor, family, juvenile and adults' crimes, victim-offender …), restorative justice, transitional justice, community justice, family conferencing, and peace processes (Casanovas and Poblet, 2008).

From a technological point of view, RJ may be defined as well as the substantive and formal structure that allows users (citizens, consumers, customers, clients, managers, and officials) to participate in the making of their own regulation and legal outcomes through all the mixed and plural strategies of the Semantic Web framework. This implies the coexistence of legal and social norms, rights and duties to be shared by subjects (artificial or natural agents) in a flexible and dynamic structured environment (Casanovas, 2009).

There are rights to be protected and duties to be put in place. But these rights and duties belong to a new regulatory framework, because the networked information environment has definitively transformed the marketplace. The Internet is evolving towards a network of things (contents), and not only of linked websites. Cooperation, mobile use, crowdsourcing and services orientation constitute the next step for the World Wide Web.

This has been recently referred as to "the Metropolis model" (Kazman and Chei, 2009): "businesses are shifting from a 'goods-dominant' view, in which tangible output and discrete transactions are central, to a service dominant view, in which intangibility, exchange processes, and relationships are central". In the Metropolis model, service-dominant logic views customers not as passive but as proactive agents, "as co-creators of value".

The new regulatory landscape constitute the natural environment of the relational justice field, where scenarios and contexts are shaped from a hybrid use of different technologies by a multitude of different users (citizens, customers, officers, agents or MAS, Multi-Agent Systems). In the following sections, we will situate broadly the Ontomedia Project among the ODR developments.

2. Recent trends in Web 2.0

In the very spirit of its present developments, the notion of "Web 2.0" has a half-baked, conversational, and collaborative genealogy. Quoting Scott Dietzen, Eric Knorr welcomed Web 2.0 in December 2003 as a "universal, standards-based integration platform" (Knorr, 2003). Shortly after, the term popped up in a brainstorming session between Dale Dougherty (co-founder of O'Reilly Media) and Craig Cline, and reached larger audiences after the O'Reilly Media Web 2.0 conference in late 2004. The notion would then spread rapidly to become one of the most successful paradigms of the recent Internet era.

Perhaps as the clue of its nearly immediate success, there was neither clear consensus on what Web 2.0 was nor where the precise boundaries lied across. Again, and following discussions with other commenters, O'Reilly posted in a forum a compact definition of Web 2.0 which included as a chief rule for success "to build applications that harness network effects to get better the more people use them" (O'Reilly, 2006). And, indeed, as people started using them, the focus gradually shifted towards the social component of Web 2.0, to the point that Web 2.0 became equivalent to "the Social Web". Today's Social Web breeds an ever-growing number of online communities that share all types of contents (documents, images, videos, music, etc.), knowledge, and expertise in a number of areas. Some recent figures by Nielsen Online may give an idea of the impressive growth rate of online social communities: (i) from a time spent perspective, member communities surpassed e-mail for the first time in February 2009; (ii) previously, video audiences had already surpassed e-mail audiences in November 2007 (roughly 100 million users at the end of that year); (iii) "new moms" (younger, one child), are much more likely to visit social networking sites and publish or own a blog than most other online users". For instance, new moms "are 85% more likely to spend time with Facebook compared to the average online consumer" (Nielsen, 2009). To Nielsen analysts, "becoming a mother is a dramatic inflection point and drives women to the Web in search of advice and a desire to connect with others in her shoes".

To what extend are these trends relevant for online dispute resolution (ODR)? Is ODR to become the default justice system of the Social Web in the next future? Furthermore, can ODR mechanisms provide sufficient levels of reputation, trust, and enforceability so as to become main stream? Clearly, online communities and electronic institutions create new spaces for interaction, but also open new avenues for the emergence of grievances, claims, and disputes. In the pages that follow we will try to offer some answers by providing some recent examples and describing our particular contribution to the field, the Ontomedia project.

3. ODR 2.0

Ricoh Online Dispute Resolution (ODR) is an umbrella domain that covers a full range of processes (i.e. negotiation, early neutral evaluation, conciliation, mediation, and arbitration) to handle disputes online. While it was sometimes viewed as the online equivalent of ADR (Alternative Dispute Resolution) processes, there is a growing consensus in specialized literature that considers ODR more than just the delivery of alternative dispute resolution (ADR) services through the Internet, especially since Ethan Katsh (2001) first suggested giving technology the role of a "four party".

In this line, the emergence of a vast range of both new terminologies and typologies to systematize current ODR practices proves that the domain is becoming a branch of dispute resolution in its own right. Especially when the judicial system alternative is perceived too costly or inappropriate for a number of reasons (nature and/or value of the dispute, physical location of the parties, etc.) ODR has the potential to become an efficient default system. This is precisely the case for online communities such as e-Bay, whose dispute resolution services deal with roughly 40 million cases each year (Rule, 2008). Overall, in recent research on ODR services we have identified up to twenty major service providers, most of them working on private schemes (Poblet et al., 2009a) (Fig. 1). Even though they differ significantly on case figures, procedures, or business models, they all tend to deal with small value claims and procedural costs can be kept relatively low. In contrast, and with some exception (Gabarró, 2009) little is known on users' satisfaction towards ODR services.

In 2006, Colin Rule welcomed 2.0 technologies and forecasted that "ODR will be one of the biggest beneficiaries of these new technologies, because they are squarely aimed at ODR's core functionality areas: communication, collaboration, and interactivity" (Rule, 2006). However, he also warned that "too many ODR providers rely on outdated platforms and technology because they are reluctant to make the investments in time and resources needed to bring their platforms up to Web 2.0 standards" (Hattotuwa, 2008a). Sanjanah Hattotuwa (2008b) went a step further anticipating unwanted consequences of ODR lagging behind the curve of Web 2.0,

"[T]he most obvious being that ODR itself may cease to exist. With the ubiquity of broadband wired and wireless connectivity, the ability to roll-out dispute resolution service online is possibly going to be seen as a normal service provision of ADR service providers, just like automated online tech support is now part and parcel of customer support mechanisms of many large software companies."

Generally, the current platforms that populate the ODR market have in common some basic features: proprietary software, stable versions, PC-based, and predetermined roles (i.e. the services provider, the mediator, the parties, etc.). Beyond these common traits, ODR services differ in scope (either addressed to specific domains or open to any type of dispute), techniques offered (assisted negotiation, mediation, conciliation, recommendation, arbitration, etc.), degree of sophistication (from facilitating online forms and procedures to case management, assignment of online mediators, or professional training), communication channels (synchronic, asynchronic, or both) and business models. Recently, some fifteen ODR service providers have been reviewed by the CEN in order to facilitate interoperability schemes (CEN 2009) Table 1 below summarizes basic features of twenty ODR providers.

Table 1. Basic features of ODR service providers. Source: CWBM, Poblet et al. (2009a)

Products	AdR&eS	BBB	Cyber Settle eBay	Der Internet Ombudsmann	DisputeManager	ECODIR	Electronic Courthouse	iQuas Confianza Online	Juripax	MARS	Mediateur du net	Mediation Room	National Arbitration Forum	Net Neutrals	ODRWorld	PayPal	Risolvi Online	Smart Settle	Square Trade
Owner	WebMediaNet	Council of Better Business Bureaus	CyberSettle	Der Internet Ombudsman	Singapore Mediation Centre	European Commission	Electronic Courthouse	AECEM AUTOCONTROL Confianza Online Consorcios Audiovisuales Red.es	Juripax	MARS	Le Forum des droits sur l'internet	Mediation Room	National Arbitration Forum	NetNeutrals & Ass.	ODRWorld	PayPal	Milano Chamber Commerce	iCan Systems	Square Trade
Country	USA	USA, Can	USA	Austria	Singapur	Europe	USA	Spain, Andorra	Holland	USA	France	UK	USA	USA	UK, India	US	Italy	USA	USA
Domain	e-T	e-T	G	e-T	e-T, dn	e-T	G	e-T, dn, Iar	G	e-T	e-T, dn, Iar	G	G	T	G	e-T	e-T	G	Gel
Negotiation	X	X	X		X	X	X		X			X		X	X	X	X	X	
Mediation	X	X	X		X	X	X		X	X	X	X	X	X	X	X	X	X	X
Arbitration	X	X	X	X	X		X		X	X		X	X	X	X		X	X	X
Complaints	X	X	X	X	X		X		X			X	X	X	X			X	X
Conciliation																			X
Recommendation	X				X	X	X	X			X	X	X	X	X		X	X	X
Mediators' roast	X	X		X	X					X		X		X				X	X
Trustmark	X				X					X		X	4	X				X	
Training		1			X			2		X		3							
Other services	X	X	X		X	X	X	X	X	X	X	X	X	X	X	X	X	X	X
Control of flows	X	X	X				X	X	X	X		X		X	X			X	
Registry of cases	X	X	X				X	X	X	X		X		X	X	X	X	X	
Structured forms	X	X			X	X	X	X						X	X		X	X	X
Messages to parties	X	X	X		X	X	X	X	X	X	X	X	X	X	X	X	X	X	
Asynchronous communication																			
Synchronic communication (chat, videoconference)		X	X		X			X	X	X		X	X	X	X		X	X	
Confidential registries		X	X			X	X	X				X		X			X	X	
Optimization algorithm																		X	
Cross-offers algorithm		X	X		X		X	X		X	X					X	X	X	
Web provider	X	X	X	X	X	X	X	X		X	X	X		X		X	X		
ODR simplified	X	X	X		X	X	X			X		X	X		X				X
Sophisticated ODR																			
Licenses selling																		X	X

G generic domains   e-T electronic Transactions (B2C, B2B, C2C)   dn. Domain names   Iar Internet related rights (privacy, access, copyright)   T eBay specific transactions   Gel Electric appliances guarantees

Other services   1. Standards   2. Premediation   3. Psychometric profiling   4. Express mediation and arbitration

ODR services do not only provide the framework, the tools, and the procedures to deal with disputes, but also create their own "soft law", precedents, and even enforcement mechanisms: in eBay, buyers and sellers may submit their dispute to the Paypal Resolution Center, which will be able to block the money transfers until a consensual decision is reached or the Center delivers a final decision; in the Wikipedia, where mediation is normally used for disputes about article content and arbitration mostly applies to disputes about user conduct, editors can temporarily or indefinitely blocked depending on the seriousness of the case.

New horizons and opportunities for ODR have incredibly expanded over the last three years with the emergence of new web tools and services focusing on conflict prevention, conflict tracking, debate, or negotiation. For the sake of clarity, we will distinguish here two different sets of tools: (i) open source platforms and (ii) mashups. Even though different in nature and purpose, they all have in common featured aspects of state-of-the-art Web 2.0: open source software, free access, multiplatform facilities, and crowdsourced data.

2.1. OPEN SOURCE PLATFORMS

– *Ushahidi* —"testimony" in Swahili— is a free, open source platform that allows its users to gather distributed data via SMS, email or web and visualize it on a map or timeline.[1] Through Ushahidi people report real time information of events such as political disruption or natural disasters and the platform aggregates this incoming information for use in a crisis response. The website was created at the beginning of 2008 as a simple mashup, using user-generated reports and Google Maps to map reports of violence in Kenya after the post-election fallout. Ushahidi has recently released the open Beta version of its platform and has been used in different projects in India, Congo, and South Africa.
– *Swift* is a free and open source toolset for crowdsourced situational awareness.[2] The first use of Swift has been as a complement to Ushahidi to monitor the Indian 2009 Elections. Swift embraces Semantic Web open standards such as FOAF, iCal, Dublin Core, as well as open publishing endpoints such as Freebase to add structure to crisis data and make them shareable.
– *RapidSMS* is an open source web-based platform for data collection, logistics coordination, and communication developed by the Innovations and Development team of UNICEF.[3] With the RapidSMS web interface,

---

[1] http://www.ushahidi.com/
[2] http://swiftapp.org/
[3] http://www.unicefinnovation.org/mobile-and-sms.php

multiple users can simultaneously access the system to view incoming data as it arrives, export new data-sets, and send text messages to users.

2.2. MASHUPS

- *Vikalpa* is a Sri Lanka citizen journalism initiative that in May 2008 launched a micro-site on Twitter with short reports on election related violence and malpractices. Reports were generated by the citizen journalist network in the Eastern Province of the country.4 The micro-blogging initiative was complemented with a Google Maps based solution for the Centre for Monitoring Election Violence (CMEV) to locate election related incidents on a map (Hattotuwa, 2008b).
- *WarViews*: Visualizing and Animating Geographic Data on Conflict. WarViews is a project of The Swiss Federal Institute of Technology that has developed an interface for the exploration of GIS data on conflict. WarViews is offered in two different versions: a static version that runs in a web browser and allows the user to switch between different data sets, and a dynamic version based on Google Earth that can time-animate geographic data such that the development over time can be monitored (Weidmann et al., 2009). WarViews targets both researchers and practitioners in the conflict management and resolution domains.
- *WikiCrimes* is an initiative at the University of Fortaleza (Brazil) that allows posting and accessing criminal occurrences in a Google map.

4. The Ontomedia Project

People in need for help and assistance —as the new mums example shows— look for help in social communities and specialized web sites. This is where Ontomedia aims at contributing. From the Ontomedia standpoint, both Web 2.0 and Web 3.0 technologies can make significant advances into the ODR field, helping professionals to gather resources relevant to the mediation services they are providing, and helping users to share and contribute to harness the connective intelligence about ODR that can be found on the Web.

The main objective of Ontomedia is to allow users and professionals to meet in a community-driven Web portal where contents are provided by users. Nevertheless, our focus is on mediation users (mediators and parties) rather than on content itself. Thus, and following a consumer-first approach (Gabarró, 2009) we expect mediation users to create the contents and the

---

4 http://www.vikalpa.org/archives/category/languages/english/

semantics that reflect how present their cases, how they interact with the mediators and the other parties, and how they experience the mediation process. While Ontomedia works with a Core Mediation Ontology (CMO) (Poblet, 2009b) that models the main concepts and relationships in mediation, we intend not to anticipate the needs of the users and impose formal semantic structures in advance. Rather, our aim is let the users define their needs and then elaborate semantic models that evolve as a by-product of the mediation processes.

We have described elsewhere the core-ontology (Poblet et al. 2009b) and the functionalities of Ontomedia (information, repository, training, communication, management) (Poblet et al. 2010). Fig. 1 shows a fragment of the ontology (phases of mediation):

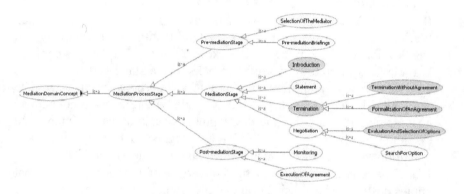

Figure 1: Fragment of the Ontomedia ontology in successive stages

Ontomedia assists mediation users and professionals assistance at different levels:

– **Information retrieval on previous cases**. Users and mediators will be able to consult previous cases, duly anonymized to ensure privacy and compliance with current legislation. Retrieval will be enhanced by one or more ontologies.
– **Definition of a case**. To control the mediation process, the Core Mediation Ontology (CMO) models the basic concepts and relationships in mediation and creates templates to guide users and mediators throughout the process.
– **Mediation**. Ontomedia will have videoconferencing facilities including different tools to provide mediators with information on the mood of the users (analyzing their voice, their movements, and their reactions).
– **Annotation**. The system will be able to annotate the contents of the multimedia objects, being those texts, video, audio objects. These

annotations will be further used to categorized and increase the case corpus. The annotations will be automatically realized against a set of ontologies on mediation and about the specific sub-domains.

– **Tagging**. Ontomedia needs its users to enhance the contents. Every piece of information is susceptible of being tagged, creating thus mediation folksonomies that can be later used also in the information retrieval stage. Users will be able to tag, comment and suggest, creating online communities around their cases and their problems.

Fig. 2 shows the overall Ontomedia cycle:

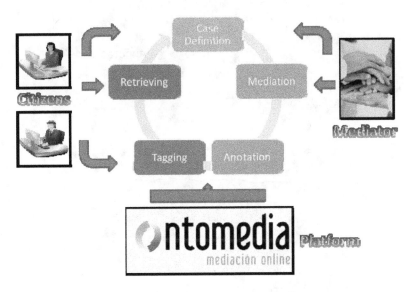

Figure 2. Ontomedia case lifecycle

5. Web Oriented Architecture, enhanced interaction and Multimedia

Mediation users and professionals can use any kind of devices to access the portal (computers, mobiles), and in any format suitable to their purposes (text, speech, video, pictures). Users will therefore be able to participate in online mediation services as they do in a face-to-face basis, but with the advantages of distributed and even remote access.

In Ontomedia we also foresee the application of mediation services as tasks within a mediation process that will be formally described by means of both process ontologies and mediation ontologies. These services will be described, stored and made accessible through a service bus that will ensure end to end communication between consumers and providers, as well as a semantic execution engine that takes care of the execution of semantically enhanced mediation processes.

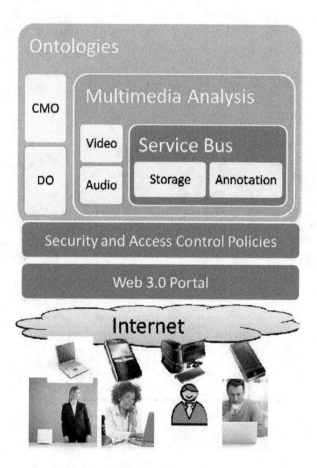

Figure 3: Ontomedia layered architcture

Ontologies will be used to annotate and analyze any type of content. The multimedia analysis aims at enhancing the information a mediator receives during a mediation session, capturing mood changes of the parties and any other psychological information inputs. All types of metadata will be automatically extracted and stored to be further used within the mediation process.

Ontomedia will also develop tools to invite users to exploit the advantages of sharing information and experiences with others. In this way, users will be able to tag and store content that are useful or interesting to them, and to find similar cases. In doing so, they will be able to create social communities of people with common interests. And, related to those utilities, Ontomedia will provide a mashable suite of features that will allow users to locate similar cases to theirs. The semantic geographical location of those cases and its representation in a map is a trivial feature.

What seems more interesting from a user perspective is the possibility to have tag clouds of concepts related with each case and a timeline of concepts against a case. The set of Web 3.0 features that will be enabled and accessible to users of the ONTOMEDIA platform can be summarized here:

1. *Annotation of all types of contents.* With this feature, a user can easily know if another case has some conceptual similarity with hers. Given a case, a useful visualization feature is the representation of those concepts more relevant in a case as a tag cloud. Just clicking in one concept or other in the tag cloud will show you a set of cases that also are related to that concept.

2. Jointly with the annotation, *some metadata extraction is automatically conducted,* including geographical position of cases, time location and named entity recognition: (i) geo-location allows users to track similar cases, given the set of concepts related to the issues. The tag cloud will always show the concepts that are relevant to cases appearing in the map. Categorization and segmentation will be possible by means of several icons and with just a glimpse the user of the platform will have a tool for visualization and conceptual identification; (ii) with time location, users will have a timeline. Timelines can show the location of cases against time with respect a particular concept (the apparition of a case related to a concept in a particular time). With this feature, users will be able to see the evolution of the frequency of cases where a concept is concerned; (iii) where NER (Named Entity Recognition) is concerned, the platform will be able to detect where well-known entities are mentioned.

3. In Ontomedia, well-known entities are *concepts that transcend domain ontologies* like person names, organizations, dates, places, figures and some others. The power behind this feature is that doing so, we will be able to connect well-know entities with well-know facts as those defined with the LOD (Linked Open Data) principles (Berners-Lee, 2006). Where the name of a person is mentioned, if it exists, we will retrieve her FOAF5

---

[5] FOAF. Friend of a Friend. http://www.foaf-project.org/

profile. Where a place is mentioned, we will extract the GeoName6 information available, and so on. This information can be used within Ontomedia to add formal restrictions and reason over it. Each concept, each piece of information, each resource is susceptible to have a comment from any user. Users are encouraged to participate within the platform and to build it jointly with other users, as professional mediators are as well. From this second point of view, multimedia content and management constitute an important issue.

Let's go this last issue. Managing mediation is far from easy. Empathy, emotions, culture and professional practice shape the interactions and the communicative flow. It has been much discussed recently whether emotions alter face-to-face interactions when they are computer-mediated. We recently established the state of the art (Poblet and Casanovas, 2007). Several studies have shown that emotional content situates and intensifies the strength of cognitive and expressive skills (Ben Ze'ev, 2004). Thus, linguistic rationality is not the single kernel of the argumentation process. Rational arguments go through what the ancient rhetoric knew as *stasis* and *ekphrasis*, based on the perceptual and visual behavior among participants (Casanovas, 2010).

What we are building up in Ontomedia, then, are some devices to visualize emotions through facial reading, and some ways to reconstruct the visual abduction of narratives (Gracia et al. 2010a, 2010b). As the reader will see in the next papers in this same volume, we are following two different strategies: (i) diarization, and (ii) semantic annotation (González-Conejero, 2010). In this way, the mediator may have some additional non-intuitive information about the distance of the agreement and the feelings of the participants.

Still, empowering professional mediators' skills is not an easy task, and we have no evidence yet about whether or not these tools will be useful and used. Moreover, this attempt is not free of ethical issues and concerns about privacy, neutrality and impartiality. However, even in this exploratory stage, we think that this is the kind of knowledge that is needed to enhance relational justice through the web.

6. Conclusions

Despite the conceptual vagueness of the definitions, both Web 2.0 and Web 3.0 developments offer new forms to interact with the Web that are most relevant to ODR. To be sure, some of their critical features—openness, standardization, free access, connectedness, crowdsourcing

---

[6] Geonames. http://www.geonames.org/about.html

effects, etc.— make it possible to enrich ODR services in a wider perspective. The Ontomedia project attempts to learn from these innovations so as to provide an easy-to-use web platform for both mediation domain experts and end-users. A distinctive aspect of Ontomedia, nevertheless, is the application of Semantic Web technologies to enhance online mediation processes. On the one hand, Ontomedia will use basic ontologies to annotate any kind of content (either textual or multimedia) to facilitate users to participate in the process and search any useful information on related cases. On the other, a semantic execution engine will take care of the execution of the semantically enhanced mediation processes.

Acknowledgements

The research presented in this paper has been developed within the framework of two different projects: (i) ONTOMEDIA: Platform of Web Services for Online Mediation, Spanish Ministry of Industry, Tourism and Commerce (Plan AVANZA I+D, TSI-020501-2008, 2008-2010); (ii) ONTOMEDIA: Semantic Web, Ontologies and ODR: Platform of Web Services for Online Mediation (2009-2011), Spanish Ministry of Science and Innovation (CSO-2008-05536-SOCI).

References

Ben Ze'ev, A. (2004), *Love Online: Emotions on the Internet*, Cambridge University Press.

Berners-Lee, T. (2006), *Linked Data*, available at http://www.w3.org/DesignIssues/LinkedData.html (accessed 1 September 2009).

Casanovas, P., Poblet, M. (2008), *Concepts and Fields of Relational Justice*, in P. Casanovas, G. Sartor, N. Casellas, R. Rubino, "Computable Models of the La. Languages, Dialogues, Games, Ontologies", LNAI 4884, Ed. Springer, Heidelberg, Berlin, pp. 323-335.

Casanovas, P. (2009), *The Future of Law: Relational Justice and Next Generation of Web Services*, in M. Fernández-Barrera, N. Nunes Gomes de Andrade, P. de Filippi, M. Viola de Azevedo Cunha, G. Sartor, P. Casanovas (Eds.), European Press Academic Publishing, Florence, pp. 137-156.

Casanovas, P. (2010a), *Legal Electronic Institutions and Ontomedia: Dialogue, Inventio, and Relational Justice Scenarios,* in Casanovas P., Pagallo U., Sartor G., Ajani G. (Eds.), "AI Approaches to the Complexity of Legal Systems" *(AICOL I-II*, LNAI 6237, Springer Verlag.

Gabarró, S. (2009) *Online Dispute Resolution in e-Commerce: A Study of European ODR Providers Offering Mediation in B2C*. MA Thesis, available at http://idt.uab.es/publications/publications.htm (accessed 12 August 2009).

González-Conejero, J. (2010), *Legal Multimedia. Management and Semantic Annotation for Improved Search and Retrieval,* in this same volume (*Intelligent Multimedia*).

Gracia, C.; Binefa, X.; Poblet, M. (2010a). *Emotional Speech Analysis in the Mediation and Court Environments*, in this same volume (*Intelligent Multimedia*).

Gracia, C.; Binefa, X.; Casanovas, P. (2010b), *Diarization for the Annotation of Legal Videos*, in this same volume (*Intelligent Multimedia*).

Hattotuwa, S. (2008) *The Future of Online Dispute Resolution (ODR): Technologies to Keep an Eye On*, Crystal Ball Session at the 2008 Online Dispute Resolution Forum, June 22, 2008, available at: http://ict4peace.wordpress.com/2008/06/ (accessed 13 May 2009).

Hattotuwa, (2008), S. *Maps of election violence and malpractices in Eastern province elections*, 10th May, http://ict4peace.wordpress.com/2008/05/10/maps-of-election-violence-and-malpractices-eastern-province-elections-sri-lanka-10th-may-2008/

Katsh, E., Rifkin, J. (2001), *Online Dispute Resolution: Resolving Conflicts in Cyberspace*. Jossey-Bass Inc., San Francisco.

Kazman, R., H-M Chen, H.M. (2009), *The Metropolis Model: A New Logic for the Development of Crowdsourced Systems*, Communications of the ACM, July, pp. 78-84.

Knorr, E. (2003) *2004 - The Year of Web Services*, IT magazine CIO, December 2003, p. 90, available at http://www.cio.com/article/32050/2004_The_Year_of_Web_Services?page=1 (accessed 1 September 2009).

Nielsen Online (2009), *The global online media landscape: Identifying opportunities in a challenging market*, April 2009, available at http://nielsen-online.com/emc/0904_report/nielsen-online-global-lanscapefinal1.pdf (accessed 12 May 2009).

O'Reilly, T. (2006) *Web 2.0 Compact Definition: Trying Again*, available at http://radar.oreilly.com/archives/2006/12/web-20-compact.html (accessed 12 May 2009).

Poblet M., Casanovas P. (2007), *Emotions in ODR*, International Review of Law, Computers & Technology, Vol. 21, Num. 2, pp. 145-155.

Poblet, M., Noriega, P., López, C., Suquet, J. (2009a) *ODR y mediación en línea: estado del arte y escenarios de uso*. In P. Casanovas, J. Magre, L. Díaz, M. Poblet (eds.) "Materiales para el Libro Blanco de Mediación en Cataluña". Barcelona, Generalitat de Catalunya, Colección Justicia y Sociedad, pp. 159-169.

Poblet, M., Casellas, N., Torralba, S., Casanovas, P. (2009b) *Modelling Expert Knowledge in the Mediation Domain: A Mediation Core Ontology*. Proceedings of the Workshop on Legal Ontologies and Artificial Intelligence Techniques (LOAIT09), available at http://ftp.informatik.rwth-aachen.de/Publications/CEUR-WS/Vol-465/ (accessed 1 September 2009).

Poblet, M., Casanovas P, López-Cobo M, Cabrerizo, A, Prieto J.A (2010), *Mediation, ODR, and the Web 2.0: A Case for Relational Justice* , in Casanovas P., Pagallo U., Sartor G., Ajani G. (Eds.), "AI Approaches to the Complexity of Legal Systems" *(AICOL I-II*, LNAI 6237, Springer Verlag.

Rule, C. (2006), *ODR and Web 2.0*, available at http://www.odr.info/colin/smu/odr%20and%20web%202.doc (accessed 11 May 2009).

Rule, C. (2008) *Making Peace on eBay: Resolving Disputes in the World's Largest Marketplace*, ACResolution Magazine, Fall

Sweeney, P. (2009), *Consumer-First to Build the Semantic Web*, available at http://corp.primalfusion.com/blog/?p=109 (accessed 4 September 2009).

Weidmann , N.B., Kuse, D. *WarViews: Visualizing and Animating Geographic Data on Civil War*. International Studies Perspectives, Vol. 10 Num. 1, pp. 36-48 (2009).

Emotional Speech Analysis in Mediation and Court Environments

Ciro Gracia[*], Xavier Binefa[*], Marta Poblet[°]
[*]*Universitat Pompeu Fabra, Barcelona*
[°] *ICREA Researcher at the UAB Institute of Law and Technology, Universitat Autònoma de Barcelona*

Abstract. When people communicate, their states of mind are coupled with the explicit content of the messages being transmitted. The implicit information conveyed by mental states is essential to correctly understand and frame the communication messages. In mediation, professional mediators include empathy as a fundamental skill when dealing with the relational and emotional aspects of a case. In court environments, emotion analysis intends to point out stress or fear as indicators of the truthfulness of certain asserts. In commercial environments, such as call-centers, automatic emotional analysis through speech is focused to detect deception or frustration. Computational analysis of emotions focuses on gathering information from speech, facial expressions, body poses and movements to predict emotional states. Specifically, speech analysis has been reported as a valuable procedure for emotional state recognition. While some studies focus on the analysis of speech features to classify emotional states, others concentrate on determining the optimal classification performance. In this paper we analyze current approaches to computational analysis of emotions through speech and consider the replication of their techniques and findings in the domains of mediation and legal multimedia.

Keywords: Emotions, Speech, Legal Multimedia, Legal Discourse, Signal Processing, Pattern Recognition.

1. Introduction

The study of cognitive and social aspects of human emotions has proved most successful during the last decades. In fact, the ability to infer others' emotional states has been pointed out as a fundamental skill in many commercial and social scenarios, where human relationship aspects have a critical weight. In the dispute resolution domain and, more specifically, in the mediation field, professional mediators use their ability to recognize emotions to improve or promote dialog between parties, thus fostering potential agreements. A good mediator is someone expected to equally work with both the emotional and relational aspects of a case, beyond the commonly known issues of the matter.

In law enforcement scenarios, as in legal multimedia, there is interest for detecting evidences of stress in voice. It is known that persons under stress suffer physical symptoms, as muscular micro-temblors in the speech production apparatus, which are reflected in the speech signal. Measuring this stress evidences provides information about possible untruthfulness or degree of potential threat in a flexible and non intrusive way. These applications are especially interesting because some emotional states fall into the sympathetic nervous system, producing an almost universal mechanical and predictable response.

Emotional speech recognition can be specifically related to the field of automatic emotion analysis, within the broad area of human-computer interaction (HCI). Automatic emotion analysis merges computer science techniques coming from the pattern recognition field, with other different areas of knowledge, such as psychology, neurology, or linguistic analysis, thus becoming a promising and interdisciplinary research field.

From a pattern recognition point of view, the analysis of human emotions is a relatively new field. Piccard published in 1997 an essay on affective computing which introduced the world of emotions and its roles inside human-computer communication (Picard, 1997). The idea of being capable of recognizing the emotional state of humans by analyzing its non verbal communication attracted the interest of pattern recognition researchers all over the world. Strategies using different sources of information, as speech analysis, facial expression, body movements and pose, were therefore introduced and experimentally studied.

Amongst those different approaches, we will focus our attention on the analysis of human speech. Human communication is heavily based on speech which, in many cases, also contains a fundamental part of human non-verbal communication, coded, for example, in elements such as intonation patterns, loudness, and a wide collection of other behavioral cues. Additionally, with the coming of digital multimedia, speech became one of the most cheap and flexible data sources for analysis. It also provided an easy, non-intrusive way to obtain emotional samples and data to be analyzed, even beating in this sense video recordings, where the presence of a camera pointing at a subject affects things as its reactions or its predisposition for showing its emotional states.

Emotion analysis from speech uses different methods for analyzing the speech signal, generally focusing on the non-verbal aspects of the speech. The analysis is complex insofar speech mixes verbal and non-verbal communication and, although both are—to some extent—independent from each other, there is still discussion about the lines separating them.

Advances in emotion recognition require databases for training, testing and validation. Several databases have been constructed, within different scenarios and with a range of different languages, most of them released from year 2000 onwards (Ververidis and Kotropulos, 2006). In section 2 we include a brief description of the factors describing emotional databases and the complexity of emotional database construction. In section 3 we describe some major approaches to signal processing techniques in order to obtain useful features, which are a discrete set of descriptors of the audio stream, for the task of emotion recognition. Section 4 contains a description of the recent approaches to feature selection and a classification used for speech emotion recognition. Finally, Section 5 shows experimental results of automatic techniques for emotion recognition. Based on these results, we discuss the replication of this techniques and findings in the domains of mediation and legal multimedia.

2. Emotional Databases

Emotional speech databases must take into account a set of factors in order not to bias or introduce distortion in data. Elements defining the scope of the database, the variety of contexts of the data, requirements of applicability, naturalness of emotions, copyrights and manual data labelling are not easy to conjugate. In fact, the existing surveys can be divided in two classes: those summarising and comparing the newly appearing databases, and those who shade light into the problems and decisions for constructing adequate emotion speech databases (Ververidis and Kotropulos, 2003, 2006; Douglas-Cowie *et al.*, 2003).

Among the factors affecting the database construction decisions are the number of speakers, the language and gender of the speakers, their dialects, and most important, the emotions to be included and how to obtain them truthfully. The emotional categories present in real life constitute a very complex taxonomy that can grow up to 64 classes. This variety notwithstanding, the research on emotional speech recognition has to be limited to certain emotions to be operational. Thus, most of the emotional speech data collections usually encompass no more than five or six emotions. Furthermore, as it is commonly agreed on, there are some primitive emotions that are more universal than others.

In practice, most of the available databases rely on models that describe the basic axis of an emotion. Most of them include emotions such as fear, sadness, joy, anger or neutrality. Figure 1 below shows a model for emotion categorisation frequently used in the computer science world (Osgood *et al*, 1957). According to this model, the computation of emotions is conceptualized as involving three major dimensions of connotative meaning: arousal, valence, and power.

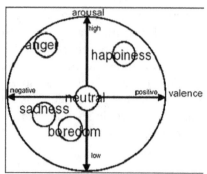

Figure 1: Basic emotional states projected on the arousal and valence axis

The easiest way to collect emotional speech is by having actors simulating such desired emotions. The difficulty regarding this approach is that, strikingly enough, so little is known about the relationship between faked and spontaneous emotional speech. There are many reasons to suspect that there are systematic differences between acted and natural emotional speech, such as the differences already reported in the natural and posed facial expressions from visual cues (Valstar *et al.*, 2007). Acted speech is often "previously thought", not improvised—as most of the human speech is—leading to unnatural smoothness in the word flow: a "read" speech effect, which is known to have distinctive characteristics respect to spontaneous speech. It also typically takes place in a non-interactive monologue, so that interpersonal effects are not present. Some studies show that well acted emotional speech can be classified by humans, showing high accuracy for some emotions like anger, boredom or interest. Nevertheless, the differences from posed and non-posed speech and the ability of humans to distinguish them are not yet referred. In any case, for such a study, a database containing spontaneous speech examples would be required for an appropriate comparison.

Collecting spontaneous emotional speech is therefore not an easy task, since makes it difficult to fulfil some further requirements: namely, phonetic balance, required for some speech synthesis techniques, the control of the words and expressions used, or having similar recording sets and acquisition environments. Lost of spontaneity is the price of consistent analysis. Other problems arise from ethics and copyright issues, particularly with natural data. Natural emotional data are often very personal, and subjects may object to allow its diffusion. Radio and television provide rich sources, as chat shows and documentaries do, but their use also raises serious copyright problems. A long-term solution to these problems may be 'bootstrapping', or using truly natural material to guide the production of material that is acted, but genuinely close to nature.

Labelling and describing emotional databases also remain difficult tasks. Sometimes there is a varying emotional intensity, a coincidence of different emotions, different interpretations of the expression shown (depending on the person listening to the audio), etc. Unfaithfulness of the labelling puts statistic tractability of data within a compromise. A common reference method for labelling is to let different people classify emotional speech and only keep samples showing at least a certain degree of consensus.

Other contextual variables referring to the emotional database construction problem are expressed next. First, the modality of data: facial expressions shown in visual information carry fundamental information for emotion recognition. Then, including or not visual information will be an important variable. Secondly, there is the language used in the database: since different languages produce different phonetic and acoustic features, the studies based on the acoustic features will produce different models and different results. Furthermore, many signs of emotion are often defined by syntactic patterns and emotionally marked words, which depend on the language. For example, a study of English words with 'emotional connotation' can be found in the Semantic Atlas of Emotional Concepts (Averill, 1975). Thirdly, the recording setup: different microphones or the level of noise present during the recording affects the performance and generality of the different methods.

Finally, the accessibility of the constructed database is a key factor in order to promote research, algorithm comparison over same data, and to drive progress towards a better understanding and automatic handling of emotional speech.

3. Audio Signal Features Describing Emotional Speech

The first step towards automatic speech emotion classification is to extract relevant and measurable characteristics from the raw audio stream: the spectrogram. The selection of such features is crucial since their objective is to greatly reduce the amount of data to be analysed but still retain all the information relevant for emotion detection.

In fact, a wide variety of characteristics describing speech signal can be computed. Some are focused in short time statistics of spectrogram, while others reflect vocal tract description. Most of them are based on short term analysis of speech signal, which is very common in signal processing and automatic speech recognition. Also, most of the features are related to intonation characteristics, its temporal evolution or its short term basic statistics including mean, variance, maximum and minimum of several variables. Pitch (also known as F0) is a very important element, since both its tracking along the different time samples and its mean value strongly determine some of the stress emotions such as anger or fear. Other features related to speech recognition have been explored and try to estimate vocal tract characteristics that reflect phonetic content. Mel Filtered Cepstral Coefficients have been one of the most successful features in speech recognition due to its capability of representing human auditory response. Obtaining a clear vocal tract response improves the quality of the information about articulation effort, a characteristic of stressed voice. Different studies analyze and compare a wide range of features and its capability to classify basic emotions given a fixed classifier (Ververidis, Kotropoulos and Pitas, 2004). Yet, there is still much discussion on which features can be valuable to efficiently recognise basic emotional states. This motivates an exhaustive analysis, using feature selection algorithms to determine optimal feature sets for the multiclass emotion recognition task.

3.1 VOICE STRESS CHARACTERISTICS

Voice Stress Analysis (VSA) technology has already been introduced to the deceit detection field. It has been originated from the concept of micro muscle tremors (MMT) which was considered to be a source of stress detection. In moments of stress, especially if a person is exposed to jeopardy, the body prepares itself for fight or flight by increasing the readiness of its muscles to spring into action. This in turns causes the muscle vibrations to increase.

The micro tremors occur in the muscles that construct the vocal tract, being transmitted also through the speech. Voice stress studies cover a wide range of natural stressed speech origins, from dangerous situations, as aircraft/helicopter cockpit recordings, astronauts communications, law enforcement, emergencies call centres, etc. In general, stressed voice reflects some of the Lombard effect characteristics which include the involuntary tendency of speakers to increase the intensity of their voice to enhance its audibility, increasing phonetic fundamental frequencies and shifting formant centre frequencies. Pitch (F0) has been one of the most successfully studied acoustic descriptors of stressed speech. Short term perturbations, long term variability and higher mean value of F0 value reflects a significant increase with the stress level (F0 range can increase by even 3 octaves), but include large individual differences.

3.2 OTHER EMOTION CUES

Contour trends (Ververidis and Kotropoulos, 2006) are one of the fundamental tools to study the temporal evolution of the signal characteristics. Contour trends reflect some physical semantics on certain emotions. For example, pitch and intensity trends can be extracted in several ways by segmenting the signal in turns levels or syllabic units.

Inside each segment, statistics about its mean value, its rising or falling slope and plateaux are extracted and analysed. The speech rate is defined as the inverse duration of the voiced part of speech. The number of syllabic units in time is also used for the detection of certain emotion cues.

For example, anger usually produces higher energy and pitch levels. Differences between genders are remarkable in terms of the intensity of the energy and speech levels and in the speech rate: males express anger with slow speech rate while females employ fast speech rate under similar circumstances. In contrast, disgust and sadness usually show a low pitch level and a flat-like pitch contour.

The emotional state of fear is correlated with a high pitch level and a raised intensity level. Figure 2 summarize some basic cues for basic emotions covered in the emotional database of the University of Maribor

Table I. Cues analyzed by using 26 different features (DSPLAB of the University of Maribor)			
	Values over average	Value near average	Value near average
Anger	Mean F0 Maximal F0 Standard deviation of DF0 Duration of syllables	Duration of fricatives	Duration of vocals Duration of plosives Duration of consonants Minimal DF0
Disgust	Duration of fricatives	Duration of vocals Duration of consonants Duration of plosives	Mean F0 Maximal F0 Duration of syllables Maximal DF0 DF0 range
Fear	Maximal DF0 Duration of plosives	DF0 range Duration of fricatives	Mean F0 Maximal F0 Minimal DF0 Standard deviation of DF0 Duration of syllables Duration of vocals Duration of consonants
Neutral (slow/soft)	Maximal F0 Standard deviation of DF0 Maximal DF0 DF0 range	Mean F0 Duration of vocals	Duration of syllables Duration of plosives Duration of fricatives Duration of consonants
Joy	Mean F0 Maximal F0 Standard deviation of DF0 Duration of syllables	Minimal DF0	Duration of vocals Duration of fricatives Duration of consonants Duration of plosives
Neutral (fast/loud)	Maximal DF0 DF0 range Duration of plosives	Duration of syllables Standard deviation of DF0 Duration of vocals	Mean F0 Duration of syllables
Surprise	Mean F0 Maximal F0 Minimal DF0 Standard deviation of DF0 Mean F03 Duration of syllables		Duration of vocals Duration of fricatives Duration of consonants Duration of plosives
Sadness	Duration of fricatives Duration of consonants Duration of plosives		Mean F0 Maximal F0 Minimal DF0 Standard deviation of DF0 Maximal DF0 DF0 range Duration of syllables Duration of vocals

4. Approaches to Emotional Speech Classification

Different approaches have been taken in order to classify emotional speech. Depending on the nature of the problem, it is possible to distinguish between the following situations: (i) speaker dependent recognition, where data from different emotional states on different phonetic contexts are uttered by the same speaker during the same or different sessions, and (ii) speaker independent recognition, where different speakers, which may have different contexts like gender or age, produce the data.

Speaker independent emotion recognition has been reported to be a difficult task, while speaker dependent recognition gets better results, which can have an 80-90% of success. In turns, speaker independent systems show a recognition rate between 50-55%. This is a naturally complex facet of speech emotion recognition since even humans are not able to obtain a higher recognition performance in a speaker-independent modality. Schuller *et al.* showed that the recognition performance of 12 human subjects dropped from 87.3% for the task of determining the expressed emotions of known persons to 64.7% for those expressed by an unknown subject (Schuller *et al.*, 2005)

Several approaches to emotion recognition on speech have been directed to explore and select the most adequate pattern recognition techniques to address the problems of feature selection and classification. Some studies have been centred in exploring massive sets of features in order to obtain a subset that optimally classifies different emotions. It is a non-trivial task, since using the whole set of features is not a good option. A smaller feature vector provides a better generalization performance [14] and reduces the well-known problem of the curse of dimensionality. Several different methods has been proposed for tackling the problem of feature selection, as: In [15] Schuller designed a genetic algorithm that generated features by combining low level descriptors with systematic derivation. Descriptive statistical analysis is used to find an optimal representation within the feature space. The feature set depends on the used classifier. In [5] correlation-based exclusion was used in order to exclude highly correlated features. Discriminant analysis has also been applied in its heteroscedastic form in order to maximize the separation between emotion classes while reducing the dimensionality of the feature space in [4].

Different tactics has been followed in order to choose the temporal scope of the features. Vlasenko *et al.* have combined short-time frame-level analysis with turns or chunk level analysis (Vlasenko *et al.*, 2007). Features modelling phoneme, word or sentence scopes are applied to speech emotion classification by Schuller *et al.* (Schuller *et al*, 2008). They use a very large feature space combined with the use of feature selection algorithms. Results show that features modelling larger time units are beneficial for emotion recognition, especially after assigning the optimal scope level to each specific emotion. Voiced versus non voiced sounds for emotional speech classification have also recently being explored showing that speaker independent features can be obtained by performing a hierarchical classification of emotions (Kim *et al.*, 2008, 2009). This procedure reportedly produces lower confusions between anger/joy and neutral/sadness.

Classification schemes for emotion recognition have acquired wide variability. Several classification schemes have been proposed in to model emotional speech, from both the generative and the discriminative point of view. Furthermore, some approaches combine generative and discriminative techniques in order to model temporal sequences of features or to obtain combined properties from both methods.

Gaussian Mixture Models (GMM) have been one of the most used techniques for classifying acoustic vectors in speaker/gender recognition, but its inability to model temporal sequences produced their combination with other models. For example, GMM and Support Vector Machines (SVM) have been applied jointly in several forms. Thus, Hu *et. al* have built a universal background model of speech using a GMM (Hu *et. al,* 2007). To classify emotional speech, the universal model is adapted to the new coming utterance, and the resulting parameters are a high dimensional vector, further classified by a SVM adapted to multiclass classification. Chandrakala and Sekhar present another example of combination of generative models and SVM for speech emotion recognition where different generative models as GMM and Hidden Markov Models (HMM) are modelled for each of M training emotional utterances. Then each training utterance is scored by the M models, building a vector of a fixed length. Finally, a SVM classifier uses these vectors to model boundaries between classes (Chandrakala and Sekhar, 2009).

Other recent techniques include multisurface proximal SVM (Yang and Pu, 2008) Boosted GMM (Tang *et al.*, 2009) or hierarchical classification using GMM (Kim *et al.*, 2008) and they all reported good recognition results for speaker independent task.

5. Discussion

We have presented the current problems and some of the facing approaches for the task of emotion recognition through speech. Although emotions are not still well understood, the recent advances in emotional speech databases and machine learning approaches have provided a feasible way to perform initial applications.

Emotions also play a role in Internet and digital multimedia. Internet email has fostered a revolution in textual communication by providing a costless and fast way for international messaging. Similarly, videoconferencing and voice IP have a promising future empowering interpersonal information exchange.

Negotiation, mediation and emotions are not ignorant to each other either. For some years now, the analysis of the role and impact of emotions on negotiation and mediation processes has provided a fertile terrain for research (see, for instance, Jones and Bodtker 2001; Fischer and Shapiro, 2005; Jones, 2005; Kopelmana et al. 2006; Li and Roloff, 2006; Sinaceur and Tiedens, 2006; Van Kleef et al, 2006; Jameson, 2007; Steinel et al. 2007; Van Kleef, 2008; Overbeck et al., 2010). Similarly, the judicial and legal domains at large have benefitted from the study of emotions in different legal settings (i.e. Blumenthal 2005; Daicoff, 2005, Maroney, 2006; Wessell et al., 2006). From this point of view future mediators may find it as a fundamental tool to extend its relationship capacities. In this scenario, tools that analyze voice or video data from the emotional point of view could be a valuable allied for the management of mediators relational aspects. We summarized tools that will track videoconferencing speech, trying to represent it into an emotional space, helping the mediator to judge the emotional flow of the communication. To provide emotional saliency can be a valuable tool for review and navigate mediation multimedia in order to find out especially remarkable parts. In our previous works with legal multimedia (Binefa et al., 2007), we explored the characteristics of legal multimedia and how to extract patterns from it. Emotional speech analysis on legal multimedia can also become a fruitful way for semantic annotation, as emotions carry semantics that are very interesting in order to further analyze behaviours or remarkable events.

Acknowledgements

This work has been funded by the Spanish projects: (i) ONTOMEDIA: Platform of Web Services for Online Mediation, Spanish Ministry of Industry, Tourism and Commerce (Plan AVANZA I+D, TSI-020501-2008, 2008-2010), (ii) ONTOMEDIA. Web Semántica, ontologías y ODR: plataforma de servicios web para la mediación on line. CSO-2008-05536-SOCI, Spanish MInisytry of Science and Innovation.

References

Averill, J. R. (1975) *A Semantic Atlas of Emotional Concepts*, American Psychological Association, *JSAS Catalog of Selected Documents in Psychology:* 5, 330.

Binefa, X., Gracia, C., Monton, M., Carrabina, J., Montero, C., Serrano, J., Blázquez, M., Benjamins, V.R., Teodoro, E., Poblet, M., Casanovas, P. (2007), *Developing Ontologies for Legal Multimedia Applications*, LOAIT 2007, pp. 87-101.

Blumenthal, J.A. (2005), *Law and the emotions: the problems of affective forecasting*, Ind. L.J., Vol. 80, p. 155.

Chandrakala, C. and Chandra Sekhar, C. (2009), *Combination of generative models and SVM based classifier for speech emotion recognition*, Proceedings of International Joint Conference on Neural Networks, Atlanta, Georgia, USA, June 14-19, 2009, pp. 1374-1379.

Daicoff, S. (2005) *Law as a Healing Profession: The "Comprehensive Law Movement"*, Bepress Legal Series, Paper 1331, available at http://law.cwru.edu/lectures/files/2008-2009/20090410_Daicoff_excerpt.pdf (accessed May 17).

Douglas-Cowie, E. Campbell, N. Cowie, R., Roach, P. (2003), *Emotional speech: Towards a new generation of databases*. Speech Communication Journal, Vol. 40, pp. 33-603.

Fisher, R. and Shapiro, D. (2005), *Beyond Reason: Using Emotions As You Negotiate*. New York: Viking Press.

Hu, H. Ming-Xing, X., Wu, W. (2007) *GMM supervector based SVM with spectral features for speech emotion recognition*, Proceedings of the International Conference on Acoustics, Speech, and Signal Processing, Vol. 4, pp. 413–416.

Jameson, J.K., Bodtker, A.M., Porch, D.M., Jordan, W.J. (2007), *Exploring the role of emotion in conflict transformation*, Conflict Resolution Quarterly, Vol. 27, No. 2: pp. 167-192, DOI: 10.1002/crq.254.

Jones, T. S. (2005), Emotion in mediation: implications, applications, opportunities, and challenges, in M. Herrman (ed.), *Blackwell Handbook of Mediation:Theory and Practice*. New York: Blackwell.

Jones, T. S. and Bodtker, A. M. (2001). *Mediating with Heart in Mind: Addressing Emotion in Mediation Practice*, Negotiation Journal, Vol. 17, No. 3, pp. 207–244.

Kim, E. H., Hyun, K.H., Kim, H.H., Kwak, Y.K (2008), *Speech Emotion Recognition Separately from Voiced and Unvoiced Sound for Emotional Interaction Robot*, International Conference on Control, Automation and Systems 2008, pp. 2014-2019.

Kim, E. H., Hyun, K.H., Kim, H.H., Kwak, Y.K (2009), *Improved emotion recognition with a novel speaker-independent feature*, IEEE/ASME Transactions on Mechatronics, Vol. 14, No. 3, June 2009, pp. 317-325.

Kopelmana, S, Rosette, A.S., Thompsonc, L. (2006), *The three faces of Eve: Strategic displays of positive, negative, and neutral emotions in negotiations*, Organizational Behavior and Human Decision Processes, Vol. 99: pp. 81–101.

Li, S. and Roloff, M. E. (2006), *Strategic emotion in negotiation: cognition, emotion, and culture*, in G. Riva, M. T. Anguera, B. K. Wiederhold, and F. Mantovani (eds.), *From Communication to Presence: Cognition, Emotions, and Culture Towards the Ultimate Communicative Experience*, Amsterdam: IOS Press, 2006.

Maroney, T.A. (2006), *Law and emotion: a proposed taxonomy of an emerging field*, Law and Human Behavior, Vol. 30, pp.119–142, DOI 10.1007/s10979-006-9029-9.

Moataz, M. H., El Ayadi, M., Kamel, S., Karray, F. (2007), *Speech emotion recognition using Gaussian mixture vector autoregressive models*. IEEE International Conference on Acoustics, Speech and Signal Processing 2007. (ICASSP 2007), pp. 957-960.

Osgood, C. E., Suci, J. G., Tannenbaum, P. H. (1957), *The Measurement of Meaning*, Urbana, IL: Univ. Illinois, 1957, pp. 31–75.

Overbeck, J.R., Neale, M.A., Govan, C. L. (2010), *I feel, therefore you act: Intrapersonal and interpersonal effects of emotion on negotiation as a function of social power*, Organizational Behavior and Human Decision Processes (in press).

Picard, R.W. (1997), *Affective computing*, MIT Press, Cambridge, Mass.

Schuller, B, Reiter, S., Muller, R. Al-Hames, M., Lang, M., Rigoll, G. (2005) *Speaker Independent Speech Emotion Recognition by Ensemble Classification*, ICME, 2005 IEEE International Conference on Multimedia and Expo, pp.864-867.

Schuller, B., Reiter, S., Rigoll, G. (2006) *Evolutionary feature generation in speech emotion recognition*, ICME 2006: pp. 5-8.

Schuller, B., Vlasenko, B., Arsic, D., Rigoll, G., Wendemuth, A. (2008) *Combining speech recognition and acoustic word emotion models for robust text-independent emotion recognition*. ICME 2008: IEEE International Conference on Multimedia & Expo, pp. 1333-1336.

Sinaceur, M. and Tiedens, L. Z. (2006). *Get Mad and Get More Than Even: When and Why Anger Expression Is Effective in Negotiations*, Journal of Experimental Social Psychology, Vol. 42, No. 3, pp. 314–322.

Steinel, W, Van Kleef, G.A., Harinck, F. (2008), *Are you talking to me?! Separating the people from the problem when expressing emotions in negotiation*, Journal of Experimental Social Psychology, Vol. 44: pp. 362–369.

Tang, H., Chu, S.M., Hasegawa-Johnson, M., Huang, T:S: (2009), *Emotion recognition from speech via boosted Gaussian mixture models*, ICME 2009.

Valstar, M.F., Gunes, H., Pantic, M. (2007), *How to distinguish posed from spontaneous smiles using geometric features*, ICMI 2007, pp. 38-45.

Van Kleef, G.A. (2008) *Emotion in Conflict and Negotiation: Introducing the Emotions as Social Information (EASI) Model*, in N. M. Ashkanasy and C. L. Cooper (eds.) *Research Companion to Emotion in Organizations*. Massachusetts: Edward Elgar Publishing: pp. 392-404.

Van Kleef, G.A., Carsten K., De Dreul, W., Pietroni, D., Manstead, A.S.D. (2006), *Power and emotion in negotiation: Power moderates the interpersonal effects of anger and happiness on concession making*, European Journal of Social Psychology, Vol. 36, pp. 557–581, DOI: 10.1002/ejsp.320.

Ververidis, D. and Kotropoulos, C. (2003) *A review of emotional speech databases,* Proceedings of the 9th Panhellenic Conference in Informatics 2003.

Ververidis, D., Kotropoulos, C., Pitas, I. (2004), *Automatic emotional speech classification*, in Proc. 2004 IEEE Int. Conf. Acoustics, Speech and Signal Processing, Vol. 1, pp. 593-596.

Ververidis, D. and Kotropoulos, C. (2006), *Emotional speech recognition: Resources, features, and methods*, Speech Communication Journal, Vol. 48, No. 9, 1162-1181.

Vlasenko, B., Schuller, B. Wendemuth, A., Rigoll, G. (2007), *Combining Frame and Turn-Level Information for Robust Recognition of Emotions within Speech.* InterSpeech conference 2007, pp. pp. 2225–2228.

Wessel1, E.; Guri, C.; Drevland1, C.B., Eilertsen1, D.E., Magnussen, S. (2006), *Credibility of the Emotional Witness: A Study of Ratings by Court Judges, Law and Human Behavior*, Vol. 30: pp. 221–230, DOI 10.1007/s10979-006-9024-1

Witten I. and Frank, E. (2000), *Data mining*, Los Altos, CA: Morgan Kaufflan.

Yang, Ch. and Pu, Y. (2008), *Efficient speech emotion recognition based on multisurface proximal support vector machine*, 2008 IEEE Conference on Robotics, Automation and Mechatronics, pp. 55-60.

Diarization for the Annotation of Legal Videos

Ciro Gracia[*], Xavier Binefa[*], Emma Teodoro[°], Núria Galera[°]
[*]Universitat Pompeu Fabra, Barcelona, Spain
[°]UAB Institute of Law and Technology, Universitat Autònoma de Barcelona, Spain

Abstract. In this paper we analyze legal hearing recordings generated at the Spanish Civil Law Courts, and we present a tool for annotation and navigation across these records. This tool is based on data recovering the legal structure of hearings. To grasp this structure automatically, we apply and compare different audio diarization algorithms to obtain the temporal boundaries of the speakers and their tracking across the hearing. Previous work on legal data will help us to apply diarization techniques into web services platforms (Ontomedia).

Keywords: Legal Multimedia, Diarization, Speech analysis, Gaussian Mixture Models

1. Introduction

For some years now, all civil hearings are tape-recorded in Spain. Under the Spanish Civil Procedure Act (1/2000), these videotapes become official records. All proceedings must incorporate them, and lawyers have to obtain them from the court, as they are distributed to the parties by the Court clerks.

Unfortunately, the content of the CDs is not generated to feed the existing legal large databases (public or private), and there are no tools in the market yet to help lawyers and judges with their daily management. They are forced to store and retrieve this multimedia information from the CDs they receive with any single case, one by one.

To make a prototype for video retrieval and classification, a detailed analysis of the legal structure of the hearings may provide information about which are the potential semantically rich patterns. Recognizing these patterns allows not only a more efficient navigation for query and referencing, but also a higher level interface that speeds up case analysis. In this paper we present the annotation and navigation tools, based on the recovering of the legal proceedings from the oral hearings. We also discuss some approaches to audio diarization as a first step to extract key metadata for efficient navigation. This paper follows up the analysis already performed elsewhere (Binefa et al. 2007, Casanovas et al. 2009). Research projects around Ontomedia allowed us keep researching on legal video segmentation and audio diarization. We will summarize some lessons learned in court hearing analyses, to apply automate methods to extract information from the Ontomedia interactive mediation processes.

Automated information extraction constitutes the challenge we face in this paper.

2. Defining semantically rich patterns in Legal Multimedia

As IDT researchers discovered during the acquisition knowledge process, Spanish civil oral hearings are not being recorded following documented guidelines. Written procedure acts, such as the Spanish LEC, provide a judicial program and agenda that are only partially followed in Court. Furthermore, all recordings do not exhibit the same properties, as on the whole they do not suggest that there is a formalized standard.

Technical implementation of recoding varies from court to court, and it is obvious that sound and video quality criteria should be optimized for storage. Usual quality configuration includes 8kHz mono sound and 320x288 pixels resolution on a wide field of view image encoded at 8 frames per second. Despite different technical quality configurations varying from court to court, usually civil hearing recordings share the camera point of view, and the common court room distribution. The camera position and orientation always ensures that neither the judge nor the rest of the court members appear in the camera field.

Inside this multimedia representation of the hearings, there are several semantically rich patterns. These patterns must provide enough context information to allow fast navigation and querying. Most of the valuable information comes from the structural elements of the hearings. Oral hearings are a moderated environment where certain procedures and rules govern the sequence evolution.

This feature can be exploited to define which existing patterns are useful to infer the legal structure of the hearing. Three major elements perform a powerful improvement for navigation capabilities of legal multimedia: (i) interventions, (ii) phase inference, and (iii) specific terminology spotting. Hearings are primarily characterized for being mostly a moderated environment where each participant has specific taking turns.

These spoken interventions provide a first structure level on the multimedia data. Interventions can be defined as a "someone is talking". In that sense, interventions provide: (i) a graphical representation which contains semantical meaning related to the speaker's specific roles; (ii) the representation of the oral hearing structure regarding the order and duration of the interventions. For example the cross-interrogation by lawyers to witnesses could be easily identified as the edition of a set of interrelated interventions.

2.1. KNOWLEDGE ACQUISITION

Stemming from the official videotapes, we worked on detailed transcriptions of 15 different civil oral hearings. We set up a focus group of 3 researchers and 3 professional lawyers and solicitors. Using standard eliciting techniques (namely, interviews, e-mail discussions and brain-storming), focusing on their legal professional knowledge (LPK), we obtained expressions and legal concepts actually used in court. We inserted these procedural and legal expressions within the different stages of the structured hearings. As a result of applying eliciting techniques, researchers and lawyers identified roughly 900 terms and legal practical expressions.

Our analysis of the audiovisual records shows that the actual development of civil hearings differs considerably from the provisions made by the law (i.e. we detected stages of the hearings that were not identified by de 1/2000 Act). The structure of the general proceedings contained in procedural statutes and regulations is not the same structure implemented in court. The procedural dynamics of hearings as they are performed follows patterns and rules shaped by practical constraints and routines.

To face these difficulties, we represented four types of oral hearings in workflows. Workflows are conceived as flexible and adapted structures able to contain (and interact with) other structures of practical knowledge (i.e. typologies, keywords lists, and content groups).

The basic units of workflows are procedural stages. Procedural stages may include: actions (red rombus) which imply to move forward or backwards to another stage; procedural legal concepts (green boxes); and content of legal concepts (orange boxes). Table I shows a typology of the civil hearings, and Figure 1 represents e.g. the development of hearings of precautionary and provisional measures (*Medidas Cautelares y Provisonales*)

Table I. Table of Spanish civil hearings

Preliminary hearing *Audiencia previa*	Preliminary hearing *Audiencia previa*
Ordinary proceedings *Juicio ordinario*	Ordinary proceedings *Juicio ordinario*
Verbal proceedings *Juicio verbal*	Verbal proceedings *Juicio verbal*
	Proceedings regarding the capacity of persons (special proceedings) *Procesos sobre capacidad de las personas (procesos especiales)*
	Matrimonial proceedings (special proceedings) *Procesos matrimoniales y menores (procesos especiales)*
	Judicial division of states *División judicial de patrimonios*

	Exchange proceedings (special proceedings) *Procedimiento cambiario (procesos especiales)*
	Summon proceedings (special proceedings) *Procedimiento monitorio (procesos especiales)*
	Mortgage proceedings *Procedimientos hipotecarios*
	Extraordinary appeal for procedural infringements and cassation proceedings *Recurso extraordinario por infracción procesal y casación*
	Opposition to judicial determination of fees for undue fees *Impugnación tasación de costas por honorarios indebidos*
	Opposition to enforcement *Oposición a la ejecución*
Precautionary and provisional measures *Medidas cautelares y provisionales*	Precautionary measures *Medidas cautelares*
	Provisional measures *Medidas provisionales*

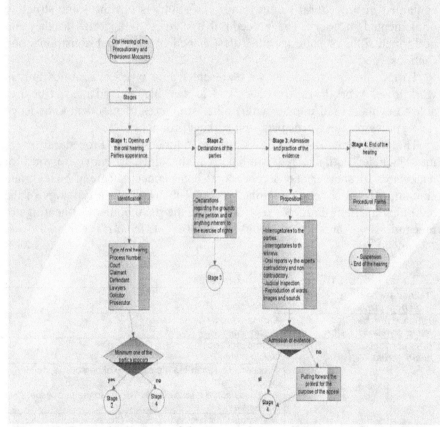

Figure 1. General structure of the Precautionary and Provisional hearings.

Stages can be used for group interventions into buckets. Each of them represents a specific part of the hearing procedure and provides a legal contextualization of the procedure development and its characteristics. For instance, in an overview of a hearing where stages are graphically represented and easily identifiable, the presence or absence of some stages (for example, practice of means of evidence) and their durations (number of interventions or minutes) provide information for navigation, hearing characteristics and analysis. The legal domain, as many other knowledge areas, includes specific terms which can be tracked on the speech signal.

Many elements recall on the acoustic signal as information source as far as video signal carries poor information. Some events can be easily recognized from video signal, e.g. elements that include movement or important changes in people's position. For example, when a witness enters the court room to testify or when a lawyer approaches to the judge's table to show documentation. However, the real challenge comes from their automatic extraction from the records.

2.2. INFORMATION EXTRACTION

The objective of this section is to discuss technical alternatives for extracting the three major elements described previously (interventions, phase inference, and specific terminology).

Detecting legal vocabulary from speech signal can be seen as a procedure referred in the signal processing literature as "word spotting" where an automatic speech recognition system (ASR) is trained to recognize a set of specific (small vocabulary) words (W.Kraaij, 1998). Acoustic template models can be also acquired by the navigation interface and searched exhaustively on the record producing a similarity function from which a set of plausible candidates can be suggested (Rabiner, 1993). More general approaches use general domain ASR systems for translate acoustic signal into text and further applying text processing techniques.

Stage inference requires a model of the legal casuistic obtained from empirical data which can take the form of a flow chart or automata. After a set of empirical observations, a set of Stages characteristics and the set of events that characterize the transitions between them are built, and a deterministic or stochastic model is stated ad hoc.

Other possibilities include the description of multimedia as a rich set of features and use automatic learning for the statistical differences between stage sequences. Similar techniques are often applied in human sequence evaluation, although the features defining stages should be very high level in order to obtain generalizable results (Cai, 2008; Peeters, 2003).

Interventions represent a speaker segmentation task which can be diarized. It will be described in depth in the next section.

2.3. THE PROTOTYPE SYSTEM

To explore the possibilities that improve navigation, we have developed a media exploration user interface that is heavily supported by a graphical visualization of speaker's indexing of the oral hearing. The user interface is based on a graphical representation of the interventions and the segmentation of the stages.

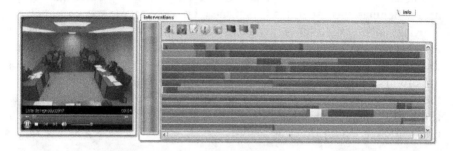

Figure 1. Media exploration graphical user interface. Horizontal segments represent speaker interventions. Vertical Column segments represent Phases presents in the media. Iconic representations of speakers help to filter interventions.

The interventions are represented as a set of horizontal segments, each one in a color that identifies the speaker owner. Stages are represented as columns with different sections, each one representing a filter operation on the displayed interventions. Different speakers can be identified by color or by an iconic representation that allows filter interventions by just displaying the speech segments of a given speaker. This graphical interface allows easy navigation and the basis for further annotation or documentation handling.

We have described it as an example of graphical exploitation of the patterns listed in the previous section. We have found that this kind of interfaces is appreciated by this specific group of users, so we have encouraged implementing speaker diarization as one of the basic elements for media annotation.

3. Diarization

The goal of diarization is to locate homogeneous regions within audio segments and consistently label them for speaker's identity, background noise, music, etc (Angueraphd, 2004). This labeled media finds applications in numerous speech processing tasks, such as speaker adapted speech recognition, speaker detection, speaker identification, and audio document retrieval.

In a legal multimedia context, this task can be seen as the process which detects speaker's turns and regroups those uttered by the same speaker. The scenario application does not involve music and other types of sources. Usually, signal processing literature often refers to this simplified version of diarization as speaker segmentation and typically subdivides the problem into a subset of problems and techniques depending on the prior knowledge of the environment. Most of the supervised approaches use previous knowledge on the number of the speakers, the infrastructure calibration and samples from speakers' voices to build models for later classification and selection. Blindly approaches do not assume any prior information and use metric approaches and clustering to estimate turn boundaries, the number of speakers and regroup speaker segments (Hyoung, 2005).

3.1. GENERAL OVERVIEW

To determine when each participant is speaking in a recording implies detecting boundaries between interventions, as well as identifying the speaker between these boundaries. Preliminary speech detection must be performed to segregate speech content from non speech content such as background noise in order to avoid further misdetections and distortions. The issues related to the segments of diarization are twofold: detecting the audio boundaries of the speakers and recognizing the segments belonging to the same speaker. From now on, we will refer to them as intervention segmentation and speaker identification. Detecting boundaries between speaker's interventions can be faced following two approaches which depend on the prior knowledge of the environment. On the one hand, metric-base methods measure the similarity between two neighboring speech regions and try to determine where an abrupt change in the speech characteristics is detected. This approach estimates boundaries where abrupt changes appear, usually pointing to speaker turns or a change point between speakers by finding homogeneous acoustic regions (Rodriguez, 2007). Given the set of segments, each one is assumed to belong to a sole speaker, so that the process to determine the number of speakers and which segments belong to the sole speaker must be faced without prior knowledge. The unsupervised approach classically faces this problem by hierarchical bottom-up clustering techniques, where a distance or dissimilarity criterium between each pair of segments is computed and the method puts together the two clusters which are closest (most similar), resulting in a new partition of the data. This process is computed in an iterative fashion until a certain stop criterium is reached (Hyoung, 2005). The number of estimated speakers corresponds to the resulting number of clusters, and the segments belonging to each speaker are the different segments belonging to each cluster.

On the other hand, model-based segmentation relies on statistical models, e.g. Gaussian Mixture Models (GMM). These models are constructed for a fixed set of acoustic classes, such as anchor speaker, music, etc. from a training corpus. The incoming audio stream can be classified by maximum likelihood selection. Segment boundaries are assumed where a change in the acoustic class occurs (Kemp, 2000).

3.2. IMPLEMENTATION AND ALTERNATIVES

Diarization is a process usually applied to multimedia data as an offline process, but results can be easily improved adding specific control element to the recording environment. In legal multimedia, oral hearings usually involve a small and quasi fixed amount of roles: judge and court staff, lawyers of both sides and an unknown number of third parties which play a similar semantic role (witnesses). This relative small amount of elements and its variability allow to incorporate specific microphones and record each channel separately, making possible an easy online indexing just by activity detection on each channel.

Generally, diarization requires detecting activity as a preprocessing step, non speech noises add disturbance to posterior processes increasing the overall error, the number of participants in the media also increases error and processing time as mismatch in speaker identification tends to increase with the number of different speakers (population increases) (Reynolds, 1992; Reynolds, 1995). Having the possibility to spread different recording channels among different roles or participants allows increasing posterior diarization accuracy as well as an easy online indexing.

4. Speech Analysis

Speech signal contains patterns inside its temporal variability, and such patterns extend over a very wide range of time scales. This variability patterns are much clearer to analyze in frequency domain. Short time Fourier transform is a major tool for speech frequency domain analysis producing a representation commonly called spectrogram. One of the most successful approaches to sound signal analysis for segregation and recognition of acoustic events is the one that aims to analyze and reproduce the natural hearing process of human auditory system or also called human perception.

The study of human auditory system aims at determining the factors that allow humans to solve difficult situations where they are able to segment, segregate, recognize, track and synthesize individual sources from a mixture of channels of sound streams (Hayking, 2005). Nowadays the signal processing techniques that extract human perception adapted features are the most used in speaker recognition/identification. Most of these features are based in Filter bank processing techniques as human auditory system behavior can be modeled by a set of critical band filter. Mel frequency cepstral coefficients (MFCC) are probably most common features extracted from speech signal for speech recognition and speaker recognition. Their physco-acoustic approach is based in the melodic scale of frequency which was proposed by Newman and Volkman in 1937. Melodic scale represents the perceptual scale of pitches judged by listeners to be equal in distance from one to another. Mapping between melodic scale and Hz is defined as:

$$Mel(hz) = 2592 * \lg_{10}\left(1 + \frac{hz}{700}\right)$$

MFCC perform a band pass filtering on power spectrum where an optional number of band pass filters are placed equally into Melodic scale warping by this way Fourier frequency axis (Roch, ; Zhang, 2003; Stern, 2006).

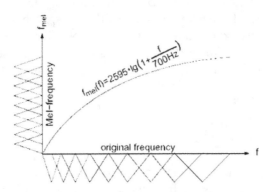

Figure 2. Frequency axis warping by melodic scale , filters equally spaced into Melodic scale results in logarithmic filters in Hertz frequency scale.

A common configuration can be found as consisting of 24 triangular shaped filters covering audible frequency range. The resulting coefficients are derived to Cepstral representation by taking the Discrete cosine Transform. Cepstral representation (Bogert, 1966; Childers, 1977; Oppenheim, 2004; Roch) refers to a representation where periodicity inside power spectra is analyzed, this analysis is closely related to homomorphic system theory developed by Oppenheim in middle sixties applied to the Source-filter model of speech production.

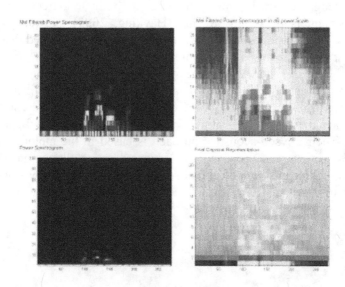

Fig. 3. MFCC Processing by Images

Posterior dimensionality reductions techniques can be addressed to keep most of the significant information while reducing noisy information. In our approach we have chosen framework for speech signal processing based in a 128-Melodic bank filtering and a posterior Principal component analysis in order to keep 10 principal dimensions to perform posterior training and classification.

5.1. SEGMENTATION

Segmentation has the objective of detecting speaker change point. Inside every speech region, a distance is computed between two adjacent given length windows. By sliding both windows on the whole audio stream, a distance curve is obtained. Peaks above a threshold in this curve are thus considered as speaker change points.

Most of the common distance metrics for change point detection are based on model Gaussian distribution for data on both adjacent windows. Methods try to compare both sides in terms of distribution overlapping, hypothesis testing or by model selection criterion. Classic metric functions are Kullback-Leiber, hostelling T2, Generalized likelihood ratio and Bayesian Information Criterion (Kemp, 2000). We have chosen Crossed BIC as an efficient implementation of BIC for segmentation, which has been reported adequate for broadcast news diarization (Rodriguez, 2007; Anguera, 2004).

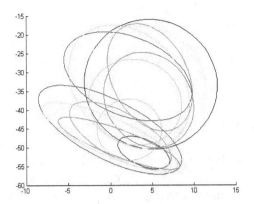

Figure 4. Sample Speakers Gaussian mixture modeling, it shows a high degree of overlapping between models.

Our Model Based segmentation is performed by using 15 seconds of speech samples from each participant in the media. A well known widely applied statistical model is used for approximate probability density for each participant acoustic features. This learning process in based on a Gaussian mixture modeling, followed by consecutive pruning stages to produce an acoustic modeling based only in each speaker's specific characteristics.

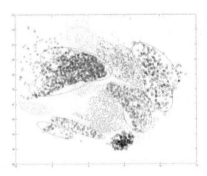

Figure 5. Sample Speakers Mixture Modeling after pruning

The selective use of feature vectors (Shrikanth, 2006) consists on reducing the overlap between speaker models. This normally implies discarding features that are common in speaker training data sets like some short silences or some turbulent phonemes. The influence of such common features to model overlap to model overlap is especially critical when the training utterance length is limited. A method to reduce model overlap consists of generating the models and filtering the features of the next learning set, just leaving features that are correctly classified using maximum likelihood methods, and recomputing iteratively the model until the accuracy achieves the required level. Discarded features are keep to build a complementary model, during maximum likelihood classification feature vectors belonging to this model will be discarded. This approach pretends to make robust decisions by selecting only robustly assignable feature vectors.

4.2. HYBRID MODEL

Using a hybrid model, the diarization becomes a two step process: segmentation and identification. From the segmentation point of view, metric approaches are interesting as they are more efficient to compute and do not make prior assumptions of the acoustic classes. While model approaches are more precise, they do not generalize acoustic conditions absent in the models. Identifying which of the speech segments are owned by the same speaker can be seen as a speaker identification task, in which taking advantage of the prior build models, a maximum likelihood classification task is performed. Grouping same speaker with neither prior information nor assumptions typically require working with long utterances to ensure sufficient statistics (Viet-Bac Le, 2007). Most of them are related with covariance estimation of dissimilarity criterions and all the data must be available before grouping can start. However, the prior speaker model requirement is acceptable given that Speaker Identification techniques can provide a very high accuracy, allow online operation and do not require such long utterances.

4.3. EXPERIMENTS

We performed experiments evaluating the diarization error (DER) as the percentage of wrongly assigned time versus total time. Experiment corpus compromises files of legal media content. Inside these data files 7 speakers (3 females and 4 males) participate in 60 minutes of audio signal. Speakers change point detection obtained from the diarization are compared to manually annotated boundaries, considering a margin of half a second of tolerance. We show precision (PRC) and recall (RCL) measures coming from standard information retrieval techniques to evaluate the performance of both methods for boundary detection: hybrid and model. Recall takes into account the completeness of the retrieval and precision measures of the purity of the retrieval.

Method	Diarization Error
Metric segmentation	0.15
Model segmentation	0.18

Method	Boundary Precision	Boundary Recall
Metric segmentation	0.66	0.6
Model segmentation	0.36	0.53

Generated boundaries and labeling were incorporated to the navigation interface and were evaluated by final users on navigation task over tested recordings. The evaluation of diarization applied to the navigation interface resulted in helpful information to further improve the exploring and navigation capabilities of the final users on this media application.

5. Conclusions

In this paper we have presented an overview of legal multimedia documents obtained from civil oral hearings in Spain. We have also presented an analysis of its potential to boost legal professionals' capabilities on case management and hearing analysis. We defined which patterns inside the media can provide the best legal structure description and we presented an interface for its graphical presentation. We have introduced diarization as a powerful information source for navigation and a general overview of methods for its computation. We have also summarized some results from the hybrid approach to further develop the navigation interface.

Acknowledgements

This work has been developed within the framework of two different projects: (i) ONTOMEDIA: Platform of Web Services for Online Mediation, TSI-020501-2008); (ii) ONTOMEDIA: Semantic Web, Ontologies and ODR: Platform of Web Services for Online Mediation (CSO-2008-05536-SOCI). These projects lean on the results of FIT-350101-2006-26.

References

Anguera, X. (2003). *Robust Speaker Segmentation and Clustering for Meetings*, presented as PhD Thesis proposal in UPC (Barcelona, Spain).

Binefa, Xavier; Gracia, Ciro; Monton, Marius; Carrabina, Jordi; Montero, Carlos;Serrano, Javier; Blzquez, Mercedes; Benjamins, Richard v.; Teodoro, Emma;Poblet, Marta; Casanovas, Pompeu. *Developing ontologies for legal multimedia applications* (2007). In P. Casanovas, M.A. Biasiotti, E. Francesconi, M.T. Sagri (Eds.) "Proceedings of LOAIT 07 II Workshop on Legal Ontologies and Artificial Intelligence Techniques", pp. 87-102.

Bogert, B. P., Healy M.J.R., Tukey, J.W. (1984), *The quefrency analysis of time series for echoes: cepstrum, pseudo-autocovariance, cross-cepstrum and saphe-cracking.* In Rosenblatt, M. (Ed.), "Proceedings of the Symposium on Time Series Analysis", Wiley, New York, pp. 209-243.

Cai, R., Lu, L., Hanjalic, A. (2008). *Co-Clustering for auditory scene categorization,* IEEE Transactions on multimedia.

Casanovas, P., Binefa, X., Gracia, C., Montero, M., Carrabina, J., Serrano, J., Blzquez,M., Lpez-Cobo, J.M., Teodoro, E., Galera, N., Poblet, M. (2009), *The e-Sentencias pro-totype. Developing ontologies for legal multimedia applications in the Spanish Civil Courts.* In Casanovas, P.; Breuker, J.; Klein, M.; Francesconi, E. (eds) "Channeling the legal informational ood. Legal Ontologies and the Semantic Web", IOS Press, Amsterdam, pp. 199-219.

Childers, D.G., Skinner, D.P., Kemerait R.C. (1977), *The Cepstrum: A Guide to Processing,* "Proceedings of the IEEE", Vol. 65, No. 10, October, pp. 1428-1443.

Haykin, S., Chen, Z. (2005). *The Cocktail Party Problem Review.* Neural computation, Num. 17.

Hernando, J., Anguita, J. XBIC (2004). *Nueva medida para segmentacion del locutor hacia el indexado automatico de la señal de voz.* In "III Jornadas en Tecnologías del Habla".

Hyoung-Gook, K., Moreau, N., Sikora, T. (2006). *MPEG-7 Audio and Beyond Audio Content Indexing and Retrieval.* John Wiley and Sons.

Kemp, T., Schmidt, M., Westphal, M., Waibel, A. (2000). *Strategies for automatic segmentation of audio data.* Proc. Icassp

Kinnunen T. (2003), *Spectral Features for Automatic Text-Independent Speaker Recognition,* Joensuun Ylipisto.

Kraaij, W., van Gent, J., Ekkelenkamp, R., and van Leeuwen, D. (1998), *Phoneme based spoken document retrieval.* In "Proceedings of the fourteenth Twente Workshop on Language Technology TWLT-14", University of Twente, pp. 141-143.

Kwon , S, Narayanan, S. (2006), *Robust Speaker Identification based on selective use of feature vectors,* Pattern Recognition Letters, Num. 28 , pp. 85-89.

Kwon, S., Narayanan S., (2005, *Unsupervised Speaker Indexing Using Generic Models.* IEEE Transactions on Speech and Audio Processing, Vol. 13 No. 5 September.

Le, V.B., Mella, O., Fohr, D. (2007), *Speaker Diarization using Normalized Cross Likelihood Ratio.* In "10th International Conference on Speech Communication and Technology (Interspeech-Eurospeech07)".

Oppenheim, A.V., Schafe R.W. (2004), *From Frequency to Quefrency: A history of the Cepstrum*. Dsp History in IEE signal processing magazine

Peeters, G. and Rodet, X. (2003), *Hierarchical gaussian tree with inertia ratio maximization for the classification of large musical instrument databases*. "Proc.of the 6th Int. Conference on Digital Audio EFFects (DAFX-03)", London UK.

Rabiner, L.R., Juang, B.H. (1993), *Fundamentals of speech recognition*, Prentice Hall.

Reynolds A., Rose C (1995), *Robust Text-Independent Speaker Identification Using Gaussian Mixture Speaker Model*, IEEE Transactions on Speech and Audio Processing Vol. 3.

Reynolds, D.A. (1992), A *gaussian mixture modeling approach to text-independent speaker identification*, PhD thesis, Georgia Institute of Technology, August.

Roch, M. *Cepstral Processing Lectures*. San Diego State University.

Rodriguez, L.J (2007), *A Simple But Effective Approach to Speaker Traking in Broadcast News*, LNCS 4478, "Third Iberian Conference" IbPRIA, Vol.2, pp. 48-55.

Stern, R.M., (2006), *Signal processing for robust speech recognition*. Department of Electrical and Computer Engineering and School of Computer Science Carnegie Mellon University.

Yu Zhang, Y. (2003), Presentation. Seminar Speech Recognition - Mel-spectrum computation.

Legal Multimedia Management and Semantic Annotation for Improved Search and Retrieval

Jorge González-Conejero, Emma Teodoro, Nuria Galera
Universitat Autònoma de Barcelona
Institute of Law and Technology
UAB-IDT, Cerdanyola del Vallès, 08290 SPAIN
{jorge.gonzalez.conejero, emma.teodoro, nuria.galera}@uab.es

Abstract. In this work, we study the possibilities of multimedia management and automatic annotation focused on legal domain. In this field, professionals are used to consume the most part of their time searching and retrieving legal information. For instance, in scenarios as e-discovery and e-learning search and retrieval of the multimedia contents are the basis of the whole applications. In addition, the legal multimedia explosion increases the need of store these files in a structured form to facilitate the access to this information in an efficient and effective way. Furthermore, the improvements achieved by sensors and video recorders in the last years increase the size of these files, producing an enormous demand of storage capability. JPEG2000 and MPEG-7 are international standards by the ISO/IEC organization that allow to reduce, in some degrees, the amount of data needed to store these files. These standards also permit to include the semantic annotation in the considered file formats, and to access to this information without the need to decompress the contained video or image. How to obtain the semantic information from multimedia is also studied as well as the different techniques to exploit and combine this information.

Keywords: Legal multimedia, semantic-based search and retrieval, JPEG2000 and MPEG-7

1. Introduction

Nowadays, legal professionals are used to consume an important part of their time searching, retrieving, and managing legal information. However, the recent explosion of multimedia legal contents has resulted in rising costs and requires more management capacities than ever before. Improving the functionalities for search, retrieval, and management of multimedia legal documents is paramount to fully unlock the potential of those contents for legal practice and to develop specific management solutions for different profiles of legal users (Brickell and Langer, 2009).

The multimedia files carries a meaning which can be very versatile. For a human the meaning of the message is immediate, but for a computer that is far from true. This discrepancy is commonly referred to as the *semantic gap* (Smeulders et al., 2000). Semantic multimedia annotation is the process of automatically detecting the presence of a concept in an image or video stream. In the literature, there are several works that address the multimedia annotation based on their meaning for different fields. In (Ballan et al., 2010) an approach for automatic annotation and retrieval of video content is presented, based on ontologies, rule learning with first order logic, and semantic concept classifiers. An automatic video retrieval method based on high-level concept detectors is presented in (Snoek et al., 2007), defining a set of machine learned concept detectors enriched with semantic descriptions. In (Zha et al., 2007) a more general and comprehensive ontology to annotate video contents is described. Usually, an ontology consists of lexicon, properties, and relations. In this work LSCOM (Snoek et al., 2006) is used to construct the lexicon, describe concept property as the weights of different modalities which are obtained manually or by data-driven approach, and model two types of concept relations. The work (Gonzàlez et al., 2008) presents a Cognitive Vision System which explains the human behavior of monitored scenes using natural language texts. Here, the trajectories of human agents are obtained to generate textual interpretations of their motion, also inferring the conceptual relationship of each agent. The human behavior model is based on Situation Graph Trees.

Nevertheless, there is no available systems within the judicial domain to automatically index, tag, or annotate audiovisual files taking into account the requirements from judicial procedures. The annotation process for multimedia files produced by the judicial domain has several important benefits for law professionals. One of the most important features is that the annotation facilitates the search based on the meaning of the multimedia files, improving the legal frameworks and applications focused on, for instance, e-learning (Xin, 2009) and e-discovery (Baron and Thompson, 2007).

Figure 1 depicts an example of a general scheme to process multimedia files extracting semantic information. This scheme consists of three main stages. The first one is the extraction of events and concepts from videos and images. Exploiting high-level concepts and low-level descriptors we can achieve an automatic video retrieval method, see for instance (Snoek et al., 2007). The second stage applies a compression to the multimedia files to reduce the storage requirements and stores the semantic information in the same file, see (González-Conejero, 2010). The last stage is aimed to extract the main concepts of the user query to match the semantic information extracted from the multimedia files.

The aim of this work is to discuss the possibilities of annotate the legal multimedia contents and how these annotated files are managed. Recalling Figure 1, we study the composition of the three stages: annotation, management, and extracting concepts from the user query that fits into the legal multimedia field.

The paper is organized as follows: Section 2 explores the suitability of two international standards, JPEG2000 and MPEG-7, to manage multimedia files produced by the judicial procedures and the concepts and events extracted from these files; Section 3 studies how different features and semantic events/concepts are extracted from the multimedia files; finally, Section 4 summarizes the work and points out some conclusions.

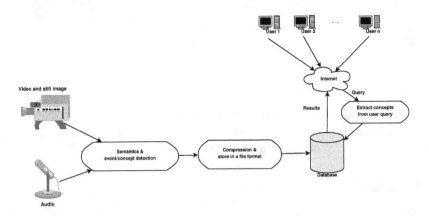

Figure 1. Main scheme for annotation of still image and video files.

2. Legal Multimedia Management

In this work, we are focused on the improving of search and retrieval applications in legal multimedia datasets. Nevertheless, how this multimedia files and the extracted semantic events/concepts are stored are also important topics. The widely use of multimedia files in the judicial domain and the improvements achieved by sensors and video recorders in the last years produce an enormous demand of storage capability. Images and videos usually contain highly redundant information, which can be exploited to compress and reduce, in some degrees, the amount of data needed to store these files. Apart from compression, the manipulation of multimedia currently requires other advanced features. Some of these features are the availability to transmit images and videos interactively over the network, to support error resilience or even to supply capabilities of watermarking and fingerprinting. Encoding systems must take these needs into account to provide a flexible framework that allows an efficient management.

A general description of the compression process is depicted in Figure 2. The input image is encoded, and the produced binary file is stored in a database (or similar) and/or transmitted over the network. Then, the original image is recovered at the client side through the decoder framework. In this Section, we describe two different coding systems that are able to: 1) achieve high coding performance; 2) provide an efficient management of the multimedia files; and 3) store semantic information in their specific file formats. JPEG2000 (Taubman and Marcellin, 2002) and MPEG-7 (Chang et al., 2001)

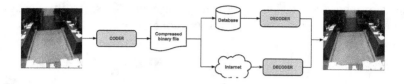

Figure 2. General compression scheme.

are standards from the International Standard Organization (ISO) and fulfills most of the requirements from the judicial field. The next sections contain a brief description of both coding systems.

2.1. JPEG2000

JPEG2000 is one of the latest standards developed by the Joint Photographic Experts Group (JPEG) and is structured in 13 different parts, addressing the encoding, transmission, security, and manipulation of still images and video. Since a description of the JPEG2000 is not the aim of this work, the interested reader is referred to: (Skodras et al., 2001) and (Rabbani and Joshi, 2002). Table I summarizes the most important parts of the JPEG2000 standard for the legal multimedia management. In our previous work, (González-Conejero, 2010), the suitability of these parts in the management of the legal multimedia contents and the inclusion of semantics in the JPEG2000 file formats are discussed. In addition, a centralized scheme to store in a database all of these files in a JPEG2000 file format is proposed.

Table I. Brief description of the 5 parts of the JPEG2000 standard suitable to manage legal multimedia contents.

— **Part 1 Core coding system**: description of the minimal decoder and a simple file format. It is the basis of the other parts.

— **Part 2 Extensions**: extensions of the core coding system, providing advanced coding features which can be used to enhance the coding performance or to manipulate unusual data types.

— **Part 3 Motion JPEG2000**: supports the manipulation of image sequences (motion).

— **Part 6 Compound image file format**: additional file format for tailored and compound documents.

— **Part 8 Secure JPEG2000**: description of a file syntax for interpreting secure image data and a normative process for registering security tools.

— **Part 9 Interactivity tools, APIs and protocols**: description of the transmission protocol JPIP, devised to interactively transmit JPEG2000 images.

2.2. MPEG-7

MPEG-7 is formally known as Multimedia Content Description Interface. While the prior standards focus on coding representation of audio and visual content, MPEG-7 focuses on description of multimedia content. MPEG-7 complements the existing MPEG standards suite and aims to be applicable to many existing formats, which include non-MPEG format and non-compressed formats as well. Table II summarizes the most important parts of the MPEG-7 standard suitable to manage legal multimedia files. In the literature there are several works that describe the different parts of the MPEG-7 standard, see for instance (Avaro and Salembier, 2001), (Hunter, 2001) and (Sikora, 2001).

Table II. Brief description of the 5 parts of the MPEG-7 standard suitable to manage legal multimedia contents.

- **Part 1 Systems**: specifies system level functionalities, such as preparation of MPEG-7 descriptions for transport/storage, synchronization of content descriptions, and development of conformance decoders.

- **Part 2 Description Definition Language**: is a derived by extension of XML schema to address other requirements specific to MPEG-7.

- **Part 3 Visual**: specifies features such as color, texture, shape and motion. Other elements required are structure, viewpoint, localization, and temporal.

- **Part 4 Audio**: addresses different classes of audio.

- **Part 5 Multimedia Description Schemes**: specifies a high-level framework that allows generic description of all kinds of multimedia.

3. Multimedia annotation

The need to review documents imposes considerable overhead in terms of cost and time, and challenges the capacity for legal system to perform search and retrieval matters effectively. In Spain, the Civil Procedure Act of January 7th, 2000 (1/2000) introduces the video recording of oral hearings. Consequently, Spanish civil courts are currently producing a massive number of multimedia files that have substituted the written transcripts and have become part of the judicial file, together with suits, indictments, injunctions, judgments and pieces of evidence. Lawyers, prosecutors and judges need to access these contents when preparing similar cases or when appealing to superior courts.

Inclusion of semantic fields and the semantic-based search and retrieval has been one of the long-term goals of multimedia computing to bridge the above mentioned *semantic gap*. In addition, the automatization of this annotation is an important feature in the legal multimedia domain due to the enormous quantity of multimedia files generated. Nowadays, this annotation has to been done manually, and the excess of work of the different employees in the court could penalize this step. Next sections studies the state-of-the-art of the multimedia annotation files and the suitability for the legal multimedia domain. Here, how the files are automatically annotated are described. Another important topic is how to match the query of the user and the annotation of the multimedia files (semantic gap from user query).

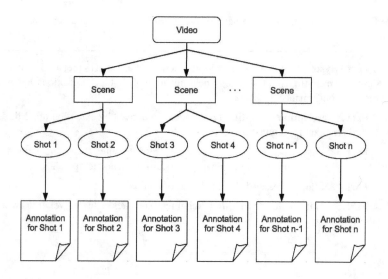

Figure 3. The video is divided in different shots concerning the meaning of every scene.

3.1. VIDEO ANNOTATION

The video annotation begins with the detection of events and concepts. Here, video events are defined as the interesting events which capture the users' attention (i.e. something that happen in the video as a "car accident" or "goal in a soccer match"); whereas the concepts refer to high-level semantic features, like "news", "sports", etc. Most of the state-of-the-art event detection frameworks were conduced toward the videos with poor structure or without story units, such as surveillance and medical videos (Zhu et al., 2005). On the other hand, the concept extraction scheme is widely used on videos which have structured contents, for instance broadcast news. Another example of field that has structured contents is the judicial domain, where its procedures are divided into ruled different parts that compose the entire process. However, the routines and constrains of daily practice in court result in a far more complex typology, revealing interesting differences between the formal provisions of the law and the actual development of the procedures. The *e-Sentencias* project (Casanovas et al., 2009) made an important effort to tackle this issue, defining an scheme of the typology of civil hearings in Spain as emerged in daily practice. The e-Sentencias also presents a framework to annotate and facilitates the navigation of the user across the different recordings of judicial oral hearings.

Semantic annotation involves temporal partitioning of the video sequence into meaningful units which serve as the basis for concept extraction and semantic annotation. Every meaningful part of the video is named as *shot* and it will be the minimum self-contained, well-defined and accessible unit. There are several works in the literature that address this issue, for instance (Amiri and Fathy, 2009) and (Meng et al., 2009). Shots are annotated with the semantic concept that each scene represents in their space of time. Figure 3 depicts a scheme of this process.

Approaches for deriving semantics based on low level features, such as color, texture and local descriptors, have shown their limitations in bridge the semantic gap. Modern approaches enable semantic search by generating a set of concept detectors to extract semantics from low level features. In (Hauptmann et al., 2007) how many concepts would be needed, and how they should be selected and used is studied. For different simulations in a broadcast news dataset they find that good retrieval can be achieved even when detection accuracy is low, if sufficiently many concepts are combined. Whereas the low level concepts are determined by the video features, concepts and detectors that learn from the mapping between a set of low level visual features and concept from examples have to be designed. The common idea in this topic is to apply a machine-learning technique, usually a Support Vector Machine (SVM), to automatically learn this mapping from the data. Other popular solutions is to apply a Bag-of-Words approach (Sivic and Zisserman, 2003) in which an image or video frame is represented as a bag of quantized descriptors referred to as visual-words. Then, this representation is used to compute histograms of visual-words frequencies used to train appropriate classifiers. Another approach proved for detection of specific object classes as "face" or "person" are (Viola and Jones, 2004) and (Jamieson et al., 2010).

On the other hand, exploitation of the semantic relationships between concepts is receiving a large attention from the researchers in this field, due to it can improve the detection accuracy of concepts and provides a richer semantic annotation of a video. Ontologies are expected to improve the computer systems detection even complex concepts and events from visual data. They organize semantic heterogeneity of information, using a formal representation, and provide a common vocabulary that encodes semantics and supports reasoning. Several works in the literature add ontologies combined with other features to improve the concepts detection. For instance, (Zha et al., 2007), (Wei et al., 2008) and (Snoek et al., 2007).

Figure 4 depicts a scheme of the hierarchy of the semantic annotation. From bottom to top of the figure: first step contains the multimedia files, from these files we can extract low-level descriptors as pixels, textures, speech recognition, etc. In the upper level, concepts used to the semantic annotation are defined. Finally, the user level contains the user query. Another important issue in semantic search and retrieval field is how to manage the user query. The accuracy of the user describing the query text to match the concepts extracted is a well-known problem. The richness of the vocabulary is also a problem for humans describing video in words. A variety of terms are used to describe the same video fragment by different users, or by same user in different contexts. Use ontologies to structure terms employed by users can make descriptions more consistent and can aid the user in selecting the terms for a semantic search.

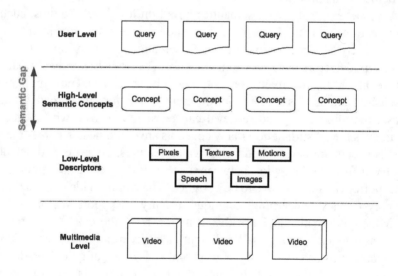

Figure 4. Video annotation scheme.

3.2. STILL IMAGE ANNOTATION

The annotation of still images is a more complex process than the video annotation. The semantic meaning is more easy to extract when a complete scene could be analyzed. Nevertheless, in a still image the only information is the objects within the image. Image annotation can not be performed by simply manually associating words to each image, firstly because it would be a very tedious task with the exponential increasing quantity of digital images and secondly because their content can not be fully described by a list of words.

Extraction of visual information directly from the images is required, nevertheless, bridging the semantic gap between the target semantic classes and the available low level visual descriptors is an unsolved problem. Consequently, it is crucial to select an appropriate set of visual descriptors that capture the particular properties of a specific domain and the features of each image class. For instance, local color descriptors, global color histograms, edge direction histograms, etc. The second crucial problem is to combine the low level descriptors in such a way that the results obtained with individual descriptors are improved.

In the literature, there are systems designed to learn meaningful correspondences between words and appearance models from cluttered images of multiple objects. Many approaches associate a caption word with a probability distribution over a feature space dominated by color and texture. This type of representation is less reliant on perceptual grouping than a shape model or a structured appearance model due to color and texture are robust to segmentation errors and the features configuration is not critical. There are several works that address the learning of configurations and problems of perceptual grouping. In (Barnard et al., 2003) a ranking scheme for potential merges of regions based on a similarity of word-regions associations. In a similar fashion, (Quattoni et al., 2007) use the co-occurrence of caption words and visual features to merge together equal features. Nevertheless, these models contain no spatial relationships between parts that would allow them to represent true part configurations. The work (Carbonetto et al., 2004) can successfully recognize a set of adjacent regions with widely varying appearance as being associated with a given word. The multiresolution statistical model introduced in (Li and Wang, 2003) can represent configurations of visual features across multiple scales. Here, each semantic class is associated with a layout for the entire image, where the division in parts is predefined. However, this system does not perform grouping. Other works avoid the perceptual grouping problem by focusing on domains where exists detailed prior knowledge of the appearance of the objects of interest, as in the task of matching names with faces, for instance see (Viola and Jones, 2004).

3.3. MULTIMEDIA ANNOTATION AND MPEG-7

All the information generated by the annotation process have to be stored in the multimedia files under a concrete file format, as we stated in Section 2. Figure 5 depicts a brief scheme of how the semantics/metadata is stored in concrete parts of the final file format. In the literature, most of the works concerning this issue pose the problem of the inclusion of semantics/metadata in the MPEG-7. So, in this section we are focused on this standard that store the information produced by the annotation process carried out to the multimedia files. MPEG-7 can be used to create complex and comprehensive metadata descriptions of multimedia content. It is also defined in terms of an XML schema, however, the semantics have no formal grounding. There are description tools for diverse types of annotations on different semantic levels, ranging from very low-level features, such as visual or audio, to more abstract descriptions. The flexibility of MPEG-7 relies on structuring tools, which allow descriptions to be associated with arbitrary multimedia segments or regions, using different levels of abstraction.

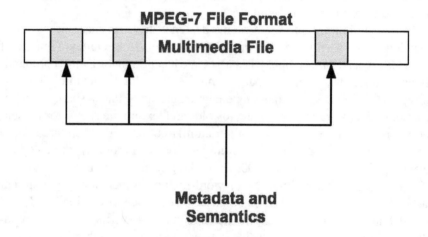

Figure 5. The semantic information is stored in the MPEG-7 file format.

Several works that relate the MPEG-7 standard and the semantics are presented in the literature. (Graves and Lalmas, 2002) proposes a model for video retrieval based upon the inference network model. The document network is constructed using video metadata encoded through MPEG-7 and captures information pertaining to the structural, conceptual and contextual aspects. For image classification, in (Spyrou et al., 2005) three content-based techniques based on fusing various low-level MPEG-7 visual descriptors are presented. One of this three techniques is based on neurofuzzy network, in this case fuzzy rules can be extracted in an effort to bridge the semantic gap between the low-level descriptors and the high level semantics of the image. In the video databases field, videos have to be presented in a compact and discriminative way to perform an efficient matching and retrieval of documents. In (Bertini et al., 2006) a method to obtain video representation to pose this issue is presented and it is based on features and descriptors taken from the MPEG-7 standard. Finally, (Bailer et al., 2006) proposes an approach for expressing semantics explicitly by formalizing the semantic constraints of a profile using ontologies and rules, enabling interoperability and automatic use for MPEG-7 based applications.

4. Summary

Legal professionals consume the most part of their time searching and retrieving legal information. Furthermore, the explosion of legal multimedia contents in the judicial domain produces an enormous quantity of this files that have to been stored in a way that facilitates the search process. E-discovery and e-learning are fields that also need to store the information in a structured manner to improve the search and retrieving applications. This work is aimed to study the automatic annotation of legal multimedia contents based on their semantic meaning, and how this annotation is stored in an international standard file format as JPEG2000 or MPEG-7. Taking advantage of both international standards, a compression process is also applied to reduce the amount of information needed to store all the multimedia files.

The JPEG2000 coding system is one of the latest standards proposed by the Joint Photographic Experts Group (JPEG). It is composed by 13 different parts addressing the encoding, transmission and manipulation of still images and video. Six different parts of the JPEG2000 are suitable to manage legal multimedia files. On the other hand, the Moving Pictures Experts Group (MPEG) committee has developed many standards for still image and video compression. The last one is the MPEG-7 that improves the MPEG-4 including: Description Definition Language, audio-visual Descriptor, and Description Schemes. All of them aimed to define, at different levels, syntax and semantic capabilities. While the prior standards from the MPEG committee focus on coding audio and visual content, MPEG-7 focuses on multimedia.

Semantic-based search and retrieval has been an important issue for years in the multimedia computing universe. Multimedia files have associated a meaning which can be very versatile. Semantic multimedia annotation is the process of automatically detecting the presence of a concept in an image or video stream. The annotation of video and images have similar problems, however, to annotate an image is more complex than a video due to videos have scenes that facilitates the detection of high-level concepts and events. Another important topic of research in this field is the extraction of concepts from the user query, where ontologies can help users to describe videos in words.

The annotation process of a video begins with a segmentation that split the video in different temporal partitions, named as "*shots*", in function of the different meaning of scenes in the video. Most works in the literature try to bridge the semantic gap between the low-level descriptors (such as texture, pixel, audio, etc.) and high-level concepts (such as sport, news, car accident, etc.). Although the use of a machine-learning technique as a Support Vector Machine (SVM) provides good results, other approaches, for instance either Bag-of-Words, or detection of different classes (faces, outdoor/indoor, etc) are used too, providing them acceptable results. In addition, the exploitation of semantic relationships between concepts is also an important field, since it can improves the detection accuracy. In the annotation of still images there are two crucial problems. The first is to select an appropriate set of visual descriptors that capture the particular properties of a specific domain and the features of each image class. The second crucial problem is how to combine the low-level descriptors in a fashion that the results obtained with individual descriptors are improved. There are several approaches to pose this problem such as models based on either the shape or structured appearance, or a distribution probability associated with a caption word. Other works address the learning of configurations and problems of perceptual grouping.

Finally, we can conclude that the management of legal multimedia files through the standards JPEG2000 and MPEG-7 can improve the storage requirements and the semantics/metadata management produced by the annotation process. Through both standards, the amount of storage requirements is reduced and the semantics/metadata information added to the final file could be accessed without the need of decompress the whole image or video. Furthermore, the existent techniques to carry out the semantic-based annotation of legal multimedia files can improve the search and retrieval applications for different legal fields as e-discovery and e-learning. The state-of-the-art summarized in this work is fully applicable to the legal domain. However, the particularities of the judicial procedures, for instance, the closed structure of oral hearings, have to been taken into account to improve the concept detection.

Acknowledgements

This work has been partially supported by the Spanish Government (Ministerio de Ciencia e Innovación and Ministerio de Industria, Turismo y Comercio) under Grants TSI-020501-2008-131 and CSO2008-05536.

References

Brickell, J. L. and Langer, A. M. (2009). Adapting to the Data Explosion: Ensuring Justice for all. In *IEEE International Conference on Systems, Man and Cibernetics Society*, pages 86–90. IEEE.

Smeulders, A., Worring, M., Santini, S., Gupta, A., and Jain, R. (2000). Content-Based Image Retrieval at the End of the Early Years. *IEEE Transactions on Pattern Analysis and Machine Intelligence*, 22(12):1349–1380.

Ballan, L., Bertini, M., Del Bimbo, A., and Serra, G. (2010). Video Annotation and Retrieval Using Ontologies and Rule Learning. *IEEE Multimedia*, In press.

Snoek, C. G., Huurnink, B., Hollink, L., de Rijke, M., Schreiber, G., and Worring, M. (2007). Adding semantics to detectors for video retrieval. *IEEE Transactions on Multimedia*, 9(5):975–986.

Zha, Z.-J., Mei, T., Wang, Z., and Hua, X.-S. (2007). Building a comprehensive ontology to refine video concept detection. In *Proceedings of the international workshop on multimedia information retrieval*, pages 227–236.

Snoek, C. G., Worring, M., van Gemert, J., Geusebroek, J., and Smeulders, A. (2006). The challenge problem for automated detection of 101 semantic concepts in multimedia. In *MULTIMEDIA'06: Proceedings of the 14th annual ACM international conference on Multimedia*, pages 421–430, NY, USA.

Gonzàlez, J., Rowe, D., Varona, J., and Roca, F. X. (2008). Understanding dynamic scenes based on human sequence evaluation. *Image and Vision Computing*, 27(10):1433 – 1444.

Xin, C. (2009). E-learning Applications and Challenges. In *International Conference on Future Information Technology and Management Engineering*, pages 580–583. IEEE.

Baron, J. R. and Thompson, P. (2007). The Search Problem Posed by Large Heterogeneous Data Sets in Litigation: Possible Future Approaches to Research. In *International Conference on Artificial Intelligence and Law*, pages 141–147. ACM.

González-Conejero, J. (2010). Legal Multimedia Management through JPEG2000 framework. *Lecture Notes in Artificial Intelligence*, AI approaches to the complexity of legal systems(In press).

Taubman, D. and Marcellin, M. (2002). *JPEG2000: Image Compression Fundamentals, Standards, and Practice*, volume 642. Kluwer International Series in Engineering and Computer Science.

Chang, S.-F., Sikora, T., and Puri, A. (2001). Overview of the MPEG-7 standard. *IEEE Transactions on Circuits and Systems for Video Technology*, 11(6):688–695.

Skodras, A., Christopoulos, C., and Ebrahimi, T. (2001). The JPEG 2000 still image compression standard. *IEEE Signal Processing Magazine*, 18(5):36–58.

Rabbani, M. and Joshi, R. (2002). An overview of the JPEG 2000 still image compression standard. *Signal Processing: Image Communication*, 17(1):3–48.

Avaro, O. and Salembier, P. (2001). Mpeg-7 Systems: Overview. *IEEE Transactions on Circuits and Systems for Video Technology*, 11(6):760–764.

Hunter, J. (2001). An Overview of the MPEG-7 Description Definition Language (DDL). *IEEE Transactions on Circuits and Systems for Video Technology*, 11(6):765–772.

Sikora, T. (2001). The MPEG-7 Visual Standard for Content Description – An Overview. *IEEE Transactions on Circuits and Systems for Video Technology*, 11(6):696–702.

Zhu, X., Wu, X., Elmagarmid, A., Feng, Z., and Wu, L. (2005). Video data mining: Semantic indexing and event detection from the association perspective. *IEEE Transactions on Knowledge and Data Engineering*, 17(5):665–677.

Casanovas, P., Binefa, X., Gracia, C., Teodoro, E., Galera, N., Blázquez, M., Poblet, M., Carrabina, J., Monton, M., Montero, C., Serrano, J., and López-Cobo, J. M. (2009). *Law, ontologies and the semantic web: Channeling the Legal Information Flood*, volume 188 of *Frontiers in Artificial Intelligence and Applications*, chapter The e-Sentencias Prototype: A Procedural Ontology for Legal Multimedia Applications, pages 199–219. IOS Press, Amsterdam, Netherlands.

Amiri, A. and Fathy, M. (2009). Video Shot Boundary Detection Using QR-Decomposition and Gaussian Transition Detection. *EURASIP Journal on Advances in Signal Processing*, 2009(Article ID 509438):1–12.

Meng, Y., Wang, L.-G., and Mao, L.-Z. (2009). A shot boundary detection algorithm based on Particle Swarm Optimization Classifier. In *International Conference on Machine Learning and Cybernetics*, volume 3, pages 1671 – 1676, Baoding, China.

Hauptmann, A., Yan, R., Lin, W.-H., Christel, M., and Wactlar, H. (2007). Can High-Level Concepts Fill the Semantic Gap in Video Retrieval? A Case Study With Broadcast News. *IEEE Transactions on Multimedia*, 9(5):958–966.

Sivic, J. and Zisserman, A. (2003). Video Google: A Text Retrieval Approach to Object Matching in Videos. In *Proceedings of the Ninth International Conference on Computer Vision*, volume 2, pages 1470–1477, Nice, France. IEEE Computer Society.

Viola, P. and Jones, M. (2004). Robust real-time face detection. *International Journal of Computer Vision*, 57(2):137–154.

Jamieson, M., Fazly, A., Stevenson, S., Dickinson, S., and Wachsmuth, S. (2010). Using Language to Learn Structured Appearance Models for Image Annotation. *IEEE Transactions on Pattern Analysis and Machine Intelligence*, 32(1):148–164.

Wei, X.-Y., Ngo, C.-W., and Jiang, Y.-G. (2008). Selection of Concept Detectors for Video Search by Ontology-Enriched Semantic Spaces. *IEEE Transactions on Multimedia*, 10(6):1085–1096.

Barnard, K., Duygulu, P., Guru, R., Gabbur, P., and Forsyth, D. (2003). The Effects of Segmentation and Feature Choice in a Translation Model of Object Recognition. In *IEEE Conference on Computer Vision and Pattern Recognition*, pages 675–682.

Quattoni, A., Collins, M., and Darrell, T. (2007). Learning visual representations using images with captions. In *IEEE Conference on Computer Vision and Pattern Recognition*. IEEE CS.

Carbonetto, P., de Freitas, N., and Barnard, K. (2004). A Statistical Model for General Contextual Object Recognition. In *European Conference Computer Vision*.

Li, J. and Wang, J. (2003). Automatic Linguistic Indexing of Pictures by a Statistical Modeling Approach. *IEEE Transactions Pattern Analysis and Machine Intelligence*, 25(9):1075–1088.

Graves, A. and Lalmas, M. (2002). Video Retrieval using an MPEG-7 Based Inference Network. In *Proceedings of the 25th annual international ACM SIGIR conference on Research and development in information retrieval*, pages 339–346.

Spyrou, E., Le Borgne, H., Mailis, T., Cooke, E., Avrithis, Y., and O'Connor, N. (2005). Fusing mpeg-7 visual descriptors for image classification. *Lecture Notes in Computer Science*, 3697:847–852.

Bertini, M., Del Bimbo, A., and Nunziati, W. (2006). Video Clip Matching Using MPEG-7 Descriptors and Edit Distance. *Lecture Notes in Computer Science*, 4071:133–142.

Bailer, W., Hausenblas, M., Hofmair, P., and Schalatte, R. (2006). Enabling multimedia metadata interoperability by defining formal semantics of mpeg-7 profiles. *Lecture Notes in Computer Science*, 4306:41–55.

Author Index

EUROPEAN PRESS ACADEMIC PUBLISHING – EPAP
http://www.e-p-a-p.com
http://www.europeanpress.eu
orders@e-p-a-p.com